FIRE
AND
RESCUE

Other books from the same authors

Neil Wallington:

FIREMAN!
A personal account

FIREMEN AT WAR

'999'
The accident and crash rescue work of the Fire Service

IMAGES OF FIRE
150 years of firefighting

LIVING DANGEROUSLY
Firefighters

FIREFIGHTER!

Sally Holloway:

LONDON'S NOBLE FIRE BRIGADES

MOORGATE
Anatomy of a railway disaster

COURAGE HIGH!
A history of firefighting in London

DEDICATION

To the men and women of the British Fire Service, in recognition of their dedication and bravery in the service of fellow citizens in cities, towns and villages across the United Kingdom.

Patrick Stephens Limited, an imprint of Haynes Publishing, has published authoritative, quality books for enthusiasts for more than 25 years. During that time the company has established a reputation as one of the world's leading publishers of books on aviation, maritime, military, model-making, motor cycling, motoring, motor racing, railway and railway modelling subjects. Readers or authors with suggestions for books they would like to see published are invited to write to: The Editorial Director, Patrick Stephens Limited, Sparkford, Nr. Yeovil, Somerset BA22 7JJ.

FIRE AND RESCUE

Into action with brigades throughout Britain

NEIL WALLINGTON AND SALLY HOLLOWAY

PSL

Patrick Stephens Limited

It is so nice to know, in this hard society, that we still have the backing of a wonderful emergency service and that we can rest assured they are still there and well and truly care when they are called upon...

Extract from a thank you letter received from a resident in Horsham, West Sussex, after the Brigade's attendance at an incident.

First published in 1994

British Library cataloguing-in-publication data:
A catalogue record for this book is available from the British Library

ISBN: 1 85260 486 7

Library of Congress catalog card no. 94 77769

Patrick Stephens Limited is an imprint of Haynes Publishing, Sparkford, Nr. Yeovil, Somerset BA22 7JJ

Typeset and designed by Stonecastle Graphics Limited, Marden, Kent.

Printed by Imprimerie Pollina s.a., Luçon, France.

CONTENTS

ACKNOWLEDGEMENTS

In writing this book, we have received a great deal of assistance from the Chief Fire Officers and personnel of fire brigades throughout the UK and we are most grateful to them. There have also been a number of people who have especially assisted in ferreting out information and photographs relating to specific incidents within their own brigades, often spending their off-duty time in doing this. We would, therefore, like to thank, particularly - and in no significant order for they all helped :

Chief Officer James Cassaday (Guernsey); Leading Firefighter Gary Chapman (Cornwall); Divisional Officer David Stout (Cleveland); Assistant Chief Officer Nigel Campion (Leicestershire); Assistant Divisional Officer Neil Cheyne and Sub Officer Roger Hansard (Lincolnshire); Chief Fire Officer Geoff Sayers (Peterborough Volunteers); Sub Officer Trevor Byford (Suffolk); Leading Firefighter Steve Hill (Tyne and Wear); Andrew Shaw and Edward Ockenden (West Midlands); Brian Saville and Andrew Hanson (West Yorkshire); Sub Officer Martin Jarrett (Shropshire); Divisional Officer John Drew and Roger Hislop (Wiltshire); Firemaster J.B.Stiff, Sub Officer Smith (Dumfries and Galloway); Iain Wishart (Fife); Sub Officer Roddy McInnes (Tayside); Station Officer Alan Fleming, Divisional Officer Brian Scott, Station Officer Alistair Swift, Leading Firefighter Denis Scott, Divisional Officer Ian Barron (Grampian); Chief Fire Officer P.A.Gribbin and C.G. Rooney (Manchester); Station Officer Eddie Hunt (Buckinghamshire); Rosemary Maslen and Jane Eckert (Royal Berkshire); Ron Bentley (Palace of Westminster); Station Officer Robertson (Cumbria); Station Officer Taylor (Central); Eric Whitaker; Assistant Divisional Officer Derek Brannan, Station Officer David Cooper, Station Officer Brian Chisholm (Lothian and Borders); J.J. O'Sullivan (British Airways); Deputy Senior Airport Fire Officer Laurie Moss (BAA, Gatwick); Nina Ridgewell (Essex); Alistair MacDonald (FBS); Eddie McArd (Isle of Man); Station Officer Steve Broadhurst (Merseyside); Dennis Holmes (Jersey); Geoff Cooper, Tom White, Cyril Daniel, Claud Evernden (Kent); Deputy Chief Fire Officer Peter Holland, Senior Divisional Officer Jim Hindle, SDO John Dobbs (Lancashire); Assistant Divisional Officer Paul Bowen (Staffordshire); The Royal Humane Society; The Society for the Protection of Life from Fire; Martin Jarrett (Shropshire); Mike Smyth (East Sussex); Graham Curtis (West Sussex); Assistant Divisional Officer Steve Elkins, Steve Osborne-Brown (Hampshire); Mike Drewett (Surrey); Mrs Nesta Orr (Northern Ireland); Dave Farr and Blue Watch (Twickenham, London); Joe Kennedy, Denis Morgan, Colin Williamson (London).

The authors readily acknowledge the use of source material contained in the following fire service publications: *In Attendance*; *Fire*; *Fire Prevention*; *Fire Engineers Journal*; *Fire Cover*, and the various regular house magazines of many British fire brigades.

GLOSSARY AND RANKS

Aerial: A fire engine able to reach up to upper floors of buildings. Can be either a turntable ladder or hydraulic platform. Maximum height around 100ft (30 metres).

Breathing apparatus control point: At a fire, entry into the smoke is strictly controlled, usually through one point only. Firefighters always go in in teams and leave tallies of their air cylinder contents which enable a close watch to be kept when a team is due out. An emergency crew of firefighters ready rigged in BA always stands by in case of need.

FIRE STATION DUTY SYSTEMS:

Day Manning: a system which uses professional firefighters who make up the fire engine crew during daylight hours but respond on bleeper call from their homes near to the fire station at night.

Nucleus manned: Stations where several professional firefighters are based, with most of the rest of the crew being drawn from retained personnel (qv).

Part-time or retained: Stations in smaller towns and more rural areas where the crew is entirely made up of part-time firefighters who follow their normal jobs within the close area of the fire station, and turn out from their homes at nights and weekends in response to a bleeper call.

Make up: The standard term for a fire or rescue situation where more fire engines and personnel are needed.

Over the border: '999' calls where part or all of the attendance is made up from fire engines and firefighters from an adjacent brigade.

Pre determined attendance (PDA): The number of fire engines despatched to an address dependent upon the prevalent fire risk factor. A city centre fire call will see up to four pumps plus aerial. At the other end of the scale a rural fire call may be attended by one water tender.

Shout: An emergency call.

Stop message: Radio message sent to Fire Control to indicate that a fire or other emergency is under control and no further assistance is needed.

Supernumerary: Fire engines normally have a crew of five or six, while aerial and other special appliances have two or three. Any firefighter crewing above these levels is said to be supernumerary.

Water tender: The general workhorse fire engine of the British fire service. Equipment includes 400 gallons (1800 litres) of water, high pressure small bore hose reels, hose lengths, breathing apparatus, various ladders up to 45ft (13.5 metres), foam, floodlighting, high-powered rescue and cutting tools, chemical protective clothing. Can also be termed a pump.

RANKS IN THE BRITISH FIRE SERVICE

Fireman/Firefighter
Crew member of fire engine.

Leading Fireman/Firefighter
In charge of fire engine.

Sub Officer
In charge of watch (shift) and fire engine.

Station Officer
In charge of station.

Assistant Divisional Officer
In charge of larger station/several stations.

Divisional Officer
In charge of group of stations (a division).

Senior Divisional Officer
In charge of large division.

Assistant Chief Officer
Based at headquarters and responsible for wide range of support activities. Also takes command at large incidents.

Deputy Chief Fire Officer
As for ACO but deputises for CFO.

Chief Fire Officer
In command of brigade and responsible to the fire authority.

ABBREVIATIONS

AFFF Aqueous film forming foam
BA Breathing apparatus
BACV Breathing apparatus control van
BAT Breathing apparatus tender
BL Breakdown lorry
Car Staff car
Risk Categories
- A high risk, inner city with industrial sites;
- B large-to-medium size town;
- C suburban/semi-rural;
- D rural.

CaV Canteen van
CIU Chemical incident unit
CU Control unit
DU Driving unit
ELU Emergency lighting unit
EST Combined emergency tender/salvage tender
ESU Emergency support unit
ET Emergency tender
FBt Fireboat
FEV Foam equipment vehicle
FoT Foam tender
FoTr Foam trailer
FoU Foam unit
FPTr Fire prevention trailer
FST Foam salvage tender
FTk Foam tanker
FWP Featherweight pump
Gen Generator
GPL General Purpose lorry
HC Hose carrier
HEF High expansion foam
HFT Combined hose layer/carrier/ foam tender
HL Hose layer
HP Hydraulic platform (height in brackets)
HPP Hydraulic platform with booster pump
HR Hose reel
HRT Hose reel tender
HX High expansion foam
L4P Light 4 wheel drive vehicle with pump
L4R Light 4 wheel drive vehicle (rescue)
L4T Light 4 wheel drive vehicle with hose reel
L4V Light 4 wheel drive vehicle
LPP Light portable pump
Lu Lighting unit
LuTr Lighting unit trailer
MR Mobile radio
MW Mobile workshop
P Pump (fire engine with 35ft/10.6m ladder)
PCV Personnel carrying vehicle
PHP Pump hydraulic platform
PL Pump (fire engine with 45ft/13.5m ladder)
PP Portable pump
PST Pump salvage tender
RAV Road accident vehicle
RIV Rapid intervention vehicle
RP Rescue pump
RTA Road traffic accident
RV Rescue vehicle
SP Salvage pump
ST Salvage tender
STr Salvage trailer
SV Service vehicle
T Tender
TL Turntable ladder (height in brackets)
TLP Turntable ladder pump
TSU Technical support unit
TV Towing vehicle
WCar Staff car with radio
WrC Water carrier
WrL Water Tender with 45ft/13.5m ladder
WrT Water Tender with 35ft/10.6m ladder

INTRODUCTION

Horror sweeps the country when disaster strikes: The inferno at Bradford football ground, broadcast live on television as the fans ran in terror from the flames that were roaring through the frantically emptying stands. The King's Cross Underground disaster where the exhausted fire crews wrestled to drag unconscious travellers from the smoke clogged tunnels – and lost a gallant station officer, killed in the rescue efforts. The breathless hell of the aircraft crash at Manchester Airport, the tangled chaos of motorway pile-ups. Firefighters sweating in heat of more than 20 degrees centigrade and minimum oxygen to disentangle the mangled corpses of an underground train crash, 40 feet below the ground and crushed into a dead end tunnel. So foetid was the atmosphere that all workers had to be inoculated before they could descend and decontaminated when they staggered back up into the daylight. That was Moorgate.

On a smaller scale, again and again, we see the pathetic ruins of small homes, charred and smoke-stained, from which friends and neighbours have not managed to rescue families overcome by heat, flames and all too often the toxic fumes of illegally foam-filled armchairs and sofas – fires often started by accident or a moment of carelessness.

It's not all a matter of chance. In 1992 (the last year for which figures are available) there were 26,300 arson attacks in the UK. Each year, criminals or mentally disturbed people fall to the temptation of lighting fires, either in an effort to solve a financial nightmare or for the sheer thrill of seeing the flames and fire engines.

Every year nearly 1,000 people, including a number of children, die, and nearly 15,000 are injured throughout the country when what the Victorians nicknamed 'The Fire Fiend' strikes again.

Coping with this never ending problem are our firefighters, men and women with the vocation to save others at whatever cost to themselves. There are 56,000 in Britain, highly trained and waiting for the bells to go down in 2,600 fire stations nationwide, in 67 fire brigades. For every call that comes, the adrenalin pumps through their whole bodies as the sirens wail and the appliances leap from their bays and roar into action. Awaiting them could be a false alarm (there were 150,000 malicious false alarms in 1991, an increase of 75 per cent in 10 years). But if it's 'for real' the job will be, at the very least, uncomfortable. The firefighters could be hot, cold, soaked to the skin, choked on smoke and fumes. At worst they may face the agony of major burns – and even the ultimate sacrifice, a painful death. One Chief Officer described the fate of two of his firemen, trapped in the collapsed basement of a fashionable London restaurant as it blazed above them. Hauled out by their mates, they were rushed to hospital. 'There', he recalled, 'they were hung suspended above their beds for there was not an area of their bodies which was not burned. Mercifully, after two days, they died.'

The firefighter's work is dirty, dangerous, uncomfortable, and challenging. But over the centuries have emerged a huge wealth of yarns. We have sought them out, asking about the variety of 'shouts' – tragic, unusual, funny, unthinkable – which affect every region and those 'specials' which live in the memory and become the legends of the service. In every case the response has been the same: 'This is all part of our job – nobody thinks of being a hero'. But heroes they are, and from every county we have tried to draw a selection which reflects the inimitable spirit of Britain's firefighters and their service.

In preparing this book, we send our grateful thanks to all the Chief Officers and their staffs who have responded to our request for help with such kindness and enthusiasm, and have often given up their own spare time to provide much of the material from which the book has been produced.

CHAPTER 1

A HELL OF A JOB

SOUTHERN AREA

When Essex County Fire Service – one of the largest in the country – wanted to know what the public thought of its work, it carried out an opinion poll. Again and again the question to passers-by in the street 'what does a firefighter do?' brought a blank look, or the stammered reply 'they rescue cats from trees don't they?'.

Admittedly some were quicker off the mark. Many spoke of heroism and courage, but few could begin to list the work of the fire service for which they pay as part of their local and national taxes. Nor could they understand what made men and women take on such a challenge, although one man reckoned, almost wistfully, 'it must be a hell of a job'.

Hell of a job it is, being roasted at fires, frozen in icy water rescues; life-threatening as they dive into ruined buildings regardless of the hazard of further cascades of masonry; health-threatening when there are unknown chemicals involved; hair-raising when they hover on the end of a helicopter line above a burning supertanker or oil rig.

But firefighters say it is the 'hell of a job' element that attracts them, whether they are whole-time, retained or volunteers. 'It gives you a purpose in life', said one. 'I had a succession of jobs, nothing for more than 12 months, until I joined the Service', said another. 'I've been in it now for seven years and I wouldn't do anything else.' 'It's the team work – depending on each other, even for your survival', said a third. 'It's the feel of the adrenalin surging every time the bells go down, the engine roars out and you tear down the road with the two-tone howling, not knowing what you'll find at the end. You may be facing something you've never come across before and you have to react immediately.' 'It's the thrill of seeing children wave as the fire engine goes past.' 'There can't be anything more satisfactory than knowing that you've saved someone's life.' 'Wherever you go, firefighters are mates. They say it's the best club in the world.'

Nobody got round to mentioning the possibility of losing their lives, as so many firefighters have done over the centuries, in the cause of saving others.

In earlier days and, indeed, until the country faced fire attacks from the air for the very first time, in the First World War, Britain's fire protection came from small local brigades. They used pumps and 'squirts' like garden syringes at first, then primitive fire engines, later to be horse-drawn and steam-powered and finally, petrol-powered. In 1938, just before the Second World War started, there were more than 1,600 fire brigades, many of them manned (as they are to this day) by local volunteers or retained staff but with no nationally unified training, uniform or equipment. Not until 1941, at the peak of the war, was a National Fire Service established, under the control of the Home Office.

After the war fierce arguments raged between those who saw the virtues of national control and those who valued the local service, for its knowledge of the peculiar hazards of its own area and its skill and experience in dealing with these. Local knowledge won. In 1948 the NFS was dissolved.

Today, Britain is divided into Regions

for Fire and Civil Defence. Within each Region are the Counties, each with its own Fire Brigade which often is called 'Fire and Rescue Service' as increasingly – and in some cases overwhelmingly – its work is concerned more with rescue than fire. Rescue can mean anything from nuclear leaks, RTAs (Road Traffic Accidents), train crashes, or air disasters to refinery explosions. Or it might be a call to free a child who has jammed its head through the railings (more likely, these days, to have stuck its finger in a supermarket trolley), or release people trapped in a lift that's stuck at the top of a tower block. So many Londoners forgot their house keys, and took it for granted that the fire brigade would attend to let them in, that by 1990 a charge of £113 plus VAT had to be imposed as an aid to the memory in cases where there were no extenuating circumstances.

Basic training is the same throughout the country: Tough, technical and extremely thorough. It covers far more than hurling water indiscriminately into 'incidents' when it could cause more damage than a fire, or 'scooshing' an unidentified chemical into the sewers which might pollute a river or cause a subterranean explosion. The Fire Service College at Moreton-in-Marsh provides courses in every aspect of firefighting for brigades throughout Britain, as well as training at international level.

What the firefighters face when they leave training school could be any type of general incident, or it might be something which would only happen in their own part of the country.

Taking Britain county by county, Kent is a good example.

KENT

There was a time – well within living memory – when Kent was called the Garden of England. In those days, the Weald rolled away in a succession of orchards and hop gardens, dotted here and there with cottages and oast houses. Like so many other counties, it has a long tradition of local fire brigades. Woe betide any book on firefighting in Kent that failed to mention the volunteer firemen who were the pride of the county in days gone by, particularly the 'Hunting Brigade' of Wingham. Harry Klopper describes them in his book *To Fire Committed*:

'On receipt of a fire call, maroons were sent up and people streamed into the streets to see the appropriate district officer, splendidly arrayed in hunting kit and mounted on a horse, galloping at full speed over meadows and fields to the fire ground. He was followed by a manual

Folkestone, Kent, firemen line up in the early 1920s with their latest equipment – a covered stretcher, ambulance with solid tyres and two forms of breathing apparatus. The BA wearers were connected with the outside world by lengths of piping, fed with air by the pumping action of their colleagues (far left and right). (Tom White, Kent Fire Brigade Museum)

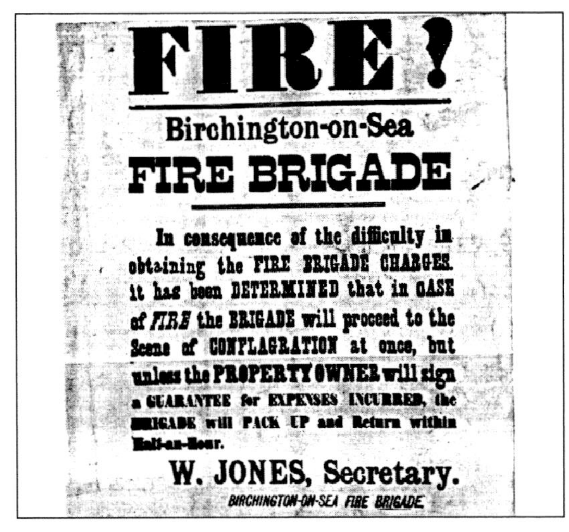

FIRE!

Birchington-on-Sea

FIRE BRIGADE

In consequence of the difficulty in obtaining the FIRE BRIGADE CHARGES it has been DETERMINED that in CASE of FIRE the BRIGADE will proceed to the Scene of CONFLAGRATION at once, but unless the PROPERTY OWNER will sign a GUARANTEE for EXPENSES INCURRED, the BRIGADE will PACK UP and Return within Half-an-Hour.

W. JONES, Secretary.

BIRCHINGTON-ON-SEA FIRE BRIGADE

'Your Money or Your Life!' An early 19th century no-nonsense warning to customers on the consequences of not paying the Fire Brigade charges. (Tom White, Kent Fire Brigade Museum)

pump, drawn by horses and manned by a lieutenant and firemen, shouting the usual warning of "Hi! Hi! Hi!". Bringing up the rear, also in full hunting gear, came the Chief Officer. Wingham people loved their fire brigade which, from time to time, provided them with a most spectacular "point to point".'

There are still many people who remember one of the stranger fires in the county. Cyril Daniel was a 22-year-old Fire Station Engineer at the time of the mysterious 'Wedding Party' disaster at Gillingham in 1929. Sixty years on, he told the story:

'Every year, the town used to hold a charity fête and traditionally the climax, as it got dark, was a mock "fireman's wedding" in a flimsy timber house which had been specially built for it. This had matchboarding walls, with a door and windows cut out on the front, and ladders between the three storeys. Two firemen, dressed as the "bride" and "groom" walked among the spectators with a naval petty officer called "auntie" going round with them. They all fooled about for a bit and then went into the house with a crowd of "guests", who were local firemen, scouts and sea cadets. After a while, red flares were lit to suggest that the house had caught fire and the Gillingham Fire Brigade, who were attending with pumps at the ready, powered in running up ladders to save them, leaving the "bride", the "groom" and "auntie" at the top window until the final dramatic rescue.

'A fireman would then check the building to make sure that everyone was safely outside before giving the signal to set the whole place alight.

'For 20 years the "ceremony" was carried out without a hitch and with everyone enjoying the fun. On this night, and nobody has ever discovered why, the fire was lit while everyone was still inside.

'It was horrific. The audience thought it was part of the act and were cheering and laughing, but my mates were among the firemen still in the building and there were all those young lads caught in an absolute inferno.

'We got the hoses trained on the house and ran our ladders up and did all we could to save them. One man fell and landed in the flames on the ground and I dived in and managed to drag him out, but he died later. The flames seared my face and neck. I had blisters hanging down; my hands were burned to the bone, but luckily my fists had been clenched round the man so the tendons were protected inside the bones otherwise, the doctors told me, I would have lost the use of both hands. Within minutes, 15 people – firemen, sea scouts and naval cadets – had been burned to death.' Despite detailed inquiries, nobody discovered why the fire was lit before time.

Cyril Daniel's injuries took 17 weeks to heal but he stayed on in the fire service and at 88 years old was still helping out in the Kent Fire Brigade Museum.

Firefighting in Kent goes back many centuries. The ancient cathedral city of Canterbury, official home of the Primate of All England, produced what must have been one of the country's earliest, if not

3,023 false alarms

Kent's calls have increased from 22,801 in 1987 – 88 to 25,298 in 1992 – 93. Of these, malicious false alarms rose from 2,666 in 1987 to 3,023 in 1992 – 93.

Firefighters have always paid special tribute to comrades lost in action. Here, an early petrol-powered fire engine bears the coffin of a Faversham (Kent) colleague, killed in the 'Fireman's Wedding' tragedy at Gillingham in 1929, on his last journey. (Tom White, Kent Fire Brigade Museum)

the most reliable, firemen, in the form of an early archbishop.

The famous monk historian, the Venerable Bede, wrote about a particularly bad fire in Canterbury in the year 624 AD:

'The great fire reached the Church of the Four Crowned Martyrs, the casting of water would not stop it and it came rushing towards the Cathedral. Archbishop Mellitus, suffering from gout, had himself carried there and, flaming with divine love and sanctity, prayed, whereupon the wind miraculously changed and blew the fire away'.

Would that to-day's fires might be dealt with so simply. In restoring the Cathedral after another fire, which came much closer and caused great damage, the monks refused to allow anything to be put up within fire-raising distance of the great edifice. That probably saved it again when fire broke out on many later occasions, and particularly dangerously in 1992.

Kent Fire Brigade was called to 'smoke issuing from a building in the paved part of Canterbury High Street' (the centre of the ancient city). It was the start of an 18-hour attendance with 15 pumps. The first report, from the Sub Officer on duty with Red Watch, Canterbury, said that a three-storey building used as shops and offices was well alight on the second floor and roof. The fire had, in fact, probably started in an overheated extension cable, in the back of a hair salon on the first floor and spread quickly through the old building into adjoining shops. Access for the fire crews was particularly difficult as the buildings were surrounded on three sides by other shops, including a large department store.

Because of this problem and heavy smoke, the officer in charge increased the pumps from 10 to 15. But before long, the fire had burst through the roof so that crews in breathing apparatus who had been fighting close to the flames were withdrawn to safety.

One of the major difficulties facing the fire officers in charge was that many of the buildings dated back to medieval times and, over the centuries, had been damaged and restored after previous fires with no particular regard to fire prevention. This left them vulnerable to the outbreak in 1992.

With increased water power, the fire was eventually brought under control and there was no doubt that Kent's fire crews had saved a large part of the old city from destruction, including many listed buildings.

Today though, apart from a few

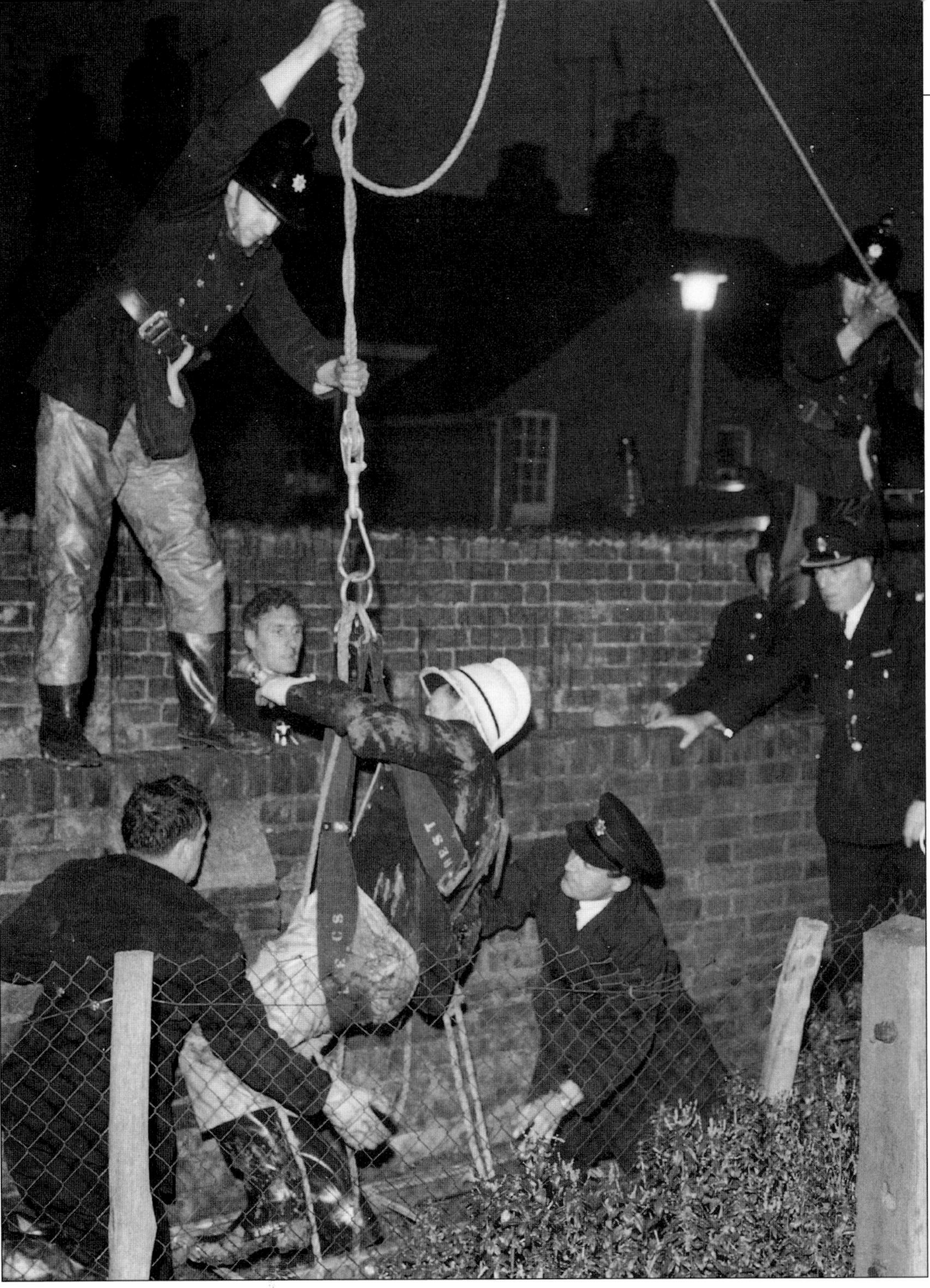

Skipping along a road in Strood on a wintry day in November 1967, a young child turned round to find its mother had vanished from sight. The woman had been following along the footpath when one of Kent's mysterious 'dene holes' had opened beneath her feet. Here, muddy, exhausted and shocked, a fire officer is hauled from the hole to report that after descending for 100 feet he had reached the bottom and found only a fast running stream. There was no sign of the young mother, who has never been seen since. (Chatham News & Standard)

remaining areas of fruit and hop growing, Kent has changed from being The Garden of England to the Gateway to Europe, and resembles a giant industrial estate, cut through by motorways. Its southern boundary borders the English Channel, and it boasts Britain's first international fire station, within metres of the entrance to the Channel Tunnel.

With nearly 18 million passengers a year passing through the port of Dover, 250 ships passing through the Straits every day, plus 50 tankers and 200 ferry journeys, this sea traffic alone brings hazards. Kent crews may also be asked to assist elsewhere. They flew to the Zeebrugge disaster, helping with the rescue work and, later, the unhappy task of bringing the bodies ashore.

A challenging 'shout' came when a giant supertanker caught fire and was abandoned by all but one of its crew in the Channel off the Kent coast. For some time, the giant ship wallowed in the mid-

Kent Fire Brigade has these specialist inshore estuary boats stationed at Strood, Whitstable and Sheerness to deal with incidents involving shipping in the Thames Estuary – a responsibility which they share with Essex County Fire and Rescue Service. (Kent Fire Brigade)

dle of one of the busiest shipping lanes in the world, until Kent flew out a special firefighting crew by helicopter. After landing on deck and putting out the fire they kept the vessel on course until it could be taken over by professional seamen again.

As well as using the RAF's emergency service from Manston, the Kent Brigade shares two firefighting tugs and three 'estuary boats' (two Dell Quay Rigid Raiders and one Zodiac Inflatable) with Essex Fire and Rescue Service, across the Thames estuary from Kent's northern border. Crews from both brigades train on board. Essex is responsible for shipping sailing up the Thames, and Kent for the seabound craft.

Fog on the motorway always brings a spate of pile-ups, because traffic is travelling too fast for the road conditions. But one of the more unusual motorway incidents happened on a clear day in 1993 when a car, driven by a driving instructor, with his teenage son in the passenger seat, got sandwiched between a coach and the vehicles behind it. The first firefighters on the scene could have been excused for thinking that this was a two-vehicle crash. The car had been shunted forward and crushed so far into the luggage bay of the coach that it had almost disappeared. All that could be seen was part of the back bumper. Tragically, the driver had been killed, but with skill and patience the fire crews cut away the enveloping metal of the coach, and then the car inside, and after several hours of expert and delicate work

Had more flying bombs than London

Kent's fire services were kept at work almost non-stop during the Second World War. Much of the Battle of Britain was fought over the county as RAF Spitfires struggled to keep Hitler's bombers at bay. Many of the aircraft shot down in the fray, fell on Kentish soil.

Later, Kent was given the nickname 'Bomb Alley' as V1 'flying bombs' rattled through its airspace on the way to London. Many of these were shot down and many V1s, launched indiscriminately from bases across the Channel, landed in Kent.

In September 1944 the *Kent Messenger* published an article showing that of 8,000 flying bombs sent over by the Germans, 2,400 fell on or were destroyed in Kent – 200 more than in London. Over 1,000 came down in the sea off the Kentish coast between Lydd and Folkestone. At least 152 people had been killed and 1,700 injured. Later, when the V1 rockets took the place of the flying bombs, 1,054 fell on English soil, about half in the London Region but, Kent claims, the first and last rockets of the war landed on them – and many more in between. They also believe that the last civilian to be killed by wartime bombing was at Orpington, Kent, on 28 March 1945.

Fire crews, called to a multiple shunt on the M20 in November 1993, were momentarily puzzled, then horrified to realise that a third car, a Ford Sierra, had been crushed into the luggage area of the coach. Doctors, nurses and ambulance crews helped as the firemen carefully cut their way through to the car. Sadly, the driver had died but his 17-year-old son survived. (Roger Johnson, Kent Messenger)

they managed to release the teenager, who was injured and in deep shock, to be raced to hospital by a waiting ambulance.

As a rule, road accidents involve road transport. But it was a different story in May 1993 when a Robin light aircraft took off from Rochester Airport, turned back with engine trouble but failed to reach the runway. The pilot decided his only hope was to try a forced landing on the coast-bound carriageway of the M2 motorway, which was full of traffic. He took the chance, chose a small gap and glided in – just clipping a coach full of German tourists, heading for lunch in Canterbury. Firefighters arrived fast with three pumps, a hoselayer and a foam unit, to find the pilot, Paul Wisely, still conscious but trapped in the cockpit with 25 gallons of aviation fuel leaking from the tanks. While one crew laid a carpet of foam, others cut him free. He was taken to hospital with back injuries. 'It was a miracle that nobody was killed.' That was the verdict of the officer-in-charge of the incident, ADO Graham Gash. 'By good luck there was that small gap in the traffic and the only other vehicle involved was the coach, which was slightly damaged by the debris.'

Kent's pride in having such a rare event on its 'patch' was slightly dented when, the following week, an executive jet with two pilots on board, coming in to land at Eastleigh Airport on Hampshire's ground, missed the runway and landed on the M27 motorway.

EAST SUSSEX

'Sussex by the Sea' is the famous song of this rolling southern English county with its sheltering shoulder of The Downs, its rich farmland, bluebell woods and chalk cliffs. But the county also has busy towns and industrial sites not only on the coast but inland, with all the problems they bring.

The whole area is so large that it has been divided in half – East and West. Cheerful and breezy Brighton with its adjoining neighbour, Hove, is one of the larger towns, famous for its theatres, its night life and its great hotels.

It was one of the largest and most luxurious, the white-fronted Grand Hotel on the sea front near the pier, that was chosen by the Conservative Party for their annual conference in October 1984. The IRA had been active and, with the Prime Minister, Mrs Thatcher, many of her Cabinet Ministers, members of the government and MPs attending, maximum security was enforced.

The hotel was searched again and again for explosive devices. All had gone well and most of the delegates were sound asleep in the comfort of their rooms at a quarter to three in the morning when there was an enormous explosion and the whole centre of the building collapsed. A 'workman' with an Irish accent had managed to hide a powerful bomb beneath the floorboards of one of the bedrooms.

One of the first officers on the scene was Leading Fireman David Norris of Green Watch, Preston Circus Fire Station. He wrote down, in his own words, what happened:

'As crewmen on the Green Watch Pump Escape that night we were "tipped out" to what we thought was just another automatic alarm call. The Tannoy crackled "Pump escape, water tender and turntable ladder to fire alarm ringing, Grand Hotel ..." On the road within a minute and driving down the deserted London Road, our blue flashing lights mirrored in the shop fronts, a radio message brought us to life: "Report of an explosion – Grand Hotel".

'Driving along the sea front it seemed to be misty up ahead. It was a large dust cloud which was soon forgotten as we looked in horror at the devastation before us.

'A gaping hole, several rooms wide and at least two floors high in the front of the hotel... debris strewn across the road and on to the beach... curtains hanging from the promenade lights. The strangest ghostly silence was only interrupted by the monotonous ringing of the hotel's fire bell.

'For a few moments we were in shock, unable to believe what had happened, but we very quickly moved into action. The pump escape crew decided to put the escape ladder up to the right of the main entrance in the hope of rescuing people. There was no fire but the water tender crew laid out hoses for any possible outbreak. The turntable ladder towered above us, peering into the gaping hole for survivors. We were soon joined by fire crews from other areas.

'As I helped with the escape ladder I heard voices coming from the basement. Down the few steps I found a man and a woman huddled together. Miraculously, they had fallen together from the sixth floor and barely suffered a scratch. The woman was very distressed so I carried her out to a waiting ambulance then, with a blanket, returned for the man. He was naked except for a thick coating of dust and we walked out together and across the promenade which was, by now, the first aid post.

'I called for torches from other crews and when they came, we went back to the basement, calling out and pausing for replies. As we made our way up through the wreckage, the Prime Minister, surrounded by Special Branch, passed us on the stairs. She paused to say "Delighted to see you!" before being ushered out. She looked immaculate – not a hair out of place'.

Passing the fifth floor, where other crews were rescuing trapped delegates, they heard cries between the fifth and sixth floors, somewhere on the edge of the chasm which the bomb had created. 'Two of us were lowered on ropes into this deep hole and, guided by the sound, began digging, mostly with our hands, until we uncovered a man's head. He was in an upright position, still in bed and not too badly injured as far as we could tell. We spent the next two and half hours digging. It seemed like 20 minutes, cracking jokes and generally chatting to him. As we dug, electricity cables were arcing round us and the dust was choking.' They released the man at 0600 hours. 'I went down for refreshments. It was only then that I realised the time and suddenly felt exhausted. By now there must have been more than 100 firemen on the scene. We

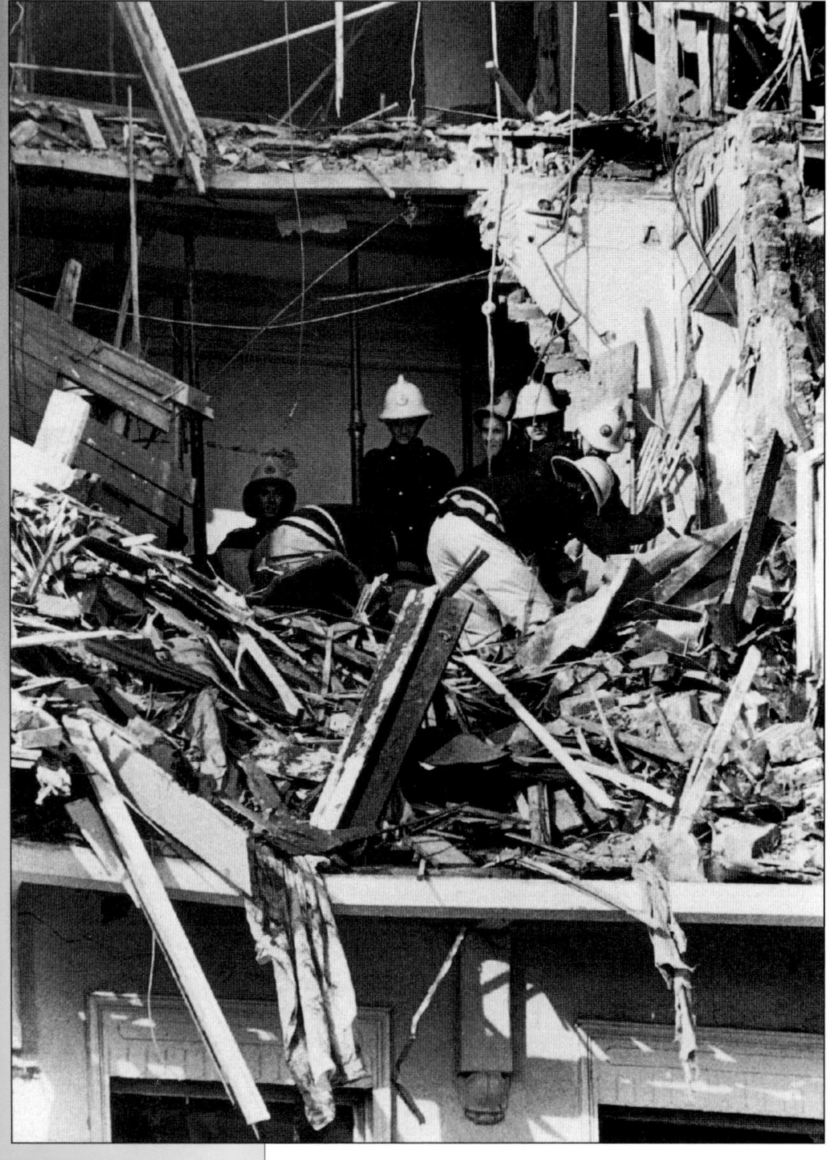

Brighton firefighters were secured by ropes as they struggled to dig out the injured, trapped high up in the wreckage after an IRA bomb blew out the centre of the Grand Hotel, Brighton, during the Conservative Party Conference in 1984. Without the ropes, they could have slipped and fallen into the bomb crater which went down to the basement. (Brighton Evening Argus)

were relieved by Red Watch just after 9 am, returning to Preston Circus dusty and weary. We wouldn't have missed it for anything.'

At the height of the incident, 115 firefighters from East and West Sussex were struggling with the rescue work and a total of 15 pumping appliances, two turntable ladders, two hydraulic platforms, three rescue vehicles, one control unit and a lighting unit were in attendance.

Later, Station Officer Fred Bishop was awarded the MBE for his work. This included rescuing Mr Norman Tebbitt, who was badly trapped (and marked the incident with his widely reported plea 'get off my bloody foot Fred!'). Eight firefighters from East Sussex and one from West Sussex received letters of commendation from the Chief Officer.

Not all the 'lodgings' along this stretch of the coast are grand hotels of course. In Hove, immediately west of Brighton, the dreaded call of 'Fire with Persons' ticked out on the teleprinter at 0230 hours one April morning for an older house in the town. Terraced and tall, this bore the worrying initials after the address of 'HMO' – 'House of Multiple Occupation'. It had, in fact, been divided into six self-contained flats; they had inflammable gloss paint on the dividing half-walls and many open doorways. On the third floor, a party had been in full swing until the shout of 'Fire!' went up.

Hove firefighters raced to the scene with a Station Officer in charge of two pumps and a hydraulic platform. Parked cars obstructed both sides of the road, making access difficult, and the sight which greeted them chilled the blood. Flames fluttered like banners from the upstairs windows, threatening the floors above and the roof, where adults and children were scrabbling at the slates in an attempt to reach the neighbouring houses. Three smashed bodies were quickly discovered lying in the outside basement area, while another victim was crawling up the steps with blood pouring from a severe head injury. All had fallen as they tried to shin down the drainpipes or jump from the unbearable heat of the blazing rooms. More followed by the minute.

Acrid smoke billowed round. The senior fire officer called base to 'Make Pumps Four' as other firefighters helped police manhandle the parked cars away to make room for the turntable ladder to put down its jacks close enough to the house to start rescue work.

At the same time the first crews, wearing BA had smashed their way through the front door with axes. They put out a fire blazing in a sofa behind the door, then headed for the stairs in what a later official report described as 'punishing conditions', clawing their way up towards the seat of the blaze as the flames licked round their steel-tipped boots and the stairs crumbled beneath them. At one stage the fire was so fierce, and the risk of the whole house collapsing so great, that all the firefighters were temporarily called out of the building, only to swarm back as soon as it was declared safe.

Outside, ladders had been quickly pitched against the front and back walls and the first rescues were well in hand. Other firefighters raced to adjoining roofs, dragging their hoses up behind them and directing the jets across to stop the fire from spreading sideways to other houses in the terrace. For two hours they fought, bringing out survivors and, all too often, as they turned over the sodden ashes, discovering the blackened bodies of party-goers and their neighbouring flatmates.

Dawn was coming up over the grey sea as the 'stop' went out at 0519 hours. The wearied crews of eight pumps and two aerial ladders damped down the remains while their officers joined with Sussex Police to trace how it had started.

They'd had their suspicions from the very start. The fire had burned with remarkable speed, and several people had been seen leaving the house just before the first screams were heard. Initially, it seemed likely that the blaze had started under the stairs, cutting them off as an escape route. As the research continued, the final horror of the disaster became known: five people dead; 11 in hospital with serious injuries and burns; one firefighter injured.

Eventually the authorities were convinced that the fire had been deliberately started in the sofa behind the front door, but why? The answer came quickly and oddly, in a fatal car crash two days after the tragedy. The driver, an airline steward, had confessed to a friend that he had set the sofa ablaze with his cigarette lighter. He gave no explanation and died in the crash.

Most firefighters will assure you that brave deeds on call-outs are usually part of a joint effort. Early on a June morning in 1992, a call went out for an armed siege in which a man had already injured the woman he was holding hostage on the top floor of a three-storey block of flats. There was little they could do at first – this was a police job – and by mid-afternoon they were wondering how much longer they would be waiting around when smoke began to pour from the flat.

Immediately, Ldg Ff Phillip Berry and Ff Mark Brown of Blue Watch, Hastings, were detailed to enter the building to fight the fire and search for the two people involved. They had hardly got through the front door when police warned them that a unexploded stun grenade, fired by police marksmen, had fallen 'somewhere on the staircase'. Despite this, and under the constant surveillance of armed police, they continued into the smoke-logged flat still searching for the man and his hostage and at the same time putting out the fire.

In the ensuing smoke and confusion the woman was taken from the building by the police. The man, who had been found lying in a bath of water with a hose in his mouth, leading to the open air, was brought out by the firefighters. Both men were awarded the Queen's Commendation for Brave Conduct. Two more firefighters, Stn/O Robin Haggar and Ldg Ff Laurence Adey, both of The Ridge, Hastings, received the County Fire Officer's Commendation.

But in an equally bizarre incident it was the personal courage of one man alone which saved his crew. Ff John Peck of Blue Watch, Roedean Fire Station, was among the team called to an incident at Chesham Place, Brighton, in November 1992. As the firemen entered the building they were suddenly attacked by a man wielding a Samurai sword not unlike one which had, in London, been used to cut off the hand of a policeman. Without hesitating, John Peck dived in and managed to disarm the man with (in the words of the

> ***'They were suddenly attacked by a man wielding a Samurai sword'***

County Fire Officer's Commendation) 'little regard for his own safety and in the very best traditions of the fire service. Firefighter Peck's actions were commendable and meritorious'.

WEST SUSSEX

Snap, crackle, pop turned to crash, bang, wallop when fire struck the huge Sainsbury superstore on the edge of Chichester in West Sussex Fire Brigade's patch just before Christmas on 16 December 1993.

For much of the time, West Sussex is a peaceful area of farms and rivers. There are no major motorways to cause trouble, although plenty of busy roads joining such Channel coast resorts as Worthing, Chichester, Littlehampton and Bognor Regis. On the eastern edge of the county, Gatwick Airport is one of the brigade's biggest potential hazards and a special Gatwick Liaison Officer from West Sussex is always on duty at nearby Crawley Fire Station. Apart from this, harvest fires have been one of the bigger headaches facing its firefighters, particularly when the burning fields are close enough to houses and hospitals to bring problems with smoke when the wind is blowing in the wrong direction.

Luckily, the wind was blowing towards open country when the Sainsbury fire began. It was thought to have started among potato crisp cartons in a store room at the back of the huge building. The store had only been open for a few years and its staff had been well drilled in what to do should fire break out. Their particular concern, the management had stressed, must be for people – to get the customers and themselves safely out of the building. This rule was followed to the letter. As the fire alarms sounded, the 300 customers and 200 staff moved quietly, if somewhat apprehensively, to the car park.

When the fire was first reported to Chichester fire station, 1¼ miles away, two appliances were mobilised. But these were rapidly increased to four, six, 15 and then 25 fire engines and, as the flames roared and thick black smoke poured up to the winter skies, they were joined by two breathing apparatus control units, three hydraulic platforms, a hoselayer and a foam tender, all in the hands of more than 150 firefighters.

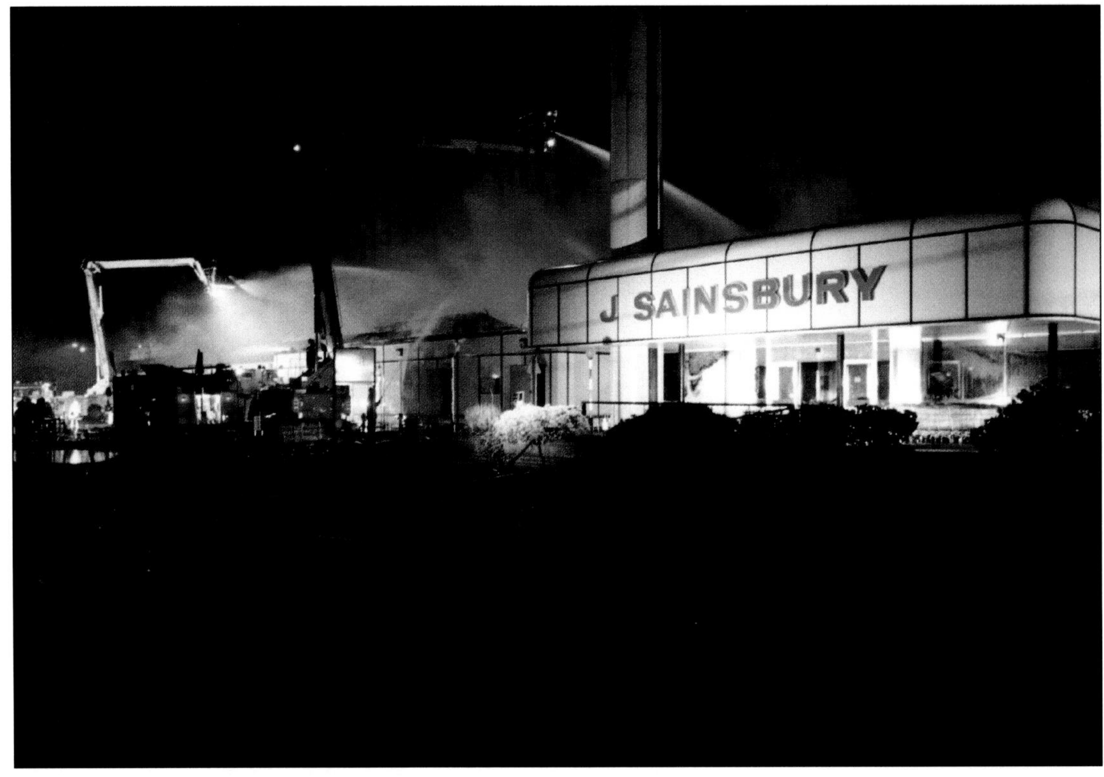

A huge fire, believed to have started in a box of potato crisps, swept the Chichester branch of Sainsbury's just before Christmas, 16 December 1993. (West Sussex Fire Brigade)

Adding to the danger was a nearby petrol station: a foam tender with two appliances were detailed to protect this. Smoke had poured over the nearby A27 road and that, too, had to be closed.

At first, crews attacked the flames from inside the huge building, which measured about 110 yards by 110 yards (100 metres by 100 metres). But within 15 minutes the fire had broken through the ceiling of the bulk storage area at the rear and into the store itself. It was spreading so fast in the space between the ceiling and the roof that the crews found the dense black smoke dropping down to waist level. At this stage the packaged goods, from 'deli' to detergents, were beginning to go up in flames. Showers of molten and burning bitumen were falling from the roof and there was every chance of a flashover with its killer fireball. Certain that everyone who had been in the store was safely outside, the crews were withdrawn for their own safety and continued the attack from outside.

There was no shortage of ammunition for the battle. Apart from a good supply from the mains, there was open water available from a nearby river and lake. At the height of the blaze, 15 jets were aimed at the building along with four ground monitors and three high pressure monitors.

Soon after 1750 hours the message went through that the fire had been surrounded and, optimistically, a 'stop' message followed at 1847 hours – but an hour later, crews began work inside the store again as pockets of fire flared up in the wreckage. Damping down, and the turning over of ashes, went on until the following morning to make sure that no further outbreaks were likely. Inspections continued for two days. Not until lunch time – 1338 hours – on 18 December was the final 'stop' sent out.

Intensive investigations by the brigade's experts suggested that the most likely cause of the fire was 'deliberate ignition'. Chief Fire Officer Kenneth Lloyd suggested that the absence of a sprinkler system, plus the huge open area of roof space, had both helped the flames to spread so rapidly. He congratulated the store for its evacuation procedure which had allowed everyone in the building to reach safety so quickly.

Less than a month later, abundance of water became superabundance as the January floods cascaded over the whole of this part of the south coast of England. Worst hit of all was Chichester, with its ancient Cathedral, its popular modern theatre and its busy shopping centre and market. An operation which started around 1630 hours on 4 January 1994 with a call for help with 'substantial flooding in the area of the Four Chestnuts public house' turned into a full-scale action. Rain saturated the chalk of the South Downs and poured into towns and villages, blocking main roads and flooding huge areas of low-lying land – including,

Investigate plane crashes abroad

Few people realise how much international work is carried out by UK fire brigades. West Sussex works closely with Gatwick Airport Fire Service on everything from incidents of all kinds relating to the 'village' of airport buildings to those concerning aircraft. Added to this, they have joined together to investigate major incidents at other airports in an effort to learn any lessons which might be useful for emergency planning.

Senior officers from both fire services travelled in 1992 to Portugal to inquire into the DC10 crash at Faro, and in 1993 to Warsaw where an Airbus had crashed. Their reports were circulated to other airports and emergency services for information.

Went back for the duty frees

If an aircraft is evacuated on landing at Gatwick the fire crews stand by to lay a carpet of foam on the outside of the plane and to help passengers as they slide down the chutes. One crew was amazed to see the travellers emerging from a giant airliner which had just made an emergency landing. 'We couldn't believe our eyes', they laughed. 'As soon as they hit the ground they leapt to their feet, ran to the front of the plane and climbed back in to get the duty frees they had left behind!'

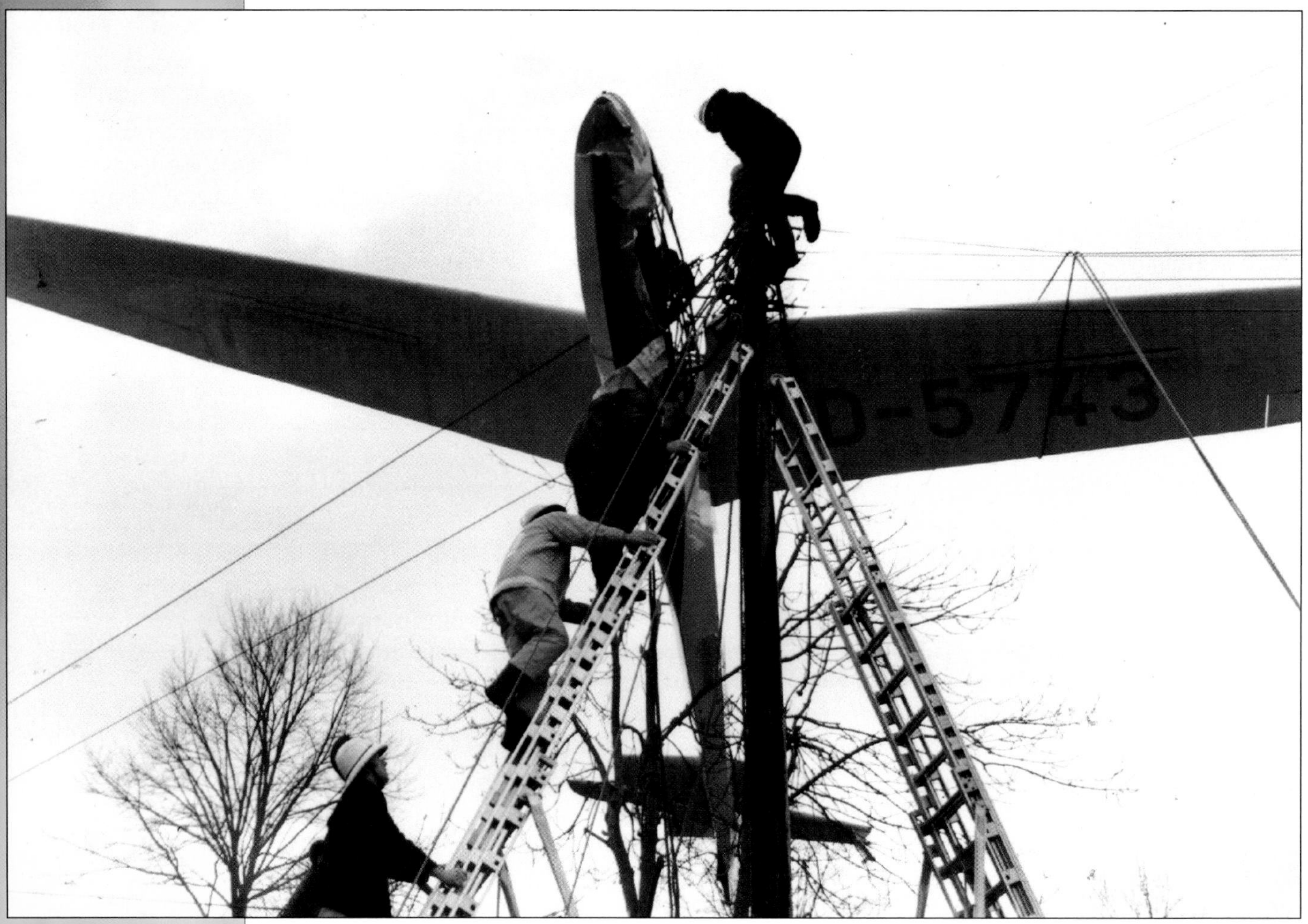

The end of the lesson. A trainee glider pilot was coming in to land at Storrington, West Sussex, when a sudden gust of wind blew the plane into a treetop. West Sussex firemen had to fasten the wings securely to prevent the aircraft from falling before putting up two ladders and bringing the young pilot and her instructor to safety. (West Sussex Fire Brigade)

ironically, the area around the ruins of the Sainsbury building.

By 6 January, the fire brigade was already combining with the Rivers Authority to see how much water could be pumped into the nearby canal. But a quick helicopter trip to survey the scene made it clear that the canal was already too full to accommodate much more water.

A day later, the full emergency was under way. Fixed pipes were put in place overnight with barriers, ramps and cones to help people get into shops and offices. It was obvious, as the rain continued to pour, that more equipment was needed, and a call for help was sent to the Army stores in the Midlands where the Green Goddess appliances were stored. Ten of these old stand-by 'work horses' were driven south, along with 200 lengths of fixed piping. Next night, Staffordshire fire personnel brought down a further 10 emergency pumps and 1,200 lengths of fixed piping to clear the floods, by now knee deep in some places, and divert them out to the sea. The weekend brought no let-up in the storms.

On the Monday the mud embankments which had been shovelled into place were beginning to give way, and every possible means of support was brought to stop them from breaching. Plywood sheets, tidy bins and a whole desert of sandbags were forced into position. The rescue workers, including, by now, personnel from the Hampshire Fire Training School, Royal Navy divers, Highways workers, District Council and National Rivers Authority staff, all held their breath as the tide came in and the rain still fell.

The campaign continued. A fine balance was kept between the amount of protection which might be given to one area without forcing the torrents into another and the task of finding outlets to carry the diverted streams down into the sea when the tide was not so high that it would be forced back inland again.

For almost the whole of January, West Sussex was dealing with flooding, not just in Chichester but throughout the county. At the end of the month came the equally massive task of clearing up.

Both the floods and the Sainsbury fire brought mountains of paperwork for the back-up staff who support all fire brigades today. Meanwhile, the crews returned to their normal assortment of answering calls to the community. Some idea of the variety of these was given in the Annual Report by the Chief Fire Officer, Kenneth Lloyd. They included fires in thatched cottage roofs; large country houses; a furniture workshop at Knepp Castle; a Dutch barn containing 1,500 bales of hay; 400 tonnes of straw at another farm; bales of paper being loaded on to a ship in Shoreham Harbour, hazardous in the extreme when burning sheets of loose paper, blown by a brisk wind, fluttered round the firemen and started satellite outbreaks; fire in the engine room of a ship moored at Littlehampton; and an assortment of chemical incidents.

Animals, as ever, figured large in the annual statistics. Sussex firefighters worked for two hours in flood water to rescue three calves when the River Arun burst its banks at Pulborough. In the same village, they manhandled a flock of more than 50 sheep out of another flood and penned them safely in a nearby – drier – field.

SURREY

Like many counties, Surrey wants its recruits to be prepared for the variety of 'shouts' they are likely to come up against. With this in mind – and the added information it can give to more experienced firefighters – they have set up their own video unit, run by an expert, Mike Drewett, who goes out to an assortment of incidents throughout the year. The variety has been remarkable.

Freak gales on 27 March 1988 brought 173 emergency calls to their Reigate Control in 24 hours, at the rate of one every four minutes.

It could not have been a worse start to the day when a Bedford van carrying workers to a building site was crushed under a falling beech tree on the A217 at Kingswood, near Banstead. Surrey sent four appliances, and three more came in from adjoining West Sussex, but three people had been killed by the impact of the tree.

While they were dealing with this, calls were coming in from all over the county about fallen trees blocking roads and damaging property. One was exceptional.

The three-coach 0843 train from East Grinstead to Victoria had started late and left the small country station at Dormans soon after 0900 hours. The driver gained speed and was travelling at some 40 mph when he negotiated a gradual bend and saw, with horror, a huge tree lying across the rails ahead. Instantly, he slammed on his emergency brakes (one passenger recalled the train shuddering as it slowed), but despite his quick reaction the corner

Milk of human kindness flows after meeting

Retained and volunteer firefighters who train in their spare time when not doing their own paid jobs, are always of immense value to brigades throughout the country. In the more remote parts of Britain, they form the major part of the fire service, and bring their own special expertise to the role as well as the knowledge of fire-fighting. They often become close friends when off duty.

Typically, in one rural Surrey station, the crew were having their general meeting when one of them, a farmer, was called home for a sudden calving. All the crew went with him and when the healthy calf was born it was named 'General' after the disturbed meeting. Another part-timer who was an electronics expert from the nearby university, fixed everyone's televisions if they went wrong. In Cumbria the retained crews include a vicar and a barmaid, while Highlands and Islands have only one full-time station and 99 whole-time firefighters. The rest of the stations are retained or volunteer, manned by 381 part-time firefighters and 931 volunteers. Among them are several women, including a hairdresser from Skye.

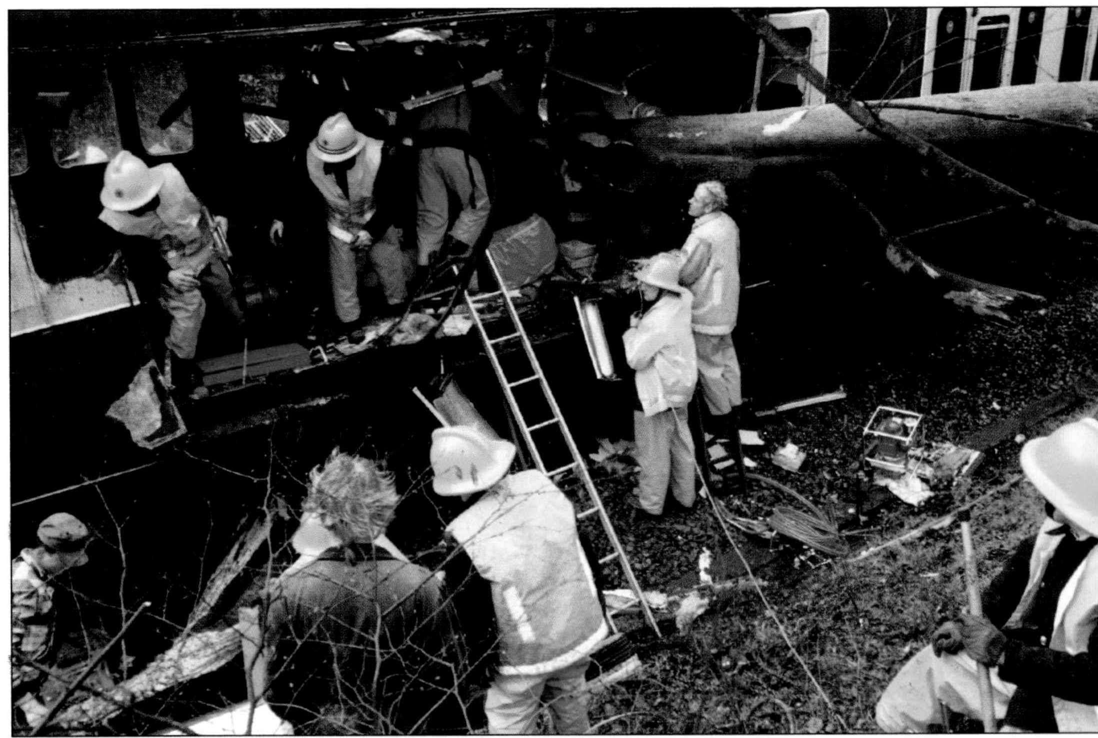

Fire crews and medics struggle to release an injured man, trapped when this tree was struck by the front of a train, spun round and pierced a carriage, smashing its way out on the other side and flinging another passenger on to the far embankment. He survived as did the trapped fellow passenger. (Mike Drewett, Surrey Fire and Rescue Service)

of his cab smashed into the treetop. Instead of sliding along the rails, the tree whirled round horizontally. Its roots cannoned into one of the carriages, smashing through and out the other side, hurling one man out across the track and on to the far embankment, injured but still alive.

Inside the carriage the shocked commuters scrambled back from the huge trunk. However, one man, 41-year-old Mr Reginald Steer, was pinned by his legs. He had four teeth knocked out, deep cuts across his face, and a piece of the metal seat-back penetrating his groin and the back of his leg.

Local workers who had heard the crash called the emergency services and the Dormans station master to warn him – but by then another train was approaching the scene. The guard of the crashed train already had this in mind and was racing along the track waving a red flag. He stopped the second train 41 metres – less than 50 yards – from the wreckage.

Emergency services were all on the scene within 10 minutes. Some rushed to the injured survivor still lying on the embankment. He was taken to hospital and eventually recovered. Others helped the passengers from the wrecked carriage and set about releasing Mr Steer. With a medical team in attendance the fire crews used hydraulic lifting gear and blocks to ease the pressure of the tree from his legs. A Tirfor winch was brought in to draw it away, along with the metal which was still pinning him down.

It took nearly two hours of meticulously careful work to avoid any further injury

Right: *A fire officer and doctor tended the Chertsey print worker while firefighters and engineers combined to produce a suitable tool to release his trapped hand from the plastic covered toughened steel rollers of his machine.* (Mike Drewett, Surrey Fire and Rescue Service)

and release him. To cries of 'that's it!' 'well done' 'take it easy!' 'keep his feet together!' 'careful!' they lowered him on to a stretcher – but the job was not yet over. As they carried him back down the line to the station, the gale was still lashing across. It knocked them off balance whipping away the blankets covering him and tearing at the drips which had been inserted by the doctors. Eventually he was safely stowed in a waiting ambulance and rushed to hospital. There he had 40 stitches in the gashes which cut the length and breadth of his face, and his other injures were treated.

Later, the firefighters were touched to receive a letter from Mr and Mrs Steer, thanking them warmly for all they had done.

Barely two weeks later, on 11 April 1988, a loaded BP tanker which had just left its depot in Walton-on-Thames was driving through the town when it was involved in an accident. It overturned, rolled on to a car and trapped a woman inside. As the tanker split open, 30,000 litres of diesel and petrol spewed out and poured down the road, into the drainage system and on to the Thames. For a brief period a square mile area near the town centre was under threat of an enormous explosion, but without regard for their own safety a team of firefighters went in and rescued the woman trapped in the car. As they worked to extricate her, other fire crews attacked with foam, pouring it out

Invented rescue tools

Dedicated Control staff and unique tools, invented and made on the spot by Surrey firefighters and specialist engineers, all contributed to the success of an agonising operation at a printing plant in Chertsey in July 1992. At the end of the working day, a print worker who had been cleaning his machine got the fingers of his right hand trapped to the first knuckle between two hardened steel rollers.

The crews arrived quickly and administered pain killers to the shocked man, but found the rollers too tough for any of their normal equipment to penetrate. While a doctor cared for the victim, the crews and engineers devised an implement for prising the rollers apart and releasing him. Although they had been doing the work on the spot, they paid special tribute later to their Control staff who, they said, had played a great part in tracking down the experts who helped them.

Like many other fire brigades, West Midlands have computerised their Control Room, but the operators still talk to members of the public who make a '999' fire call and have the responsible job of calming them down, making sure that they give a clear address and, if possible, have someone standing outside the scene of the fire to guide in the crews. (West Midlands Fire Service)

Not an alpine Christmas but spring in Walton-on-Thames where firefighters risked their lives to save a woman from this wrecked car when a tanker carrying diesel and petrol overturned on to it. As they worked, other firefighters were pouring a gigantic carpet of foam on the fuel which had leaked from the tanker and poured through the town, bringing imminent risk of a devastating explosion. (Mike Drewett, Surrey Fire and Rescue Service)

from great monitors until the town looked like a snow scene in the Alps.

Altogether, 70 firefighters were involved in making the area safe and helping to minimise the pollution of the river. As one of their officers said: 'It was extremely dangerous, particularly at the beginning. There could have been a major explosion at any time. The risk was very, very high'.

ROYAL BERKSHIRE

Without doubt, the great fire of Windsor Castle in November 1992, was the most important and spectacular event ever to hit Royal Berkshire's Fire and Rescue Service. It happened when their Chief Fire Officer, Garth Scotford, was visiting Australia, so that command of the fire-fighting was in the hands of the Deputy Chief Fire Officer, David Harper.

The Castle was no stranger to fire. Over the centuries since its building was started by William the Conqueror soon after 1066 there had been an assortment of outbreaks. These included one major conflagration in 1853 when rescue efforts were led by Queen Victoria's husband, Prince Albert. Most of the smaller incidents were dealt with by its own fire brigade, helped, if necessary, by Windsor's town firemen. But in recent years, co-operation with the Royal Berkshire Fire and Rescue Service had been increased, particularly after the Royal Household took over responsibility for fire safety. Regular meetings were held, plus an annual exercise, to cover all aspects of fire safety.

It was, then, something of a surprise when Royal Berks HQ received a call at 1137 hours on 20 November 1992 to a fire in the Queen's private chapel at 'Special Address One'- the code name for Windsor Castle.

According to the pre-arranged plans, five appliances including an HP (Hydraulic Platform) were immediately sent from nearby Slough. They arrived seven minutes later to be confronted by a full pipe band marching round the Castle quadrangle, apparently unaware of any problems.

> *Advice offered by successive fire officers had been ignored*

But a problem there was. The first officer took a rapid and comprehensive glance at the rising smoke, then put out a radio call for seven more appliances. The Castle's own fire brigade was on hand to help and advise the Berkshire officers, particularly in finding their way round the rabbit warren of rooms and passages. By just after mid-day there were 20 assorted fire engines on the spot and by 1300 hours Berkshire's Deputy Chief Fire Officer, David Harper, had taken over and was calling for more back-up.

Already the news had been put out on radio and television. As winter's early dusk settled, the flames and smoke could be seen for miles as the fire roared through the magnificent State Apartments.

Within minutes of the fire crews arriving, the valuable collection of pictures, furnishings and ornaments were being removed by Castle staff, helped by troops brought in hastily from nearby barracks. Some 370 people were involved in the salvage work and pre-arranged plans were working to the letter. Every item carried out along chains of helpers, was carefully photographed and logged before being taken off for safe storage. Because of this, very few pieces from the priceless Royal collection were lost to the flames.

The buildings were a different matter. For years, much of the advice offered by successive fire officers, which could only be given on a 'goodwill' basis, had been ignored. It was tragic that when, at last, steps were being taken to try to improve fire safety, it was too late. The flames

Windsor Castle blazing against the night sky in November 1992. Fire crews from Royal Berkshire and the surrounding areas fought the flames as a lone piper, among the crowds watching from over the river, played a lament. (Royal Berkshire Fire and Rescue Service)

Lone piper laments

Among the thousands of sightseers who poured to nearby Eton and Datchet to watch the Windsor fire, one man recalled standing in a meadow by the edge of the River Thames which flows below the Castle walls. 'It was dark and very cold, and a mist had risen so that you could only see the top half of people's bodies, reflected in the flames. They were standing in absolute silence which was only broken by the sound of a lone piper who had come down and was playing a lament. It was heartbreaking.'

found their way into the huge gaps above the magnificent plasterwork ceilings and roared through. The Queen arrived just as the fire officers had decided to vent the roof at the worst point to allow the fire to go up, with a chimney effect, in an attempt to slow down its progress sideways.

'I had a difficult job persuading Her Majesty that it was not as bad as it looked', said Mr Harper. His too was the task of briefing the Royal Family and VIPs as they hurried to the scene. But, as he said later, 'advising the Queen that there was no need to evacuate her private rooms was the hardest decision of my career'.

HM The Queen discusses the damage with Royal Berkshire's SDO Lynn Ashfield. (Royal Berkshire Fire and Rescue Service)

At the height of the fire there were two alternatives: to hurl more water in (and there was no shortage as the Castle has its own supply), or to set up fire breaks. The fire was still spreading fast and needed what David Harper called 'very aggressive firefighting'. This involved more 'venting' as well as creating fire breaks and attacking with 31 jets plus three great monitors, aimed with devastating accuracy from the top of three hydraulic platforms, high above the walls.

Help was pouring in from the surrounding counties. The first contingency had arrived soon after 1300 hours, and at one stage there was not a single Royal Berkshire appliance in any of its fire stations – they had all raced to the Castle. In total, 79 appliances and 700 firefighters attended from nine different county brigades including some as far away as Gloucestershire and Hertfordshire. At one point an off-duty London fireman, driving along the nearby M4, was flabbergasted to see the pump escape from Soho, London's heartland, racing towards the Castle 'on the bell'.

'We never knew where the next crew was coming from,' explained one officer. 'I found myself looking round for help and finding a turntable ladder from one county, an escape from another. It was an amazing turn-out.' Breathing apparatus was essential. In the course of the fire, 80 sets were in use and 750 cylinders were supplied.

Miraculously – again – only one firefighter was injured. Two more men, in BA, had taken their hose into one of the State rooms when, almost with a sixth sense, they looked up and hurled themselves against the wall as the vast ceiling above them, heavy now with water, crashed down on the very point where they had been standing.

One of the added problems – apart from dealing with the world's press, which had poured in and been 'penned' in the Castle's (dry!) moat – was feeding the 700 firefighters who needed food, and particularly drink, to prevent dehydration as they sweated in the heat. At one stage, the

Salvation Army's canteen, which is always on hand at major incidents, was supported by the WRVS and Windsor's local hotels and restaurants. Several burger bars and pizza houses stayed open all night to help with the food supplies.

The flames continued far into the night, with the TV eyes and ears of the world following their awful progress. The 'stop' came in the small hours of the next morning – but crews were damping down for seven days afterwards. Despite the intensity of the fire, the ancient Castle walls were said to have stood up remarkably well. To help pay for the reconstruction, the Queen later opened Buckingham Palace to the public for a limited period of paying tours.

Luckily, incidents of this size are rare – anywhere in the country. But for Royal Berkshire there are always a variety of calls to its major motorways, the M3 and M4, and to a wide range of 'shouts', from nuclear establishments to farms and rivers. It was a river incident which one Berkshire firefighter, later a Station Officer, remembers most vividly.

Fireman Ken Kay had, at 23 years old, only two years' service under his belt when the call came through to his station in December 1976: 'car submerged in the river; children trapped'.

Taking up the story himself, years later, he recalled: 'If you believe in fate, this was it and I'll never forget that night – cold, dark, raining. I shouldn't have been on at the time. I was riding supernumerary on a TL, but I happened to be standing next to the Station Commander when I heard the words "children trapped". I said "Do you mind if I go sir?" and for some reason he said "OK. Hop into my car".

'By now the first two pumps were away and we trailed them the mile or so down the road to Kings Meadows and the lock. There were two entrances. They went to the further one. We saw a policeman at the end of the first track and drove towards him. He was quite worked up and shouting "They're in there! In there!" and pointing at the river. The car was just disappearing below the surface; we could see the bubbles and there was an eerie red glow under water where the rear lights were still on.

'There was only one thing for it. I stripped down to my underpants and duck-dived in. The water was freezing cold. I felt for the door handles but couldn't find them. The cold was grabbing me and I had to surface, breathe and dive down again. The car had stirred up the mud, the water was murky and I still couldn't find the door handles. Again, I had to surface and this time I called for BA equipment. I believe that this was the first time ever that BA intended for use at fires was used under water.

'The crews had raced back to the scene. They fitted the BA and face mask

Pity we can't take our boots off! Firefighters – male and female – take a break during the battle to save the castle. (Royal Berkshire Fire and Rescue Service)

Learning the lessons

The saga of the Windsor Castle fire was made into a one and a half hour presentation by the Royal Berkshire Fire and Rescue Service. This describes how the fire developed, and includes the original fire brigade radio and telephone messages, on-site video footage, extracts from news bulletins, diagrams, illustrations of past fires in the Castle, and a background of appropriate music.

It has been used for training, to explain the way in which the fire developed and how it was dealt with by the fire service.

and held me back long enough to fasten a line to me. I dived again. This time I crouched on the car roof and thought “I must treat this logically. Where are the handles likely to be?” I felt my way down to the wheel arches and then made my way back to the door. The handles were recessed, but now I tried to open the door. Either it was locked or the water pressure was holding it firm. In the end I got my knees against the door frame and pulled with all my strength. Slowly, like a spoon coming out of treacle, it opened and I looked inside. It was glowing strangely white now – the interior light had come on.

‘I clambered in and felt around until I grasped a bundle of wet rags floating above my head. It was a woman. I dragged her out and up to the surface where the crews began resuscitation. The car had been underwater for about 15 minutes, but next time down I found another woman and got her back to the crews who set to work on her. I was so cold now that I could hardly think, but I had it on my mind that there were still children in the car.

‘I dived again, knelt on the front seat and leaned into the back groping at more sodden material and tearing at it to release the bodies. By now my arms and legs were losing all feeling and I realised that unless I got out quickly I would collapse with hypothermia. Still I scrabbled at the fabric but eventually gave up. Luckily the line was still intact. It saved my life. I just managed to scramble clear of the car so they could haul me to the surface.

‘I was shaking from head to foot with the cold and the crews half-carried me over to the pump and stood me by the warm engine to try to thaw me out. Someone gave me a cup of hot coffee but my hands were shaking so much I couldn’t drink it. Next thing I knew I was back at the fire station being put into a hot bath and while I was there, they came back with the message that I had rescued a mother and daughter, one about 60 the other around 30 years old and both still alive. They had been Christmas shopping and hadn’t realised that they had parked on the edge of the river. Heading for home, the driver had backed the car into the water.

‘But above all, they confirmed that there were no children in the car. After that, I stopped shaking. Only later did they tell me that in my desperation to find the children I had thought were there, I had ripped all the fabric off the back seat.’

The two women survived, but the mother died a month later from complications following pneumonia.

Fireman Kay had a longer trip a year later when he went to Buckingham Palace to receive the Queen’s Gallantry Medal. He still maintains that he couldn’t have done it alone. ‘All the crews were involved, the resuscitators, the Thames Conservancy who helped get the women ashore, the ambulance people. You don’t just do these things alone.’

Behind every County fire service are the often forgotten members of the Control Room staff who form the link between the public dialling ‘999’ and the firefighting crews. Their work involves not only making sure that they have the exact location of the fire accurately logged, but often in dealing with a very agitated caller – and in some cases, a child.

Leading Fire Control Operator Alan Webster of Royal Berkshire took just such a call at noon on 29 July 1993. Schools were on summer holiday and a 13-year-old girl, left in charge of her two brothers, aged 11 and six, and her five-year-old sister, had been upstairs with them when she smelt smoke. Dashing to the landing, she found the kitchen was on fire and they were trapped on the first floor.

‘She was remarkably cool,’ said a fire officer later. ‘She ushered the younger children into the front bedroom where there was a telephone, shut the door and dialled 999.’ Alan Webster called out the nearest fire crew and, realising her predicament, began talking the girl through the situation. As with all ‘999’ calls, the conversation was logged on tape.

‘Have you closed the door?’ – ‘yes’.

'Can you see any smoke coming through?' – 'Just a bit.' 'Can you get your brothers to put the bedding up against the door, pack the pillows round the edges to stop the smoke coming through?' Quietly he told her to get the children close to the window. He heard the younger ones crying and told her to tell them not to worry, to open the window and listen for the fire engine, to explain that it was on its way. He was as relieved as the girl must have been when he heard the sound of the two-tone getting louder, the fire engine stopping and the comforting 'clunk' as the ladder struck the front wall of the house. All the children were rescued and later the Chief Officer wrote a friendly letter congratulating Alan on his professionalism in the way he dealt with the call.

BUCKINGHAMSHIRE

Compared with the excitements of the bigger counties, Buckinghamshire tends to think of its incidents as 'rather bread and butter', although its major motorways – the M40 and the M25 – provide all too frequent jams after pile-ups. This was another area which changed its old name of 'fire brigade' to Fire and Rescue Service because it found itself dealing with rescues almost as much as fires.

It was, at one time, a very rural county with a lot of small farms. This brought a regular crop of fires in barns and haystacks, particularly with spontaneous combustion if the hay was stored while it was slightly damp. Heat built up inside the stacks and eventually burst into flame. Today a fire is more likely to be caused by children playing with matches, or tramps dossing down for the night and throwing away a cigarette end.

Now, public attitudes and farming methods have both changed. 'We get quite a lot of arson and, of course, fires in the equipment used on some of the bigger farms these days', explained a Bucks officer. 'For years, they've been pulling down hedges and making bigger and bigger fields. These need bigger farm gear, including enormous combine harvesters,

Nuclear farming

It isn't unusual to see Bucks firefighters plodding incongruously across the rural landscape in full protective clothing as they approach incidents involving big combine harvesters.

These giant machines are often guided automatically up and down the enormous fields by sophisticated equipment which includes small quantities of radioactive material. This is safe enough under normal circumstances but presents a headache to the emergency services if the equipment is broken open in an accident.

and if these catch fire, the fire service has to be called. Then, again, the grain is stored in huge grain driers and these too, can cause problems.

'You never know what you're going to come up against – from cutting a metal tube off a child's finger to coping with a chemical incident on a motorway. We have also had a fairly major hazard among the many furniture factories which have gathered, traditionally, in and around High Wycombe.'

HAMPSHIRE

Many a fire officer has stepped back from an incident and trembled at the thought of what might have been. 'It was a bloody miracle' is a regular catchphrase after a particularly lucky escape.

It certainly had all the appearances of a lucky coincidence, if not a full miracle, when an executive Citation 550 jet came in to land at Eastleigh Airport, just outside Southampton, on Wednesday 26 May 1993.

Time was on their side. It was 0630 hours when the pilot and co-pilot battled their way down towards the runway. A motorist, approaching this stretch of the M27 said 'conditions were atrocious. We'd been hit by two thunderstorms in succession. Before each one struck there was a bout of gusting winds and then each poured down an inch of torrential rain. There were great rumbles of thunder and lightning flashes all over the sky'.

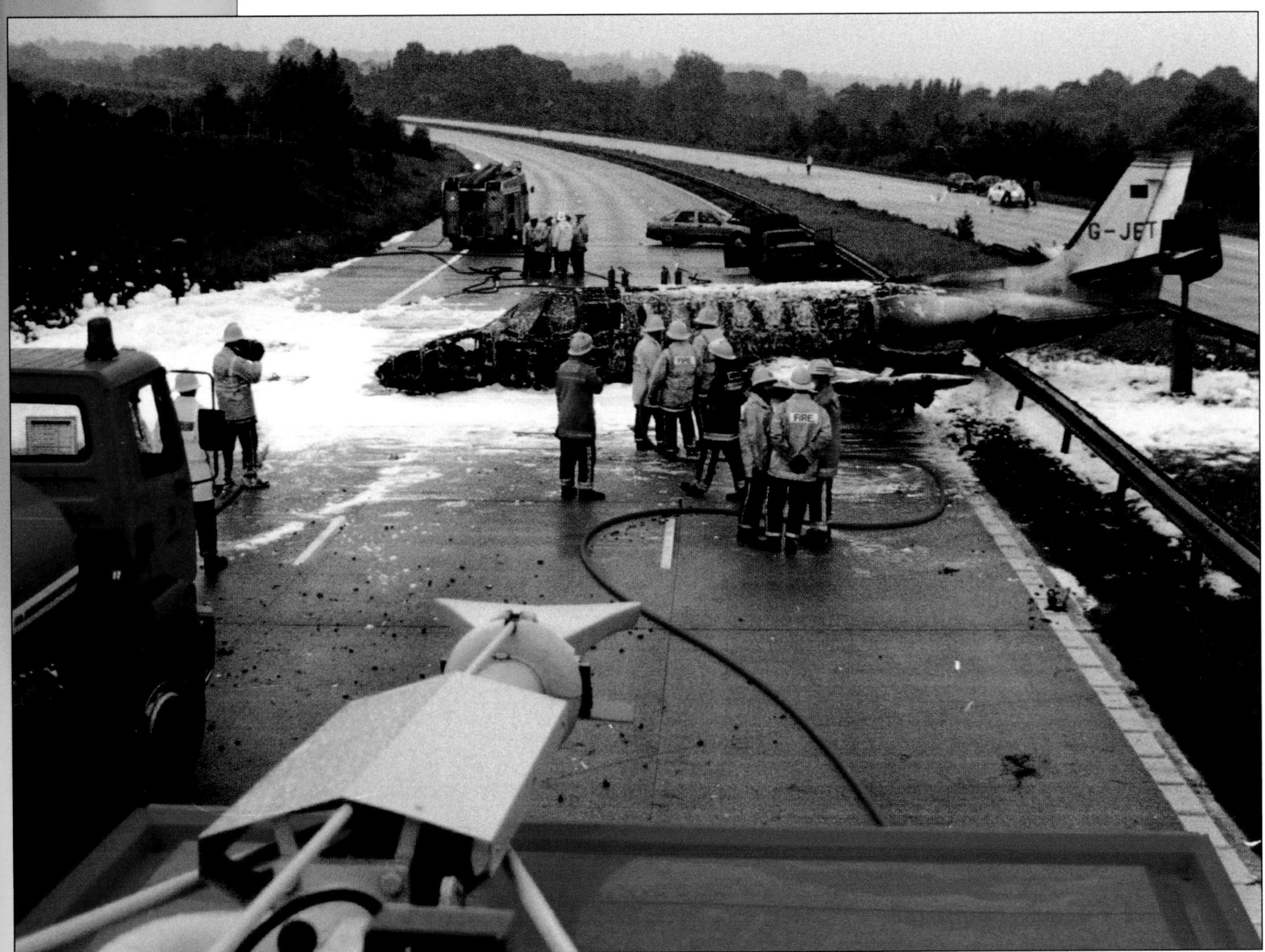

Miracle on the M27. Air crew from this executive jet and early morning motorists, near Southampton, were lucky to escape when the plane missed the runway at Eastleigh Airport at the height of a sudden thunderstorm in May 1993 and landed on the motorway. By coincidence, the accident happened only days before local emergency services had planned to hold a live emergency exercise at the airfield. (Hampshire Fire and Rescue Service)

Eastleigh was not officially open until 0700 hours. Airport firefighters were outside, checking their equipment as the plane skimmed over their heads and they realised that it was going to land, not on the airfield but beyond the perimeter fence on the M27 motorway.

Immediately, they swung into action, chasing the plane as it lost height and following it out on to the road. The two pilots dropped from the cockpit and ran for cover in the brief seconds left to them before the fuselage burst into flames. But almost immediately, the firefighters had turned their monitors on and soused the plane and road surface with foam.

Luck was again with them. Had the incident happened half an hour later the road would have been busy with early commuter traffic. Had the jet crash-landed another hundred yards further on it would have hit the Ford Motor Company's factory car park.

The miracle extended to the two cars which had been on the motorway at the time, a Renault 18 and a Ford Sierra. The Renault was being driven by 35-year-old Roy Davis, on his way to work. He said later that he had only just joined the motorway when his car was hit and burst into flames. For a moment, he thought he had hit the car ahead – he didn't even see the plane before it 'winged' him. The car's central locking system was activated by the impact and for a short time he was trapped in the now burning vehicle. Somehow he managed to scramble out and could only remember smelling the aircraft fuel, spreading across the road towards him before losing consciousness and being taken to hospital with head and hip injuries.

The two men in the Sierra were even luckier. Steve Huthwaite and Dale Antell had just come off the night shift at Ford's and were horrified to see the plane flying straight at them. It hit the car a glancing blow, but enough to roll it over, trapping them inside. Remarkably, they both escaped with shock and, for one, a broken thumb.

Firemen were said, in an old poem, to have 'courage high and hearts aglow'. They needed both courage and adrenalin when they faced a fire, believed to have been started deliberately, in trucks parked in a compound near the Wella Building in Lister Road, Basingstoke, in the small hours of 24 May 1983. Their load – hundreds of highly inflammable aerosol cans.

Hampshire Fire and Rescue Service logged 150 calls as terrified residents watched nervously as the exploding aerosols shot like demented fireworks in all directions, some of them up to 100 feet in the sky. Crews from Basingstoke Fire Station were first on the scene and the 10 firefighters rapidly assessed the situation. With cool courage, they decided that the first essential was to remove two tractor units attached to trailers which were already on fire. Despite the risk of explosion they held their ground and managed to uncouple the tractors and drive them to safety while the rest of the crew tackled the blazing trailers – and dodged the flying aerosols.

The fire, which, had it not been contained, could have spread to a neighbouring factory with more risk of explosions, was eventually extinguished. But it had burned with such intensity that it was four hours before the wrecked trucks were cool enough for police to search them to find clues which might lead to the arsonist.

When it comes to recalling past dramas, the people of Basingstoke will remember for years the great fire on 16 April 1991 when the Churchill Plaza, a 14-storey office block went up in flames in the heart of the town, and a senior officer owed his life to the courage of his men.

This was a terrifying fire. At one stage the whole top section of the modern blue glass building, which stood out as a landmark, was lit from within as the heat blew out the windows, showering the firefighters with broken glass. The firemen's lift, installed to save crews from having to mount the staircase to the top of the block in the event of fire, was put out of action almost immediately and crews had to struggle up the tower of stairs in heat and smoke, dragging hoses and equipment behind them.

The first '999' call had reached Control at 2142 hours. Four minutes later the first fire crews had reached the scene and begun to assess the situation. They were told that the fire was on the 9th floor and took the firemen's lift there, but as they searched the open plan offices, they could feel heat rising from below. In fact, the seat of the fire was among the office equipment on the 8th floor and already,

A single burning aerosol can kill as it explodes and shoots through the air. Basingstoke firefighters were all too aware of the fact as they ducked and dived in their effort to fight fires, believed to have been started deliberately, in two lorries and two juggernaut trailers packed with hair products. According to local residents, the aerosols 'were going off like rockets and flying in all directions'. (Hampshire Fire and Rescue Service)

the flames had a strong hold. As the crews battled with the flames, the heat of the fire broke glass windows on both sides of the buildings and set up such a draught that the intensity of the flames increased even more rapidly. By 2200 hours reinforcements were arriving from all over Hampshire and 90 firemen were at work in the building.

It was just before 2300 hours that three firemen, working high up on a staircase, were hit by a sudden great belch of hot black smoke. They backed down the stairs, heading for safety, when they realised that their senior officer was no longer with them. Divisional Commander Malcolm Whitehouse, in the heat of the moment, had plunged in without breathing apparatus. Fireman Vince Stapleton turned and ran back up the stairs, calling and listening for a reply. None came. Dropping down and crawling up through the smoke on his stomach, he cautiously opened the door into the 8th floor but could see nobody. It was at the top of the next flight of stairs, in thick smoke, that he caught a glimpse of the Commander, collapsed against the wall. 'I spoke to him but he didn't answer,' Vince said, 'so I got hold of him and dragged him backwards down the stairs until I met my mates, Mick Phillips and Ian Jones, coming up. The smoke was less dense here and between us, we carried him down the rest of the stairs and out into the open.' D/C Whitehouse recovered in hospital from smoke inhalation and was later able to go home to his wife and daughters.

Green Goddesses to the rescue. Two of these tough but redoubtable 'old ladies' pumped steadily for many hours on end to clear water from buildings in West Sussex and Hampshire which had been flooded by the non-stop torrential rain in January 1994. (Hampshire Fire and Rescue Service)

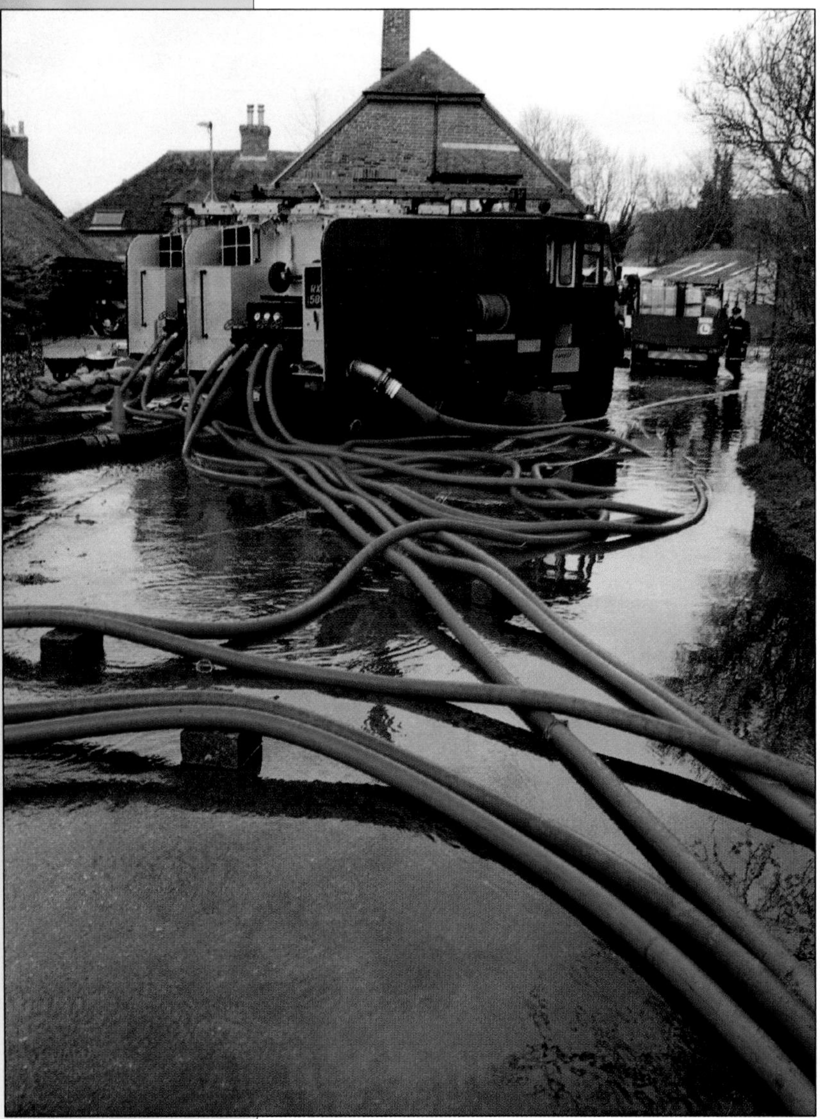

> ***'It was a wet, miserable, cold night, but this was only the prelude'***

Although the building was reckoned to be 'a monument to modern fire prevention techniques', the speed with which the fire took hold of the whole top six floors suggested otherwise. Many officers felt that the outbreak would have been contained more easily had a sprinkler system been installed.

Torrential rain had been falling, hour after hour, on 4 January 1994. Throughout the evening Hampshire's firefighters had attended 226 calls for help, most of them in the Portsmouth area. 'It was certainly one of the busiest nights since the storms of 1987 and 1990,' observed one of their officers. 'Most of the calls were to flooded gardens and roads, but some were for pumping out basements.'

It was a wet, miserable, cold night for the soaked crews, but this was only the prelude. Dawn – and many dawns to come – brought pitch black clouds rolling over the south of England and days of solid rain. Every firefighter and every appliance in the county was turned out to cope with the water which seemed to be coming at them from all sides. By the middle of the month the water table in the hills was reported to be 91.8 feet (28 metres) above normal and at saturation point. Rain poured off the land and, with no streams or rivers to direct it, cascaded down through the villages and towns to the sea. Such rivers and streams as there were had burst their banks, water meadows were flooded, and in places the whole landscape was transformed into one massive lake.

Convoys of 'Green Goddess' pumps travelled down from the Midlands to ease the strain on the local appliances. The sturdy green 'engines' had been built for long sessions without a break and they released some, at least, of the local fleet for more normal duties. But still the rain poured down.

By mid-January, the county's Chief Fire Officer, John Pearson, was reporting that the combined efforts of all the pumps was recovering six million gallons (27 million litres) of water a day (enough to supply a town the size of Winchester for a normal day) from flooded cellars, ground floors, village streets and gardens as well as from the specially erected dams which had been built, with the help of the firefighters, to protect the villages at greatest risk. In Finchdean alone, one of the worst hit places, crews were pumping three million gallons of water a day from the village and into the fields behind The George public house.

Other crews helped with the backbreaking job of filling endless sandbags and digging ditches to channel the water. They went on to plunge up to their knees – and higher – in flood water to carry the elderly and the very young to safety from homes which were too badly flooded for the sandbags to help. Some crossed the county border into West Sussex to help pump out Chichester where the old Cathedral was threatened and much of the town centre was under water.

Not until the end of January was the area clear of flood water. Then the fire service was left with the job of helping clear up and sort out the equipment. It cost Hampshire's local authority alone £2 million towards the overall expenses of the emergency.

'A bunch of bastards' is the firefighters' term for tangled hose, but few could have seen such a varied collection as these, left behind as the 1994 flood waters receded in Hampshire. Someone was in for a headache unravelling them. (Hampshire Fire and Rescue Service)

Flood water on this scale is a rare hazard, but in Hampshire the sea is never very far away, and it was a near tragedy quite close to the shore which brought bravery awards for three firefighters.

On 31 January 1993, Cosham Station Officer Keith Simmons had been spending his day off working on his boat, down at the Sailing Club in Langstone Harbour when two teenage boys called over to him that a dinghy had capsized. Glancing across, he saw the upturned boat and then realised that two middle aged men had fallen out of it and were being swept out on the tide.

Watch where you put your hands! The cow with the beady eye had wandered from its pasture in Liss, Hampshire and fallen into the swimming pool of a nearby garden. Firefighters helped its owners lure it up on to bales of hay before hauling it out in this unusual rescue in the winter of 1993. (Hampshire Fire and Rescue Service)

Very nearly overcome. Ralph Southern keeps a stiff upper lip as Tim Murrell, Assistant Chief Officer of Hampshire Fire and Rescue Service, presents him with a Certificate as youngest winner of the 'First Alert' Competition for his knowledge of fire safety. Included with the certificate was a prize of a smoke alarm. (Hampshire Fire and Rescue Service)

Firefighters had picked their way gingerly along Southampton's derelict Royal Pier after six crews from St. Mary's, Woolston and Redbridge had rushed to the scene to try to stop the remains of the structure, already damaged from a previous fire, from collapsing into Southampton Water in July 1992. They were lucky to escape when two explosions rocked the girders. Gas cylinders, left in one of the buildings, had blown up and were followed by a fireball which sent black smoke billowing across the town. (Hampshire Fire and Rescue Service)

Sparks fly as a Hampshire firefighter struggles to cut his way into a Securicor van. Raiders had forced it off the road by threatening to blow it up with a remote control device, but were thwarted as they tried to cut their way in. Their oxy-acetylene torch set fire to some of the £10 million cash inside. In the chaos the driver and his mate managed to escape and raised the alarm. Even Hampshire's finest firefighters had to call on Securicor experts before they could cut through the tough outer metal of the van, lower two firefighters in breathing apparatus into the thick smoke inside and put out the flames. (Hampshire Fire and Rescue Service)

Although he would be the first to admit that he was not a strong swimmer, he grabbed a buoyancy ring and dived into the sea. He managed to reach the younger man, 48-year-old David Lown, and bring him back to safety. Tired by the effort, he nevertheless plunged back into the freezing water and struck out for the second man, David's brother, 56-year-old Don Lown who, by this time, had been swept 500 yards off the shore. By now the fire brigade had arrived and two firemen, Russell ('Buster') Brown and Roger Moore, commandeered the nearest small dinghy and rowed off towards Keith Simmons and Don Lown, dragging them one after another into the boat. It seemed clear then that the lightweight craft would not hold four men, so Moore got into the icy water and swam alongside until they reached the beach. By this time an ambulance had arrived and Stn/O Simmons, along with the two men he had helped to save, were rushed to hospital with hypothermia and shock. Released later, Keith Simmons said that he was delighted

Dennis bell rung for roll call

On 23 November 1940, Southampton became the target for an intensive air raid, with wave after wave of German bombers raining high explosive and incendiary bombs down on to the docks and the city. It was far more than the local fire brigade could cope with and reinforcements from all the surrounding districts raced in to help.

Winchester's crew arrived at the height of the raid and were at work with their long-serving Dennis motorised fire engine when a bomb exploded almost on top of them. Three of their men were killed and several more injured. Fireman G. Robinson, who was in charge, instantly regrouped the surviving firemen and tended to the wounded before taking them to hospital himself. Being assured that they were in safe hands, he returned to his crew and carried on fighting the fires.

The old Dennis engine was damaged beyond recall. Only its brass bell survived. This was taken back to Winchester where it was engraved with the story of the firemen's courage that night and with the names of the men who died. It still hangs in Winchester City fire station and is rung every morning at 0900 hours for roll call and parade.

to have saved the two men, but admitted that he was very pleased to see the Brigade arrive on the beach. 'Without them we would all have been in trouble.'

As a result of the rescue, Stn/O Simmons was awarded a Chief Fire Officer's Commendation and the Royal Humane Society's Testimonial on Vellum. Leading Ffs Brown and Moore received Chief Officer's letters of congratulation and Letters of Appreciation from the Royal National Lifeboat Institution.

Heroes all! Cosham (Hants) Station Officer Keith Simmons (centre) meets again with fellow firefighters Russell Brown and Roger Moore who helped him rescue two middle-aged brothers when their boat overturned in Langstone Harbour on 31 January 1993 in a calm sea but with a strong ebbing tide. (Hampshire Fire and Rescue Service)

ISLE OF WIGHT

'At times the ground was so hot that it burned the soles off the firefighters' boots'. The report came after arson had apparently been responsible for a fire on the National Trust's Headon Warren heathland near Freshwater, on the Isle of Wight, on 6 August 1989.

It had been a particularly dry summer. Crews raced in from 10 stations to try to prevent the blaze from spreading across this environmentally valuable area of open land. Equipment was manhandled up the steep slopes of the rough terrain and a helicopter was flown in by coastguards from Lee-on-Solent to help. Thermal imaging cameras were used to track down and douse 'hot spots', but after 48 hours of exhausting work, parts of the fire were still gaining ground and the helicopters were keeping watch to prevent the fire crews being trapped between the flames and the cliff edge.

Suddenly, the wind changed. The sky darkened and a heavenly sprinkler system took over. Torrential rain finished off the job for the weary fire crews.

CHAPTER 2

THE COUNTRY LIFE

SOUTH WEST

DORSET

Fires on board ship are among those most feared by firefighters. The small compartments of a vessel do not allow easy access for crews seeking the seat of an outbreak, and the metal construction of a ship can easily spread a fire into unaffected parts simply through the conduction of heat along bulkheads. On top of this, ship fires tend to break out in engine and machinery rooms which are usually many decks down in the depths of the ship's hull.

The only way down to these parts is via metal companionways and ladders, around which the heat and smoke from the fire will be swirling upwards in a chimney effect. It is the heat debilitation in a large ship with many decks to penetrate that probably makes for the most physically punishing firefighting conditions anywhere. Another problem concerns ship stability. Even a modest amount of firefighting water pumped into a ship can upset its trim in the water, so before fire crews can safely tackle an on-board fire, sufficient pumping capacity has to be available to pump water out of the hull again.

It was just such a fiery and difficult situation that Dorset firefighters found themselves in on the afternoon of 28 January 1986. The first wisps of smoke coming from the hold of the 7,400 ton *MV Ebn Magid* were noticed by the ship's crew when it was about 21 miles south of Portland Bill. The freighter was carrying a general cargo including cattle feed, cocoa powder and pharmaceuticals and was bound for Tripoli out of Antwerp.

The German master of the *Ebn Magid* activated the ship's carbon-dioxide fire suppression system but this appeared to have no effect in reducing the thickening smoke coming from the cargo decks. He then made a Mayday call for assistance and several warships in the vicinity responded and escorted the *Ebn Magid* towards the Portland Royal Naval base. It was at this stage that Dorset Fire Brigade were alerted to the burning ship which was shortly to be delivered to them.

Further reports from the escorting warships led to a change of plan. The *Ebn Magid* would be anchored out in Weymouth Bay with the firefighting effort mounted there from smaller support ships alongside. Before the burning ship arrived there, the Dorset Brigade was able to assemble its resources on shore, although a fire service reconnaissance party embarked on a naval support vessel and was ready to board the *Ebn Magid* when she finally entered Weymouth Bay late that evening.

Even before the first Dorset crews ventured far down into the stricken vessel, it was obvious that a serious fire was gathering force deep within the ship's hold.

A serious fire burns deep within the freighter Ebn Magid *off Portland, Dorset, on 28 January, 1986. Firefighters working from several tenders battled to get down into the ship's holds. Access was made extremely difficult as containers with cars on top were stacked on the decks. Note the thick smoke which, added to the intense heat in the holds, made conditions particularly uncomfortable for the fire crews. Luckily, the sea was fairly calm, but 8,000 man hours were spent in firefighting before the fire was under control.* (Dorset News)

Thickening clouds of dense smoke were now showing from separate parts of the midships section.

Because of the severity of the fire and the need to put many firefighting crews on board and sustain their effort, the Royal Navy agreed to allow the *Ebn Magid* into Portland Harbour. A major firefighting operation was then mounted from a flotilla of support vessels gathered in choppy waters around the freighter. Fire pumps brought their crews to a pier area nearby and a number of support vehicles including breathing apparatus tenders were also assembled.

However, firefighting efforts led by Dorset's Chief Fire Officer, Trevor Bassett, to save the vessel and its cargo were beset with problems. Access down into the various holds for breathing apparatus crews was not easy. Not only was the *Ebn Magid*'s deck packed with containers, but many of these had cars on top. Those hatches into the hold which could be opened showed that cargo inside was stowed to within inches of the access ladders. As midnight approached and the smoke got thicker, it became evident that the cargo also included drums of highly flammable ethanol and butanol. It was a firefighter's nightmare.

The CFO's strategy was simple. The fire was thought to be in No 3 hold and to get into this with water jets would only be possible via No 2. Upper hatch covers were removed where possible and under cooling sprays firefighters first removed the flammable drums. This dangerous work took several hours. Then, several decks down, working in dreadful, hot and smoky conditions, firefighters were able to squeeze into No 2 hold and from there to close in on the seat of the fire in No 3. But there were more frustrations. Many cars found in the hold were not shown on the ship's cargo plan and they were right on top of the seat of the fire, believed to be bagged animal feed. Worse still, the ship

began to list to starboard, although this was soon corrected by pumping ballast water to port.

Due to the worsening situation, a decision was taken at about 0800 hours on the second morning to beach the *Ebn Magid* in shallow water in Portland Harbour. When this was done, she was about 764 yards (700 metres) from the beach itself. Earlier during the night the ship's lighting had failed and temperature and smoke levels within the *Ebn Magid* were approaching an intolerable level. Taking advice from a marine and salvage expert on board, the CFO withdrew all fire crews from below decks and decided to concentrate on flooding the fire-affected No 3 hold.

This was successfully carried out and by 1 February the fire had been largely extinguished, apart from a number of containers on deck which had ignited through conducted heat from below. Cooling and salvage operations continued for another three days and on 4 February the fire was out and the ship declared safe.

It had been a remarkable logistical exercise and involved over 8,000 firefighting hours. Some 34 fire pumps and seven support vehicles had attended the quayside. Personnel from every one of Dorset's 27 fire stations had been involved at some stage. Twenty-four jets and hundreds of lengths of hose had been used to pump water on board from the tenders moored alongside the *Ebn Magid*. Throughout the four days of intense firefighting, 120 breathing sets had been used, many being recharged and used again by fresh crews. The cause of the fire was believed to have been spontaneous ignition as some damp animal feed dried out.

As for the *Ebn Magid*, she survived her fiery ordeal and was eventually refloated and towed away for repairs. For their part, Dorset Fire Brigade could be forgiven for not wanting to see another ship for a very long time.

> ***Fireballs rolled menacingly up into the darkness as fresh fuel ignited***

SOMERSET

A railway crash of near disaster proportions took place on 16 May 1991, facing Somerset firefighters with a highly dangerous fire situation. In the early hours of the morning, a 660 ton (672 tonne) tanker train travelling from Milford Haven to Devon on the Great Western Inter City main line became derailed at an unmanned automatic level crossing close to the peaceful village of Bradford-on-Tone. It happened when a tanker axle snapped.

Almost all of the 22 tankers, variously loaded with petrol and diesel fuel, reared up, crashed over and were dragged along for some distance before the engine driver was able to stop the train. By then, over half the tanks were on fire. With thousands of gallons of the flammable cocktail spewing out on to the track and into the surrounding areas, the situation was dire. Fortunately, no other train was passing in the opposite direction at the time of the crash.

The train driver was able to uncouple his locomotive and drive down the track to the next signal some half mile distant to raise the alarm. By then a huge fire was lighting up the night sky and several fireballs rolled menacingly up into the darkness as fresh fuel was ignited by the spreading blaze.

When the first crew from Somerset Fire Brigade on a water tender from Wellington Fire Station approached the scene, they found the entire area lit up as if it were daytime, so fierce was the fire being fed by tons of escaping fuel. Even worse was the river of burning fuel which was running down the slope from the level crossing towards them and their fire engine, causing the tarmac to become a wall of flame.

After immediately requesting plenty of assistance, the crew prepared to mount the first firefighting attack which was clearly going to need the blanketing effect of lots of foam. More firefighters were soon arriving on the scene and foam jets were brought to bear on the inferno. Other crews were busy evacuating several farms close to the crash site. Another immediate problem was the unburnt fuel which was still gushing off the track into ditches, gullies and into the River Tone nearby.

As more police officers arrived they were deployed to the nearby villages to warn families to stay in their homes. The major risk was that those tankers not actually on fire would explode, sending lethal metal fragments and more burning fuel into the inferno.

Within an hour of the crash, the fire was still burning fiercely, but by this time over 100 firefighters were battling to control the emergency. These included most of the resources of Somerset Fire Brigade and, in addition, units mobilised from the Devon and the Avon Brigades. To combat such a large flammable fuel fire demanded vast quantities of foam compound beyond that readily available. Every firefighting foam tender in an 80-mile radius of the fire was summoned.

To provide the thousands of gallons of water per minute being used in the firefighting operation, a complicated network of hose lines was needed to bring water from distant water sources. The narrow lanes surrounding the affected area complicated this work and the speedy movement of vehicles and equipment. Soon after the first alarm, the National Rivers Authority were asked urgently to attend the accident site. They had to deal with the potential pollution not only of the River Tone and stream, but to the threat to the surrounding farmland generally. Their personnel, assisted by firefighters, were able to set up a boom across the river to trap the escaping unignited fuel.

When dawn broke the situation was coming under control, although speed restrictions remained in force on the M5 motorway not far away. By mid-morning the fire, which had spread over a wide area for several hundred yards on both sides of the railway line, was completely out. However, thousands of gallons of foam continued to be applied right across the site to prevent re-ignition. Salvage and clearing up operations went on right over the next weekend and the main railway line was not re-opened for five days. The Rivers Authority remained working at the site for many weeks in the aftermath of a crash, which could so easily have had a large loss of life had another train been passing the ill-fated tanker train on that dramatic morning.

Disarmed masked raider

One Somerset firefighter experienced both danger and the unexpected far removed from the smoke and flame of his normal working environment.

In November 1991 Firefighter Ray Fraser, attached to Yeovil Fire Station, came across an armed robbery in progress at the offices of a building society in Yeovil. Ray wrestled and disarmed the masked gunman, and then assisted in his arrest. For his gallant action, Firefighter Fraser was awarded the Queen's Commendation for Brave Conduct.

DEVON

During the winter of 1988 Devon fire crews found themselves called to a very demanding special service rescue, in a remote rural location on a valley floor near the village of Stokeinteignhead in the south of the county.

During a wild and stormy February night when the wind force rose to a frightening pitch, a large oak tree at the edge of a field was blown over. It crashed down on an old caravan which was the home of Walter, a retired farm worker. Walter, asleep at the height of the storm, found he was pinned to his bed amid the crumpled wreckage of the caravan, but miraculously appeared not to be seriously injured.

Walter lay there for several hours, occasionally crying out for help. Eventually a tractor driver on a hill above the crushed caravan noticed the fallen tree

Devon roads are always busy in high summer and it was August 1989 when this car was involved in a collision with a truck. His head injuries bandaged, the driver waits now for fire crews to cut him free from the crushed metal before he can be taken to hospital. (Mark S. Wilkins)

Arson by animal rights activists, opposed to the sale of fur coats, was blamed for this spectacular fire which destroyed much of the top three floors of Dingles department store in Plymouth in December 1989. Devon fire crews prevented the blaze from spreading to the rest of the building and others nearby. (Marc Hill)

and came down to investigate. Discovering Walter, still conscious but suffering from shock and cold, he dashed off to summon help.

When the first Devon firefighters arrived along with an ambulance crew, the immediate problem was to get down to the accident site. A narrow muddy track high above the caravan was as close as the rescuers could venture. From there on, a whole host of rescue equipment such as resuscitator, medical aid kits, hydraulic jacks, compressed air bags, air cylinders, wooden chocks, lines, and power saws all had to be manhandled down the wet and slippery hillside, over several fences and through a hedgerow.

The rescue of Walter was painstakingly slow. Due to the soft and muddy ground all around the crushed caravan, it was first necessary to rig a series of hydraulic jacks to raise the several ton weight of the oak tree a few inches. Once this was done, the Devon firefighters were able to insert a number of inflatable air bags to further raise the tree sufficiently for Walter to be cut free from the splintered woodwork and aluminium wreckage.

All this took time. The jacking operation itself had to be carried out extremely carefully. If the jacks slipped on the muddy surface, the weight of the tree could well have crushed Walter. As the rescue progressed, a medical team arrived by helicopter.

After three hours' work under the most difficult circumstances, Walter was finally freed and taken by stretcher to the helicopter for the brief flight to hospital in Exeter. Apart from some bruising, exposure and severe shock, he had survived his awful ordeal incredibly well.

A most unusual '999' call mobilised Devon firefighters attached to Holsworthy

A quick conference between officers as the Tudor archway goes up in flames and the Elizabethan heart of the ancient Devon town of Totnes is threatened by fire on 4 September 1990. At the height of the fire, 150 firefighters and 20 fire engines from all over the county were at work trying to contain the conflagration. (Devon Fire and Rescue Service)

and Hatherleigh in January 1991. The pilot of an RAF jet on a low flying training flight noticed the roof of a building on fire and radioed his base with a location and a request to call out the fire brigade. The premises concerned was a large public house out in the countryside. A gas leak and explosion had started a fire there. By the time the first crew arrived, a serious blaze had developed which required the attendance of six pumps. The public house was badly damaged.

A tripod, sling and airbag were used in the struggle to rescue this young steer from the mud at Launceston, Cornwall, on 19 June 1993. The waterlogged gully was some distance from the road and fire crews wallowed in the mire before successfully releasing the animal to drier ground. (Gary Chapman)

CORNWALL

On Sunday, 14 December 1986 at 1125 hours a '999' call was received from the police, reporting that a child had fallen into a disused mine shaft at Threemilestone, Truro. One water tender from Truro Fire Station, with Sub Officer Lean in charge, responded.

The call originated from a Mr Lewis who, with his three-and-a-half year old son, Sam, had been out walking with their two dogs. Suddenly, Sam literally disappeared before his father's eyes when he walked onto a piece of ground which covered part of an old tin mine. The earth crust covering the mine workings was thin, and the boy's weight was sufficient to cause the ground to collapse into the mine. Sam fell vertically into the mine workings with the earth and debris, and disappeared from sight. After Mr Lewis had called help he returned to the shaft and shouted to his son who, fortunately, was capable of answering him.

Divisional Officer Knight arrived at the scene before the fire engine from Truro, and was directed to the mine opening. This was alongside the perimeter fence of the main London to Penzance railway line. The opening to the mine shaft was about three feet square (0.91 metre) but partly obstructed by a concrete fencing post. All the ground around the opening was very unstable as it was undercut by the mine workings.

When the Truro water tender arrived, Divisional Officer Knight explained the situation to Sub Officer Lean and asked for lines and shovels to be brought to the shaft. Immediately, Sub Officer Lean volunteered to go into the mine. He tied a 98 foot (30 metre) general purpose line around himself and was then lowered down the shaft. When he was part way down, a second line was lowered to him. Sub Officer Lean located Sam on a ledge about 82 feet (25 metres) from the mine entrance.

The child did not appear to be injured, and the firefighter was able to reassure and comfort him while he manoeuvred him around his own body so that the child was above him, and thus protected from falling further down into the darkness. The second line was made fast to Sam and, together, they were raised up the sloping part of the shaft to the vertical opening.

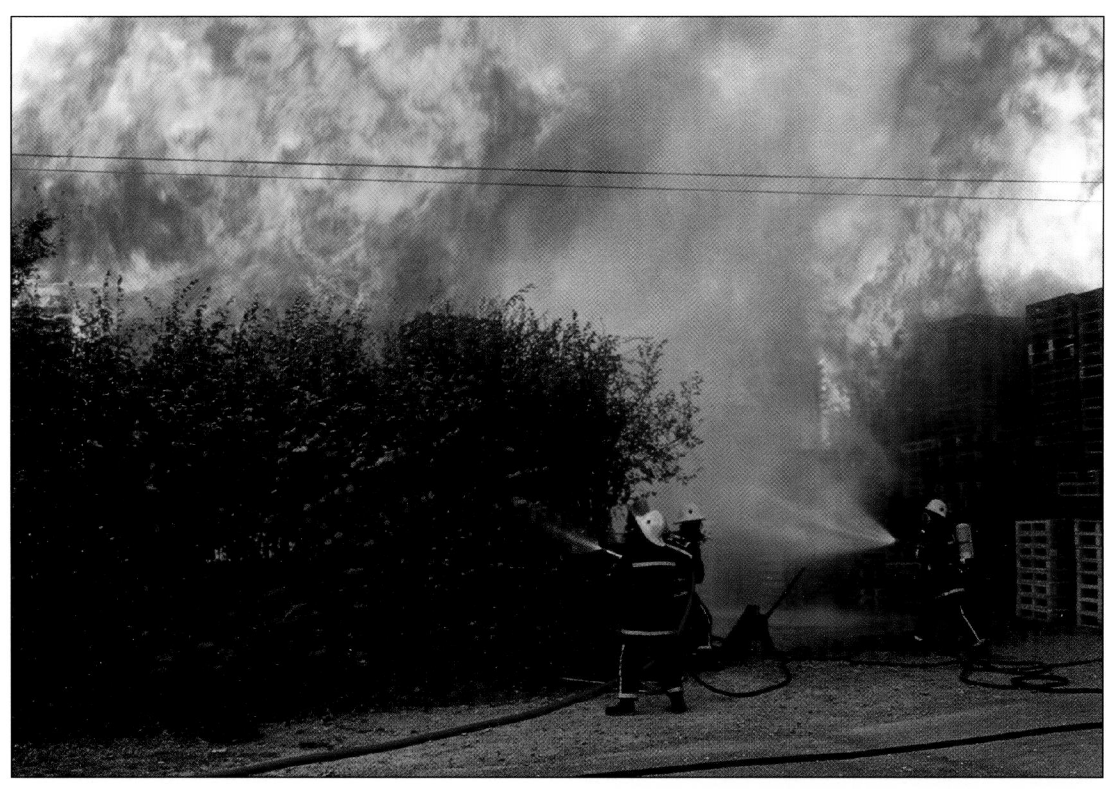

Poor water supplies hampered fire crews from Devon and Cornwall as they attacked a fire in stacked timber pallets at Chapmanswell, Devon, on 6 September 1993. The flames were so fierce that they set light to the hedge across the road to produce a wall of flame. As Launceston firefighters went into the attack, a colleague can be seen spraying them with water as a protection from the searing radiated heat. (Gary Chapman)

The child was then pulled up and out of the mine and finally the Sub Officer was hauled out to fresh air.

When Sub Officer Lean volunteered to be lowered into the mine he was fully aware of the potential danger to himself. The ground around the opening to the mine was known to be unstable as part of it had collapsed under the weight of a three-and-a-half year old boy. Sub Officer Lean was an experienced officer and would have been under no illusion about the dangerous consequences should there have been a further collapse of the mine opening. The rescue was also carried out using only equipment available on the Truro water tender and not the specialised mineshaft rescue equipment which is carried on Cornwall's emergency tenders.

The Chief Fire Officer subsequently commended the courageous actions of Sub Officer Lean.

Killed during training drill

In the ordinary course of their work, firefighters have to undertake a dangerous job but they aim to do such tasks against a background of regular training. Drills and exercises are a daily part of the on-duty routine of a firefighter and many drill scenarios are made as realistic as possible, although safety considerations must be uppermost.

Even then, the unexpected can happen, sometimes with fatal consequences. Such was the case on 5 November 1990 at Newquay Fire Station during a routine drill session using a 100 foot (30.5 metre) turntable ladder. Leading Fireman Stephen Taylor was at the top of the ladder while it was fully extended when the metal sections suffered a complete collapse. The ladder came crashing down and Stephen Taylor was killed instantly.

WILTSHIRE

In January 1992, crews of Wiltshire Fire Brigade tackled what was to be the largest fire ever to have occurred in the county since the post war brigade was formed in 1948. The first '999' call came at 0235 hours to a huge single storey hangar full of strategic military stores at RAF Hullavington. While still some two miles distant, the crews of the first responding Wiltshire appliances, from Chippenham Fire Station, could see an orange glow in the direction of the RAF base. The base firefighting unit had responded quickly

A fire loss of £40 million was recorded at this huge fire in a hangar full of military stores at RAF Hullavington in January 1992. Flames and smoke indicate better than words the scene which faced the first firefighters on the scene. The cause of the fire was arson. (Wiltshire Fire Brigade)

and were at work as the first Chippenham appliance arrived, but a strong wind was whipping the flames inside the locked and secure hangar into a fury.

The Wiltshire officer in charge immediately flashed a priority radio message back to his control for a reinforcement of 10 fire engines, such was the rate of fire spread. By the time that the crews, wearing breathing sets, had forced an entry into the burning hangar, conditions were becoming very dangerous. As the firefighters crept forward amid the swirling smoke towards the fire glow, a rolling ball of fire swept over their heads at rooftop level. Within seconds, the entire hangar was engulfed in flames. All the crews inside the massive building were rapidly withdrawn and firefighting efforts had to be continued from outside.

Eventually, 20 pumps and four aerial appliances were at the scene and over 150 firefighters, including some crews from the Avon and the Gloucestershire Brigades struggled to contain the conflagration. By 0540 hours on that freezing cold morning, Chief Fire Officer John Craig was able to send a radio message back to Wiltshire Control that the blaze was being contained, although firefighters were to remain on the scene damping down for several days to come.

Early on during the fire, the Brigade's fire investigation team had set themselves up to work closely with police colleagues to attempt to establish the cause of the massive fire. They could now move in and start their investigation. Despite the serious damage, the team were able to identify the origin of the fire amid the blackened

Alarm call

In 1990 it was reported :

'Wiltshire Fire Brigade and a local dairy in South Wilts are combining forces to promote fire alarms. Thus the cheapest alarm – at £3.99 – can be delivered to your door by your milkman!'

'You can scratch for a week after one of these incidents!' That was an experienced firefighter's comment on this view of crews in full breathing apparatus, struggling to cut a fire break in the thatched roof of this idyllic Wiltshire cottage. Burnt thatch produces tiny hot 'cinders' which get down inside the tunics. Stinging insects and even, occasionally, wasps nests are disturbed, and when the thatch is cut loose to make fire breaks, it can expand to six feet in depth. Even with BA, bits of ash get into the lungs and to crown everything, most firefighters find it takes days before they can get rid of the smell of thatch smoke from their lungs and nostrils. Hidden from view here are the firefighters working inside the roof space in even more demanding conditions. (Wiltshire Fire Brigade)

Punishing conditions faced fire crews tackling the long thatched roof of the famous, centuries old Cott Inn at Dartington, Devon, in August 1989. Piles of reeds mount up as some firefighters cut a fire break in the thatch while others tackle the end which is still burning fiercely. (Mark S. Wilkins)

Opposite: ***A terrifying fireball rises from this chemical factory at Portishead, Avon, in August 1990, when a store of phosphorus drums exploded and resulted in a 15-pump fire.*** *(County of Avon Fire Brigade)*

and steaming debris, which included the remains of over 5,000 parachutes – half the armed forces' requirements. The estimated fire loss was in the region of £40 million.

Wiltshire Police subsequently charged an RAF junior rank with starting the fire. At the trial, he was found guilty and sentenced to five years imprisonment.

Later that year another particularly dramatic emergency took place in Wiltshire, when fire broke out on the fourth floor of a terraced house in Trowbridge. When the alarm was raised, several neighbours ran to help. Two of these happened to be an off-duty firefighter and a retired member of the Wiltshire Brigade. Between them, they obtained a builder's ladder and pitched it up to the burning upper floors where it was believed a family were trapped. Despite their heroic rescue attempts, the intense heat and smoke drove them back. By that time, the first fire crew had arrived at the scene and firefighters were able to get their ladders up to windows and snatch a six-year-old boy from a blazing attic room. Sadly, despite resuscitation attempts, he died of 95 percent burns. But the boy's father was rescued down a ladder. Another man was brought down semi-conscious and badly burned.

Remarkably, the off-duty firefighter had only just returned from America where he had taken part in a fire service car crash extrication competition.

UK brigades donate £1million aid to Romanian firefighters

Wiltshire Fire crews have been busy for several years in their spare time, servicing and renovating second-hand equipment for their fellow firefighters in Romania.

After the revolution there in 1990, when President Ceausescu and his government were overthrown, the fire service there was in dire straits, lacking crews, equipment and expertise. Because of this, a delegation of five senior Romanian officers visited Britain early in 1991 on a 'Look and Learn' mission. Soon after this, the Foreign and Commonwealth Office and the Home Office in London agreed to give more practical help to Romania's firefighters, starting with a grant of £6,000 'to prime the pumps' of what became known as 'Operation Romaid'. Wiltshire's Chief Fire Officer was chosen to co-ordinate the project.

He sent his Deputy, Cyril Moseley, to Romania to discover what was happening there. The report came back that the firefighters were enthusiastic but their appliances were of 'very rudimentary design' and small gear and ancillary equipment was 'conspicuous by its absence'. They had no breathing apparatus worth mentioning and no chemical protection suits. Uniform consisted of an army steel helmet, a greatcoat and a pair of boots.

The upshot of these initial investigations was a letter in the autumn of 1991 to all Chief Fire Officers in Britain, appealing for surplus equipment and appliances. The result, says Wiltshire, 'has been and continues to be magnificent'. Most of the appliances were supplied fully serviced, but any which did need attention were worked on by Wiltshire's volunteers.

Added to this, they spent the summer of 1992 planning an overland journey of 1,450 miles to Romania with a convoy of vehicles and equipment. Since then, two more convoys, crewed not only by Wiltshire but other British brigades, have made the journey through France, Germany, Austria and Hungary to Romania, staying overnight with firefighters in each country whose help and hospitality was, they reported, 'overwhelming'.

By the summer of 1994, the total of aid provided by the British Fire Service to the Romanian Fire Service had reached £1.1 million.

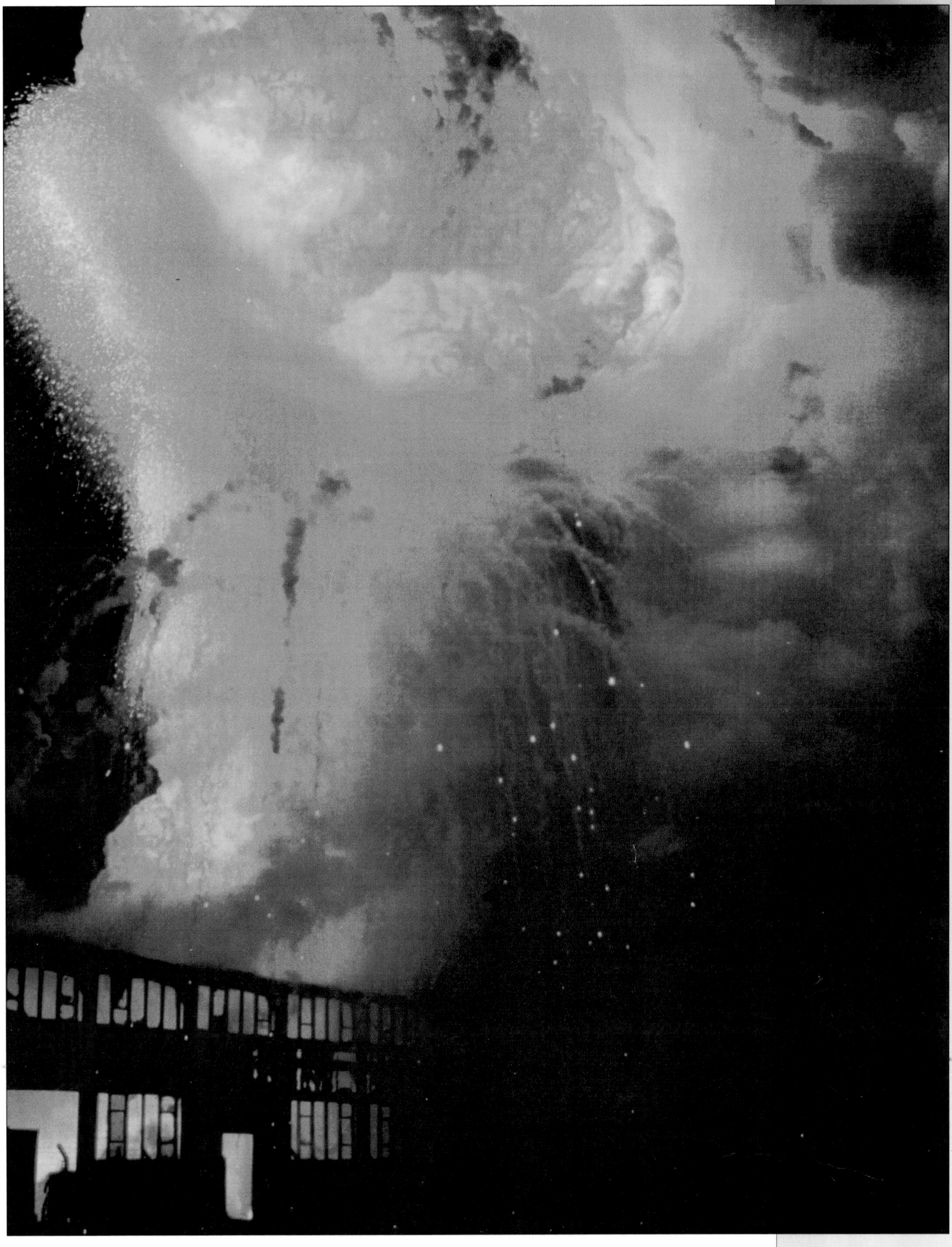

AVON

Two rescues of people who had fallen into the River Avon illustrate the wide nature of dangerous emergencies which the fire service responds to.

Around lunchtime on 16 July 1989, a number of long boats had visited the Jolly Sailor public house near Saltford Lock as part of a family birthday celebration. There were about 25 people in each boat. When one of these suddenly capsized, all its occupants were thrown into the river, apart from a 67-year-old woman who was trapped in an air bubble underneath the upturned boat.

Hearing the commotion, 27-year-old Mark Haines, who was drinking at the Jolly Sailor, came out, saw the mêlée on the river – which was over 50 feet (15.2 metres) wide and 18 feet (5.5 metres) deep – and dived to the rescue. He managed to get under the overturned boat and located the trapped woman. However, because of various obstructions, he was unable to rescue her.

Mark comforted the unfortunate woman before resurfacing and securing the upturned boat with a rope to prevent it drifting towards a nearby weir. By this time the fire service had arrived and Mr Haines was able to tell the crew precisely

Two firefighters huddle together and almost merge into one during a hot-fire training exercise using burning diesel fuel. Their uniforms carry reflective strips to aid conspicuity at night-time emergencies. Remarkably, this drill session is taking place during the daytime!

where the casualty was to be found. Two firefighters, Peter Edmonson and David Fleck, quickly donned breathing sets usually used for working in smoke, and entered the water.

Unfortunately, once under the boat neither could free the trapped woman. Firefighter Fleck remained with her while the rest of the crew carefully cut a hole in the hull of the boat. Only then was she finally extricated and lifted out to safety. She was taken to hospital and detained overnight, but survived her ordeal. Both firefighters involved in the rescue received awards from the Royal Humane Society.

A second County of Avon Fire Service river rescue took place on 3 May 1990. It well illustrates the occasional lunatic act which results in firefighters becoming involved, often at great personal risk.

A 20-year-old unemployed man, who was the worse for drink, had been thrown into the River Avon close to Pulteney Weir in Bath. At this point the river is 10 feet (3 metres) deep. The considerable undercurrent swept the youth along but he managed to cling to a ledge formed by the steel grating of the sluice gate where water was pouring over the edge. Passers-by summoned both the fire service and police.

As soon as they arrived, Firefighters Gammie and Cross were secured by safety lines and dropped into the river. Other firefighters called out encouragement to the drunken youth to hang on as the two rescuers made their way to the sluice gate. As they reached the youth on the grating, he began to struggle violently and fell back into the swirling water. Firefighter Gammie managed to pull the drunk on to the ledge again, where he continued to resist rescue. The firefighter took off his lifeline and with the help of Firefighter Cross secured it to the youth who was then dragged to safety across the current by the rest of the crew on the river bank. Once there, he was taken into police custody, examined by a police surgeon and later released when sober! The two rescuers ultimately received awards from the Royal Humane Society for their fine work.

COUNTY OF AVON
FIRE BRIGADE

GLOUCESTERSHIRE

Outbreaks of fire have no respect for public holidays as Gloucestershire firefighters were reminded during Christmas 1991. On the evening of Boxing Day, a fire broke out in an electronics factory at Tewkesbury. During the early stages of firefighting operations, leaking chemicals became involved in the spreading flames, and poisonous fumes were given off which mixed insidiously with the thick black smoke which poured out of the two-storey building.

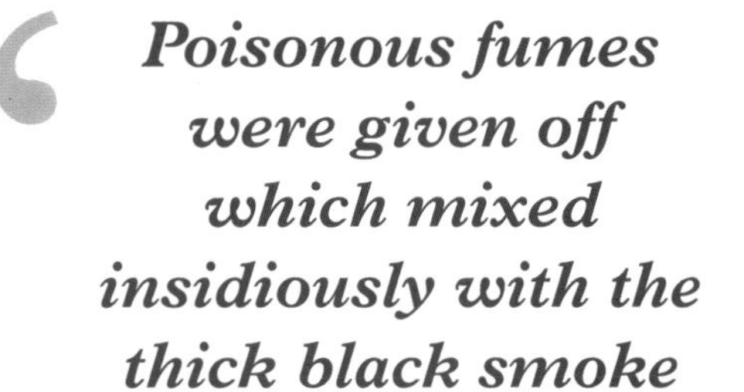
Poisonous fumes were given off which mixed insidiously with the thick black smoke

Bringing the fire under control was a difficult and dangerous operation which necessitated the extensive use of breathing sets. Even so, before the night was out nine firefighters had been overcome by the lethal smoke cocktail which swirled around the factory complex. In addition they also developed a skin irritation and had to be taken to hospital by ambulance. Fortunately, all recovered from their experience. The fire was attended by 10 pumps and other specialist tenders, crewed by 60 firefighters from Tewkesbury, Cheltenham, Winchcombe and Cirencester Fire Stations. They will all remember that particular Christmas!

JERSEY

Jersey is one of the smaller fire brigades in the UK, with 74 whole time and 42 part-time firemen and two fire stations. The small State, a jewel of the Channel Islands, is a holiday paradise with hotels, boarding houses and restaurants as well as a thriving fruit and vegetable growing industry. Jersey's early potatoes, with their short season, are a gourmet delicacy and their tomatoes are among the best in the world. Many of the growers, though, particularly those with big stores of boxes and packaging, have had their fair share of visits from the local fire brigade.

During the Second World War, life was less than sunny for the islanders when the Germans invaded and overran Jersey. They built a complicated network of huge underground tunnels to store arms and supplies and provide shelter for a hospital, power station and assortment of other necessities.

With the war over and the Germans ousted, the tunnels were closed and life went back to normal. But the underground system was a source of mystery and constant temptation to some of the Jersey teenagers, and it was on a summer afternoon in the early 1960s that a group of four lads decided to explore them from an entrance close to what had become known as the 'German Road' in St Peter's Valley.

Just before tea-time, at 1545 hours, a call came in to the local fire station from the ambulance station. One boy had staggered to the telephone to call them out to rescue his friends. Deep in the underground network they had lit a bonfire. It was now out of control and they were cut off by smoke.

There was an instant and full turn-out and by 1608 the call went out for a doctor. Smoke was pouring from the tunnel and by 1641 two firemen had to be rescued and taken to hospital, overcome by smoke and the peculiar fumes. Within minutes a Sub Officer succumbed and was rushed away for treatment. It was 1725 before a crew returned with two of the boys, both suffering from the particularly unpleasant fumes but not badly hurt. Two more were still missing.

The Brigade brought in a JCB to try to open up the entrance hole but the operation came to a halt at 1832 when a message came through from the hospital 'no person, with or without BA, to go into the tunnels'. More firemen had been taken for treatment for what appeared to be a skin irritation brought on by some unidentified gas.

The search was resumed soon after, despite medical warnings and eventually the bodies of the remaining two boys were discovered. They had succumbed to smoke from the bonfire.

It was a sombre moment as the 'stop' came through. Two boys were dead, but at least three more – John Lloyd Grimes, who had raised the alarm and the two who had been rescued – survived. One of these, John Jefferies, remembers the day all too well – and is now a full-time Jersey firefighter.

Mostly, Jersey is a peaceful haven. Yet for three years after the Second World War the island was haunted by a firebug who struck frequently and caused a succession of expensive and damaging incidents. No particular pattern emerged. He chose his victims at random, but favoured the stores of the local market gardeners where the thin wooden barrels and trays were kept for transporting potatoes and tomatoes to the mainland. One after another they went up in smoke, and despite a close watch being kept, he escaped every time like a will o' the wisp. It was a fire at the Jersey optical works which was his undoing. There, finally, he was very nearly caught. The fright must have struck home. The bug went to ground. The arson campaign was over.

Not all incidents are on land. Jersey Fire Brigade has close links with the sea and was not only the first to use the Zodiac inflatable lifeboat dinghy in action, but on one occasion was honoured by the Royal National Lifeboat Institution.

Late on a July evening in 1970 a flare burst into light above St Owen's Bay and the fire service was called to help a 25 foot craft, the *Bounty*. Conditions were bad – impossible some said. The Zodiac bounced across the water until it was within hailing distance of the distressed craft which had lost its rudder and was being pounded by the rough sea. At first, the tiny dinghy, manned by the firemen, stood by until the lifeboat and the State's launch *Duchess of Normandy* arrived, and then went in to rescue three of the crew and transfer them to the launch. The skipper refused to leave and stayed on board until daylight. The Zodiac crew, Sub Officer D. Bickley, Fireman J. Robertson and Retained Fireman T. Billot were all presented with RNLI awards later in the year.

GUERNSEY

The uproar of fire and rescue on so small and idyllic a holiday island as Guernsey seems impossible. But with a thriving tourist trade and a busy market produce industry, the island has had a fair share of

Then and Now. Guernsey firefighters show their old uniform and the high-tech outfit of modern firefighters. It includes better headgear and body protection as well as improved comfort. (States of Guernsey Fire Brigade)

incidents which, in recent years, have ranged through fires in a bulk oil storage tank and a large hotel to a string of arson attacks.

Although the Brigade is short of retained firemen particularly, it rates 'very highly' having the best in firefighting equipment on the grounds that with this, 'a small but well equipped firefighting crew can achieve surprisingly good results'. Accordingly, Guernsey fire crews are among the most up to date in uniform and equipment in the country – although they treasure their 57-year-old Sarnia II fire escape which is still going strong although not 'on the run'.

One of the most worrying 'shouts' for many years came just after lunch at 1428 hours on 11 December 1993. A call for help came through from the MV *Norman Commodore*, a 1,577 ton RoRo (Roll on, Roll off) ferry wallowing in a heavy sea, half-way on its journey from Portsmouth to Guernsey and with fire on board.

Fire at sea is always dangerous and the island's Chief Fire Officer, James Cassaday, joined the firefighting crew which took off from Guernsey Airport on a Coastguard Wessex helicopter. They found the stricken ship at 1600 hours, but by then a fixed installation on the ship had poured carbon dioxide into the danger area and was holding the fire in check. Nevertheless, three firemen were winched down on to the deck of the ship, with BA and first aid equipment to follow.

Fire Chief Cassaday joined the team which inspected the vehicle loading deck, found it heavily smoke logged and decided that it should remain sealed with its 'fire blanket' of CO_2 and that the vessel should carry on with its journey and dock to allow passengers to disembark before fire-fighting began in earnest. Unfortunately, the CO_2 was escaping through leaks in the bow and stern loading doors, and the temperature began to rise rapidly as the fire took hold again.

Despite this and the shifting cargo, CFO Cassaday stuck to his decision to head for the harbour at St. Peter Port and the ship limped into the dockside safely.

Just testing! Guernsey fire crews try out some of their brigade's latest rescue equipment. Bottom left: *Thermal imaging camera capable of penetrating thick smoke and dust-laden atmospheres. It can also trace 'hot spots' in cavities, as well as determining variations in temperature in other places.* Top left: *Clan Lucas hydraulic cutting, spreading and traction device working to 8,000 lbs. Invaluable for releasing trapped victims in traffic accidents.* Top right: *Trapped Person Locator, capable of detecting and pinpointing the source of any sounds below collapsed structures using a combination of seismic and acoustic sensors.* Bottom right: *These dangling sensors can discriminate between background noise and human movement and are sensitive enough to detect the sound of heartbeats.* *(States of Guernsey Fire Brigade)*

This 57-year-old fire engine, Sarnia II, *has the doubtful distinction of being the only British fire engine to have been crewed in part by German occupying troops during the Second World War. They did this to keep an eye on the Guernsey firefighters who would, otherwise, have had a free run of their island. Today, the beloved and beautiful old lady is kept comfortably in the Occupation Museum, but still gives today's crews a run in the sun.* (States of Guernsey Fire Brigade)

As soon as passengers and crew were landed, a firefighting plan was put into action which involved opening the stern loading doors on to the loading ramp to admit two firefighting crews carrying two main jets. Their risky task was to follow a preplanned route towards the seat of the fire – but in doing this they came up against an unexpected barrier. During the rough passage, cargo trailers and vehicles had shifted and were now strewn across the deck in a sea of spilled diesel oil, petrol and assorted cargo from the trailers. Despite all their efforts, the firefighters had to draw back and the next stage, injection of high expansion foam through a top deck opening, began, followed by the long and arduous job of controlling the fire.

Some of the cars and trucks on the ferry had been towed off the vessel to create enough deck space to drive two airport fire tenders aboard. A thermal imaging camera was used to direct long throw jets, between sessions of using high and medium expansion foam.

The efforts succeeded eventually, after fire crews found a narrow gap, little more than a yard (1 metre) wide between the barrier of scattered vehicles and cargo, close to the starboard bulkhead. They struggled through this, despite the risks, to get close to the seat of the fire. It was 0830 the following day before the 'stop' message was recorded.

Altogether, 79 firefighters were involved in the operation including 17 airport firemen. Civil defence volunteers transported men and equipment to and from the harbour. In the course of the action, 171 BA sets were used as well as two powerful ground monitors and two airport fire tender monitors.

The cause of the fire was recorded as 'Unknown' but it seems likely that it was partly due to the very considerable shift of vehicles during the crossing and the spillage of cargo – and particularly of diesel oil.

Four days after the fire, a second Ro-Ro vessel entered St. Peter Port Harbour with its cargo shifted en route. Thankfully this time there was no fire at sea, but Guernsey's crews went aboard to recover a quantity of caustic soda which had spread across the deck after falling from a trailer.

CHAPTER 3

VALLEYS AND MOUNTAINS

WALES

GWENT

Dealing with domestic chimney fires is a fairly routine exercise for firefighters, but in September 1992, firefighters from Newport were called to a 180 feet (55 metres) high steel chimney stack which had caught fire.

The chimney was part of the large premises of a fibreglass manufacturer. Three cooling jets of water were brought into use, some of the water coming from a tender using water from a nearby river.

Further crews were sent to the scene to supplement the initial crews. More cooling jets were put to work, both externally around the base of the chimney stack, and inside where metal trunking from around the factory led into the chimney.

By now, the fire was increasing in severity, with a blowtorch effect, and parts of the stack were glowing red. There was a real danger of the entire structure coming crashing down onto the roof of the factory itself.

As more cooling jets of water were directed onto the outside face of the chimney, a hydraulic platform was positioned to provide high level cooling some 80 feet (24.4 metres) up. The decision was taken to open several hatches into the actual chimney and the first of these was about 30 feet (9.1 metres) up. Such was the intensity of the radiated heat that the firefighter who scaled a ladder to undo the bolts had himself to be soaked by water spray as he climbed to carry out the tricky task. Despite the heat, he undid the hatch and other firefighters started to work a water jet into the chimney interior.

The second hatch was much higher up the chimney than the first and was released by a crew working off the hydraulic platform and more water was applied through this access point. Some two hours after the first '999' call the incident was declared safe and under control.

> ***'By now the fire was increasing in severity, with a blowtorch effect'***

Dwarfed by the intensity of the flames and smoke from the huge oil storage tanks at a Milford Haven refinery in August 1983, fire crews from Dyfed and adjoining counties tackled this £10 million blaze for more than 60 hours. So much foam was used that extra supplies had to be brought down from the Midlands under police escort. (Eye Level Photographs)

Smoke and flames belch from an oil tank, on the point of rupturing, during the £10 million Amoco Oil Company fire at Milford Haven in August 1983. (Colin Kaijaks)

FOR FUN... All UK firefighters have to keep fit, and Blue Watch at Twickenham (London) take it very seriously. Apart from working out on a Multigym at their station, they visit their local rugby ground every week for training on a weighted gantry. Here, they are pulling for a gold at the World Firefighter Games in Perth, Western Australia, in 1994 and, for the third time in succession, winning it. They took first place also in their section of the tug-o-war at previous Firefighter Games in Auckland, NZ, in 1990 and Las Vegas, USA, in 1992. (Blue Watch, Twickenham, LFB)

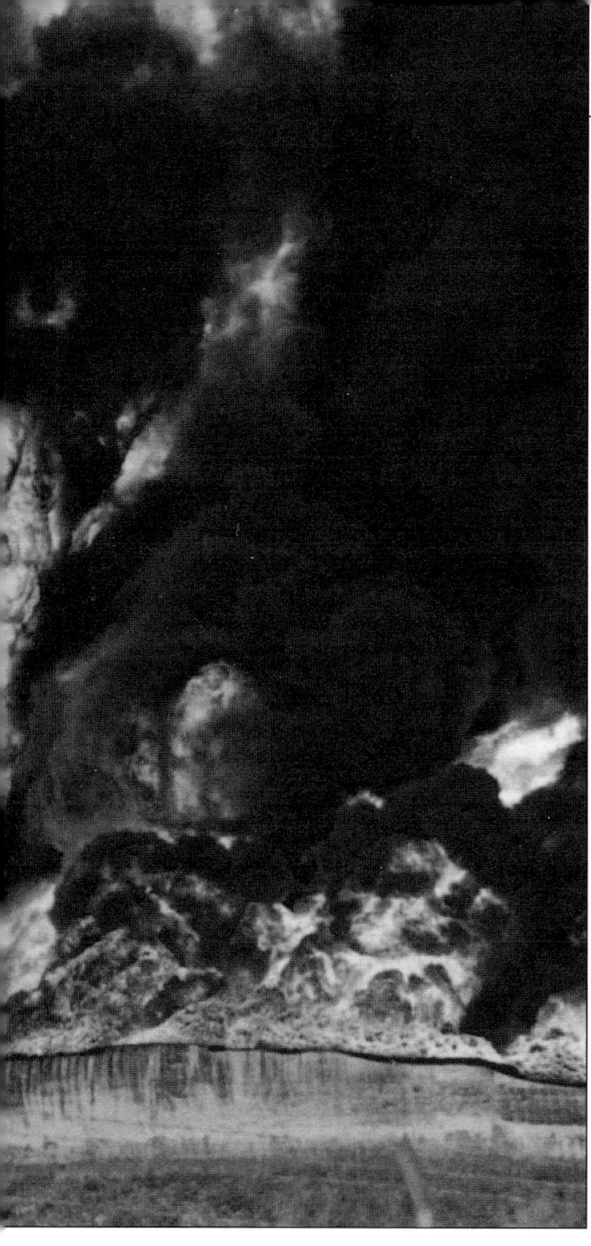

By now the chimney was leaning over some seven degrees, but the Brigade had the satisfaction of knowing that they had minimised the factory's loss of production time.

MID GLAMORGAN

Quite often an accident or crash will occur in a location where access for firefighting and rescue vehicles is difficult. A few days before Christmas 1985 Mid Glamorgan firefighters were faced with just such an emergency when a 32 ton articulated lorry skidded off the A465 Heads of the Valleys trunk road near Merthyr Tydfil.

The lorry failed to stop at temporary traffic lights at road works on a viaduct, and plunged headlong down a 100 foot (30 metres) ravine. The full impact was taken nose on by the tractor unit, which was compressed into about one quarter of its usual dimensions. The trailer came to rest directly above and in line with the cab unit, the axles perilously hanging over the cab wreckage itself. The tanker was loaded with powdered milk in paper sacks. Most of these burst open to complicate the very muddy scene.

The first '999' call brought a pump and emergency tender to the site. On their

...FOR REAL. It took every ounce of strength in this real life tug-o-war as Swansea fire crews, lifeboatmen and the RSPCA joined forces to rescue these two ponies from mudflats at Loughor Estuary, near Swansea in Wales, in the Spring of 1994. They were about to call in an RAF helicopter when, with a last heave, they won. The ponies were freed and transported to safety in a Swansea sanctuary. (Dragon Photo Agency, Swansea)

Up before the beaks

In February 1990, Mid Glamorgan firefighters came to the rescue of 100,000 day-old chicks at a poultry farm in the Rhondda Valley. A water main had burst, the farm was without water supplies of any sort and the Brigade was called in. Sufficient water was pumped to the farm to provide for the needs of the tiny chicks before normal water services were restored later in the day.

arrival the crews had to negotiate a tortuous route into the ravine to the accident beneath the viaduct.

Amazingly, the driver was still conscious, but trapped in the crushed cab of the lorry. There was no immediate sign of any other casualty.

Cutting, spreading and lighting equipment was instantly got to work to free the trapped man. But before any serious rescue attempt could begin the trailer, poised above the scene, had to be secured by cables to prevent any downward slippage. This in itself was not an easy task, as heavy continuous rain made the steep grassy banks of the gorge highly dangerous.

A second emergency tender from Pontypridd was requested to provide additional rescue equipment, as it became clear that there was likely to be another casualty somewhere within, or close to, the wreckage of the lorry and its scattered load.

The officer in charge confirmed that a medical team was needed. Progress was painfully slow in cutting open the crushed cab to extricate the driver. He remained semi-conscious throughout his rescue, although it was some time before he was able to tell his rescuers clearly that he had a colleague with him at the time of the crash.

Using the combined equipment from both the emergency tenders, the driver was eventually released and taken to hospital about an hour and three quarters after the first '999' call. Firefighters, helped by site construction workers, were then able to continue careful digging through the widespread mud and milk powder to gradually check and clear the area around the crash. A thermal imaging camera was used for this purpose.

After much cautious progress, a sec-

Smashed to smithereens, the wreckage of a 32 ton articulated lorry which plunged 100 feet down a ravine when it failed to stop at road works in Merthyr Tydfil, Wales, in December 1985. The driver survived but his mate died in the wreckage. The scene was complicated by the lorry's load of powdered milk which was strewn all over the area in a sticky, slippery mess. (Mid Glamorgan Fire Service)

ond casualty was found, pinned beneath the cab wreckage and buried under the compacted powder. Unfortunately he was dead. His body was finally released after about another 45 minutes of further cutting, lifting and digging – assisted by a contractor's overhead crane from the viaduct above.

SOUTH GLAMORGAN

Firefighter Stephen Dawson joined South Glamorgan Fire and Rescue Service and during his 16 years as a Welsh fireman saw a considerable amount of operational action in the Cardiff area. His experiences included the rescue of four people from a serious fire in Llandaff in 1982, for which he received a commendation for bravery.

However, Stephen transferred to Buckinghamshire Fire and Rescue Service and was posted to Beaconsfield Fire Station. In late August 1990, Stephen was a crew member of a Beaconsfield water tender when it responded to a '999' call. En route to the emergency the fire engine was involved in a crash and Stephen was killed.

Stephen's funeral took place back in Ely, Cardiff, where his coffin was carried on a South Glamorgan Fire and Rescue Service turntable ladder. The cortege included a water tender from the Buckinghamshire Brigade.

WEST GLAMORGAN

Most of the 750 or so annual UK fire deaths happen in the home, but it was unusual for three fire fatalities, all women, to occur within hours of each other during the same weekend in West Glamorgan.

In the first fire, which took place in a house on the Gower Peninsula in January 1991, a woman died despite a courageous yet unsuccessful rescue attempt by a policewoman. West Glamorgan firefighters clad in breathing sets battled through the intense smoke and heat to get the woman out to fresh air, and frantically tried to resuscitate her but, sadly, she never regained consciousness.

The second fatal fire, only hours later, was in a singly storey 'prefab' house in Swansea. That claimed two more lives. Neighbours spoke of the flames taking hold within minutes and firefighters could do nothing to save the women.

But this tragic Welsh weekend was not yet over. Within a few hours two more women had perished amid thick smoke in house fires in Clwyd; one in Old Colwyn and the other in Mold.

DYFED

In the space of five weeks in 1992, Dyfed firefighters successfully tackled two ship fires. Both occurred in the port of Milford Haven and in both cases the seat of the fire was in the vessel's engine room.

The first incident was on 16 November when the crew of the 2,946 ton coastal tanker *River Shannon* discovered a fire in the engine room. Within minutes the crew were mustered, the engine room sealed, and the built-in carbon dioxide fire extinguishing system activated.

By the time the first firefighting crews arrived from Milford Haven it looked to be a simple enough operation, providing that the carbon dioxide system did its job. However, it soon became apparent that the extinguishing system was not working properly. The steel deck plates of the ship were getting hotter and hotter.

Firefighters then injected high expansion foam down into the engine room. Soon after this it was thought that the main area of fire was out. However it was necessary for firefighters wearing breathing apparatus to descend steel ship's ladders, down into the heat and smoke to open up the engine room and check that this was indeed the case.

The work was physically very punishing and energy sapping. There was still much smoke, heat and humidity rising up the stairway. It enveloped the first crew as they descended. The possibility of a flashover was always present. More firefighters went down to support the first team.

In the engine room access was very

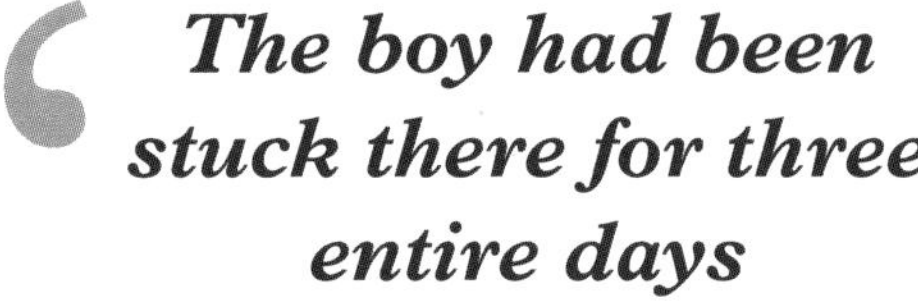
The boy had been stuck there for three entire days

restricted, but despite some small pockets of fire, the main outbreak was out. After almost five hours of hard slog, the fire was finally under control.

The second ship fire occurred on 22 December on the 1,178 ton coaster *Avinia*. This time the ship's central heating oil fired boiler had caught fire. The crews faced the same problem of enduring searing heat and acrid smoke while descending into the hull to locate and extinguish the seat of the fire.

In 1993, lengthy periods of rain following a protracted dry period brought severe flooding to parts of West Wales.

One of the worst affected areas, with 7½ inches of rain in 48 hours, was the town of Cardigan in Dyfed. Dyfed County Fire Brigade received 171 calls, 116 of them to Cardigan.

The raging floodwater swept 18 caravans into a river, trapping many occupants. Buildings were destroyed and residents clung to roofs in an attempt to escape the waters. On 34 occasions firefighters had to use their specialist training and equipment to rescue members of the public who were stranded by the high water, or to drag people from the raging torrent. All these people were in real danger of being swept to their deaths.

At the height of the operation 20 fire engines and their crews were in attendance, including the Brigade's marine rescue unit, an emergency tender and a turntable ladder. Dyfed's marine rescue unit makes the Brigade unique among the UK fire services. Four of the Brigade's inflatable rescue boats were in continuous use saving marooned residents from their water-logged homes. Meanwhile Dyfed's team of trained divers searched abandoned buildings and cars for missing persons, and performed a number of timely rescues. A turntable ladder was used as a bridge in part of the flood zone and enabled many residents, including a paraplegic, to leave their homes.

The flooding prompted a visit from the Duke of Edinburgh on 16 June and some of the first rescuers he met were Dyfed firefighters.

POWYS

Powys firefighters from Brecon Fire Station were summoned to a very unusual special service emergency on 8 September 1992. In an area of peat bog outside the remote village of Llanddew, an 11-year-old boy was trapped waist deep in mud. Incredibly, the boy had been stuck there for three entire days before his life-threatening plight was discovered.

Firefighters and ambulance personnel worked for one and a half hours in the glutinous morass, digging and preparing a rescue route to the boy who was eventually hauled out to safety. He was whisked off to hospital where he was detained for a week suffering from exhaustion, hypothermia, insect bites and swollen limbs. But he made a full recovery.

GWYNEDD

The perils and danger of emergencies involving liquid petroleum gas (lpg) were well underlined in August 1992 when an lpg tanker travelling on the A55 near Bangor caught fire. After the fire had been extinguished Gwynedd crews from Bangor, Llanfairfechan and Caernarfon stood by with protective clothing and cooling jets throughout a lengthy and dangerous operation to isolate 3.9 tons of lpg which remained in the tanker.

CLWYD

The County of Clwyd Fire Brigade were in the national news for several days during the end of February and beginning of March 1990.

Very severe weather had struck the North Wales coast, and the sea defences were breached in a number of places along the Clwyd coastline. Particularly badly

Tyre dump fire burned for years

Powys had the misfortune to suffer from the longest known burning fire in Wales. A dump at Knighton containing millions of scrap tyres burned for several years after it first caught fire in 1989. Local residents and politicians were horrified when it was reported locally that to extinguish the deep seated fire under huge piles of tyres might cost something in the region of £4 million.

affected were Towyn and Kinmel Bay, between Rhyl and Colwyn Bay. The sea flooded for a considerable distance inland throughout these communities, affecting homes and business properties alike.

Clwyd firefighters led by Chief Fire Officer Ken Hayton were soon called in to oversee the evacuation effort as the flooding threatened even worse devastation and suffering. The firefighters worked with the police and ambulance personnel, the RAF and RNLI. A large number of people, particularly the elderly, were carried from their homes and, using every available boat, taken to places of warmth and safety.

Alongside the rescue operations a huge pumping effort was mounted. This was not only to restrict the floods from spreading even further, but also to pump water out of hundreds of flooded properties. Almost every fire engine in the Clwyd Brigade was put to work. Normal fire cover in other parts of the county was provided by crews from Gwynedd, Shropshire, Cheshire and Greater Manchester Brigades.

Soon after the flooding drama, Clwyd firefighters from Prestatyn, Rhyl and Colwyn Bay found themselves called to a quarry near Prestatyn to find two teenagers stuck on a ledge on the 100 foot (30 metres) quarry face. Apparently, the foolish youths had been challenged by a friend to climb the cliff face for a £5 bet. Needless to say, the fire crews climbed to the teenagers and brought them down to safety. The conversation between the rescuers and the foolhardy youngsters can best be left to the imagination.

CHAPTER 4

THE BIG SMOKE

LONDON

Without doubt, London has the biggest area and probably a more varied selection of incidents to deal with than any other fire service in the country, if not the world. Since 1965 – when it expanded from the old London County Council area to take in the surrounding brigades of Croydon, Middlesex, East and West Ham plus parts of Kent – it has been dealing with nearly a quarter of a million fires and accidents a year, among a population of 6.8 million. London has 6,388 working firefighters, men and women, based in 114 fire stations. The River Thames Division, has a fire boat *London Phoenix* stationed on a pontoon opposite the Lambeth Headquarters.

To single out individual acts of courage among so many which take place almost daily would be unfair to the many whose work, like all firefighters the world over, demands a generous ration of 'guts'. So a selection has been made from London's long history and dealing with the almost unbelievable variety of calls which never cease to come its way.

Still remembered by many firefighters are the stories of earlier heroes. Victorian Fireman Joseph Jacobs was one of these. Called to a fire in the three-storey building of a manufacturing chemists in Wandsworth, he and another fireman, a friend called Ashby, ran their hoses up the staircase and attacked the fire from the top floor as the thick, choking smoke swirled round them.

Suddenly there was an enormous explosion and the staircase collapsed. The two men were trapped on the top floor. All the windows had been barred for safety – only a small ventilation hatch was left. Ladders were raised against the window, but there was one major problem. Ashby was slim and if he could reach the high ventilator he might get through. Jacobs was stout and realised that for him there was no escape. As the fire advanced on them he was already feeling the burns on his back. But with a superhuman thrust he lifted his mate up and managed to push him through the tiny hatch. Ashby was already badly burned himself, but as he fell, he was able to grab the top of the ladder and struggle safely to the ground. For Jacobs there was no more hope. He fell backwards into the flames and died.

George Ford was another early hero in London, in 1871. A call came to his Holborn station for a fire in a house in Grays Inn Road. As 'escape man', he ran his ladder on its wheels to the scene and pitched it against the wall. Already the residents were screaming from the windows for help. Ford managed to rescue five people, carrying them down the ladder, one by one, over his shoulder in a 'fireman's lift' before the flames began to burst from the windows. Only one woman was left behind, screaming in agony. To the hoarse cheers of the crowd, Ford, already exhausted, climbed his ladder yet again and grasped the woman. But by now the canvas cover which ran down behind the woven mesh chute at the back of the escape had caught fire and both he and the woman were enveloped in flames. Unable to hold her any longer, he had to let his fingers relax, but it was close enough to the ground for her to survive her fall.

Ford was less lucky. His axe, fixed to his belt, had become entangled in the broken mesh of the chute. There he hung, powerless to free himself, slowly roasting to death – then, with a violent effort, he managed to free the axe and fell to the ground. The force of his landing bent his brass helmet in two. His mates rushed to put out his burning clothes. He was raced to hospital and lingered in agony until he died of his injuries. A public fund, launched for his widow and children, was so well supported that the authorities decided they no longer needed to pay her a pension, so withdrew it.

Nearly a century later, a similarly brave rescue took place at the Worsley Hotel fire on Paddington Fire Station's 'patch', on Friday, 13 December 1974. At the height of the action, the centre of the building collapsed, trapping several firemen beneath burning rafters. The full story of the rescue efforts by their mates is told in TV newscaster Gordon Honeycombe's book *Red Watch*, but at one stage he describes the scene in the burning hotel as the roof collapsed :

'All Martin' (Walker) 'remembered afterwards was Harry turning towards him and a dark shadow coming down on them. His helmet came off and he was knocked to the floor. Stunned by the sudden impact, by sheer surprise, his mind was blank...the darkness was as complete as the silence. Only by blinking his eyelids did he know his eyes were open; only by smelling pungent fumes did he know he had a nose; only by moving his features and breathing did he hear any sounds above the thudding of his heart, and only by moving or trying to move his muscles and his limbs did he discover that he was sitting in a reclined position with outflung legs and his right arm by his side.

'He could not move his feet, legs, waist or trunk, only his left arm and his head. His right foot had no feeling at all. He wondered if it was broken, but although he was acutely hot and uncomfortable, he felt no pain. He saw points of fire, like flecks on his eyeballs, seemingly inches away. He felt a damply suffocating, steaming heat that stung his nostrils and throat and eyes – and he heard someone coughing far away and sighing, and a muffled voice saying – "Oh, God, what happened? Martin? Martin?" The fingers touched the fingers of his outstretched right arm and a hand grasped his and held it fast. "Harry? You all right?" His own voice sounded harsh and high. 'Harry? Harry!"...'

Martin Walker was trapped by his leg. His foot was slowly being burned away by the glowing rafter below him. Gripping his hand was his friend, Harry Pettit. Harry was completely buried under the debris and slowly dying as their mates picked their way precariously through the rubble.

Old smoke-eater had a heavenly gift

Many of the calls bring sadness and stress to fire crews. But some are yarned about for years, and grow with the telling from station to station across the metropolis, particularly if they involve the real old characters of the LFB. Charlie X was just such a character. A tough, old-style 'smoke-eater', he had a reputation for doing just enough to get by at the station, but for being first on the job when they went into action. He was, said his Divisional Officer, recalling Charlie and his reputation, 'a real scruff pot. No matter what his officers said or did, he never looked smart and he didn't seem to give a damn, but his one surprising skill was his ability to play any sort of musical instrument. He'd never been formally taught, he didn't come from that sort of family. But he could play anything – trumpet, piano, the lot'.

Charlie was on duty when the call came in for a fire in the local church. As always, he was first on the pump escape when the bells went down, and first off at the church. The crew unrolled the hoses as the vicar, incoherent with distress, exhorted them to hurry and hustled them towards the entrance. As they approached, he stopped aghast. Floating out on the clouds of smoke came the ghostly sound of organ music, beautifully played. The men drew back too – just for a moment – then plunged on into the church and followed the sound to its source. There were the ashes of the small fire, quickly extinguished by Charlie with a light hose reel, and there was Charlie himself, unable to resist the temptation, perched at the manual trying out his innate skills on the church organ.

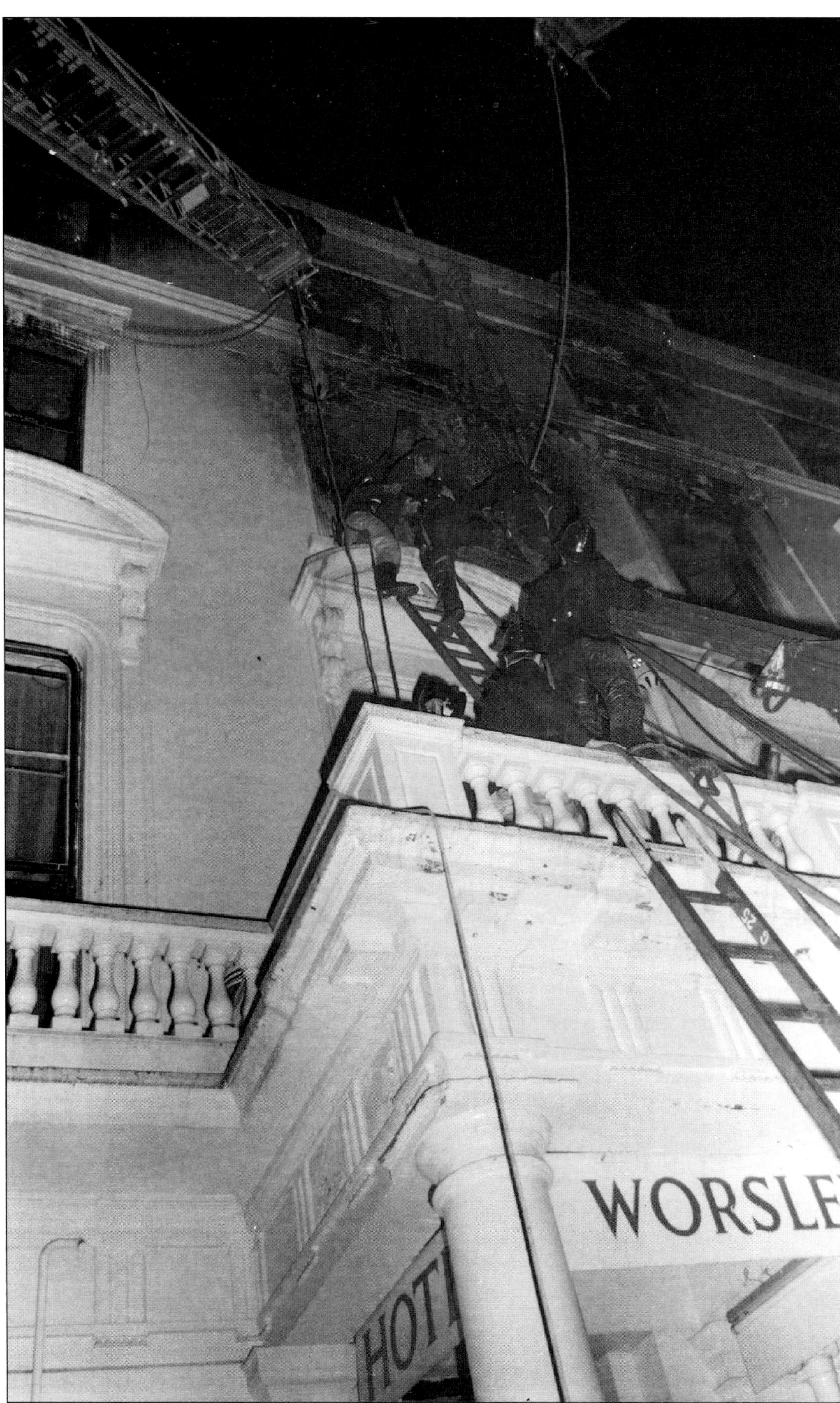

Right: ***After fighting to rescue their colleagues, trapped under a fall of burning rafters for over an hour, firemen lower them one by one down the ladder from the blackened remains of the bedroom at the Worsley Hotel fire, Maida Vale, London, in December 1974.*** *(London Fire Brigade)*

Centre: ***The fire in the Worsley Hotel had been at its height when the ceiling collapsed on a group of firemen, trapping them under the scorching rafters. After a desperate struggle, Colin Searle had to be rescued with severe back injuries, to be lifted away to hospital, still protesting that he must go back to help his mates. For one, Harry Pettit, it was too late – he had already died of his injuries.*** *(London Fire Brigade)*

Ignoring the likelihood of another collapse, they set about the frantic task of trying to rescue the two firefighters. Only Martin came out alive. He was in agonising pain – physically because much of his foot and leg had been burned away; mentally because, despite all his efforts to get free, he had not been able to rescue Harry whose body lay still now, under the debris.

Two years later, the *London Gazette* announced that eight firemen would receive awards from the Queen as a result of their courage at the Worsley Hotel fire – more than at any other single incident. Peter Lidbetter, Ron Morris, Roger Stewart and David Blair went to Buckingham Palace to receive the Queen's Gallantry Medal. Later, at a ceremony in London's County Hall, three more firemen – Ray Chilton, Eric Hall and the author Neil Wallington – were presented by the Lord Lieutenant of the County with the Queen's Commendation for Brave Conduct. Harry Pettit's posthumous Commendation was received by his widow, Pat. The Greater London Council had already honoured 22 firemen who had fought at the same fire.

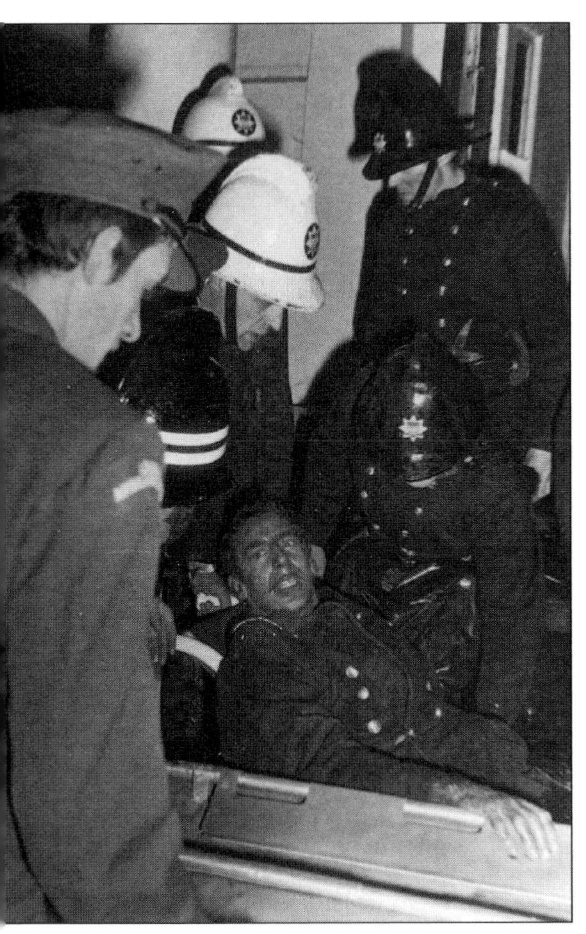

Above: **Stone stairs which had cracked and crumbled in the heat of the Worsley Hotel fire were a death trap for the firefighters who had to resort to using ladders to reach trapped residents on the upper floors.** *(London Fire Brigade)*

Part of London's problems arise from its sheer size and importance as the capital of the country. Its Underground was started more than a century ago and has developed steadily since then. Today, many of its tunnels and stations are in need of renovation and repair – work which has increased dramatically since the King's Cross disaster of 1987 when Station Officer Colin Townsley lost his life.

King's Cross was not the first sign of trouble though. Three years previously, in 1984, a man running a hot dog stall at the entrance to Oxford Circus Underground –

'When everyone rushes out, the fire brigade rushes in. If you can imagine climbing down into a burning chimney, choking on the smoke, wincing at the heat, and with no idea what you will find when you reach the bottom – that's what the London Fire Brigade crews faced when they went into the darkness of the fires at Oxford Circus Underground Station and, later, at the King's Cross disaster,' said one of their senior officers. (London Fire Brigade)

one of the biggest and busiest in the system, in the heart of London's West End – noticed smoke emerging from a ventilator which led down to the station. He called the fire brigade. The first crews to arrive found people still using the escalators despite smoke pouring up from below. They closed the station, evacuated the passengers as fast as they could and then began to descend to the lower levels.

'If you can imagine going down a chimney that's on fire, without having the remotest idea what you're going to find at the bottom, that was Oxford Circus', said one of the senior officers, after the incident. 'It was like taking an escalator down into hell. Hot, full of smoke and when we got to the bottom, there were flames as well. An assortment of lines run through at different levels, each with its platforms.

'We had to work out where the source of the fire was likely to be and while we did this, smoke was pouring through and emerging at stations like Piccadilly and Green Park, further along the line. Eventually we discovered it, blazing deep down in a wire cage which had been set up to hold workmen's equipment but had gradually filled with bits of paper and other flammable litter.'

The fire was put out and the system re-started. Horrified senior brigade officers appealed desperately for better fire prevention measures in London's Underground – but with little response.

It was with no surprise that they were called to a fire at King's Cross on 18 November 1987. But with the nearest crews at Euston out on a false alarm call, there was a slightly longer delay than there

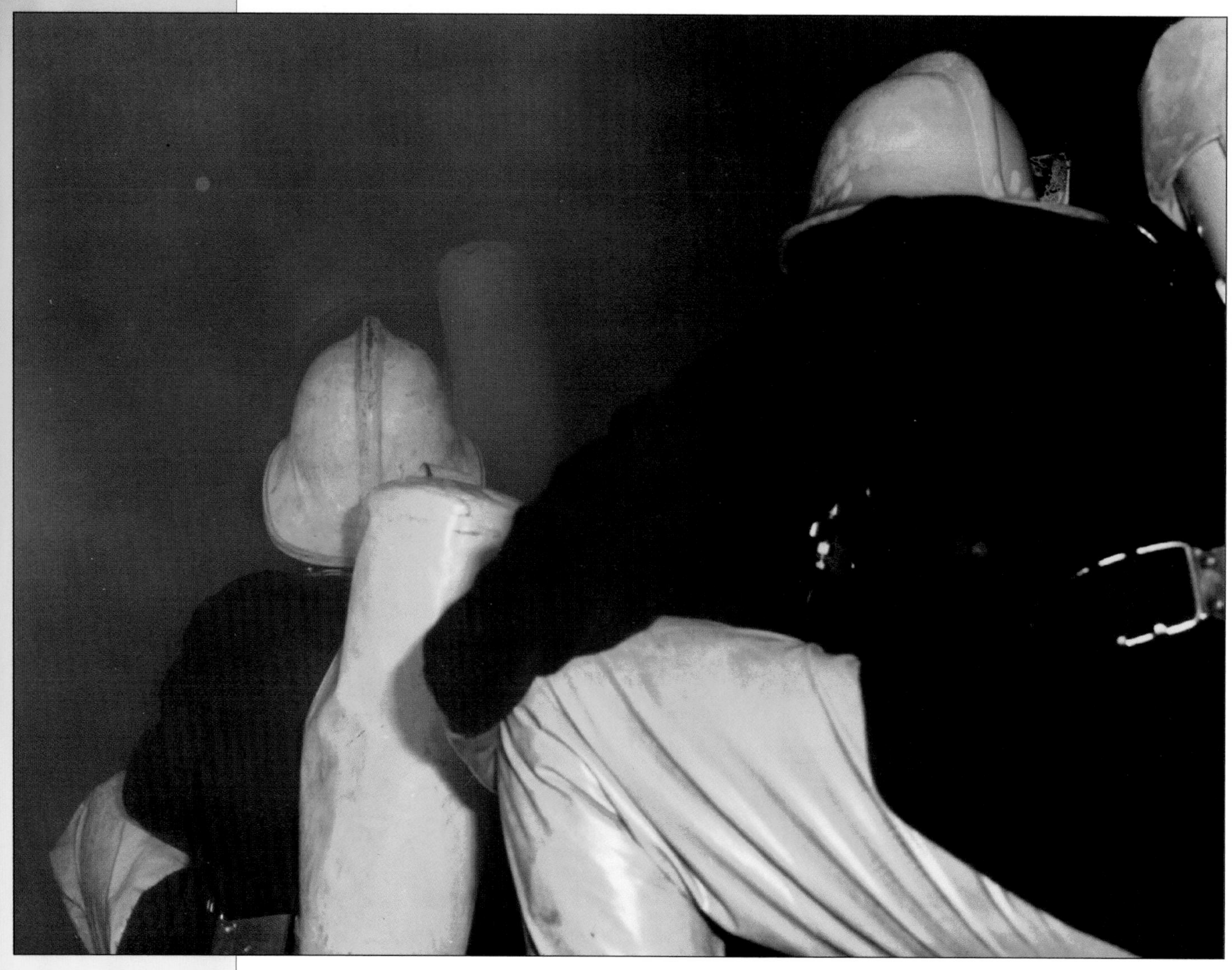

Barely visible in the gloom, a London firefighter contemplates the burn pattern from the bottom of the wood-faced escalator where the fire had started which built up into the King's Cross underground disaster of November 1987. *(London Fire Brigade)*

might otherwise have been while Soho, the next nearest crew, made its way through the rush hour traffic to the terminus.

As it transpired, they had only three minutes – 'three unforgiving minutes' as their Chief Officer, Gerald Clarkson described it at the Inquiry later – to discover what was going on and take action. Led by their Station Officer, the Soho crew plunged into the nearest Underground entrance to meet, once more, a wall of choking smoke and bewildered passengers, some still trying to get down to the platforms below. The heat was intensifying. One firefighter who had always been teased for his big ears noticed that, like a heat sensor, they were beginning to get uncomfortably hot.

It was clear that the fire was coming from below the escalators and travellers were in danger. Calling his men to go back for breathing apparatus, Soho's Station Officer Colin Townsley plunged into the smoke.

Within seconds there was a roar. A wall of flame swept across the booking hall. Fumes and gases had built up under the false ceiling and exploded now in the unpredictable phenomenon fire crews fear most – a gigantic flashover. In the blaze which followed, many passengers and firefighters suffered terrible burns. Station Officer Townsley was found dead among the people he had tried so hard to rescue.

Following King's Cross, a public inquiry was held into the cause of the fire and the way in which it was handled by the Fire Brigade. This caused great bitterness, particularly among the senior officers. As one put it: 'Men whose skill lies in

'They had three minutes to discover what was going on and take action'

The charred remains of the booking hall at the top of the escalators at King's Cross Underground Station. It was here, after the flashover and fireball, that many of the travellers were killed. Soho's gallant Station Officer, Colin Townsley, died trying to save them. (London Fire Brigade)

Farewell to a hero. Crews from Soho Fire Station carry the body of their Station Officer, Colin Townsley, in traditional style on their 'chariot of fire' to Lewisham Crematorium on 27 November 1987. Traffic came to a standstill in Central London and many onlookers were in tears as the cortège passed. Fire Officers from all over Britain lined the approach to the crematorium. Wreaths, including one in the shape of a white helmet and another in letters spelling 'GUV', were among the floral tributes. Station Officer Townsley was posthumously awarded the George Medal for gallantry. (London Fire Brigade)

facing and fighting fires, in making decisions at great speed in the face of appalling danger, based on training and experience and without necessarily knowing exactly what they were dealing with, were subjected, in some cases, to several days of cross-examination by a succession of high powered lawyers. Many of us felt that it was worse than the incident itself.

'Our men had gone in without hesitation. We had all done our utmost, literally in the heat of the moment, to save lives. We were now, with hindsight, being examined in the most minute detail on every action we had taken, by people who appeared to have no concept of what a situation such as the King's Cross fire presented in those first moments when our crews were faced with an inferno of smoke and flames and screaming victims – and with no idea what lay beyond. By all means let there be Inquiries, but not persecutions'.

As a result of the King's Cross fire, strict new legislation was brought in and London Underground was required to take immediate and far-reaching action to improve its fire safety.

But no amount of legislation would have prevented the Moorgate Underground train crash, in February 1975. Neither the Inquiry which followed in its wake, nor the inquest, could explain why a quiet, reliable and experienced train driver had, at the peak of the morning rush hour, driven his packed train at 40 mph and without braking, into the solid wall at the end of a 60 foot (18.2 metres) blind tunnel, 51 foot (15.5 metres) below the surface in the heart of the old City.

An ordinary commuter, he had been travelling in to London's Moorgate Underground Station in the rush hour when the train swept through the platform at 40 mph and hit the dead end of the terminus tunnel. Trapped for hours in the heat and dust as fire crews strove to cut away the wreckage, he nears the end of his ordeal as they manoeuvre him gently through the distorted metal and wheels to safety. (London Fire Brigade)

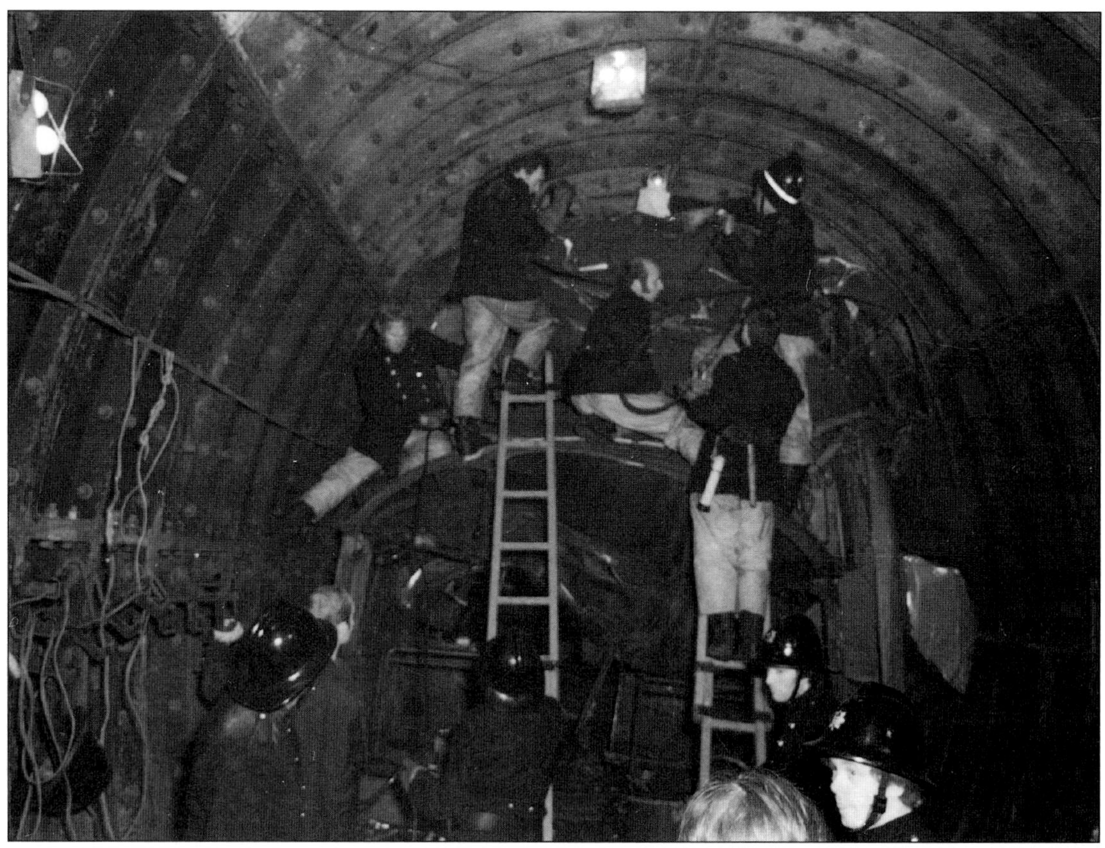

Three London Underground coaches were crushed, one on top of another, into this tunnel at Moorgate. Firemen from all over the capital worked non-stop for nearly five days before the last of the victims was released from the wreckage. (London Fire Brigade)

As the dust settled, the three front carriages – half of the train and 156 foot of metal – had been concertinaed over and under each other between the rails and the tunnel roof. In the words of a senior City Police Inspector, 'never, in our wildest imagination, had we envisaged anything like this!'

For years there had been close co-operation between all the emergency services – fire, police, ambulance, hospitals, St John's, Red Cross, WRVS, Salvation Army. The biggest nightmare had always been the thought of a jumbo-jet landing within the square mile of the City itself – or on Oxford Street, the great shopping centre of the West End. There had been no rehearsal for something like this. At Moorgate, among the dead and dying, in the soot that still swirled round the station platform, and using sheer skill, experience and unselfish co-operation, the senior officers came together and worked out a plan of action.

Communication was difficult. Most of the normal systems failed to work at such depth. Hot cutting equipment produced heat and fumes, also the risk of further injuring those who had survived but were trapped in the mangled wreckage. Supplies of specific equipment needed in such quantity were not readily available. With trains, of necessity at a standstill in the system, ventilation was nil and great tubes had to be lowered to bring in fresh air. Even so, at one early stage, the air level was tested and found to be 120F with minimal oxygen.

Despite this, all the live injured had been released from the wreckage by evening. But it took five gruesome days and nights in appalling stench and deteriorating conditions and, eventually, full decontamination procedure and injections against possible infection for all the fire-fighters involved, before the last of the dead – the train driver – was released. In all, 42 people died and 82 were injured.

All the emergency services learned the lessons of Moorgate. But the greatest skill of all, perhaps, was their remarkable ability to work together at speed and to maximum effect, when confronted with the unknown.

For individual courage, mention must go to Harry Errington of Soho, one of the few members of the London Fire Service to have been awarded the George Cross – the highest decoration for bravery.

A quiet man, Harry had joined the Auxiliary Fire Service, the 'AFS', at the start of the Second World War and managed to settle down into the brash and lively life of Soho Fire Station in the centre of London's 'red light' district. At first, it was a matter of training and standing by. But in September 1940 the German air raids on London began, first on the docks and then on the rest of the capital. Soho crews, along with some of the families who lived nearby, took shelter in Jackson's underground garage. This was close enough to the fire station to be able to get out when the calls came – and they came frequently as the bombs rained down.

On the night of 17 September, they had settled down on the concrete floor to snatch what sleep they could when suddenly, the building above them took a direct hit. The huge bomb exploded on the ground floor and as the building collapsed, a fireball flashed across the basement – so hot that it set light to the oxygen in the lungs of the people who had been sleeping there. Cars and taxis, parked in the garage above, fell through the floor and caught fire, adding to the inferno. All the civilians and seven firemen were killed instantly.

Harry Errington had been blasted 20 feet (6 metres) across the floor and badly burned. For a moment he was stunned, then made for the staircase, only to find that it had been blocked by rubble. He remembered another exit, a side door, ran for it and was escaping into the fresh air when he heard, above the crackle and roar of the flames, the screams of his mate, John Hollingshead, burned too, and buried to the waist in concrete blocks.

'For a moment I hesitated and I was about to go on when I realised that I would never again be able to live with myself if I didn't go back,' he recalled, many years later. 'I grabbed a blanket, put it over my head and ran back.' The jagged blocks were so hot that not only was his skin burned but it came away from the flesh in torn strips. Still he worked on until he released the man, but as he carried him to the door he saw another friend, John Terry, lying against a wall with a radiator across his feet, bleeding from a head wound.

He continued out with John Hollingshead, into the immediate safety of a back courtyard, then plunged back into the flames, lifted the radiator from Terry's feet and half frog-marched him out to safety. Hollingshead was taken to the Middlesex Hospital, half a mile away, but Harry Errington supported Terry, half dragging him, to the Women's Hospital in nearby Soho Square. On the way, in this nightmare sequence, another bomb landed covering them in dust and debris – but they made it to the hospital. All three survived. However it was the end of firefighting for Harry. He had been so badly hurt that he could no longer stay in the fire service.

Dust, debris and general inferno do sometimes face firefighters in their course of duty. When the signals failed outside Clapham Junction in south west London on 12 December 1988, the resulting crash between two trains full of rush-hour commuters killed 35 passengers and injured a further 500. It was a scene of hellish carnage.

Sandwiched between two other shattered carriages, London fire crews work to extricate passengers still trapped after the major rail crash at Clapham Junction, south west London, in December 1988. Many were rescued, but 35 died and 500 were injured in the busy commuter train which crashed at the height of the rush hour. (Derek Robinson)

Initially, teachers and boys from the nearby Emanuel School scrambled down the steep railway embankment to try to help the passengers stumbling round the track which, at this point, runs through a cutting. Their place was quickly taken by crews from Battersea, and then from many parts of London. Men and women firefighters struggled for as long as five hours in difficult and dangerous conditions to disentangle the injured from the twisted metal of the carriages, and it was seven hours before the last identifiable body was taken away from the scene.

Ten awards including one Letter of Commendation and nine Letters of Congratulation from the Chief Officer, were made after the incident.

For sheer, spine tingling courage, the rescue from a fifth floor flat in Park Royal, north west London, takes some beating. Thick smoke was pouring from the windows, high in an eight-storey block, on a cold December evening in 1985 when the Brigade arrived. While some went in from the front, three firefighters ran to the back of the block and discovered a young woman with a baby in her arms, perched on her kitchen window sill, screaming in terror and calling out that there were other children inside. They pitched a ladder against the wall but it was eight feet too short. Desperately they pushed the base further in until it was almost vertical – but it was still short of the sill.

By now, the stabilisers were useless. The fire crew called on the crowd of onlookers to help hold the ladder virtually upright and the first firefighter, Leading Fireman Steve Davies, ran to the top – only to find it was still 18 inches short of the window. He managed to haul himself up and after quickly reassuring the mother that she would be rescued immediately, plunged into the dense smoke and heat to search for the children.

It was then that Firefighter Alan Garside, who had reached the top of the ladder, realised that there was no alternative but to stand, without support, on the top rung, take the baby from the mother's arms and bring it to safety. It was dark. The only light came from the flames and a nearby street lamp. It was cold and pouring with rain. But, balancing himself as firmly as he could, he took the child, clutched it to him and carried it down to safety.

His place was taken by Stn/O Charles Gardner who followed Davies into the flat where they discovered the two children, coughing and crying with smoke and fright. They carried them down then went back for the mother who was, by now, hysterical with fear. Between them, the men calmed her and began the task of persuading her on to the ladder and encouraging her to climb down. With their constant support she managed well until, half way, when the ladder was shaking so much that she froze, paralysed with fright. There was only one solution. One fireman had to hang on to her from the side while the other took her feet in his hands and moved them, rung by rung, down the ladder to the ground.

All three firefighters received the Chief Officer's Letter of Congratulation.

Animals are no strangers to the fire service. Over and over again, they are

Willy/won't he need the bolt-croppers?

Occasionally Lambeth Fire Station, at London's HQ, gets a call to St Thomas's Hospital, just down the road. Usually it's to help cut free a child with its finger stuck in a toy or a supermarket trolley, but early in 1994 it was something else. A patient had arrived in Casualty with a padlock firmly gripped round his private parts. There was no explanation other than the fact that he'd fixed it there himself and then realised that he didn't have the key for it.

Doctors and nurses had done their best, but to no avail. Lambeth's finest did their best, but were just producing the massive bolt-croppers when, as the patient paled with horror, the Station Officer, who had been quietly sorting through his statutory collection of Keys That Will Open Anything, discovered that he had a key which would fit the padlock. The bolt-croppers were superfluous. Colour returned to the man's cheeks and the local paper was able to run a success story under the headline: 'Free Willie!'

mentioned in reports – and not just cats stuck in trees, although there is the traditional tale of the cat which was rescued with difficulty from a perilous perch, high in a tree, by a gallant firefighter who brought it safely to the ground, said his farewells, climbed aboard the fire engine – and watched in horror as the animal leapt from its grateful owner's arms and dived beneath the wheels as the appliance backed away. The crew rushed out to give it the kiss of life but it was, alas, in the rhyming slang of the fire brigade 'brown bread'. Others have been more lucky.

Horses seem determined to get themselves into awkward situations, in ditches, bogs or canals. They have a particular penchant for stinking and slimy slurry pits on cold winter nights. It was daylight though, when the 'shout' came through to

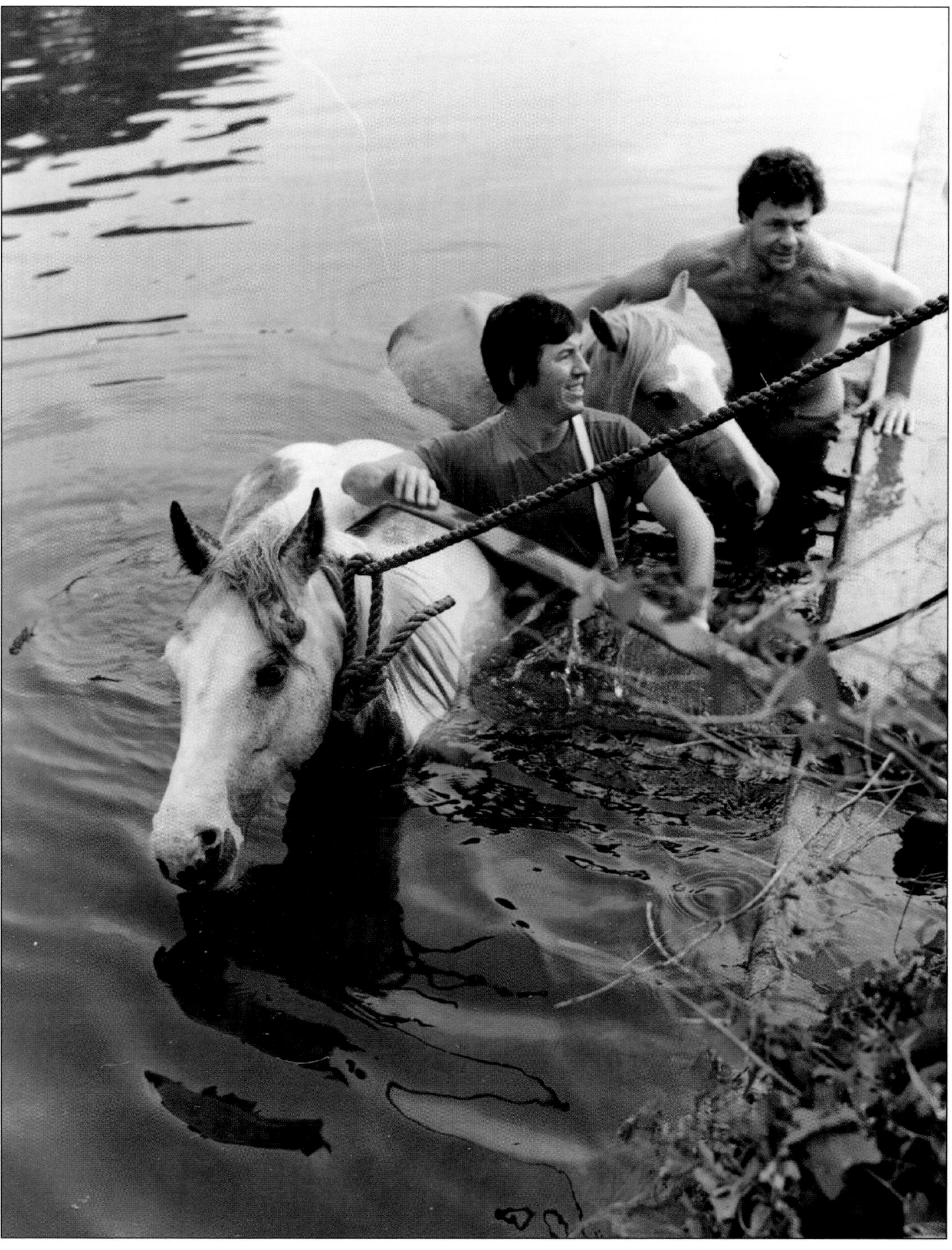

Two ponies from a group which had fallen into a culvert at Tottenham, London, could have drowned had they not been rescued by local firefighters on 28 September 1984. (London Fire Brigade)

Stand by for lift off! A hydraulic platform was transformed into a makeshift crane to rescue the horses. One firefighter stripped to his underpants and worked for more than an hour in the cold water to help save the animals.
(London Fire Brigade)

Tottenham Red Watch in September 1984 – four horses trapped in a steep sided culvert close to a reservoir. Arriving at the site, they surveyed the scene. The four horses included a foal, a sizeable grey and two more, 'one large and one enormous', up to their shoulders in water. Fireman Peter Johnson was only just back from playing a soccer match for the LFB in Newcastle and had still been in 'civvies' when the bells went down. As he said later, he'd only gone along for the ride and to make up the crew. Instead, he found himself 'volunteered' to remove his best suit and lower himself down into the water in his underpants.

With another stripped-down firefighter, Leslie Barnes, they managed to struggle through the freezing liquid mud and get a couple of hoses under the foal which was then hauled to the bank and corralled in a field. The second horse was lured out on the further side which meant another firefighter only had a half mile walk to lead it back to its field.

Meanwhile reinforcements had arrived with lifejackets for the rescuers. 'You try swimming under a trapped horse, wearing a lifejacket,' observed Fireman Johnson. The lifejackets were removed and eventually a van arrived with two horse slings. By this time, the men had been in the water for nearly two hours, but they swam beneath the animals with the slings and eventually managed to fasten them. It was 'chocks away' for the first horse, which sailed into the air and was safely set down on firm ground. Now came the turn of the huge mare. Steadily and gently swaying, she was winched aloft. Fireman Johnson stood, head back and vastly relieved, watching her slowly rise above him. She too was relieved. Lifting her tail she deposited a grateful and accurately aimed reward of best manure – on his upturned face.

These are the lighter moments but, all too often, a rescue demands every ounce of determination and guts not to flinch at horrors that would make the average man or woman in the street run a mile.

Leading Firefighter Gary Paul was among the crew of Ilford Fire Station in London, called out to a fire in a baker's shop, late on a January night in 1990. Smoke was pouring from the first floor. After smashing the front door the crews, wearing breathing apparatus, plunged into the smoke and heat and dashed upstairs. In the back bedroom they found a man so badly blackened and burned that they thought he must be dead. They carried him down and Gary Paul, with a colleague, laid him on the ground and quickly assessed the situation.

He was like a cinder, his arms, torso and face all crusted and blistered, but they set to work and were rewarded, at last, with a faint pulse. Paul realised that they must now maintain the breathing with mouth to mouth resuscitation, but there was a problem. The man's lips had been welded together by the heat. Kneeling alongside him, the fireman managed gently to prise the lips apart sufficiently to start respirex treatment and keep it going until the ambulance arrived. The reward was considerable – it took a long stay in hospital but the man survived.

Embankments, railway lines, bridges – and electricity pylons – are all among the sites chosen by potential suicides for their last moments on earth.

For anyone who has wondered what rescuers talk about as they try to save the victims from suicidal situations, a London fireman 'spilled the beans' in a note to the LFB house magazine *London Firefighter*. Tower Bridge has been popular for these dives, but his crew had been called to a 'jumper' who had selected for his final moments Hammersmith Bridge, which spans the Oxford and Cambridge Boat Race stretch of the River Thames in London. The man sat now, 80 feet (24.3 metres) above the road and river, threatening to hurl himself down at the drop of a ladder.

With a line knotted in a round turn and two half hitches ('four might have been a bit safer') and tied to his belt, the fireman clambered up the iron ladder inside the stanchion of the bridge and emerged from a trapdoor, whereupon the man took fright and climbed even higher. 'I beseeched him "please be careful – you'll fall and hurt yourself!"' but there was no immediate response until, reluctantly, he agreed that if the rescuer wouldn't move, neither would he. They sat chatting.

'Nice morning isn't it? Do you come here often?'

'Once should be enough!'

Talked him down from the pylon – in Gaelic

A cool head for heights has always been essential for any firefighter. However it's not necessarily for standing on a high ladder, fighting flames. Just before Christmas in 1969, an Irishman with major psychiatric problems climbed a giant electricity pylon in the middle of a playing field in east London. When the Fire Brigade arrived, he was sitting astride an insulator between two live high tension cables, 130 feet above the ground. It was, inevitably, a bitter cold day with torrential rain and an icy wind blowing, so that the man – who had already removed his trousers – was shivering with cold and fright. The first move was to get the power cut off.

Calling from below, the fire crew tried then to persuade him down, but without success. The officer in charge of Poplar's turntable ladder tried to reach him but the ladder was too short and they couldn't seem to 'get through' to him by shouting. By this time Assistant Divisional Officer Liam Hackett had arrived on the scene. He too tried to talk to the man and suddenly realised that it was not just his mental problem that was causing difficulties. He changed tactics and began a fresh effort, but this time in Gaelic. It worked. ADO Hackett and an engineer from the Electricity Generating Board climbed up with a lowering line and a blanket, but it took considerably more chat in his native tongue before the deranged climber was persuaded to allow himself to be 'walked' and lowered down the side of the pylon to the head of the turntable ladder, where he was hauled aboard and lowered the last 50 feet (15 metres) to the ground.

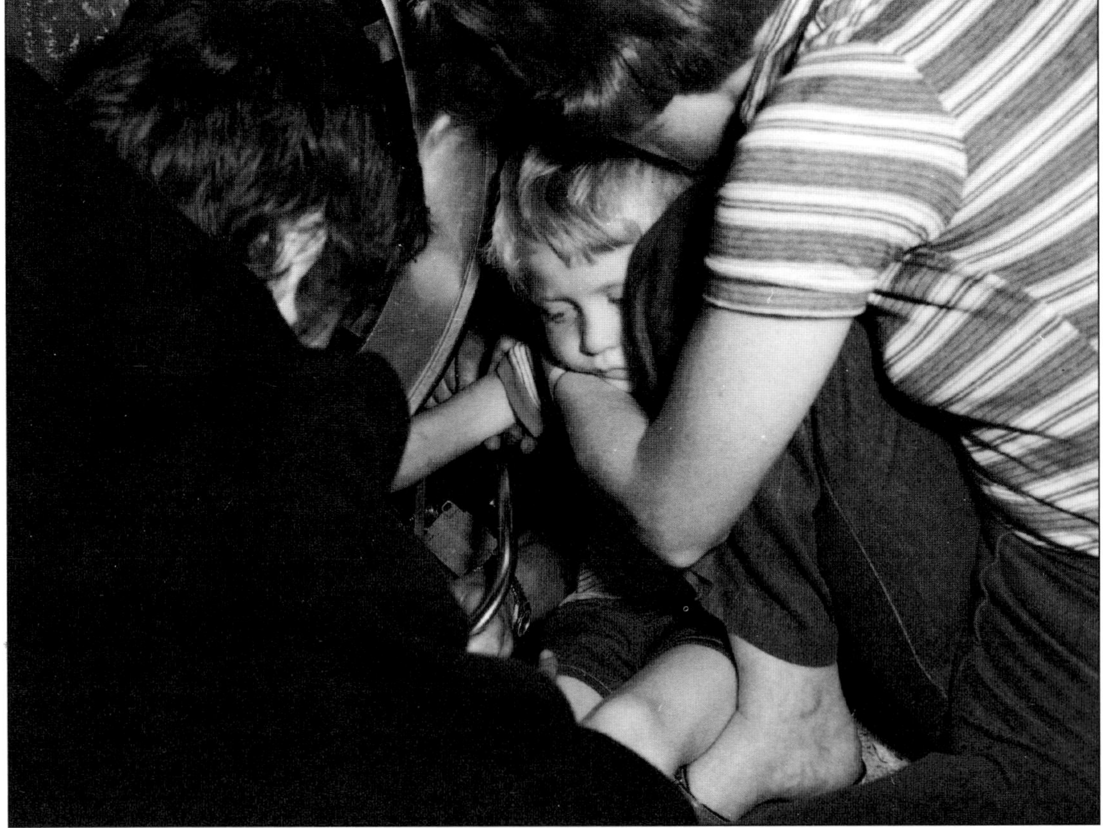

Comforted by his mother, the small shopper waits stoically while firemen release his arm from an escalator in a Wembley store in July 1976. Remarkably, he was not seriously hurt. (London Fire Brigade)

Even the bravest firefighter quaked at the knees when the call came to rescue an injured crane driver 11 storeys up in a block of high-rise flats being built in Maida Vale, London, in 1968. The jib of the crane had snapped in gale force winds, trapping the driver in his cabin. The crane and the scaffolding were not all that was shaking as the crews climbed out into the elements, high above the rooftops, to ease the driver to safety. (London Fire Brigade)

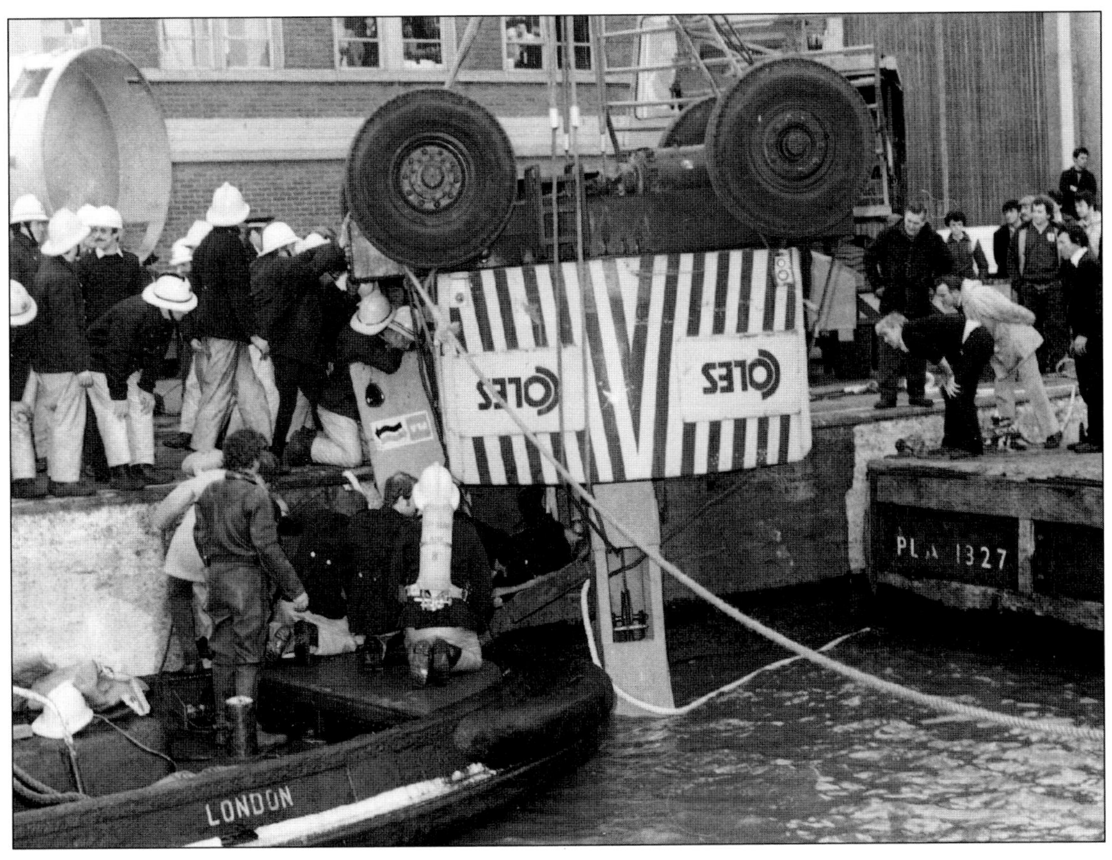

When this crane capsized on the edge of a wharf in London's docks the senior officer on duty, 'Joe' Kennedy, insisted on taking over the task of going down into the driver's cabin to lead the efforts to release the driver, although the whole crane was in imminent danger of capsizing into the dock. The operation was successful and the man was eventually released and taken to hospital. (London Fire Brigade)

Left: *Thermal imaging cameras – believed to be used operationally for the first time – and Vibraphones were among the fire crews' technical equipment used in their urgent attempts to trace victims of a gas explosion which virtually destroyed this block of flats in Putney, south west London, in 1985.*

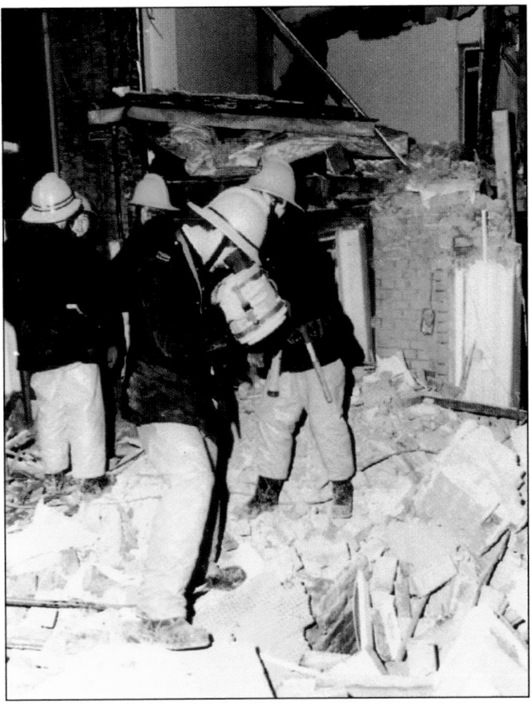

A firefighter at the Putney explosion using the 'new' thermal imaging camera as crews wait for him to track down victims in the rubble.

> *They navigated into Dunkirk thanks to the black smoke*

There was a pause and more chat, during which the 'jumper' admitted that he had problems. Not women, drink or the job, but tranquillisers. The firefighter asked :

'Have you got the trancs with you?'

'Yes, they're here,' came the reply.

'Do us a favour mate, my nerves are shot to hell with all this, pass me a couple over will you?'

All this seemed to touch a mutual chord and although no tranquillisers were taken, the chat continued for more than an hour until the man took pity on the firefighter, his insteps cramped from standing on the iron ladder. He threw him his tobacco pouch and together they rolled cigarettes. After a puff or two the fireman spoke again :

'George', he said (they were, by now, on first name terms), 'you can't do this to me. I've got a wife, three kids, a big black dog, a rabbit, two hamsters and three goldfish, all dependant on me, and if my mortgage goes up another half per cent I'll be up there with you. If you have a shred of human decency left you'll come down immediately.'

It worked. The 'jumper' gave in. Together they climbed down. A warm ambulance was waiting. Within minutes, the man was back in the psychiatric ward of the local hospital.

London firefighters may be up in arms at the huge array of incidents which have not been covered in this chapter, but space will only allow for a sample of the exceptional range of road, rail, toxic, explosive, underground, river and even air incidents which the London Fire Brigade faces during the course of each year.

No mention of bravery in the capital would be complete, however, without a note about the *Massey Shaw*, the old fireboat which holds pride of place in the annals of the River Service. In 1940 she was still comparatively young when the call went out nationally for small boats to

A runaway crane caused this havoc at Hendon, in north west London, on 6 January 1987. Fire crews rescued several people trapped in the wreckage but, incredibly, there were no serious injuries. (London Fire Brigade)

sail to Dunkirk to help evacuate thousands of British soldiers, early in the Second World War.

With a volunteered crew of full-time professional firemen and Auxiliary Fire Service men (including a former film producer and a City company director) the vessel was prepared in just a few hours. This included nipping down the Old Kent Road to buy her a compass. There was no time even to 'swing the ship' to record her magnetic deviation before they left and began the journey down river to the coast. At Ramsgate they took a young naval officer on board, then pointed the *Massey Shaw*'s bow across the Channel. They navigated into Dunkirk thanks to the columns of black smoke rising from the burning town and, under bombardment and machine gun fire, began taking troops on board.

The *Massey*, built for river work, made three valiant crossings, bringing back several hundred exhausted and wounded troops and, on the last journey home, rescuing 40 survivors from a nearby French ship which had been blown up by a mine. Only as they set off on this last journey did they discover that their little ship had not be de-gaussed – treated to deflect magnetic mines.

Years later, a wartime German fighter pilot met a *Massey Shaw* man and admitted that he had been about to machine gun her decks when he saw what he thought was a big gun pointing towards him and beat a hasty retreat. Only later did he discover that she was a fireboat and this was her water monitor.

Some time after the war, the *Massey* herself was rescued when a group of London firefighters discovered her, semi-derelict, and set about resuscitating her. By fund-raising for their expenses and giving up much of their spare time, the members of the *Massey Shaw* Preservation Society have brought the little ship back to active life and were able to take her back across the Channel for the 50th anniversary of the Dunkirk evacuation.

Intruder caused palace coo!

Embarrassing situations are nothing new to the fire service. But there was still quite a surprise awaiting the crews who were called to Charing Cross Police Station in London, at 0849 hours on a chill February morning in 1994.

An American paraglider had landed on the roof of Buckingham Palace, stripped naked, and proceeded to paint his groin area with green paint which, he told the police who rushed up to grab him, was radioactive.

After an arm's length check-up by a pink-faced firefighter with a survey meter, the London Fire Brigade was able to give the reassuring news that while the man may have had the wind up, he was certainly not radioactive.

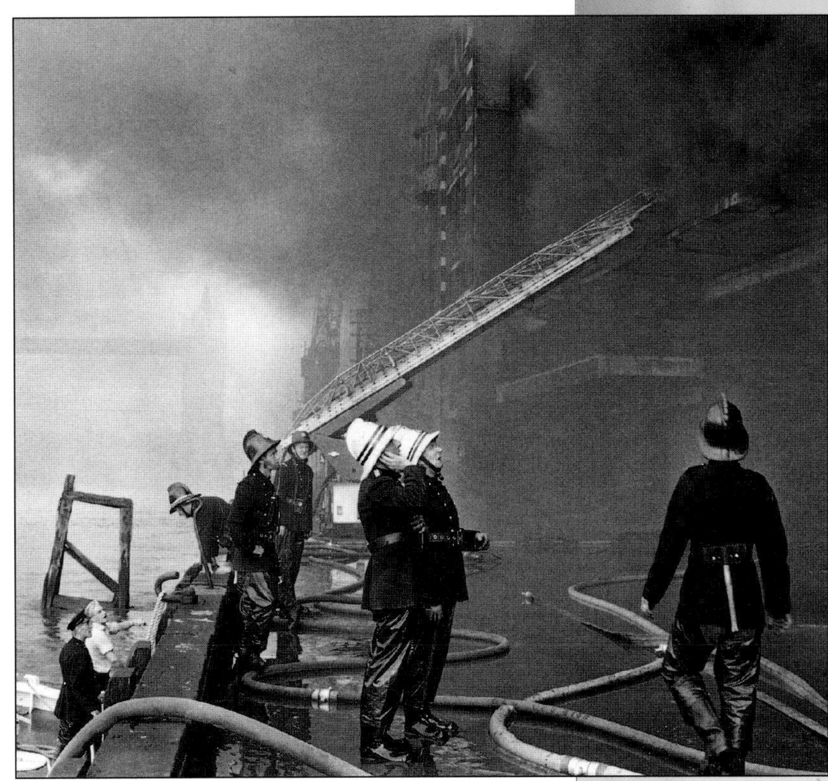

Senior officers survey the scene in a 1971 fire at an old, cork-lined cold storage warehouse on the edge of the Thames near Tower Bridge as the fireboat Massey Shaw *comes alongside, ropes meticulously coiled, to offer assistance. Note the high shine on the boots and 'wet legs' – hours of work and shoe polish went into achieving the mirror finish.* (London Fire Brigade)

CHAPTER 5

ESSEX TO THE WASH

EASTERN

NORFOLK

One of the worst scenarios faced by firefighters is a fire involving chemicals or other hazardous materials. This magnifies the 'ordinary' risks which crews already have to contend with. Chemicals on fire invariably add to the thick toxic smoke which not only fills the burning building but hangs low over the surrounding area as well.

Such was the situation on 11 October 1991. A hydrochloric acid fog was just one of many problems endured by firefighters during a three-day fight to control a massive fire in a plastics factory in Thetford, Norfolk.

Crews were beginning to get the fire under control on the second day when an unusual phenomenon occurred. Thick fog descended on the area; the wind dropped and toxic gases from the fire plume mixed with the surrounding fog causing a weak hydrochloric acid fog which necessitated a withdrawal of crews for about four hours until the monitoring safety team agreed that the fog had lifted and it was safe to return.

However, by this time the fire had intensified again and a massive attack had to be mounted to try and complete firefighting operations before the expected return of the fog that evening.

Firefighters toiled for long hours over the three days, yet the brigade maintained its usual service to the rest of the county (including coping with a double fatal road traffic accident just outside Thetford at the height of the blaze). Many off-duty staff reported for work, including control personnel who had the enormous task of

Firefighting teams at work on a huge fire in a chemicals warehouse in Thetford, Norfolk on 11 October 1991. Thick black smoke masks the fact that it is mid-afternoon. (Norfolk Fire Service)

mobilising appliances, finding the resources requested from the fireground, and providing the many back-up moves of appliances and crews required.

Further major problems related to water shortages and a lack of knowledge of the stored contents until several hours into the incident.

At the height of the fire, approximately 1,000 tons of waste plastic, including pvc, polyethylene, polypropylene, ABS (a mixture of acrylonytrile, butadienne and styrene) and polystyrene was burning fiercely across an area of about two acres.

A total of 51 appliances attended with 235 personnel from Norfolk, Suffolk and Cambridgeshire.

A relay was set up to bring water from the river nearly two miles away, involving 15 pumping appliances. The fire was difficult to extinguish not only because the fumes meant that breathing apparatus crews had to wear chemical protection suits, but also because all the machinery in the factory became bonded together by melted plastic, including two articulated trailers.

The situation was further complicated by the fact that the factory backed on to Thetford Forest and was next to other industrial units. More firefighting resources had to be deployed to prevent fire spread.

Gases given off by the fire included hydrogen chloride, styrene, chlorine and traces of cyanide. Variable wind conditions throughout the operation led to crews occasionally being exposed to the smoke and, as a result, 45 firefighters were taken to hospital for minor chest complaints and skin irritations. Some firefighters also suffered from exhaustion, although all but one were quickly released.

Serious problems occurred with breathing apparatus and appliances, especially the Norwich hydraulic platform which was severely damaged. Fortunately the wind direction took the smoke plume away from the town, but there were a number of complaints from the public regarding strong smells.

Great difficulties were experienced in tackling large heaps of plastic which had solidified. Large mechanical diggers had to be brought in to break these apart so that firefighters could deal with remaining pockets of fire.

The Thetford fire was truly without precedent in Norfolk. Well over 500 personnel (including relief crews) were used, and many had little or no sleep during that period.

SUFFOLK

Shire county firefighters are accustomed to dealing with animals when a farm fire breaks out. Even so, there was a surprise for Suffolk fire crews when they responded in October 1990 to a '999' fire call to a pig farm at Wetheringsett. A serious fire was in progress when the first fire engine

Swam pushing boat to rescue flood victims

The East Coast floods of January 1953 saw numerous individual acts of bravery. One of these involved a lone fireman who was later awarded the George Medal.

Leading Fireman Fred Sadd was in charge of a crew from Gorleston Fire Station. He led a rescue team and waded out to families stranded in their homes, where they perched on wardrobes and watched in fear as the waters continued to rise.

Swimming from house to house on a flooded estate, he called out to those trapped inside, 'Don't panic. I will be back with a boat.' But when he found a boat there were no oars, so Fred pushed the boat ahead of him as he swam back in the icy waters.

It was pitch dark and the water was rough. Fred stumbled from house to house, freeing trapped people and helping them into his boat. He eventually rescued 10 people, including five children, before he collapsed from exhaustion.

A little later he plunged back into the floods and brought back 15 more people.

After his retirement Fred Sadd remained in the area until he died in 1987.

arrived, and firefighters were told that 1,000 pigs were inside the burning buildings. Sadly, despite the strenuous efforts of crews from Debenham, Eye, Stowmarket, Needham Market and Framlingham, virtually all the pigs perished amid the flames.

Another Suffolk emergency which involved a human life and death situation took place in February 1992 and illustrates the teamwork nature of rescue work.

While hunting for antique bottles around the area of a disused trench in Willy Snaith Road, Newmarket, a young man moved into the bottom of the deep trench to continue his search. Almost immediately the trench sides collapsed, burying the bottle collector up to his neck in soil.

There he remained, trapped for some time, before his cries for help were heard by a passer-by who raised the alarm. Two fire engines from Newmarket and Bury St Edmunds were despatched. When they arrived at the scene, all that could be seen was the man's head and left shoulder above the compacted soil. The story is taken up by Sub Officer Trevor Byford who was in charge of the Bury St Edmunds crew :

'The soil was very dry at the point of collapse. Consequently there was a large overhang above the trapped man which threatened to fall down at any time. This required the rapid use of an airbag to hold the overhang up. A hydraulic spreader was used to lift the weight of a large boulder of earth off the casualty's chest, and due to the confined available space in which to scoop out the crumbling soil, progress was very slow.

'Two doctors were now at the scene and rendered medical assistance as the rescue progressed with four firefighters working down in the trench using a wide range of lifting and spreading equipment. Cracks in the surrounding soil were growing all the time but after an hour's sweat and toil, the trapped man was finally free and lifted out.'

The casualty was rushed to hospital where he was treated for his injuries and released. Suffolk's Chief Fire Officer subsequently commended four of the rescue crews, including Sub Officer Byford. They also received a teamwork award from the Royal Humane Society. The two doctors' courage was also recognised.

ESSEX

Land, sea and air define the areas in which Essex County Fire and Rescue Service operates. Reaching out across the Thames estuary, it joins forces with Kent to monitor 'incidents' by fire launches in the busy shipping lanes that lead from the Dover Straits and the North Sea up to Tilbury and from there to London. On its northern border, the busy port of Harwich sees more than three million travellers a year off on their journeys to Holland, Belgium and Scandinavia. Many will have arrived by road or rail, through Essex's 'patch' and, under the latest procedures, will stay within its field of operation for 50 miles out to sea beyond the county's coastline.

This combined role brought its senior officers the problem of what sort of protection their firefighters needed for their new range of duties. Working from boats or helicopters, they could be facing extreme heat in the case of shipboard fires or extreme cold if they landed in the sea. The survival suits which they came up with give protection against heat, cold and wet.

'The survival suits they came up with give protection against heat, cold and wet'

Essex also includes within its territory the growing Stansted Airport.

With new towns, new shopping complexes and an assortment of industrial sites as well as a backing area of farmland, its fire crews need to be ready for anything.

'Anything' in March 1994 turned out

to be a call to one of the area's biggest oil refineries.

Firefighters have been wary of oil storage fires since they first began to make their appearance in the early 1900s. Dudgeon's Wharf, in East London, had been a landmark in this form of hazard since the day in July 1969 when a London Fire Brigade Sub Officer, four firemen and a civilian, dealing with a small outbreak of fire in an empty 20,000 gallon oil storage tank, were killed when it suddenly exploded. A public enquiry followed and as a result, legislation was passed to make sure that all empty tanks were cleared of vapour or gas before any sort of maintenance work began.

Essex firefighters must have had it at the back of their minds when, just before 1700 hours on 8 March 1994, they were called to a large oil refinery where, according to the first call, fire had broken out in a crude oil processing unit, under maintenance and empty. The tank was about 100 foot (30.4 metres) high and raised some 10 foot (3 metres) above the ground. The fire had apparently been started by sparks from the workmen's hot cutting equipment showering on to some three foot thick filters below and setting them alight. From here, it had spread to the scaffold boarding and by the time the refinery's firefighters arrived it was well away, burning merrily at about 80 foot (24.3 metres) up inside the sealed container. ADO Kelvin Hardingham surveyed the huge tank, towering above him and takes up the story :

'The only way in was through a series of small manhole covers around the sides of the tank, each about 21 inches (52 cm) across. Two of the refinery crewmen, wearing breathing apparatus, wriggled through one of these covers, boots first at about 50 feet (15 metres) above ground. The first man lowered himself on to a narrow walkway just below the entry hole but slipped and tumbled down 20 feet (6 metres) to the bottom.

'The whole tank was full of black smoke – we could see it billowing out as we arrived – and the second man could hear the oxygen hissing from his mate's BA which was evidently leaking. He managed to get down and found his colleague lying injured and trapped behind a fixed ladder.

'By this time we had arrived and

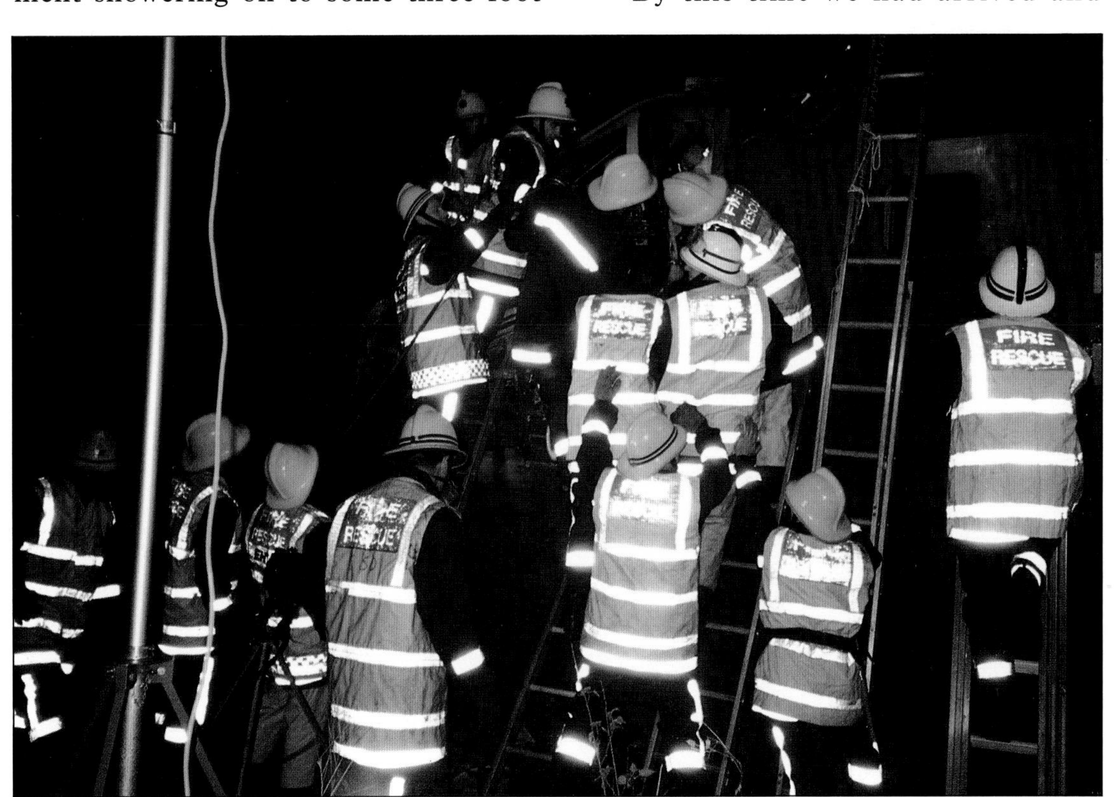

Like swarming wasps, luminous safety jackets glow in the dark as fire crews from Grays, Tilbury and Chelmsford struggle to cut the driver free after two Class 37 diesel locomotives, in tandem, were in collision with a row of flat-bed rail wagons in a siding near Grays Station on 29 November 1991. The buffers of the first wagon had penetrated the front of the first locomotive, pushing the main frame and controls into the driver's cab and compressing the driver against the bulkhead. A fireman who had worked with British Rail before joining the fire service proved invaluable in assessing any special risks inside the locomotive. Winches and heavy cutting gear had to be used, but here, the driver is about to be released and taken to hospital. (Essex Fire and Rescue Service)

Day turns to night as dense black smoke rises above a factory full of gifts and toys in Eastwood, Essex, on 6 December 1993. A lone firefighter ignores the danger of possible explosions as he calmly directs a jet into the roof of the burning building where, among the toys at risk, were copies of television's inflatable 'Mr Blobby', ready for the Christmas shopping spree. (Essex Fire and Rescue Service)

assessed the situation. We called for air line units and tried to lower them down to the two men. Conditions were appalling, we couldn't see a thing. Our crew went into the tank, with great difficulty, wriggling through the hole with full BA and as they got inside they could hear the whistle going on the injured man's BA. Because of the leak, his equipment had lost a lot of air and we only had 10 minutes to get him out. It was a real race against time. The men worked fast but he only had two minutes left when we finally got the line to him'.

One team helped his colleague out, the rest stayed down in the darkness and smoke, with the fire still burning above them, until they were able to release him from under the ladder.

'Getting him out was a nightmare, the sides were slippery and there was no way they could use a stretcher. In the end and with great difficulty, they manhandled him up and managed to manoeuvre him through the hole.' Even then, there was only a narrow single walkway but they carefully strapped him into a stretcher and had him winched down by crane to an ambulance. He was taken to hospital with a broken arm, exhaustion and shock while the Essex men climbed back in and put out the fire – which had burned throughout the rescue.

It took about two hours to get the man out safely and another hour to extinguish the fire. None of the Essex firefighters was hurt, but, in the restrained words of ADO Hardingham: 'I think that, by the end, everyone was rather fatigued.'

Chalk pits are one of the hazards in Essex. It was a Grays house owner who called out the Fire Brigade around teatime one April evening in 1993. Children had come running from a quarry behind his back garden crying for help because one of their friends had been buried by a landslide.

Apparently five youngsters had been playing in and around a hut which had been carved into the side of the quarry some years before. Below it was a sheer incline of some 100 feet (30.4 metres) to the bottom. There had been heavy rain in the previous days which had evidently loosened the soil above the hut and below an oak tree growing there. As the children played, the ground moved, the tree fell and 13-year-old Adam Oake was completely buried in a landslide of limestone and soil. His friends frantically dug away the earth surrounding the top half of his body but the lower half was submerged in tightly packed chalk.

As soon as the fire crew reached the scene, three firemen, Station Officer Nick Brazier, Leading Fireman Flower and Fireman Chandler dashed through to the back of the garden and clambered along the chalk face to the injured boy. Leading Fireman Arthur Barley and Fireman Still followed with lines and other equipment.

The scene facing them was not hopeful. Young Adam was obviously in great pain and seemed likely to have broken both his legs.

As more chalk and soil tumbled down on their heads, three of the firemen rigged up a quick cover of broken boards to protect the boy, but as fast as the rest dug away at the chalk, more fell from above. In the end, Station Officer Brazier called for a trowel and gently dug small amounts away from the boy's limbs. By 1800 hours an ambulance had arrived and supervised Fireman Flower as he administered pain-killing gas to the lad.

By 1820 Adam's left leg was released and two firemen still perched perilously above the 100 foot (30.4 metres) drop, supported his weight while the work of trying to free his right leg continued. The early Spring evening light was fading now, rain was beginning to fall again and a paramedic who had been lowered to check on the boy had asked for the rescue to be speeded up if possible as he was concerned about the blood supply to the lower leg. They had already reckoned that he had a fractured right thigh bone.

Constantly in danger of a further landslide and of sliding into the quarry, Fireman Still and Fireman Flower held Adam upright while Stn/O Brazier and L Fmn Barley dug steadily but faster now, and mostly with their bare hands, to avoid hurting him. As darkness fell, at 1900 hours, they succeeded. Adam was free, secured safely on a 'Troll' stretcher and carefully carried back along the dangerous and slippery rock face to the waiting ambulance.

The crews, weary from the effort and the emotion of the rescue, returned to base, but their concern for Adam was such that they telephoned the hospital later that evening. A nursing sister told them that he had, indeed, fractured his femur and had a hairline crack in his pelvis – but, to their delight, she added that he was comfortable and was expected to make a full recovery.

Of the 20,000 emergency calls which Essex receives a year on average, well over

Adam Oake was completely buried in a landslide of limestone and soil

8,000 are false alarms and of these, 2,971 are 'malicious'. Added to this are fires which are clearly started deliberately.

Temporary Station Officer Norman Sparks of Harlow Fire Station was particularly incensed when his crews' lives and those of elderly people and children were put at risk again and again by the activities of a 'firebug'. At one house fire, neighbours put up a ladder and saved five people from the flames, but nobody seemed able to identify the culprit. Eventually, Norman Sparks decided to take action himself.

Working in co-operation with Harlow police he listened to recordings of the '999' calls which the 'firebug', a man, had put through after starting the fires, noting the various public telephone boxes which he had used. He studied fire reports and statements, talked to people who lived near the fires and gradually built up such a pattern of times and places that, after six months' work, he was able not only to come up with a profile which confirmed his suspicions of a man he had seen watching the firefighting at a number of these incidents, but to predict where and when he was likely to strike next.

His research proved him right. When the next call came in December 1992, fire officers surrounded the telephone box and arrested a man. There was no doubt that this was the 'firebug' – although he had been given resuscitation after posing as a hero carrying out rescues from one of the fires he had started himself.

The case ended with the man being jailed for four years on five charges of arson in Harlow. Essex Fire Chief John Sherrington commented after the case that 'Mr Spark's dedication and determined attitude to the investigations helped achieve a satisfactory result' and rewarded the firefighting detective with a Special Commendation.

HERTFORDSHIRE

Pollution prevention is beginning to figure large in the world of firefighting. Often, particularly when they are dealing with fires in industrial premises, fire brigades find that the water being used to put out the fire picks up chemicals as it drains away and can easily pollute sewers and rivers.

Hertfordshire Fire and Rescue Service made the decision not to wash down roads after fires or spillages which might cause a pollution problem. This has now been followed by other brigades on a national scale.

What happens to the water now? The latest method is to contain spillages as much as possible rather than wash them down the drains, and to do this, Herts fire crews carry special anti-pollution packs, issued by the National Rivers Authority, which contain a variety of absorbent materials to soak up oil and chemicals.

The national agreement, called the Memorandum of Understanding, covers various issues which improve the co-operation between the Rivers Authority and the fire services, who have also agreed to notify them of any incidents which might cause water pollution.

CAMBRIDGESHIRE

At 0947 hours on 22 March 1989, Cambridgeshire crews from Dogsthorpe and Stanground Fire Stations were called out to a 'tanker on fire' at a Vibroplant depot in Fengate, Peterborough.

Within minutes of their arrival there was a massive explosion which showered metal fragments and debris all around the site. The blast wrecked the fire appliances

Firefighters had just arrived at the car park adjoining a warehouse site where a vehicle fire had been reported when there was an enormous explosion. The unmarked truck had been carrying industrial explosives. One firefighter was killed. The blast damage to the fire engines and surrounding buildings was horrific. (Geoff Sayers)

Spent seven hours on lorry leaking chemicals

The dangers in the transport of hazardous goods were foremost in the minds of Cambridgeshire firefighters in June 1993 when they were called to a heavy goods vehicle which was leaking nitric acid on the southbound carriageway of the A1 near RAF Wittering.

There was a real danger of the acid coming into contact with sodium hydrosulphite carried in another container on the lorry. Eventually 155 gallons (700 litres) of nitric acid had to be decanted into another container on another vehicle. A total of 18 BA sets, two gas tight suits, six chemical protection suits and the decontamination shower were used. The A1 was closed for most of the day and major traffic jams built up. Fortunately there were no injuries but the crews spent seven hours on this taxing and potentially lethal job.

together with many cars and much plant, and devastated possibly 30 or more factories, offices and adjacent buildings.

When more firefighters arrived at the explosion site, one fireman, John Humphries, had already been killed and several others were seriously injured. Both of the fire engines first at the scene were severely damaged and the rescue tender was still on fire.

Most of the first crews were suffering from serious injury and taken into ambulances and whisked off to hospital. By now it had been established that the information on the original '999' call sheet was incorrect. An unmarked van, not a tanker, was involved. It had been carrying explosives and detonators and had caught fire in Vibroplant's yard. The initial task of the reinforcing crews was to assist in firefighting and to search and check all the buildings to ensure that all persons were accounted for. They then cleared all the rubble from Vibroplant to thoroughly check for unknown casualties.

Fortunately no fire occurred in any of the many buildings which suffered from the explosion damage. Crews remained at the scene of the tragedy until late into the evening.

The following week a full Brigade Funeral was held for Firefighter John Humphries. It was attended by many of his colleagues, still suffering from their injuries as the result of the explosion.

In the early hours of 3 July, Peterborough crews were called to Do-It-All at the Orton Centre. A stolen car had been pushed up to the fire exit doors and set alight and a serious fire was developing. However, prompt firefighting action contained the fire and there was no spread of the fire into the shop itself, only smoke damage. Not satisfied with this, the pyromaniac struck again a few weeks later, setting fire to the roof while repairs were being carried out. On this occasion 25 firefighters with five pumps again managed to check the fire after forming two breaks in the roof.

A road crash which happened soon after this fire called out Cambridgeshire crews from Dogsthorpe, Stanground and Peterborough Volunteer Fire Brigade. A car being driven by a very drunk man had left Soke Parkway, Peterborough, and ended up down an embankment. Two adults, including the driver, were released before the arrival of firefighters, but a 13-year-old girl was certified dead in the back of the car. The driver turned out to be her father and he caused a considerable disturbance at the scene while his daughter's body was being extricated.

'A stolen car had been pushed up to the fire exit doors and set alight'

Peterborough has independent 'private' Fire Brigade

The Cambridgeshire city of Peterborough has a unique aspect to its fire service organisation. There are three fire stations which protect the Peterborough area but only two of these, at Stanground and Dogsthorpe, are manned by Cambridgeshire Fire and Rescue Service firefighters.

The third fire station is that of the Peterborough Volunteer Fire Brigade which celebrates 110 years of service during 1994. Formed in 1884 by a number of gentlemen who felt that the town fire brigade had been dilatory in dealing with a large fire, the Volunteer Brigade has kept its independence through many local government reorganisations which led to the present county fire brigade national structure. Nowadays, the Volunteers operate under a contract with the Cambridgeshire Brigade as a 'private' fire brigade which provides additional fire cover to Peterborough in conjunction with the two county fire stations. The fees for this contract go to the Volunteer Brigade itself rather than its 21 members, who are drawn from a wide range of professions. They have been described as a sort of landbased lifeboat station.

The Volunteers man two pumps from their fire station located in the centre of the city. In all respects their equipment, training and procedures reflect that of local authority fire brigades across the UK.

Peterborough Volunteers' modern fire station is the fourth in the Volunteers' history and was built by the Volunteers themselves in 1984. In the same year, these unique British firemen received the freedom of the city to mark their collective service to Peterborough.

The bane of rural firefighters, particularly in hot summers, are stubble and grassland fires. On a humid afternoon on 17 August 1989, a solitary crew from Peterborough assess the situation as the fire creeps towards them from the far side of this vast field. (Cambridgeshire Fire and Rescue Service)

BEDFORDSHIRE

Every fire brigade in Britain is inspected annually by Her Majesty's Inspectors of Fire Services whose task is to ensure on behalf of the Secretary of State that Fire Brigades are being provided and working efficiently in accordance with the Fire Services Act 1947.

These inspections usually take the form of a week-long visit to each brigade by uniformed inspectors who have all held senior posts in the service.

During the 1992 HMI inspection of Bedfordshire Fire and Rescue Service, a major fire developed in Luton in a vehicle repair workshop. The Chief Fire Officer was able to take the Inspector to the scene to see fire crews at work amid the smoke at first hand and, no doubt, to demonstrate just how effective his firefighters from Luton, Dunstable and Stopsley fire stations were.

Like most other fire brigades, Bedfordshire can have periods of intense activity when abnormal factors influence the '999' call workload. A period of dry weather will cause a sudden increase in the number of grass and heathland fires which need attention, and likewise rainstorms will create flash flooding.

However, in 1992, political events thousands of miles away in India landed Bedfordshire firefighters with a serious fire to tackle at a Sikh temple in Luton early one morning. It followed an arson attack. Despite their strenuous efforts, the building was badly damaged although the crews were able to limit the spread of fire to nearby buildings.

When the Bedfordshire firefighters returned to their respective stations some hours later to shower and change into dry clothes, clean and restow their fire engines, they were probably not surprised to learn from the news bulletins that other Sikh temples around the country were similarly attacked during the night.

LINCOLNSHIRE

The dangers of firefighting are particularly well understood in Lincolnshire Fire Brigade as, although this is predominantly a rural county, it has had its share of fire service tragedy in recent years.

In the early hours of 1 September 1984, a '999' call sent two water tenders from Lincoln Fire Station to the Sunningdale Trading Estate on the outskirts of the city. As the crews neared the call location, a Smith's Crisps warehouse, a red glow was visible in the night sky. When they arrived, firefighters were faced with a fire burning underneath a loading bay canopy involving stacked cardboard and timber. The fire was also spreading to the tyres of a trailer, and flames from this were threatening a nearby diesel fuel tank.

Jets of water were soon at work to isolate the oil tank and the trailer. As the senior officer moved to check the situation inside the warehouse, he gave instructions for the 39-strong night shift to evacuate the building.

High above this shattered corrugated iron roof, two firefighters were attacking a fire in a Smith's Crisps warehouse when one of the men toppled from the cage of the hydraulic platform and, tragically, fell to his death. (Lincolnshire Fire Brigade)

It was not long before the inside of the metal loading bay door was glowing red with heat. Stacks of baled cardboard close to the door were already alight due to the intense radiated heat.

By now, more fire engines were arriving and their crews could see that the fire was spreading very rapidly. The asbestos sheeting of the warehouse roof was starting to explode, throwing fragments over considerable distances as the firefighting effort intensified.

At 0229 hours, Lincoln's 85 foot (26 metres) hydraulic platform arrived at the blaze and its crew members were instructed to site their vehicle along one side of the warehouse. They were then to raise the cage above the level of the burning roof and use the powerful water jet from the cage to attempt to create a fire break across the roof.

Around 0250 hours the two man crew of the hydraulic platform were working in the cage at roof level directing a jet of water into the fire. Both men were wearing breathing apparatus to protect them against the intense smoke, heat and fumes which swirled up from below.

Suddenly, a section of the warehouse roof collapsed inwards releasing an upward plume of heat and hot gases which caused one of the firefighters in the cage, Fireman Kemp, to fall out and plunge to the ground. He was quickly removed to a place of safety and given immediate resuscitation which continued as the fire raged on. He was rushed to Lincoln County Hospital by ambulance but, tragically, was pronounced dead on arrival.

Meanwhile, the hydraulic platform cage was quickly swung down to ground level where the other firefighter, Leading Fireman Hooker, was found to be suffering from severe burns to both his hands and back.

The fire was finally brought under

control at about 0520 hours by which time 13 pumps, other special fire engines and some 100 firefighters from across the county had battled to contain the fire. Four other firefighters suffered minor injuries.

> ***'A mother and her child were unaccounted for when the warehouse was evacuated'***

A week later, a full Brigade Funeral was held in Lincoln for Fireman Kemp which was attended by firefighters from brigades all over the country.

The second major tragedy to befall the Lincolnshire Brigade happened on the very cold and windy evening of 2 February 1992. At 1651 hours, two pumps from Gainsborough Fire Station responded to the first of 17 separate '999' calls reporting an explosion in the vicinity of a petrol filling station. Within minutes the crews were at the scene and had established that a severe fire was developing inside the premises of Paul Eyre Carpets. A young mother and her child were unaccounted for when the warehouse was evacuated.

Assistance was quickly called for by the officer in charge as the first breathing apparatus crew made an entry into the thickening smoke inside the large, two-storey building. As reinforcing crews began to arrive, including firefighters from Humberside and Nottinghamshire Brigades, the strong winds created additional difficulties, with clouds of black smoke being driven in all directions around the warehouse. Locating the deep seated fire amid the thick smoke from the burning carpets and furniture proved to be extremely difficult.

At about 1758 hours a breathing apparatus team of two from Saxilby Fire Station was due to emerge from their search for the two missing people inside the building. When they failed to show at the due time, the BA control point officer despatched a reserve BA team into the worsening situation within the warehouse where the Saxilby crew were found making their way out due to their low air supply. While this was going on amid the pitch black torrid atmosphere inside the carpet warehouse, one of the Saxilby team, Leading Firefighter Malcolm Kirton, in an exhausted state, mistakenly entered the showroom area instead of emerging into the fresh air. More searching BA teams and Malcolm's team-mate found him very soon after, but although

Rooftop hedgehog gives firemen the needle

An unusual rescue of a prickly nature proved successful for Lincolnshire firefighters when they were called to a house in Grantham where a hedgehog was stuck on the roof.

Firefighter Mark Garner, who went up onto the roof to rescue the animal, claimed that it was undertaken with a 'Hedgehog Rescue Kit' – ie roof ladder, canvas bucket and line.

The firefighter explained: 'The roof ladder was secured safely and I climbed to the ridge of the roof to find the athletic hedgehog pacing up and down. Inching slowly across the ridge I was beginning to appreciate how a jockey might feel riding in the Grand National, when the hedgehog realised I was closing in on it and put a spurt on in the opposite direction. At the halfway stage along the ridge I thought it was time to call in two of my crew down below to stretch a salvage sheet out at the end of the building in case the animal decided to take a suicidal leap.

'Progress was then made a little further along the roof until the hedgehog was just an arm's length away. I paused for a while to allow it to settle, and looked at the team with the salvage sheet pulled tight ready for my final swoop on the animal. That was it. The time had come. Now or never!

'I then swooped down onto the little creature in one swift stroke and bundled it into the canvas bucket which was still over my arm.'

Firefighter Garner later reported that, having been rescued, the hedgehog was adopted by a nearby family.

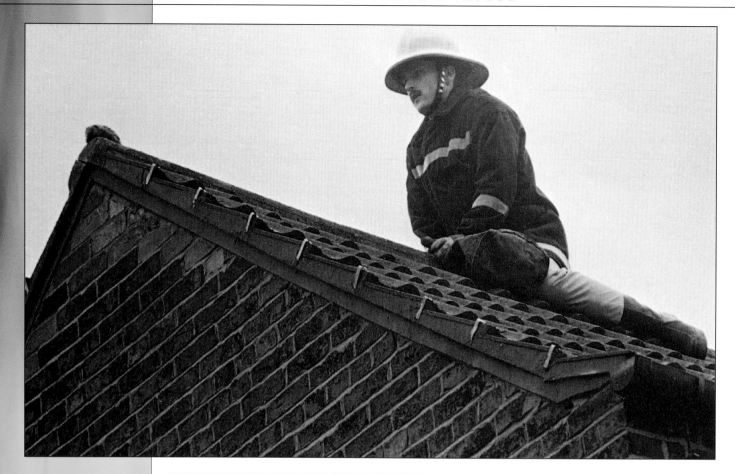

The point of no return. Firefighter Mark Garner rescues a hedgehog trapped on a rooftop in Grantham. He needed sharp wits – and a canvas bucket. (Grantham Journal)

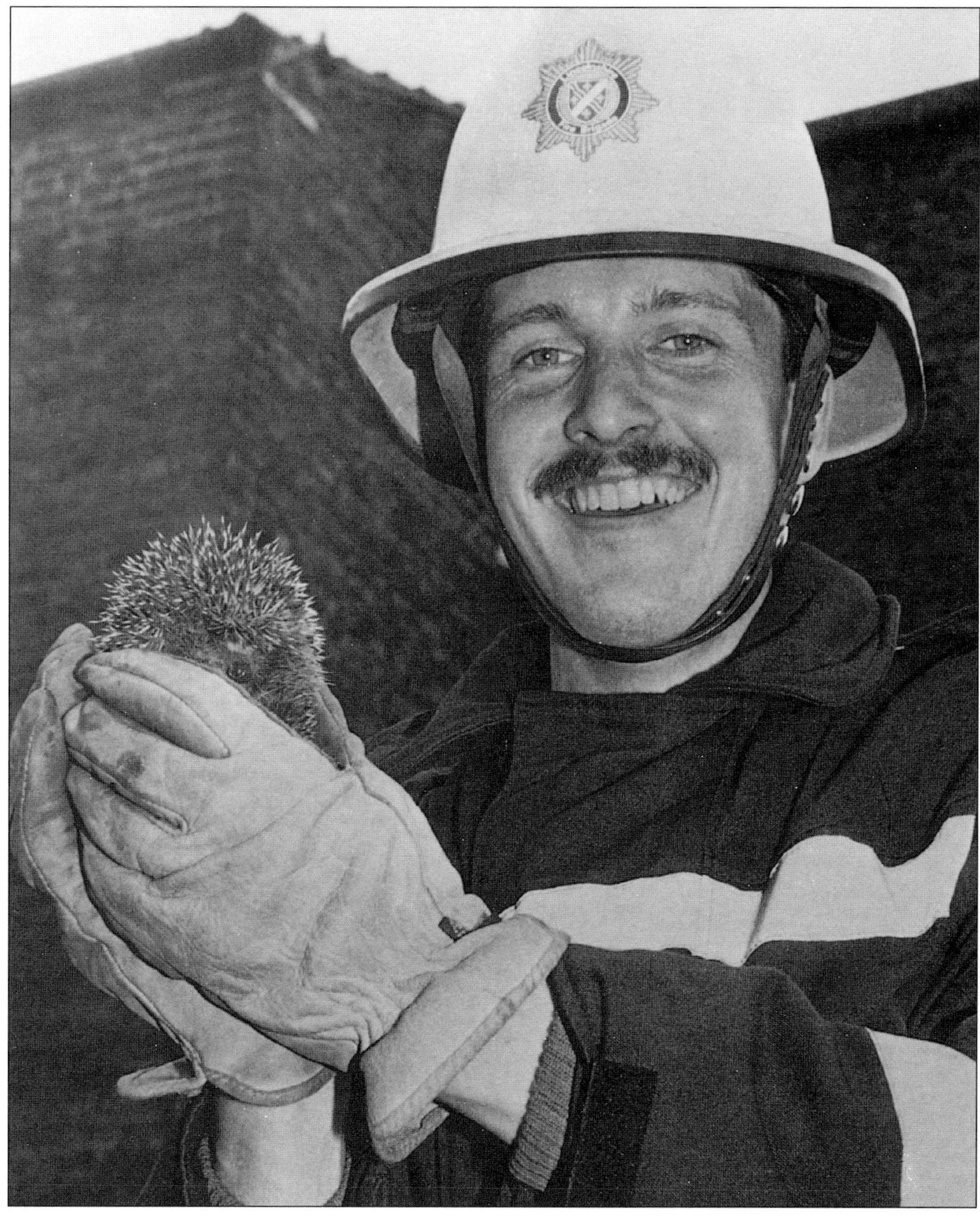

repeated attempts at resuscitation went on all the way to hospital, Malcolm was dead on arrival.

It was not until some four hours later that the fire was brought under control. Such were the dreadful conditions, both inside and outside the burning building, that 13 firefighters, including some from Humberside and Nottinghamshire, were removed to hospital suffering from smoke inhalation, minor burns and hypothermia. A number of police officers and ambulance personnel were also affected by the swirling smoke.

Malcolm Kirton was aged 37. He left a widow, a daughter aged nine and son of seven. As on the previous occasion in 1984, Lincolnshire Fire Brigade accorded the deceased firefighter a funeral with full Brigade honours and, once again, other firefighters from the length and breadth of the UK travelled to Lincoln to pay their last respects to a fellow firefighter who had given his all.

CHAPTER 6

TYKES AND TYNESIDERS

Opposite: *On 21 July 1992, West Yorkshire's fire crews tackled the biggest fire in the brigade's history when the Allied Colloids factory and warehouse covering 40 acres went up in flames. As 43 fire engines, crewed by 200 firefighters, struggled to control the flames, more chemicals ignited to produce this gigantic fireball.* (Andrew Hanson, West Yorkshire Fire Service)

NORTHERN

WEST YORKSHIRE

Firefighters from all over the West Yorkshire Fire Service area will long remember 21 July 1992 as the day of the Allied Colloids blaze at Bradford. The fire was the biggest ever dealt with in the history of the area.

Allied Colloids manufacture a range of specialised chemicals and, because of the risks within the site, its operation is regulated by legislation. The site covered an area of approximately 40 acres and consisted of factory plant, storage warehouses and offices. Some 1,600 people were employed there.

At about 1330 hours, the Allied Colloids internal emergency team were called to a report of smoke in a raw materials warehouse. Within four minutes, the team reported back to their control room that no assistance was required. All that was found were two cardboard drums of an organic compound which had started to decompose.

However, about fifty minutes later there was an explosion in the same warehouse. West Yorkshire Fire Service were called, arriving at Allied Colloids within six minutes of the '999' call. A very severe fire was already engulfing the raw materials warehouse and the senior fire officer urgently requested a further six pumps by radio.

The blaze in the warehouse was still growing in intensity when there was a flashover within the building. Escaping liquid chemicals also caught fire and became a running river of flame through the works complex. In no time the fire had spread to an open air store of plastic products and drums of chemicals. Sudden fireballs erupted over this area, some shooting orange flame and sparks over 100 foot (30 metres) up into the sky. The fire also produced a huge pall of thick black smoke which drifted down wind and rose high above the chemical factory.

Further firefighting reinforcements were called for. It was not long before 30 pumps, three aerial ladders, and 10 support tenders were at work at the Allied Colloids fire. Such was the vast quantity of firefighting water needed that 18 fire hydrants were in use, yet it was still necessary to relay water from a dam which was over a mile (1.6km) away. Residents all down the line of the plume were warned to keep their windows shut because of the toxic smoke cloud.

The fire was brought under control at

Flushed with success

After the railway authorities had spent £5,000 on refurbishing the Ladies Waiting Room at Leeds Station, the Station Master decided to ban smoking there – but in vain. The customers continued to lock themselves in, settle down in comfort and light a quick fag.

Undeterred, the Station Master lashed out on two £5 smoke detectors and reported cheerfully that 'when they go off they frighten the smokers out of their wits and an attendant then arrives to ask why they were smoking in a non-smoking area'.

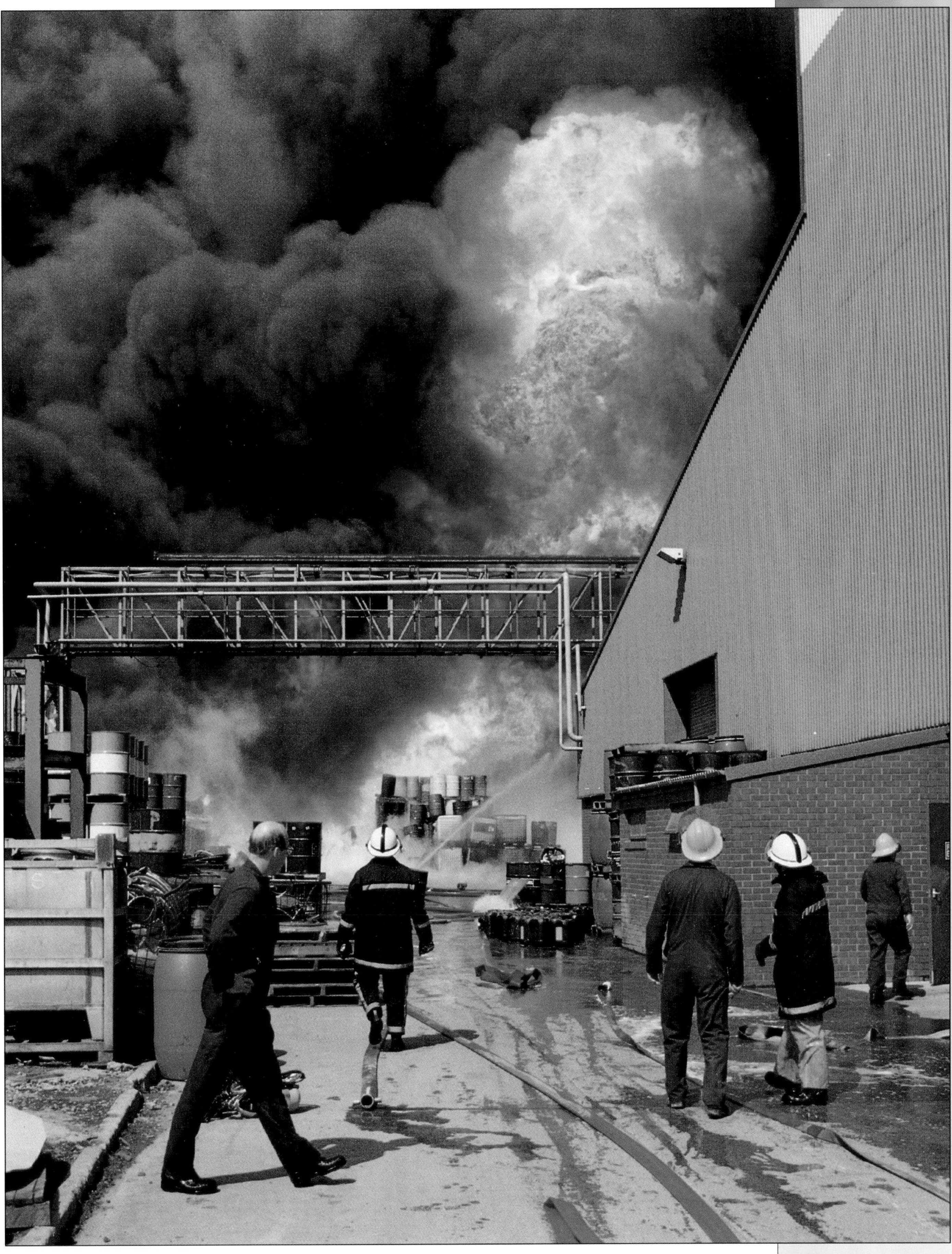

> ***Residents were warned not to eat locally grown fruit***

Bitter ending

One of the largest fires in West Yorkshire during 1991 was at J. L.Tankards Ltd, at Staincliffe, Batley. This 20 pump fire involved a large three-floor building and a number of surrounding single storey properties. A total of nine jets and two aerial appliance jets were used.

At the time of the incident the owner of the factory was returning from London having just received the Queen's Award to Industry on behalf of his Yorkshire company.

The aftermath of a huge explosion and fire at a chemical works in Castleford, Yorks, which claimed five lives on 21 September 1992. Note the severe damage to the cars parked in front of the building, caused by the fireball effect. At the height of the incident, 20 fire engines and 150 firefighters worked to control the blaze. (Brian Saville, West Yorkshire Fire Service)

about 1730 hours that evening. During the action, 39 firefighters were injured and required hospital treatment. Forty-three fire engines, crewed by more than 200 firefighters, had attended the blaze. The brigade stayed on the scene for the rest of the week. But the pollution threat remained, both through airborne contamination from the smoke and from the many hundred thousand gallons of water which had been poured onto the inferno. Days after the emergency, residents of the Bradford city area downwind of the Allied Colloids fire were warned not to eat locally grown fruit or vegetables. Even swimming in the nearby Calder and Aire rivers was forbidden.

An ethereal view of a turntable ladder in action, 100 feet above a large mill fire in Bradford in 1987. (Brian Saville, West Yorkshire Fire Service)

Below: *Steam rises from the uniforms of this breathing apparatus team as they emerge, grim-faced, from a fire in a terraced house in Brighouse, West Yorkshire, in 1986 where, despite all their efforts in the teeth of the flames, a resident has died.* (Brian Saville, West Yorkshire Fire Service)

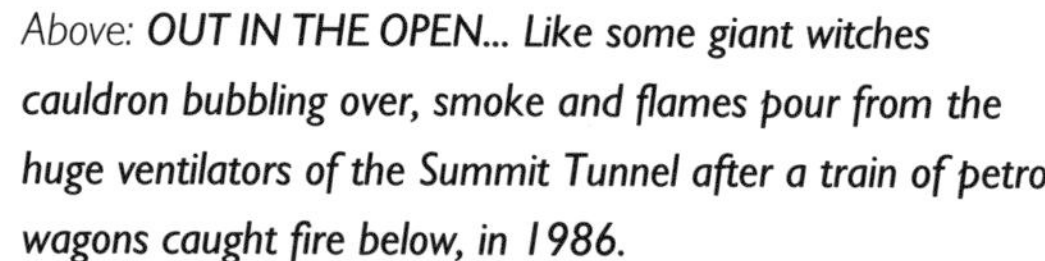

*Above: **OUT IN THE OPEN... Like some giant witches cauldron bubbling over, smoke and flames pour from the huge ventilators of the Summit Tunnel after a train of petrol wagons caught fire below, in 1986.***

...WHILE UNDERGROUND, despite the threat of a possible explosion blowing back at them from the still-burning petrol train in the middle of the tunnel, firefighters risk their lives in the smoke and heat to clear the derailed tankers and lay foam carpets to prevent the fire from spreading. *(West Yorkshire Fire Service)*

*Above: **'Don't worry, we'll get you out' the firefighter seems to be saying to the frightened calf, stuck fast in a deep mudhole at Odsal, West Yorkshire, in 1989.***

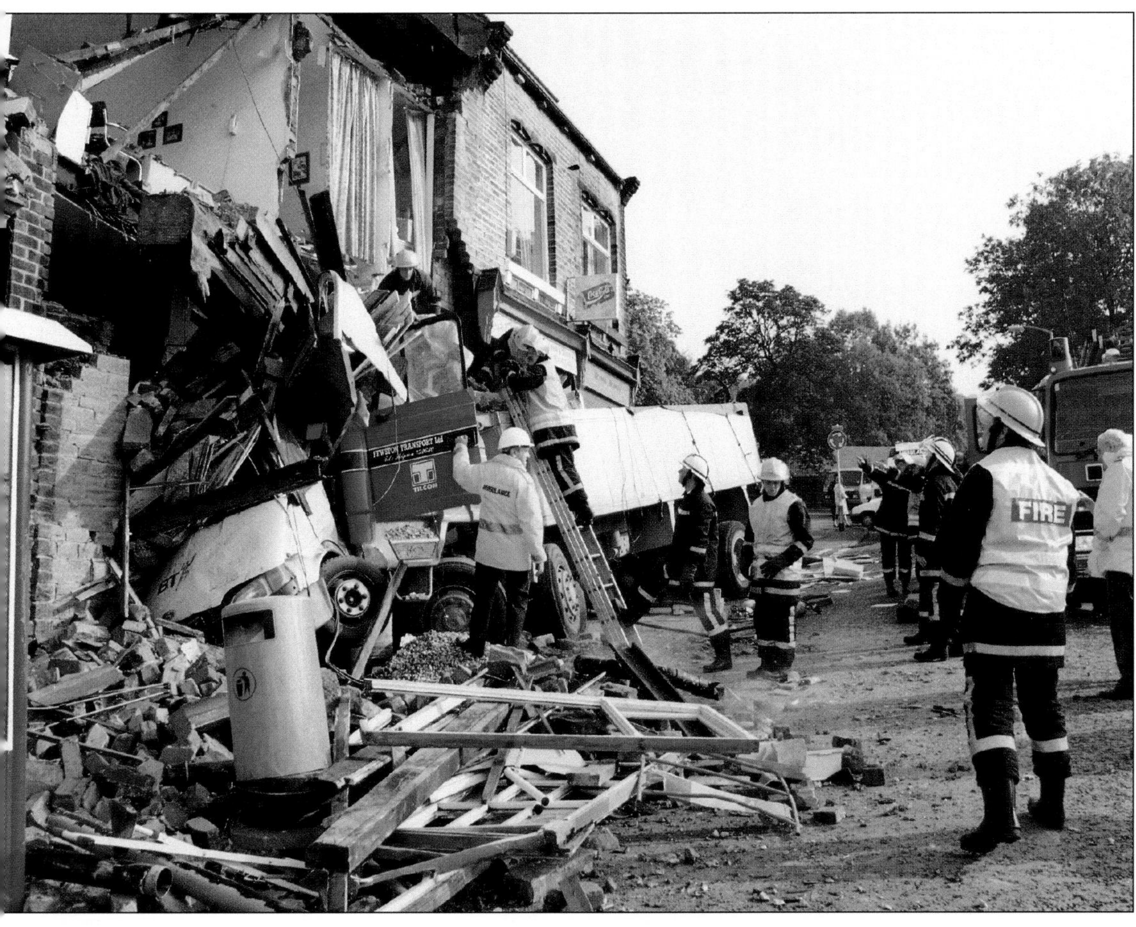

Rescue work goes on after a runaway lorry careered down a hill and crashed into a shopfront at Sowerby Bridge, Yorkshire, in September 1993. A British Telecom van was smashed into the shopfront and six people were killed in the devastating incident. (Brian Saville, West Yorkshire Fire Service)

'Gotcha!' The moment of rescue as the animal is finally released and given a quick shower.

A warehouse fire involving baled acrylic textiles spreads rapidly as crews try to cut the fire off at Heckmondwike, West Yorkshire, in April 1994. (Andrew Hanson, West Yorkshire Fire Service)

Stunned crowds huddle together in the goal mouth as fire, caused by rubbish gathered under seating, sweeps through the stands at Bradford City Football Club, in May 1985. (Bradford Telegraph & Argus)

Opposite: *Command and Control measures are an important part of firefighting. Here Chief Officer Jim Manuel briefs his senior officers at a 25-pump warehouse fire at Bradford in January 1992.* (Andrew Hanson, West Yorkshire Fire Service)

SOUTH YORKSHIRE

It is strange how some fire situations seem to repeat themselves within a short space of time and often involve the same firefighters.

Such was the case with South Yorkshire fire crews in the spring of 1993 when a lorry driver travelling east on the M62 suddenly found one of his lorry wheels on fire. He stopped the vehicle and tried to keep everyone clear as the wheel fire started to engulf the whole lorry. And well he might, for the lorry was loaded with boxes of aerosol shaving cream.

As the first firefighters at the scene began to tackle the fire, the aerosols started to explode. There were many small explosions showering cans on to huddled teams of firefighters and on to the roofs of halted cars on the motorway some 150 feet (45 metres) away. The blaze took three hours to control and the traffic queues and snarl-ups were horrendous.

Then, only a few weeks later, came a nearly identical fire when an articulated lorry, heading north up the M1 near Barnsley, collided with another lorry which was stationary on the hard shoulder. A fire quickly broke out and involved the full load of aerosol products which exploded in all directions intensifying the severity of the blaze.

When firefighters finally put the inferno out, they found amid the steaming wreckage that the intense heat had welded the tractor unit and trailer of the articulated juggernaut together. Traffic hold-ups broke all known records as police closed the M1 and diverted traffic off the motorway either side of the crash; queues stretched for miles in both directions.

> ***High winds caused sparks to fly and then settle into the dry grass to start yet more fires***

NORTH YORKSHIRE

For a brigade with a very large rural area to protect, North Yorkshire firefighters would probably consider it unusual if the brigade attended more than two 10-pump fires per year.

However, the first week of March 1992 turned this assumption on its head when the brigade went through the busiest period since its formation in 1974.

The first major fire during this hectic week was on 1 March in a large dutch barn at Sowerby, near Thirsk. The fire spread to another farm building which contained 150 pigs. Although firefighters were able to rescue many of these animals, a number had to be destroyed soon after the fire. Four fire engines attended this incident.

Less than 36 hours later, the brigade were called in the early morning to Tap Mill, Cononley, near Skipton, where the old buildings were in use as a shopping complex. Twelve pumps and two turntable ladders were needed and 90 firefighters battled to restrict the fire damage, including four crews from West Yorkshire Fire Service, and one from Lancashire County Fire Brigade.

Not 24 hours had passed when North Yorkshire pumps from York and Acomb fire stations were despatched to a fire call from the Rowntree Nestlé chocolate factory in York. This was a huge complex and the fire quickly developed to involve the seventh and eighth floors as well as the roof. Ten pumps and three turntable ladders were needed to contain the blaze, although all the fire engines attending came from the North Yorkshire Brigade apart from a West Yorkshire turntable ladder from Gipton.

As the scale of the attendance at the fire escalated, standby pumps from other brigades were sent into North Yorkshire to maintain fire cover across the county. A West Yorkshire crew from Wetherby arrived at Tadcaster Fire Station, while a Humberside pump was sent to Selby. At the height of the Rowntree blaze, North Yorkshire Fire Control moved one of their own pumps from Thirsk into York and due to all aerials being in use at the factory fire, they also moved a turntable ladder from Scarborough to York, a distance of over 41 miles!

There was no respite yet for North Yorkshire crews. Even as the Rowntree fire was coming under control, three more pumps on the county's coastline area were dealing with a large barn and stack of tyres on fire at a farm near Whitby.

The next day saw two more serious incidents. The first was when four acres of heathland caught fire on Strensall Common and crews from York and Acomb were again in the front line. Then fire was reported in a large grassland region of Ravenscar Moor near Robin Hood's Bay. Due to the widespread nature of the fire and the remote location with little water available, the crews of six pumps and two support vehicles battled for four hours into the early morning before they gained the upper hand.

Only hours after the Strensall Common fire was extinguished, another outbreak was reported on the common at a different location. So serious was the overall fire area that a total of 10 pumps were mobilised. Water had to be relayed over a considerable distance to the fire. High winds also added to the firefighters' problem, causing sparks to fly and then settle into the dry grass to start yet more fires. Over six hectares of grassland were finally destroyed and crews were drawn from as far afield as Knaresborough, Boroughbridge and Malton.

About an hour after this large fire had been in progress, a '999' caller reported a major area of moorland on fire at Sleights, near Whitby. The subsequent firefighting operation there lasted some 20 hours and tied up the crews of five pumps. A pump from Loftus Fire Station from distant Cleveland County Fire Brigade had been mobilised as part of the build-up to this fire and few weary Whitby firefighters could ever remember support needing to come such a distance.

However, it was still not the end of this frantic North Yorkshire spell. During the early evening of the following day, a fire broke out in a paint sprayer's premises at Tockwith Airfield, near York. Seventy firefighters and 10 pumps, a turntable ladder and four support vehicles were soon at the scene. The incident was complicated when acetylene cylinders became involved in the blaze and caused a risk of explosion. Fortunately, this was averted by the extensive use of cooling sprays and the fire was eventually brought under control within four hours.

Thus ended a week when North Yorkshire firefighters worked without respite to cope with a continual string of major fires. It was certainly a spell well remembered by all those involved.

HUMBERSIDE

Hotel fires can provide enormous physical challenges to firefighters, especially so when they occur at night and the building is full of sleeping guests.

This was the case in October 1990 when a fire was discovered in the Royal Station Hotel in the centre of Hull at 0230 hours. For the first fire crews the priority was to save residents trapped by the thick smoke rapidly spreading through the hotel. Sixteen residents were rescued by firefighters and taken to safety while other teams mounted a search operation amid the smoke filled corridors to ensure that every guest was accounted for.

The size of the firefighting operation quickly escalated until 30 pumps, five aerial appliances and several support tenders were drawn up around the Royal Station Hotel. Some idea of the fire and rescue effort can be gained by the fact that at one stage, 36 breathing sets were in use and 170 firefighters at work inside and around the hotel. Only two of Humberside's 31 fire stations were not involved in attendance at the fire or in subsequent standby moves to other fire stations in order to maintain cover.

Another major blaze in Hull, this time on a ship in January 1991, drew in 100 firefighters working for up to 10 hours. As at the Royal Station Hotel fire, Humberside Fire Control had to continually reassess the fire cover needs of the rest of the county as more and more fire engines were ordered on to the ship fire. During this particular protracted period, no fewer than 13 separate pumps were moved in to stand-by at other fire stations.

Humberside Fire Brigade's facilities in Hull incorporate a training school where firefighting instruction is given to a wide range of employees drawn from the industrial sector.

A recent addition to the facilities at the school is a platform and rig which simulates gas escapes on offshore installations. 'Controlled' leakages from a one tonne propane tank feed the platform and its pipework and create a very realistic level of hot fire training. It is estimated that a total of 10 tons of gas is burnt in a training year!

CLEVELAND

When it comes to fire risks on a particular brigade's area, Cleveland County Fire Brigade can claim to have more then their fair share. For located in the Middlesborough and Teeside districts are a number of very large petrochemical and chemical plants and storage depots. Among these is the principal United Kingdom Imperial Chemicals Industries petrochemical complex.

Such large risks are, of course, controlled by various safety legislation and at their Cleveland plant ICI maintain their own industrial fire brigade. Part of its role is to contain any fire or chemical leakage until the first units of the Cleveland Brigade arrive.

Great emphasis is placed upon training at the various petrochemical plants of

A small fire in a gas pipeline at an industrial works is tackled by Cleveland firefighters. The crew are working to position a heavy spray jet which is being fed by two high pressure hose lines. Teamwork, strength and a cool nerve are all on display. Note the latest fire-resistant uniforms including helmets with protective visors, now worn by British firefighters. (Cleveland County Fire Service)

Cleveland. County fire crews undertake regular exercises involving works fire teams and safety officers to ensure that if the worst happens, firefighters will be familiar with the general layout of a plant, its water supplies and access points.

Cleveland firefighters have to be particularly proficient in dealing with leakages and spillages of hazardous substances, and in the effective use of protective suits, breathing sets and the decontamination procedures once an incident has been successfully dealt with.

Teeside is the second busiest port in Europe in terms of the amount of hazardous chemicals being stored or handled at any one time. Cleveland County Fire Brigade is one of the only brigades in the UK to operate two fully fledged fireboats. These are literally floating fire engines. They are crewed by specially trained firefighters able to take either fireboat right alongside any vessel on which there is a fire or other emergency. Apart from their ability to provide powerful water jets for either firefighting or cooling purposes, the fireboats can also lift tons of water per minute through their fire pumps and send this ashore to wherever vast quantities of water may be needed.

DURHAM

Just occasionally, fire brigades are called out to rescue persons who have fallen over cliffs or down into ravines. A good example of such a rescue took place on 24 February 1991 at Gunners Bridge on the Castle Eden Nature Reserve in County Durham.

The drama started when a 13-year-old boy attempted to retrieve his hat from bushes at the top of a 90 foot (27.5 metres) deep gorge. As he reached out, the boy lost his footing and fell headlong down the steep gorge and into a fast flowing icy-cold stream at the bottom.

Fortunately, his plight was seen by

Such is the marine fire risk on the River Tees that Cleveland County Fire Brigade man two fireboats, 24 hours a day. In addition, there is a rigid inflatable high speed rescue craft. Here, the brigade's newest fireboat Cleveland Endeavour *shows off her firefighting capability out in mid-river.* (Cleveland County Fire Brigade)

passer-by Hugh O'Grady, who ran for about a mile down into the gorge, entered the stream and waded out to the boy who was suffering from head and arm injuries. At this point the stream was six feet (1.8 metres) wide and five feet (1.52 metres) deep. O'Grady, who had already detailed a second man to call for help, remained in the water to support the boy which was a particularly plucky action as he was not a swimmer.

When the first Durham Fire and Rescue team arrived, they quickly assembled their equipment before Leading Firefighters Cameron and Chapman were lowered down the ravine on lines and harnesses by other firefighters of their crew. Once in the water at the bottom, they were able to strap the boy into a special stretcher after which he was carefully raised up to the top of the gorge and a waiting ambulance. The firefighters were then able to get O'Grady from the freezing water in which he had now been immersed for about an hour.

The boy was kept in hospital overnight and then released, no doubt very thankful to his team of rescuers for his narrow escape. Both Hugh O'Grady and Leading Firefighters Cameron and Chapman received Certificates of Commendation from the Royal Humane Society for their brave actions at this dramatic incident.

Drove digger into sea to save marooned man

An unusual situation confronted a crew of firefighters from the Blue Watch of South Shields Fire Station in April 1992. While driving along the sea front they noticed an object in the water. On closer investigation, they could see that it appeared to be a submerged tractor with a man clinging to it about 100 foot (30 metres) out from the shore edge.

The crew immediately grabbed some lines and ran down the beach to the sea. Leading Firefighter Trotter tied a line around his waist and entered the water with Firefighters Lynn and Mellefont anchoring him. It was very windy with gusts up to 40 knots.

The sea was so rough it proved impossible for the team to reach the marooned tractor. Instead, they quickly commandeered a large mechanical digger which was driven into the sea, but this attempt failed as the firefighters were swept off the vehicle by the pounding waves and gusting winds.

Just at this moment, a large wave also caused the stricken man to let go of the submerged tractor and this brought him closer in to the shore. The Tyne and Wear fire crew were then able to re-enter the sea once again and struggle out far enough to reach the casualty and haul him up on to the beach and safety. The man turned out to be the driver of the tractor which, while working on the shore, had got out of its depth as the tide swept in. He was taken to hospital and survived his watery ordeal.

For their determined and successful rescue attempt, all three firefighters, together with Station Officer Hamilton who assisted them in the latter stages, were presented with a Team Parchment Award from the Royal Humane Society.

TYNE AND WEAR

Nowadays it is not unknown for fire crews to be attacked by stone throwing mobs as they attempt to tackle fires which have been lit maliciously during a period of disturbance.

Over several nights in September 1991, Tyne and Wear fire crews were called out to deal with fires started by vandals in the West Newcastle and North Shields districts of the brigade area. The first fires were lit in a kitchen shop, a youth centre, and an electricity sub station. A number of other sporadic outbreaks occurred later.

Apart from stones, firefighters and police officers found themselves being pelted by bricks and petrol bombs and on a number of occasions had to withdraw with their fire engines to avoid serious injury.

Divisional Officer Ken Horn said: 'It was extremely vicious and nasty. Several of our fire engines were damaged and had windscreens and windows smashed. We had to pull out and leave a burning pub because we were suffering so much damage'.

Assistant Chief Officer Jim Bremner said that these were scenes unprecedented in his 27 years of service. Every firefighter who went through these attacks must have wondered just what the role of the fire service was coming to.

Back amid the 'ordinary' dangers of firefighting, Tyne and Wear crews went to work in Sunderland in August 1992 when a petrol tanker overturned after its driver swerved to avoid a van. The tanker was loaded with 1,777 gallons (8,000 litres) of petrol and the leaking fuel ignited almost immediately. Worse still, the crash happened at the top of a slight rise and a burning river of fire flowed down a side street igniting many parked cars before running into a car park where the fire consumed even more vehicles. Eighty firefighters tackled the fire which spread over several streets. A huge foam carpet was laid down to extinguish the flames. At one time the blaze reached up 100 feet (30 metres) into the air. Some 42 cars were damaged although, remarkably, no serious injuries were caused.

NORTHUMBERLAND

Changing weather patterns may have been the reason why, in 1990, Northumberland Fire and Rescue Service found itself facing its worst forest fires for 50 years. This northernmost part of England, close to the Scottish border, is a land of hills and forests. For them the long, dry spells of the new weather scene brought a succession of terrifying 'incidents' as the flames roared through the pine and fir trees and smoke rolled across the countryside.

'It isn't the job of putting out the fires which gives us the most headaches,' explained a senior officer. 'Almost half our firefighters are retained or part-timers. They have other jobs to do and while they can get away for the short space of a normal fire or accident, it becomes much more difficult to take two or three weeks off – and that's how long some of these big forest fires go on, by the time we've made sure that they really are out and there are no "hot spots" lurking in a remote place which could start the whole thing off again.

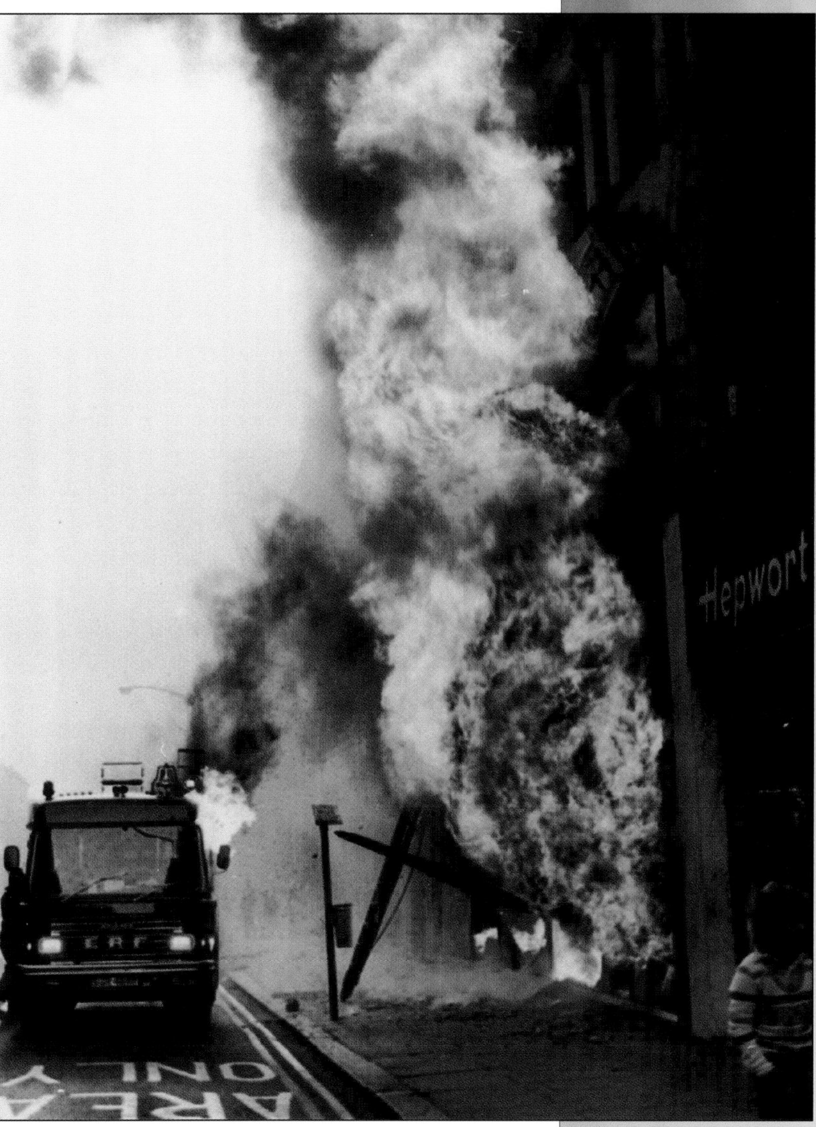

Seconds after Sub Officer Jack Stubbs had successfully rescued three shop workers down the ladder in this photograph, fire burst out through the front of the furniture shop and the intense heat set light to the side of the fire engine. The dramatic scene took place at Sunderland in October 1972. (Sunderland Echo)

'As it is, there are few firefighters who travel less than eight miles to a call and, for quite a lot, it means driving 30 to 40 miles to get to the fireground.'

Despite this, there's always an instant response when the bells go down in the local fire stations and the part-timer's bleep starts up, day or night.

Between July 1989 and April 1990 it was particularly busy. The county's firefighters faced four major forest fires and in early April 1990 there were two burning simultaneously at Simonside, Rothbury, and at Holburn Moss – within a few miles of each other.

Thrunton Woods and Holburn Moss were both major fires. The flames and smoke of Thrunton were spotted first by a forestry worker who reported it to his HQ

Carry kettle for reviving cuppa

The heat at a major forest fire can dehydrate firefighters. The hard physical work of trudging through undergrowth, hauling hosepipes, saps their energy. WRVS volunteers bring in copious supplies of tea, coffee, drinking water and squash, along with an assortment of pies and sandwiches.

'Many of the forest fires are in remote parts of the county – we've no hotels or McDonalds to drop into', explained one senior officer. 'The food and drink is brought in from the nearest point of civilisation and you're just thankful for anything that arrives.'

In cold weather, the crews are supplied with 'hot-cans' of stew or soup. Pull on the ring top and the can heats up automatically. However, all appliances are now supplied with a vital piece of equipment – an electric kettle. Powered by the generators that supply the firefighting equipment, they can be plugged in for a hot 'bevvy' whenever it's needed and there's time to stop.

and they, in turn, alerted the fire service. It would be 18 days later, at lunch time on 12 May, when the final 'stop' came. By then, 150 hectares of standing trees and 150 hectares of moorland had been damaged or totally destroyed. The worst part was not only the financial cost in terms of timber but the loss of a large area of outstandingly beautiful countryside with all the birds and animals who had disappeared in the inferno.

As the crews reported for duty, senior officers were carrying out a careful reconnaissance of the scene by helicopter, making their plans for attacking the fire and, incidentally, giving orders to close the nearby A697, already affected by thick smoke. This was not the moment for a full-scale road traffic accident.

It was clear that this was, indeed, a big fire. The flames were already eating up the trees at frightening speed and jumping from one 'crown' to another as the wind whipped through roaring, crackling, and turning the dull red of the burning trunks to bright scarlet. Showers of sparks tumbled over the fire crews, stinging their faces and eyes while the smoke and heat seared their throats and lungs.

With the survey over, the helicopter was used to damp down the front of the fire, but because it took up to eight minutes to collect water from the nearest lake, the fire service brought in an 8,000 litre portable dam from their stores and parked it where it could be filled from a water main, so that the helicopter could replenish its supply much more quickly.

Bulldozers dug fire breaks to try to stop the flames from engulfing more trees, and 'foam traces' were spread for long distances – again to try to stop the fire from spreading. Soaking the ground in water might have done the same job but in the

Smoke billows up towards the helicopter as fire officers look down on the fire ground as one of Northumberland's fell fires sweeps across, destroying plant and wildlife in this area of great natural beauty. (Northumberland Fire and Rescue Service)

intense heat, water often evaporates. Foam will hold back the fire for a longer period.

For the senior officers, everything has to be watched – and dealt with. The way in which the fire is travelling, changes in wind direction, the positioning of the men, the cutting of firebreaks and, in the case of Thrunton Woods, the discovery of live shells on the fireground. That caused something of a stir.

For Thrunton Woods the cause of the fire could never be proved, but suspicion lay heavily on some of the holidaymakers who walk and camp in the area without realising the cost of carelessly dropping a match or throwing away a lighted cigarette end.

Not all Northumberland's incidents concern their many forests. They have their fair share of RTAs. With roads which sometimes pass along precipitous edges, rescues demand a particular kind of skill and courage.

In the small hours of a Saturday morning in October 1989, Berwick Fire Station was called out on a nightmare – an RTA on the A689 at remote Tillmouth. It was a foul night, cold, wet and foggy. The driver of a saloon car carrying two passengers had skidded off the road, tumbled down a sloping 100 foot (30.5 metres) embankment and dropped over a 30 foot (9.3 metres) sheer cliff face to finish upside down on the shore of the river below. Luckily, it was seen by people in a nearby hotel and the fire and rescue crews arrived as fast as they could manage in such conditions. With one glance at the task confronting them they called for more help and a Lothian and Borders fire engine from Coldstream joined them soon afterwards.

First – how to get their crews and equipment down the slippery embankment and then the sheer cliff? They managed the slope, then the crew lowered themselves and their equipment over the sheer drop on ropes while those left on the brow of the cliff set up a generator and halogen lighting to throw some light on the scene.

For two hours they struggled with the battered car until they managed to release all three victims. But the officers had already realised that there would be no hope of bringing them all back up the cliff face. Instead, they arranged for an ambulance to wait at some distance from the incident and for a dinghy to come up to meet the crews.

Everything worked according to plan and both rescued and rescuers headed for the comfort of light and warmth – in hospital or home.

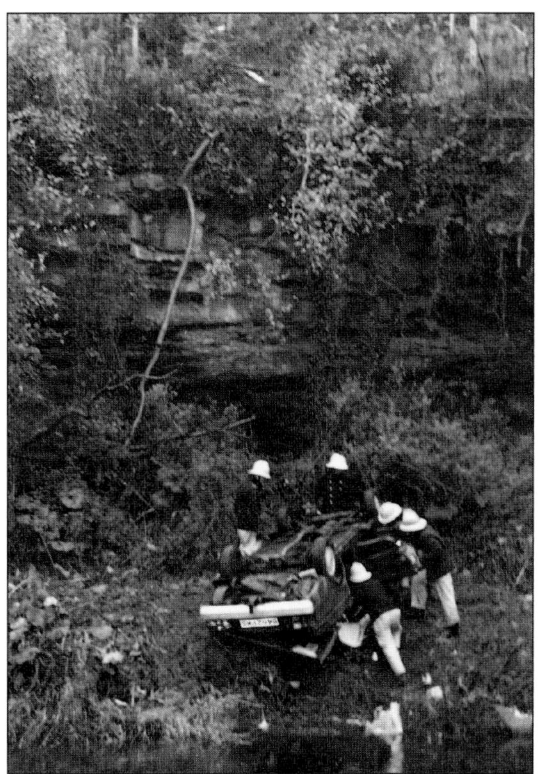

Retained crews from over the Scottish border at Coldstream joined firefighters from Berwick-on-Tweed, sliding down ropes to reach passengers trapped after a car left the road in the small hours of the morning and plunged down a 100 foot slope to the shores of the river. Other firefighters used an inflatable dinghy to transport the injured to the nearest point which an ambulance could reach, further downstream. (Northumberland Fire and Rescue Service)

Keeps tally of campers

After a spate of fires in its huge area of forests, Northumberland issued 20,000 leaflets throughout the area as part of a campaign aimed at reducing forest and moorland fires and explaining to the public what they should do if they discovered a fire.

One of the big problems for their firefighters is knowing whether people are walking or camping in the forest and possibly trapped by the flames. To help them with this, they have asked visitors to pick up a fire safety tally and display it in their parked car windscreens to show how many people are in their group before they set off into the wilds.

CHAPTER 7

INTO BIG INDUSTRY

MIDLANDS

OXFORDSHIRE

At 1038 hours on 16 March 1992 Oxfordshire Fire Service Control received the first of 17 '999' calls to a fire in an old mill being used as a printing works in the centre of Banbury.

Firefighters arrived at the scene only three minutes later and were confronted with thickening smoke pouring out of all the doors and windows of the large four-storey building. The fast developing fire was already threatening a road tanker and nearby petrol depot, and 50 residents on a caravan site close by.

Despite the heroic efforts of 130 firefighters drawn not only from Oxfordshire but Warwickshire and Northants as well, the Banbury blaze grew to become the largest fire in the area for 25 years. Damage costing in excess of £2 million was caused, and the outbreak was believed to have started when an industrial kettle developed a leak. Fortunately, there were no serious injuries. There were plenty of weary and wet fire crews though.

An unusual emergency, coincidentally also in Banbury, occurred on 24 June 1993 when a maintenance worker fell into a 100 foot (30.5 metres) silo tower at a chocolate factory. The silo was three quarters full of sugar and there was a considerable risk that it would shift and swallow up the trapped worker.

The first firefighters were able to get up on top of the silo and lower a rescue line down to the man, which he was able to put around his chest to stop him sinking further into the quicksand-like sugar. A firefighter in a breathing set then got into the silo through a side hatch and took an oxygen supply in to the trapped worker. Although he was found not to be seriously injured, the task of raising him out onto the top of the silo was far from easy. Once the rescue team got the maintenance worker on to the silo roof, he was transferred into the cage of an elevated hydraulic platform, and carefully eased down to ground level and a waiting ambulance. He was detained in hospital for 10 days but made a full recovery.

Retirement gift burned bedroom

Former firefighter Alan Humphries sprang back into action when his retirement present burst into flames and set fire to his bedroom.

Alan, previously a member of the Hereford and Worcester Fire Brigade, had not long retired from the service to run a pub near Sidmouth, Devon, when the teamaker which he was given as a parting gift caught fire.

He climbed through the smoke-logged bedroom and put out the burning teamaker with an extinguisher before the local fire crew arrived at the scene.

Mr Humphries, who runs the Coach House Hotel at Southerton with his wife Susan, said : 'It's quite ironic really. I can laugh about it now, but it really has caused quite a lot of damage.'

HEREFORD AND WORCESTER

On 7 August 1992, Hereford and Worcester firefighters tackled a spectacular and dangerous fire at an electricity power station in Hereford.

It all started when an explosion was heard at about 1100 hours and a huge sheet of orange flame shot high into the sky. This brought the first of very many '999' calls from frightened residents requesting the fire brigade.

The first fire crews arrived to find a severe fire in a large ruptured oil tank. Some distance away lay a fatally injured worker. It was not until some time later that it was discovered that he had been welding in the tank area and was blown about 200 feet (61 metres) by the sheer force of the blast.

But more drama was to follow. Some 10 minutes later, just as reinforcing firefighters started to arrive from Leominster, Ledbury, Ross-on-Wye, Fownhope and Droitwich, a second huge explosion blew a large oil tank high up into the air like some fiery meteorite. Propelled by the burning fuel inside, the burning tank cleared several buildings in a flaming arc, and then crashed down about 230 feet (70 metres) away on to a turntable ladder, causing over £100,000 worth of damage. Mercifully, at that stage the aerial fire engine was not in use and had been parked well away from the fire area.

The flying fireball also created other immediate problems. In its wake it had set alight six vehicles and a skip, and had also rained liquid fire down close to a piled stack of chemicals in drums. Added to all that, there was a pollution threat to a nearby stream.

Apart from giving hard-pressed firefighters these extra scattered fires to deal with, the main blaze in the power station still had to be conquered. A concerted attack with foam and cooling jets was necessary before firefighters eventually got the upper hand and brought the emergency under control some four hours after their arrival. Amazingly, apart from the welder, there were no serious injuries.

> ***'A huge sheet of orange flame shot high into the sky'***

WEST MIDLANDS

On the morning of 2 July 1993, it was announced in the *London Gazette* that Her Majesty the Queen had graciously approved the award of the country's highest gallantry honours to two West Midlands firefighters. Firefighter David Burns of Green Watch, Central Fire Station, Birmingham, was to receive the George Medal and Firefighter David Scott of Green Watch, Ladywood Fire Station, the Queen's Gallantry Medal.

Both these awards were in recognition of the selfless acts of great bravery performed by the two firefighters when rescuing colleagues trapped in a serious flat fire

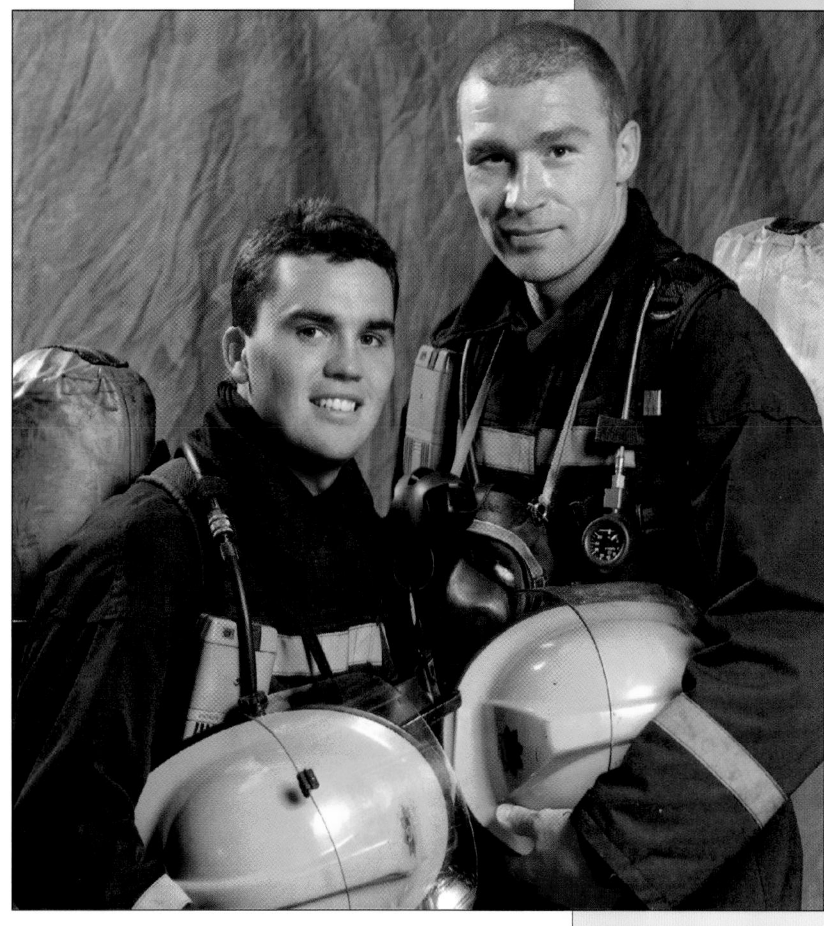

True heroes. Firefighters David Burns (right) of Green Watch, Birmingham Central Fire Station, with David Scott of Green Watch, Ladywood Fire Station. Ff Burns was awarded the George Medal for his courage in rescuing a fellow firefighter from a blazing flat in the city in July 1992, and Ff Scott received the Queen's Gallantry Medal after going back into the fire with Ff Burns and rescuing a second colleague from the burning flat where, at times, the temperature reached 900 degrees centigrade. (West Midlands Fire Service)

Not alarmed enough by risk

After a television advertising campaign by the Home Office in the early 1990s, more than 99 per cent of the population of Britain was aware of the advantage of fitting a smoke alarm.

Follow-up research showed that most of those who didn't bother to install an alarm believed that they would wake up if fire broke out in their home at night. It also showed that those who invested in an alarm were more likely to take other precautions against fire generally.

Overall, too many people continued to be complacent about fire and didn't think it would happen to them.

in Charlecote Tower, Dorking Grove, Birmingham in July 1992.

At the incident, following a probable flashover, two firefighters were trapped by a whirlwind of fire. Without thought for his own safety, David Burns responded to the cries for help from an injured colleague and entered the flat, found Firefighter Chris Ryder, and carried him single handedly from certain death away to safety. Firefighter Ryder suffered terrible burns from which he is still recovering. Firefighter Burns then returned to the flat with Firefighter David Scott to search for and rescue another colleague, Firefighter Iain McPhee, who suffered over 60 per

After dealing with a fire on the ground floor of a Birmingham warehouse, crews went upstairs and discovered this tell-tale trail of petrol leading to the cartons already stored there and now smoke-damaged. Clearly a case of arson. (West Midlands Fire Service)

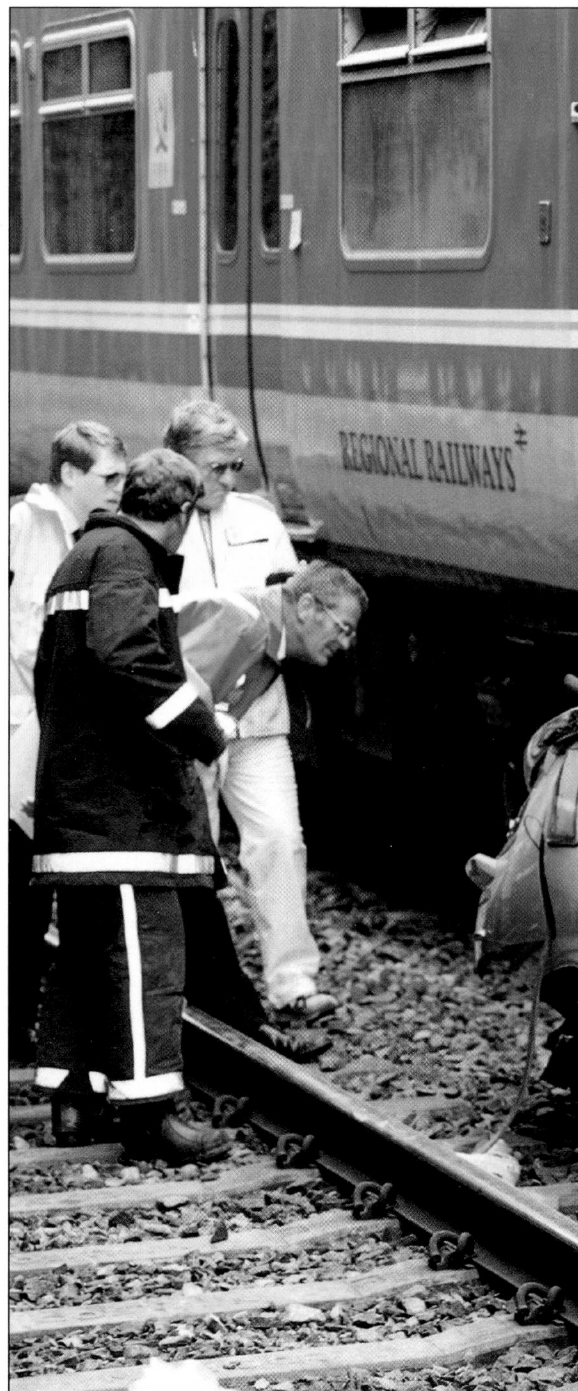

cent burns in the fire and, sadly, subsequently died from his injuries.

The fire in the flat was a particularly severe one and the temperature at ceiling level was estimated to have reached as high as 900 degrees centigrade. In carrying out the rescues both Firefighters Scott and Burns placed themselves at grave personal risk and battled through extreme heat and large quantities of smoke which reduced visibility to almost nothing.

Firefighting is all about teamwork. Many individuals that day displayed courage and determination in carrying out their duties, but the actions of these two West Midlands firefighters were truly in the finest rescue traditions of the British Fire Service.

During 1990, the West Midlands Fire Service acquired special protective suits for tackling incidents at Britain's only titanium manufacturing plant. Six heavy duty sodium suits were purchased by the plant's operator, IMI (plc) Witton, in conjunction with the Brigade. The suits, which cost a total of £4,000 were for the exclusive use of firefighters should an incident occur at the plant.

Joyriders lost control of this stolen Mini which tumbled down a railway embankment and hit the rails below as a train was passing through on 21 August 1993. Remarkably, the driver escaped but two friends were trapped in the wreckage. Fire crews could only rescue one alive. (West Midlands Fire Service)

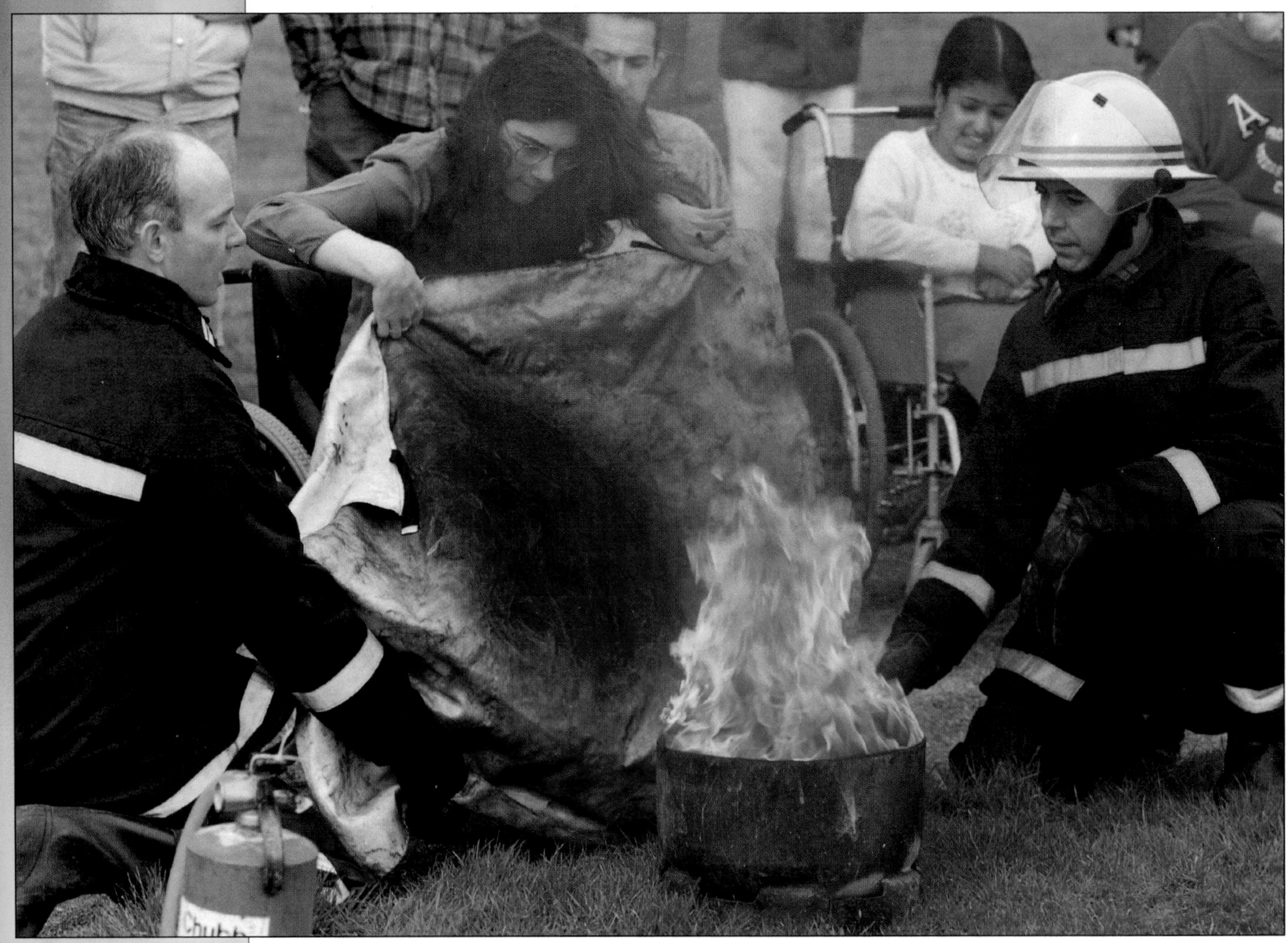

Fighting a fire when you're wheelchair-bound can be difficult and dangerous. As part of their Fire Safety education programme, West Midlands firefighters offer advice to all local people including those with special problems. (West Midlands Fire Service)

The inevitable, of course, happened. On 11 March 1994 the *Birmingham Evening Mail* reported:

> Families in hundreds of homes came within minutes of being evacuated as firefighters tackled a dangerous chemical fire in Birmingham today.
>
> The blaze at IMI's special metals plant at Witton released a cloud of toxic smoke into the air.
>
> Senior fire officers said that had they not contained the blaze in the first few minutes and the toxic cloud had grown, they would have had to evacuate the area.
>
> The company today started an internal investigation into what could have become a major public safety alert.
>
> More than 30 firefighters were called to the site when the fire broke out just after 4am.
>
> A pipe carrying a coolant used in the processing of titanium burst allowing the metal alloy, which is highly volatile in contact with air or water, to escape.
>
> It instantly heated up and started a fire, filling the plant with light grey smoke which is toxic when inhaled and can cause skin and eye irritation.
>
> Station Officer George Burfitt, of Perry Bar Fire Station, said around three gallons of the chemical had escaped from a 20 gallon tank.
>
> He added: 'If the smoke cloud had spread we would have had to evacuate the entire area. Hundreds of homes would have been affected.
>
> 'Fortunately we managed to get in and tackle the fire and leak, and then isolate the burst pipe very quickly which reduced the danger'.

SHROPSHIRE

Lightning can strike twice, although in this case it was more likely an arsonist. Shropshire Fire and Rescue Service had a tough enough time fighting the huge £165 million fire at the Central Ordnance Depot at Donnington in June 1983. They were less than pleased when they were called again in April 1988. The fires were notable as being the most expensive peace-time fires in British Fire Service history. Here, firefighters attack the flames in 1983. (Shropshire Fire and Rescue Service)

Second time round. Even more spectacular, the fire at the Central Ordnance Depot at Donnington in 1988, caused by arson. (Shropshire Fire and Rescue Service)

After the second fire, the ruins of the COD Donnington. (Shropshire Fire and Rescue Service)

DERBYSHIRE

The growing problem of arson and its risk to both firefighters and the general public was highlighted by a fatal fire in a Littlewoods department store at Chesterfield in May 1993.

The store had opened for business as usual at 0900 hours. About an hour later, a customer noticed flames licking up the sleeve of a garment in the first floor clothing department. He tried unsuccessfully to put the fire out with an extinguisher.

By this stage smoke was thickening and beginning to billow out into the shopping area and the fire alarm was sounded. As the heat and smoke on the first floor and above rapidly built up, many customers made their way down staircases to fresh air and safety. Unfortunately, a number of shoppers and staff were unable to do so and climbed out of open windows onto a ledge at first floor level.

Once they were noticed, several rescue attempts were made by members of the public. At least one of the trapped group on the ledge climbed down a drainpipe. Another unusual yet successful and quick-thinking rescue method saw a box van driven close to the building. Trestles and ladders were placed on the roof of the van and the vehicle was still in position when the fire service arrived only minutes after the first '999' call.

Firefighters immediately pitched a turntable ladder to the ledge and six people still marooned there were rescued. Other crews wearing breathing sets entered the store with water jets to fight the fire and search for shoppers reported to be trapped inside the store by the thick black smoke. It was not known at this time whether or not the building had been completely evacuated.

Assistance messages were sent to increase the number of fire engines up to 10 pumps as the fire was spreading throughout the first floor. Firefighters were finding it difficult to make progress through the store in the darkness, and their paths were impeded by the clothes racks and merchandise displays.

'Shoppers and staff climbed out of open windows onto a ledge'

The search of the first floor continued and by using four water jets and many breathing apparatus sets, teams of firefighters were gradually able to bring the fire under control. Slowly, the smoke began to thin and at about 1130 hours a breathing apparatus crew discovered two bodies lying in the cafeteria area. These were removed to a waiting ambulance. The casualties were certified dead and identified as a married couple, a man aged 80 and his wife of 74.

One of those rescued by firefighters from the first floor ledge was Joan Healey, aged 59, who worked in the store restaurant. She said: 'It was obvious that was the only way to get out, so we climbed onto the ledge. I thought my number was up. I don't usually panic but when you can't get out through the stairs and the windows on the first floor you don't have much choice. As I sat on the ledge, I kept thinking I was going to have to jump because it was getting to be life or death'.

Apart from the two dead shoppers, about 82 others suffered from smoke inhalation and shock. After an intensive police and fire service forensic investigation, a youth was arrested and charged with arson at the Littlewoods store. In November 1993, the youth was tried, found guilty and was sentenced to be detained at Her Majesty's pleasure.

LEICESTERSHIRE

One of the largest Leicestershire fires in recent years occurred on 22 January 1993. The first of over 30 '999' calls to Brigade Control was received at 0055 hours to a factory on fire in Humberstone Road, Leicester. Two pumps from Leicester's Eastern Station arrived three minutes later to find a four-storey building on fire from

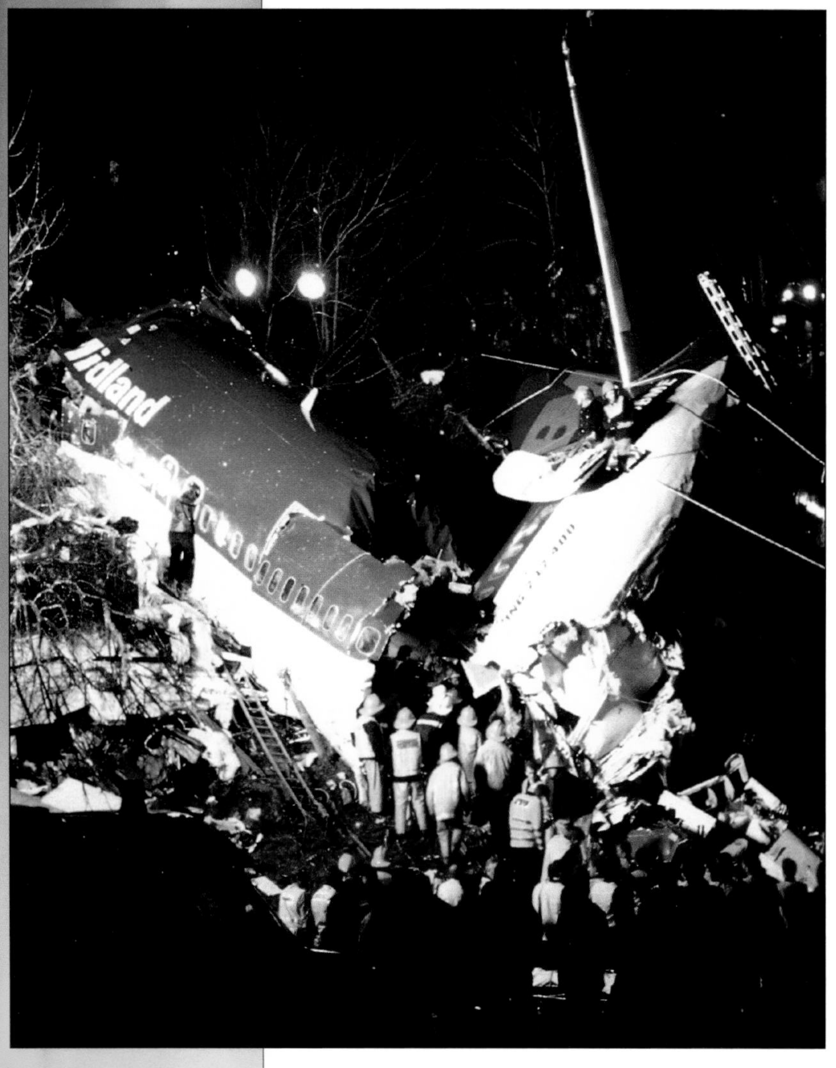

back to front and end to end. The rapid build-up of firefighters then grew as six extra pumps were called for by radio, with a turntable ladder requested one minute later at 0059. Soon they were joined by the remaining four Leicester 'city' pumps (two from Central, two from Western) plus Central's turntable ladder and emergency tender and Wigston's foam salvage tender.

Five minutes later, at 0104, as the full extent of the fire became apparent and adjoining premises were seriously threatened, more pumps and a hydraulic platform were requested. Supporting appliances came from Wigston, Syston, Coalville, Billesdon and Central, plus the command vehicle from Loughborough.

Further assistance messages followed at 0128 (make pumps 15) and 0135 (make aerial appliances three). This necessitated the attendance of more crews

Below: *The scene on 10 March 1991, after Leicestershire fire crews had put out a huge blaze in 200 scrap railway carriages spread over a large area near the city centre. Asbestos in the linings of the carriages posed an extra hazard to firefighters.* (Leicestershire Fire and Rescue Service)

Above: *On 8 January 1989, a British Midland Boeing 737 crashed into an embankment close to the M1 motorway after failing to touch down at East Midlands Airport because of an engine fire. Forty seven passengers were killed but 79 persons survived. Here the rescue operation goes on under floodlights around the crumpled aircraft.* (Leicestershire Fire and Rescue Service)

from Loughborough and from Kibworth, Hinckley and Uppingham and an 'over the border' attendance of Nuneaton's (Warwickshire) hydraulic platform. A 'fire surrounded' message was sent at 0338 and the 'stop' at 0434, by which time 13 jets were in use including three from aerial fire engines. The premises involved, a knitwear factory of four floors and basement of approximately 200 by 100 feet (60 x 30 metres), were severely damaged by fire and collapse, although adjoining buildings were saved from serious fire spread.

Firefighting efforts were hampered by the strong winds which persisted throughout the night. These carried large burning embers down on to a nearby timber yard where they started a number of small fires which needed attention from the crews.

Another taxing and rather unusual fire dealt with by Leicestershire firefighters took place on 10 March 1991. They were first called at 0412 hours to a large scrapyard on the outskirts of Leicester. There they found a serious fire all around and underneath about 200 old railway carriages stacked four high and covering an area the size of several football pitches. It took 80 firefighters and 13 pumps over eight hours to control the huge fire.

A major problem during the blaze was the suspected release of blue asbestos found in the internal linings of the old carriages. Great care was needed throughout firefighting operations, and all front-line crews wore breathing sets. Many also wore special protective clothing.

As each team was relieved by fresh firefighters, full decontamination of the relieved crews – still in their breathing sets and protective clothing – took place under special high pressure water sprays. It was not until they were pronounced clear of any asbestos contamination that they were able to get out of their firefighting gear and change into clean, dry clothing. Control of the whole emergency was a very complex task but the fire was eventually contained and a serious pollution risk to the city of Leicester was avoided.

WARWICKSHIRE

Warwickshire firefighters will long remember 6 March 1992 as a 'motorway' day – three separate emergencies crippled the entire Midlands road system.

The first incident was on the M6 near Bedworth, when a lorry full of sheep caught fire. This caused a 10 mile tailback while fire crews dealt with the fire and helped to prevent the terrified animals running loose all over the motorway.

Then a petrol tanker overturned on the M42 near Coleshill. The driver was trapped and had to be cut out of his crushed cab. A carpet of foam was quickly applied to the entire surrounding area, but fortunately the spilt fuel did not ignite. Five mile tailbacks built up in both directions.

Then, to close this hectic day, firefighters were called again to the M42 to a lorry on fire with 19.5 tons of paper on board. More horrendous traffic snarl-ups developed.

Some two weeks later, several of the Warwickshire crews involved in these inci-

Hell below earth

On 10 May 1968 Warwickshire firefighters were called to one of the most challenging incidents ever tackled by the Brigade. As part of a major sewage scheme, a large-diameter tunnel was under construction at the Finham treatment plant. Fire broke out in the tunnel at a point near the village of Baginton, where the workings were 80 feet (24 metres) underground.

The tunnel was pressurised and access to it was through a series of vertical shafts and air-locks to prevent the ingress of water. About 200 yards (183 metres) from the shaft and in punishing conditions of heat and smoke, the breathing apparatus crews from nine fire engines from Warwickshire and Coventry brigades successfully extinguished the fire which involved several hundred feet of electricity cable.

Before being commissioned and put to its intended use, the tunnel achieved a certain degree of fame when it was used as the location for the famous car chase sequence in the feature film *The Italian Job*.

dents were called to Bedworth to deal with a leak of 222 gallons (1,000 litres) of hydrofluoric acid. This emergency posed a serious threat to the population of the surrounding area, but after several hours, the leak was contained by crews in breathing sets and protective suits and that part of Warwickshire returned again to normality.

NOTTINGHAMSHIRE

Nottinghamshire, like all other fire brigades in the UK, can be on the road within seconds of receiving a clear address of the emergency via the '999' system. And if fire engines and crews are needed from an adjoining brigade's area, Nottinghamshire, like every other UK brigade, has mutual aid arrangements in place which provide for the immediate despatch of pumps to assist 'over the border'.

A fire in Mansfield in the week before Christmas 1991 quickly developed into a moderately sized incident and well illustrates the rapid build up of firefighters and fire engines needed to tackle such a blaze.

The first '999' call to a bingo hall in Mansfield town centre came soon after 0900 hours. Mansfield's two water tenders and hydraulic platform responded. Further assistance was soon called for which brought two more pumps from Ashfield, one each from Warsop and Blidworth, together with a control unit from Beeston.

> ***'He set fire to himself and ran off down the road'***

Even then, the fire was threatening other buildings and more help was requested. This brought a further water tender from Edwinstone and an 'over the border' pump from Alfreton (Derbyshire Fire and Rescue Service).

By then fire cover to this part of Nottinghamshire was getting rather thin. Nottinghamshire Fire Control moved a water tender from Alfreton and Ashfield, while another pump from Shirebrook (Derbyshire) was moved to stand by at Mansfield Fire Station.

Fire crews remained at the scene until 0400 hours the following morning. The bingo hall, which was originally a Victorian theatre, was badly damaged, but the fire was prevented from spreading to other properties in the town centre.

NORTHAMPTONSHIRE

Two apparently fairly straightforward emergencies attended by Northamptonshire fire crews during 1992 turned out to be far from run-of-the-mill.

Firefighters from Northampton dashed to an address in Thrapston in response to a '999' call in which the caller said a house, a car and two vans were all on fire. There were indeed three separate fire situations. What made this fire call rather different was that an irate man suddenly appeared and tried to stop the firefighters as they set to work to tackle the house and vehicle fires.

Worse was to follow. When the fire crews approached the fellow, he set fire to himself and ran off down the road with flames licking up around him. Several firefighters chased after him and managed to get the flames out, but by this time the man was very severely burned. The house and all three vehicles were badly damaged before the fires were brought under control.

The second incident which underlined the unexpected side of fire and rescue work, again took place in Northampton. Three water tenders and a chemical incident unit were called out to a spillage on a lorry carrying chemicals. The emergency occurred when a drum burst open and spilt its contents among other drums of chemicals on the back of the lorry.

What complicated the situation was that essential documentation was missing, which should have been on the lorry and would have immediately identified the chemicals. This basic information is normally critical in the first few minutes of a chemical emergency as firefighters need to know specifically how to deal with a wide range of solid, liquid, and gaseous hazardous substances.

Many of these chemicals can react violently with each other or when in contact with water. Fire crews have to make a rapid assessment of the level of protection they need to have in order to work safely and close to the spillage or leak itself. The precise name of the chemical or its trade name is essential, and in all of this, time is precious if the situation is to be contained and risks to the community be minimised.

Unfortunately, before the precise details of the chemicals involved in the Northampton spillage were established, 37 people had been overcome by the fumes being given off from the lorry, and several firefighters needed medical treatment before the emergency was finally declared over.

STAFFORDSHIRE

Staffordshire, almost the heart of England, has had an assortment of unusual calls over recent years, to add variety to the usual firefighting diet of motorway incidents, industrial and house fires.

High or low, Staffs were there – and at Alton Towers, in March 1989 it was up in the air when a communication cable fouled the running gear of one of the cable cars at the famous leisure park, trapping 59 holidaymakers, high above the ground.

Fire crews, attending with a hydraulic platform and turntable ladders, managed to reassure, comfort and bring 38 of the people down to earth. Special rescue teams brought the other 21 to safety using

Visitors trapped in the stranded aerial coaches at Alton Towers are helped to safety by fire crews with hydraulic aerial platforms. (Staffordshire Fire and Rescue Service)

What's quackers about that?

Flashing blue lights and a loudly quacking duck roused residents of a quiet Midlands' road in the small hours of the morning. Their eyes widened in amazement at the sight of a fireman chasing the agitated duck along the gutter with a tape recorder in his hand and then lying on his stomach holding the recorder down a storm drain hole.

All was revealed in the next few minutes. The crew had been called out by a local housewife, concerned at the state of the duck who had been leading her family of ducklings along the road in the dawn light when, one by one, they had tumbled through a wide drain grid into the watery bottom. No amount of enticement by the fire crew would bring them within reach until one of the men had a brilliant idea.

Borrowing the recorder he taped the sound of the anxious quacking, then played it back in the depths of the drain. One by one the fluffy ducklings paddled back to the mechanical 'Mum'. One by one they were grabbed by the inspired fireman. The entire brood was rescued and given a brief lecture on road safety before they set off back to the pond.

rope lines attached to the individual cable cars.

From mid air to mid-tunnel, and it was a question of which way to enter when crews were called to a fire in the Harecastle Canal Tunnel in March 1984. Oil, leaking from a diesel-powered air compressor used for repair work, had sprayed on to a hot exhaust pipe and set fire to the equipment, trapping four men in clouds of choking smoke, half way between the main entrances of the two-mile tunnel.

This stretch of the canal runs between Kidsgrove and Tunstall, so crews wearing BA entered from the Tunstall end in a boat and managed to rescue the men and put out the fire. Meanwhile crews from the Kidsgrove end had set off but with a less straightforward run. The water had become so shallow that they had to leave the boat and struggle through mud to reach a further nine workers who had gone in as a replacement shift. In all, 50 officers and men with nine appliances attended the incident. Despite the mud and smoke, it was dealt with successfully,

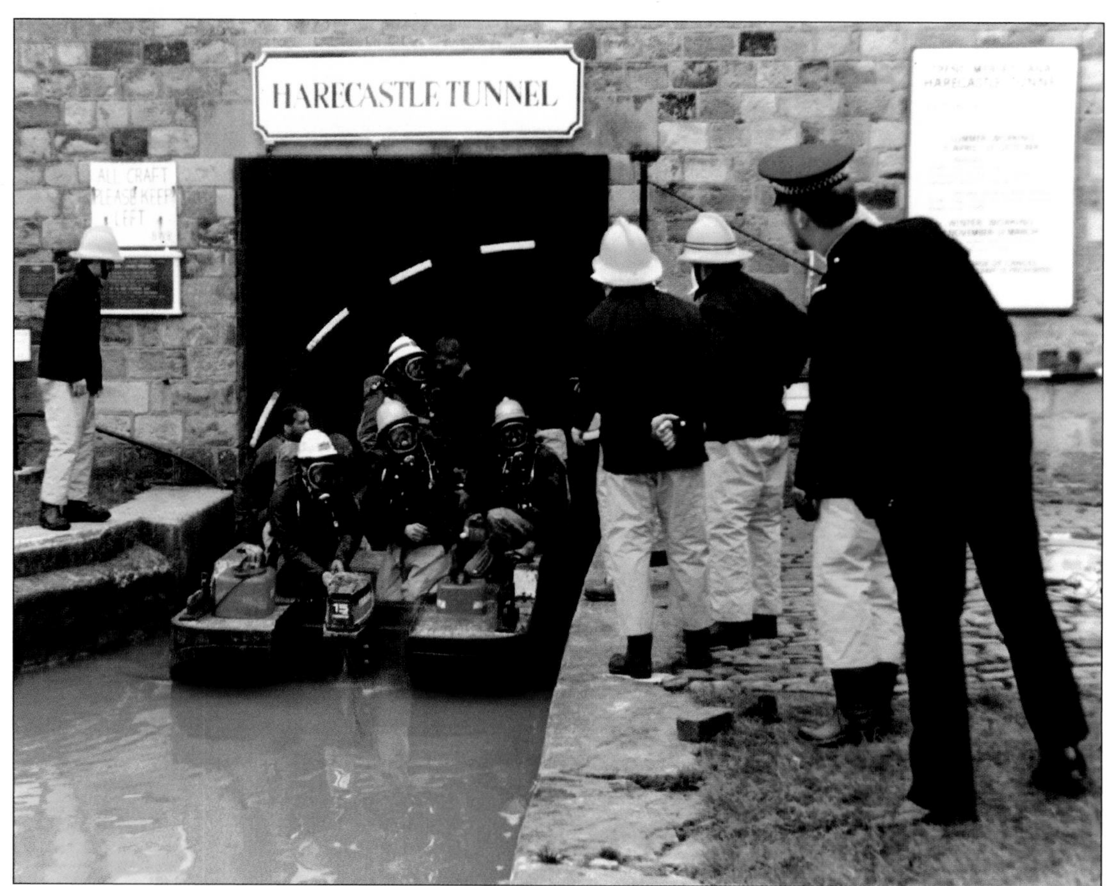

Into the daylight – and fresh air. Firefighters used an inflatable dinghy to rescue night shift workers, trapped by fire and smoke in the middle of the two-mile Harecastle Canal Tunnel between Kidsgrove and Tunstall, after leaking diesel oil sprayed a hot exhaust pipe. A total of 13 workers were taken to hospital suffering from the effects of smoke. The fire, in March 1984, was dealt with by 50 officers and firefighters. (Staffordshire Fire and Rescue Service)

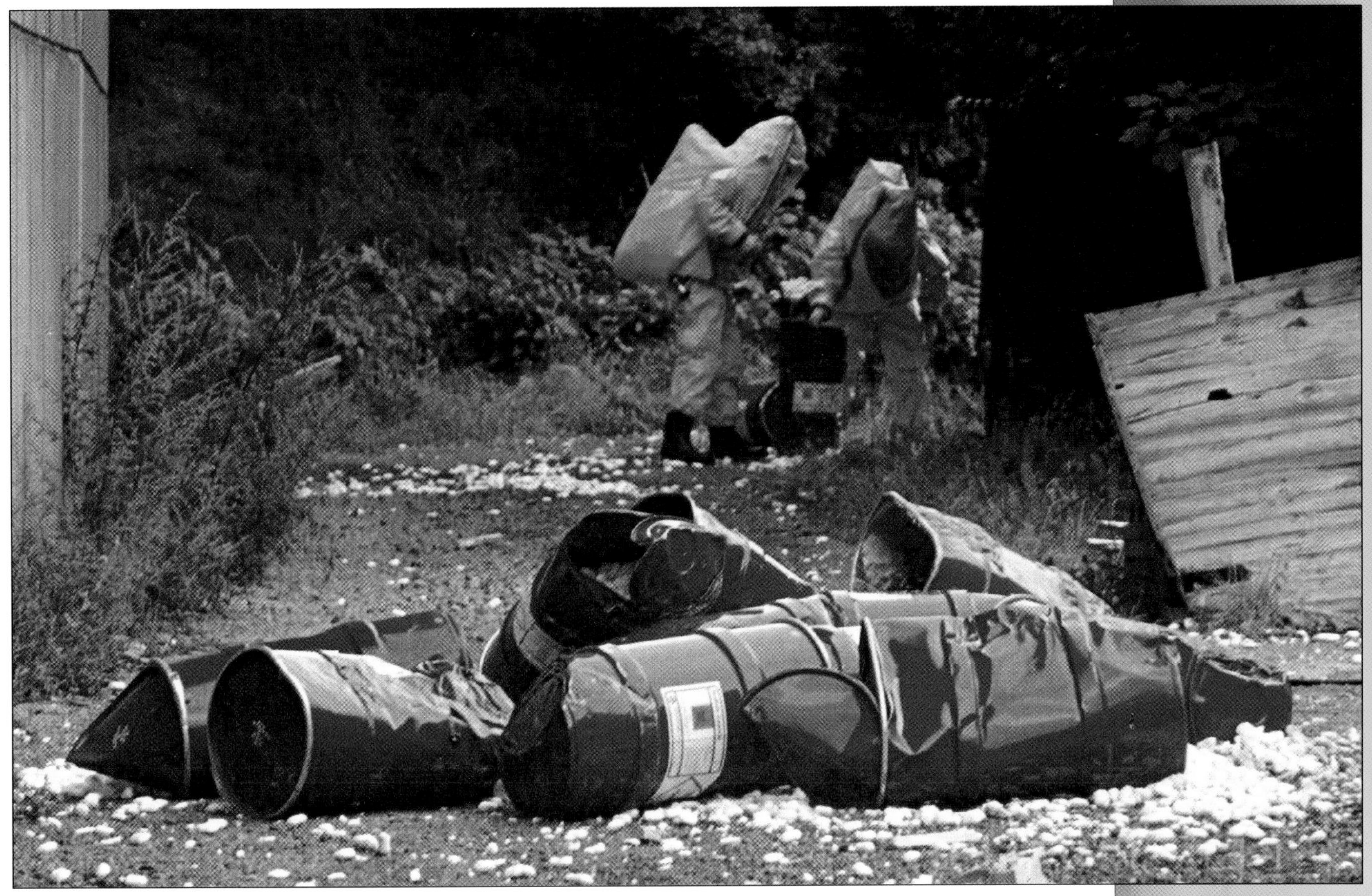

Staffordshire firefighters wore BA under their gas-tight suits as they cleared away drums of sodium cyanide which had fallen off a lorry that crashed on the A38 Branston/Claymills road above, spilling its load of lethal pellets. It took three days, from 31 July 1989, before they were certain that none of the pellets remained. (Staffordshire Fire and Rescue Service)

although the workmen and several firefighters had to be treated in hospital for the effects of smoke.

Somehow one expects major accidents to take place on motorways – but two unusual incidents which extended the skill and professionalism of Staffordshire's crews were on smaller roads.

Around lunch time (why are they so often around lunch time?) on 31 July 1989, a heavy goods vehicle was trundling along the A38 Branston/Claymills road when it collided with the roadside barriers and came to rest mounted on the guard rails of a bridge. Many of the blue metal drums in its load rolled off the truck, burst open and scattered their contents – thousands of small white pellets – over the carriageway, down the embankment and all over the road which was running below the bridge.

Training and experience have taught fire officers to take no chances with any spillage from a lorry – particularly if it looks harmless. Staffs officers kitted their crews in full protective clothing and breathing apparatus before they approached the pellets – and with good reason. Specialists, consulted to identify them, confirmed that this was a load of sodium cyanide, which needed instant protection from damp or water and the removal of absolutely every piece from the scene of the accident.

It took Staffordshire firefighters three days of intensive searching before they were satisfied that not a single cyanide pellet remained, the public were at no further risk and the area could be reopened.

Everyone who attended the incident had to be decontaminated at the scene, and all were later given blood tests at the local hospital as a precautionary measure.

In December 1988 a road accident occurred on the B5030 Uttoxeter to Rocester Road at Crakemarsh.

It was late in the afternoon on 10 December, Carl Roffey was driving his Ford Escort along the 19 foot (5.7 metres) wide country road with a friend in the

Night club rescue gives fireman the bird

Firefighter Steve Kenny of Cannock could have made a first class music hall comedian with his string of 'yarns' of firefighting epics. Highlight of them was the night in April 1991 when he was called with his Watch to a fire at the Coliseum Night Club in Stafford, and not at all sure what to expect.

'It were a big place, very popular – the only night club in the town,' he explains in his strong local accent. 'Other crews were at the front so we went round the back and smashed the door in and it was then I looked round and saw this big sheet of glass. It were just like Dudley Zoo. For one moment I thought "ayup – I bet there's blewdy pythons in there, like they have with the dancers".

'I told the gaffer and he said "get in there and see", so with that I opened the door and slid in, closing it behind me. It weren't full of snakes, it were parrots, all colours, flying around, squawking and screaming. I thought "if I put my arm out, one will jump on it and I'll just be able to walk out with it . So I put my arm out and one of them bit my bloody finger! I couldn't believe it! Here I was trying to rescue it and it bit me!

'I went back outside, got hold of a big box and grabbed these birds, one by one, and shoved them into the box – eight or nine of them in all, but I got them out into the fresh air and they were all OK. Some of them were quite valuable. The press were there with photographers and I'd have liked a picture, but I never got one.'

front passenger seat and his five-year-old daughter, India, sitting happily in the back.

Coming towards him very slowly on a straight stretch was a low loader carrying a huge, rectangular tank, later identified as a shot blasting plant assembly measuring 9 foot by 9 feet by 12 feet (2.7 metres by 2.7 metres by 3.6 metres) and weighing approx 10 tons. He was about to pass the truck, in his own lane, when the load caught a solid tree branch, the securing straps snapped, the tank toppled sideways and, a second later, had fallen on to the Escort, crushing it to the ground. First messages to the emergency services reported that at least two people had been killed. Within minutes the quiet countryside was echoing to the sound of two-tones as police, fire and ambulance crews raced to the scene, along with a 'flying squad' of doctors and nurses from the Accident and Emergency Department of North Staffordshire Royal Infirmary.

Passing motorists had already stopped and forced open the passenger door of the car enough for one man to ease his way out. His message was stark. 'You must get my mate out. He was driving – and his little girl is in the back seat.'

One motorist put his head in through the driver's window and realised that the miracle had happened. The man was still alive but desperate for news of his little daughter, India.

'I tried to see where she was but the back seat had disappeared beneath the tangled wreckage of the sides and roof of the car and the corner of the huge tank,' said the man. 'It seemed impossible to think that anyone could have survived in there, but I called and then I saw this little hand sticking out of the tangled metal. I took hold of the hand and said "Are you alright? If you can hear me, squeeze my hand". To my relief, I felt her squeezing it.'

There was no more they could do other than comfort the trapped and frightened victims in the short space of time before the emergency services arrived. Policemen, firefighters and ambulance workers all surveyed the scene with horror. A police sergeant with 14 years' experience as a traffic patrol officer at many accidents, wrote later of the tension and anxiety as they realised that the huge tank was poised so precariously on the extreme edge of the loader that it could fall at any minute.

'This rescue was so different from anything else I have met in the past, even those of horrendous magnitude such as motorway accidents,' he said. 'They are a known quantity when rescue starts, as are large fires, so that when even the most frightening circumstances prevail, rescue is carried out in a calculated manner. This was different. This was a disaster waiting to happen.'

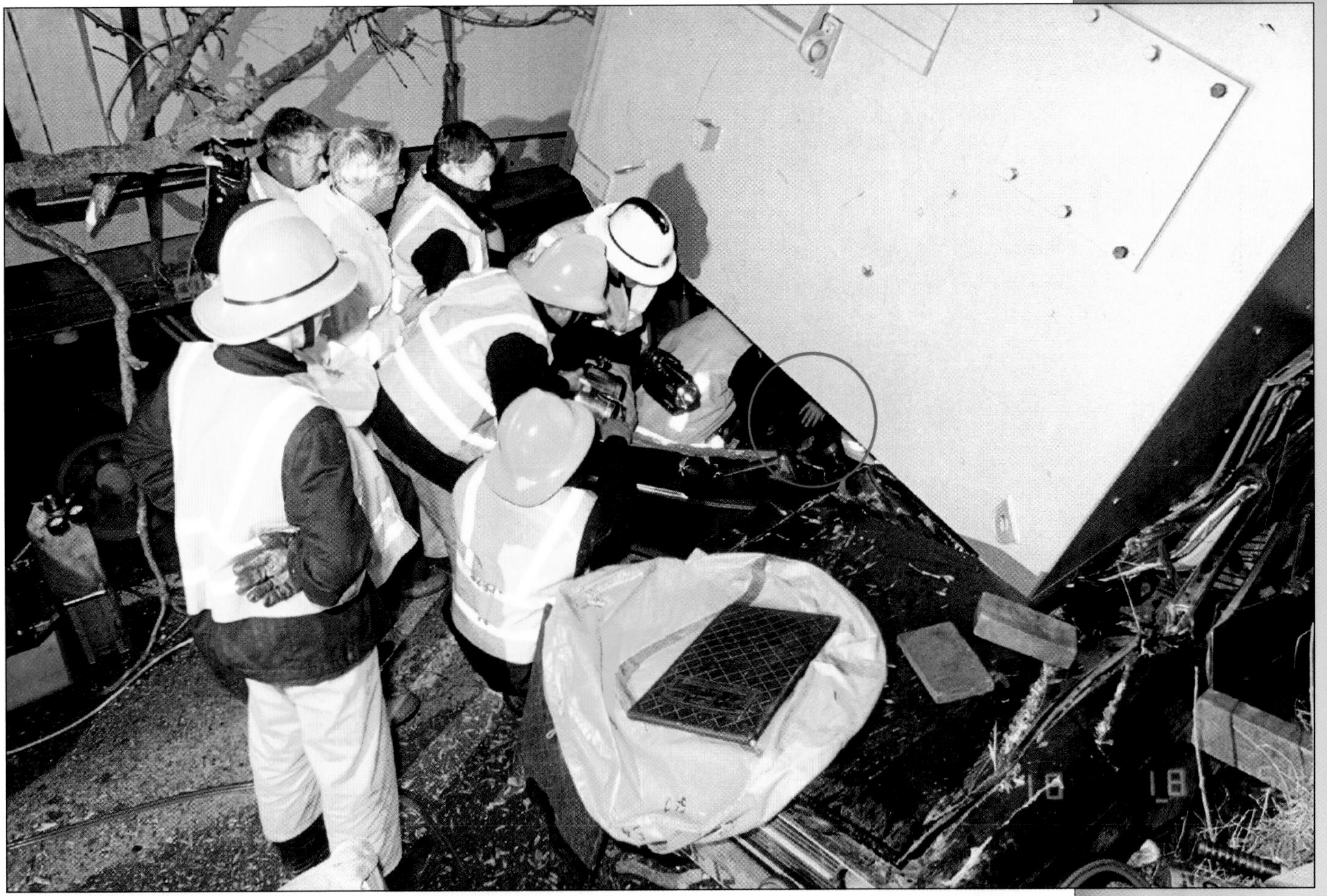

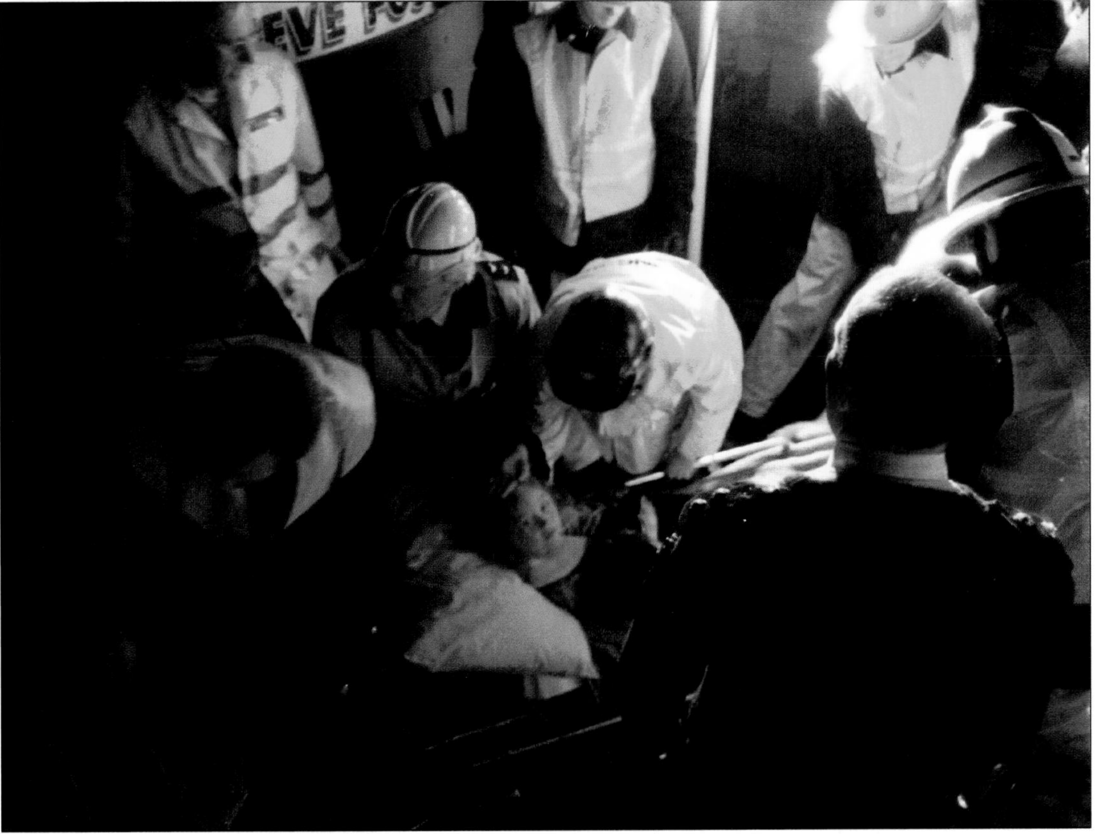

Above: ***One false move and the rest of the 10 ton tank, which had already fallen and crushed the car alongside it, could slip and kill five-year-old India Roffey and everyone trying to help in freeing her from the wreckage. All they could see of the little girl was her tiny hand (circled).***

Left: ***As the tank was slowly winched up, India was snatched from the wreckage and carried to safety by her rescuers who included Staffordshire's Chief Officer.*** *(Staffordshire Fire and Rescue Service)*

The remains of the car from which India escaped alive. *(Staffordshire Fire and Rescue Service)*

The whole rescue was taken over by Staffordshire's Chief Fire Officer, Peter Reid, who went to the scene as soon as the incident was reported to him. After a quick discussion with senior officers of the other emergency services, he cleared the area round the car of all but a handful of essential workers and went into action. Inflated bags and props were slipped under the 10 ton tank with the utmost care. The slightest false move could have tipped the last corner off the low-loader. If this happened, the rescue crews who were now bent double, cutting away the twisted metal, and the trapped father and daughter would, without any doubt, all be killed.

As they worked, India whimpered with shock and fright. Peter Reid, who had been talking to her and trying to calm her, crawled out and approached 25-year-old Sister Kathryn Clayton, from the hospital team. Spelling out the dangers, he asked her if she would be willing to go in and help comfort the little girl. Without hesitating, she followed him into the wreckage and soon the rescuers could hear her voice, quietly singing nursery rhymes and then telling India the story of Cinderella.

The work on the tank and in the wreckage continued until a sudden creak warned the Chief Officer that the danger was now too great to impose any further on the nurse. He asked her and the other rescuers to leave and took their place, alone, as the crucial moments of the rescue were reached. Slowly – so slowly – the huge tank was winched aloft enough to ease the pressure on the top of the car. As it went, the crews returned to cut away the driver's seat and reveal the little girl, tucked into the foot space between this and the back seat. With one swift move, Peter Reid snatched her to safety.

India and her father were taken by ambulance to the Infirmary but, by some miracle, neither had more than minor cuts and bruises. Days later, India and her mother were invited to meet their rescuers and see the slides and photographs of the amazing rescue.

A consultant from the medical team summed up the incident in a letter to the fire service: 'This was one of the most dangerous situations I have ever seen. I was very impressed by the professionalism and team work of the three emergency services...which made the work of our medical team very easy...With the team spirit which was shown in managing this incident, I am sure the three emergency services and the team from the North Staffordshire Accident and Emergency Department will be capable of dealing with any emergency irrespective of its size'.

Children often show remarkable resilience in desperate situations. This was the case in another incident which had faced Staffordshire crews in April 1986.

Gavin Hall, a chirpy five-year-old, had been taken by friends of his family for a morning walk at Seven Springs, part of the famous Cannock Chase area of the county, on the fine Spring morning of 27 April 1986. They had climbed to the top of a 100 foot (30.4 metre) hill and Gavin was skipping along through the bracken and undergrowth when, to their horror, he vanished. One of the group ran two and a half miles to the nearest telephone and called out the emergency services and soon all three groups plus a unit from the Mines Rescue Service, were making their way up the winding path to the top.

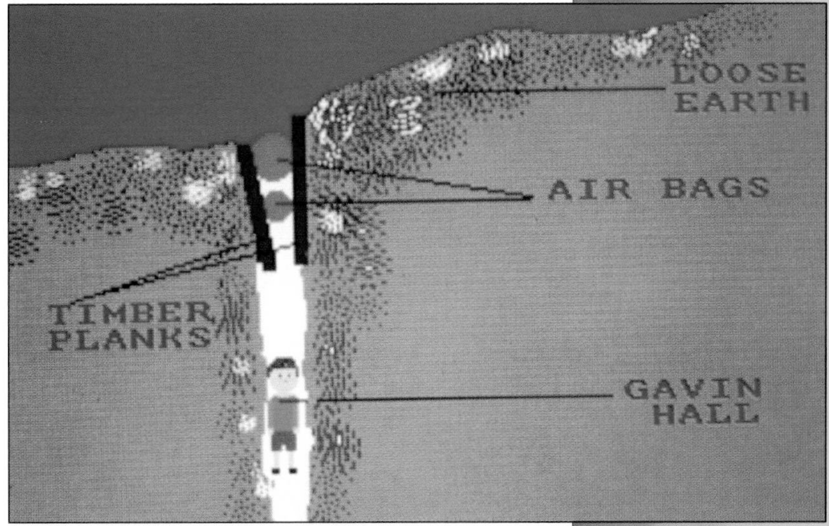

Top right: ***Protective boards, held apart by air bags, show the first stages of the rescue operation to free five-year-old Gavin Hall after he had fallen down a hidden crack in the ground when he was out walking with friends on Cannock Chase, Staffs, on 27 April 1986. In this artist's impression, Gavin was already stuck 25 feet below ground with a 75 foot drop beneath him.***

Right: ***Because Gavin's arms were trapped at his sides he was not able to reach up for a rescue line.*** *(Illustrations by Paula Nadim, graphic artist, Staffordshire F & RS Audio-Visual Department)*

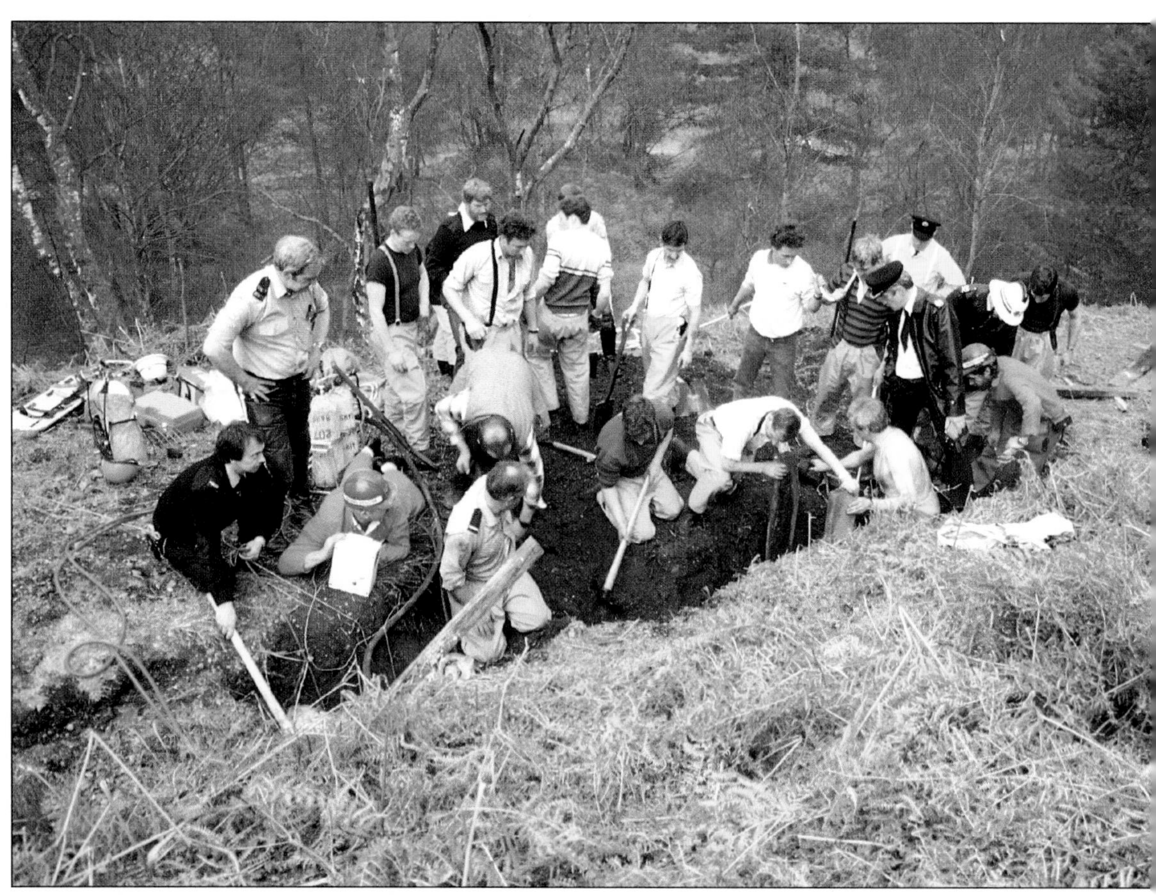

Tension and anxiety all round as rescue workers gather above the hole where a firefighter and a Mines Rescue expert are burrowing closer to the trapped boy with their bare hands. (Staffordshire Fire and Rescue Service)

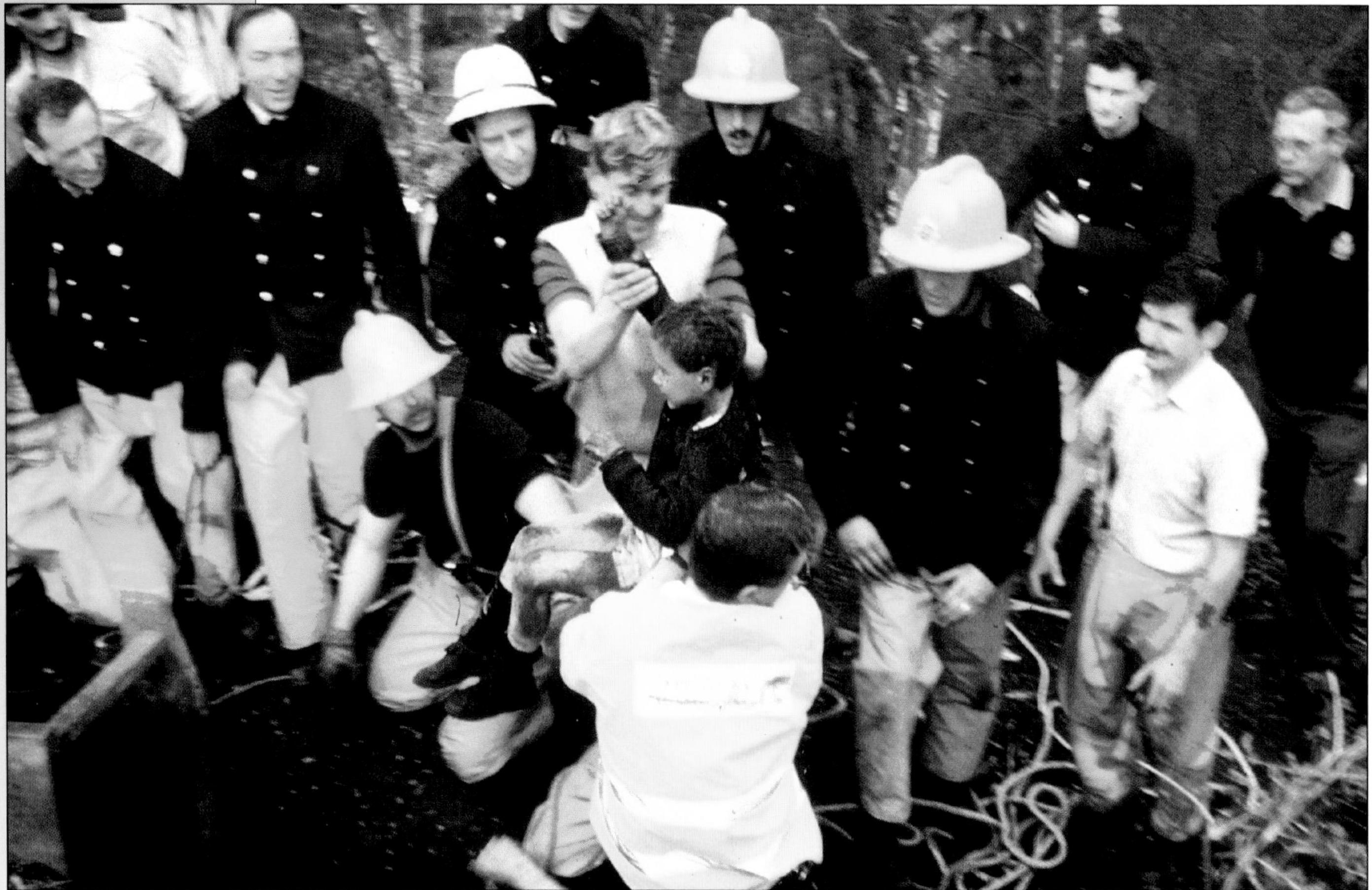

Success! After six hours of meticulously careful excavation, Gavin is lifted to safety. (Staffordshire Fire and Rescue Service)

> ***The boy was in grave danger, wedged 23 feet down***

Guided by Gavin's companions, the fire crews found a hole just over three feet (one metre) across and some 23 feet (seven metres) below they could just see Gavin's head. There was no question of dropping a line to see if he could catch it and be hauled out. In falling, his hands had been wedged firmly to his sides against the edge of the hole. Even as they peered down, earth and pebbles were being dislodged from the loose soil round the top of the hole and falling on the boy's head.

Hastily, they inflated air bags into the top of the crevice and lowered an air line to help keep him alive. Soon after this, a microphone was lowered to monitor his condition and keep him in touch with the Leading Fireman who was trying to keep his spirits up.

This was clearly going to be an unusual and difficult rescue and Staffordshire's Deputy Chief Officer at that time, Robin Richards, could not have been more suitable to take over. He held the unique distinction of being the only qualified geologist in the British Fire Service and, more than that, he knew the area.

Immediately, he realised that the hole was probably part of a larger underground fault system and ordered an exploratory hole to be dug, not far from the crack where Gavin was trapped. It confirmed his opinion – and his fear – that the boy was in grave danger, wedged 23 feet (seven metres) down with a drop of some 75 feet (23 metres) beneath him.

Already, further holes were beginning to appear in the surrounding area so no heavy equipment could be brought in. Instead, a fireman and a member of the Mines Rescue Service dug into the soft sandstone, with constant pauses for reassessment of the situation. Four hours from the moment they were called, the rescuers were able to see Gavin's head, but it was covered in dirt. A scraper on a long pole and an industrial vacuum cleaner cleared this away.

By now he was, understandably, growing weaker, but after another half hour they were able to talk to him and he rallied considerably. By 1645 he had been trapped for more than five hours. His rescuers had reached him, only to have their hopes dashed. They had freed his body but his head was still jammed in the hole. The danger here lay in the fact that if his head was released suddenly, he might fall to the bottom of the shaft. They tied safety ropes to his wrists and carried on chipping away.

Catastrophic ingratitude

When a Cannock firefighter went up a tree to rescue a black cat it was not his lucky day. The cat went higher and higher. So did the firefighter. In the end, when the cat ran out of tree, the firefighter got it by the tail and hauled it down.

Enraged at the indignity, the cat twisted in his arms and bit a lump out of his elbow, but having rescued it, the gallant firefighter was not letting go now. As the pair of them struggled to the ground, the cat, spitting and scratching, made a dive, put its claws into his leg and bit him again before high-tailing it off into the middle distance. The firefighter finished up in hospital.

On the surface, with the press and TV cameras reporting every move, the situation was quiet and tense. The chipping continued for three quarters of an hour and suddenly, his head came free. Remarkably brave, five-year-old Gavin was carried, smiling, into the fresh air at the surface. A medical team took him to hospital where he was kept in for three days observation and checks before returning home. A week later he was well enough to spend the day at Stafford Fire Station. There, it was reported, 'he was obviously suffering no ill-effects, and the pleasure of all those involved in his rescue was a delight to see'.

CHAPTER 8

COAL AND COTTON?

Many of Manchester's famous old mills have been the site of fierce fires over recent years. Here, firefighters attack a blaze in the old Phoenix Mill, Piercy Street, Ancoats, in 1956, from ground level, and also perched precariously on a turntable ladder. *(Greater Manchester Fire Service)*

NORTH WEST

GREATER MANCHESTER

'We're not all coal and cotton any more,' said one Greater Manchester firefighter, pointing to a varied list of recent incidents in their area. It's true. Many of the huge old mills which had survived are now divided up into small units housing all kinds of light industry. But if they do burn, there is a major risk for occupants and fire crews. Most of the floors are original timbers, still saturated with oil from the old mill machinery. When these burn, gases can build up and cause the incident which firefighters fear almost more than any other, the flashover, with pent-up gases exploding in a ball of fire which destroys everything in its path.

Typical of this was an incident at the old Bank of England Mills in Ancoats in

September 1986. The occupants were almost all small knitwear and clothing companies in a building noted as 'traditional', 262 feet by 131 feet (80 metres by 40 metres), up to seven floors high, and all the floors made of timber, on timber joists and cast iron columns.

At 1540 hours, the landlord of a nearby pub saw flames and smoke coming out of the fourth floor and roof of the building but decided that, as it was already well alight, somebody must have called the fire brigade. They hadn't. Meanwhile, he fetched his camcorder and videoed the scene.

At about the same time one of the businessmen inside the building, a Mr Khan, saw smoke coming up from the central lift shaft and simultaneously, the occupier of the floor above called 'Fire – get out!' Mr Khan broke the glass on the fire alarm but it failed to ring. He then thinks he dialled 999 but in his haste, can't be sure. Whatever the truth, he got the 'engaged' signal. He then dialled the telephone operator who was connecting him to the fire service when flames appeared in his room. He dropped the telephone and ran to safety.

It was not until 1551 that the fire brigade received the first alarm call. Immediately, three fire engines and a hydraulic platform were mobilised and as they were on their way they could see the smoke pouring from the building so they put out an urgent call to 'make pumps eight'.

Remarkably, the occupants of the building were slow to respond to the telltale signs of fire. A Mr Aslam, working with his staff of four on the third floor, heard a 'roaring noise' but thought it came from one of his machines, investigated, found they were all working and carried on regardless. Ten minutes later, his phone rang and as he answered it, he glanced up and saw smoke coming through his ceiling. He hadn't smelt anything burning until then. He ordered his staff from the building, dialled 999 but as the operator answered and asked where he was, he said he couldn't wait any longer, dropped the phone and left as the ceiling fell.

By now, firefighters were pouring into the building, astonished that people were still inside when the fire had obviously been going for some time and had taken such a hold. While those outside went into action, drawing water from hydrants and

Welephant makes sure kids never forget fire safety

'Welephant' is one of the biggest-ever success stories in fire safety. He was created as an entry in a children's fire safety competition in Greater Manchester in 1978 and was such an immediate success that he was officially adopted by Greater Manchester County Fire Service as its fire safety mascot in 1980.

Since then he has ventured further afield, appearing all over the country, urging children not to forget fire safety.

In 1986 he arrived in Whitehall, London, to receive Home Office approval and 'go national', being adopted by almost every fire brigade in the United Kingdom and Eire to promote fire safety.

Since then, the Welephant Club Incorporated has been formed, and the money it raises is used to provide life saving equipment for burns units in the nation's hospitals.

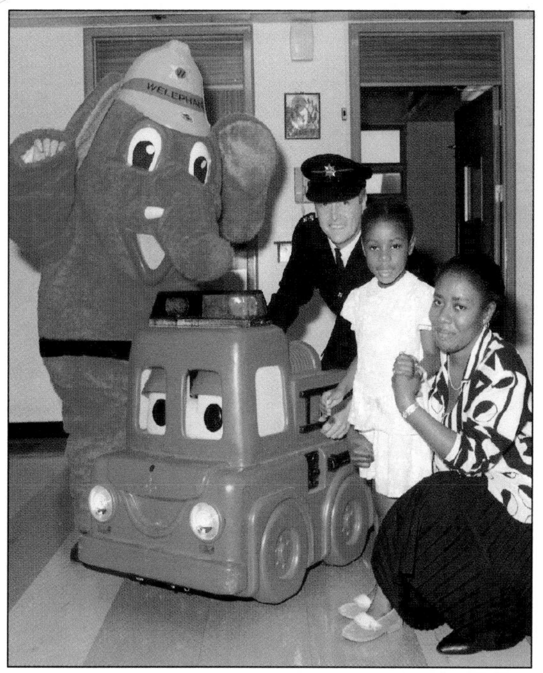

Welephant, born in Manchester as the idea of a schoolchild in a competition to help children remember fire safety, still travels the country reminding them of the dangers of fire. Here, Welephant introduces his mate, Freddy Firetruck, to two young friends. Freddy and several similar mini fire engines flash their eyes, bleep, sound a two-tone and talk to young children as part of West Midlands' fire safety education programme. (West Midlands Fire Service)

POLLARD ST
GREATER MANCHESTER FIRE SERVICE
DODGE
C434 AND

> ***Dense, toxic smoke was travelling towards a nearby housing estate***

the adjoining canal and pumping it into the building from jets and hydraulic platforms, another team dived inside, ran up the stairs and rescued 20 people who had been working on the third and fourth floors.

Despite the work of the fire crews, the building was badly damaged. Investigations which followed were not helped by the fact that the floor on which the fire had started had collapsed, but traces of 'a petroleum type liquid' were found in the floorboards. Coupled with the speed at which the fire developed, it seemed likely that someone had entered the building and deliberately set fire to it.

Another suspicious incident had resulted in a monstrous fire at B & R Hauliers in Flax Street, Salford in September 1982. Late at night, the 'lads of the village' had set light to a pile of old tyres, close to the haulier's site. Within seconds of receiving a '999' call, crews at Salford Fire Station heard a large explosion and as they drove out, they could see a mushroom shaped cloud of dense smoke – like an atom bomb – which continued to rise throughout their journey. The whole area was littered with broken glass and wreckage from the explosion.

Jumping down from the appliances, they saw that nearly one third of the roof had been blown off, the smoke 'mushroom' was still rising and, within it, was a core of burning and rapidly expanding gas, swirling and exploding in the air. At the same time, dense, toxic smoke was travelling north towards a nearby housing estate. Added to all this, they noticed a small fire in a heap of tyres, burning on open ground near the side of the store.

They found the night watchman, who was wandering around, too dazed to remember what was being stored there, but the managing director of the firm was contacted and to the fire officers' horror, but no particular surprise, word came back 'sodium chlorate', a chemical known to be highly explosive and to produce vast amounts of toxic smoke.

All crews within range were now dressed in chemical protective suits and breathing apparatus as they laid hose lines to the centre of the works yard, close to

Opposite: ***The Bank of England Mills in Ancoats was one of many old mills which have been divided up into small industrial units. Here, firefighters led workers to safety as flames, probably caused by arson, raced through the upper floors. Note the crews already at work high up in the dense smoke beyond the Dodge HP at this 20-pump fire in September 1986.*** *(Greater Manchester Fire Service)*

Fire crews damping down the ruins after a horrific chemical store fire in Flax Street, Salford, in 1982. Some drums of chemicals are still smouldering. *(Greater Manchester Fire Service)*

Firefighters had to saw through iron bars across some of the windows after fire broke out in Woolworth's store, Manchester, in May, 1979. Shoppers and staff were trapped on the upper floors and although fire crews rescued 26 people from the blazing building, 10 died in the fire and 47 members of the public plus 10 firefighters were taken to hospital. (Greater Manchester Fire Service)

the building, to feed either ground monitors or foam equipment. But for the moment they held back until they knew what chemical they were up against. While they waited, another explosion rocked the area and forced the firefighters to drag their equipment away and wait further back. This second explosion made the fire spread sideways and several smaller explosions which followed destroyed the whole roof.

Already, police were evacuating residents from the entire surrounding area as the choking fumes rolled over the flats and houses.

Quickly, word had come through with the Emergency Action Code for sodium chlorate so that the appropriate foam jets could be brought into play, but the intense heat broke up the jets. Big ground monitors were then brought in and moved up and down the building, dousing it with foam. More was still needed and by midnight, the message 'make pumps 14, foam tenders two', went out along with a call for two crews to help with the evacuation of the people living nearby.

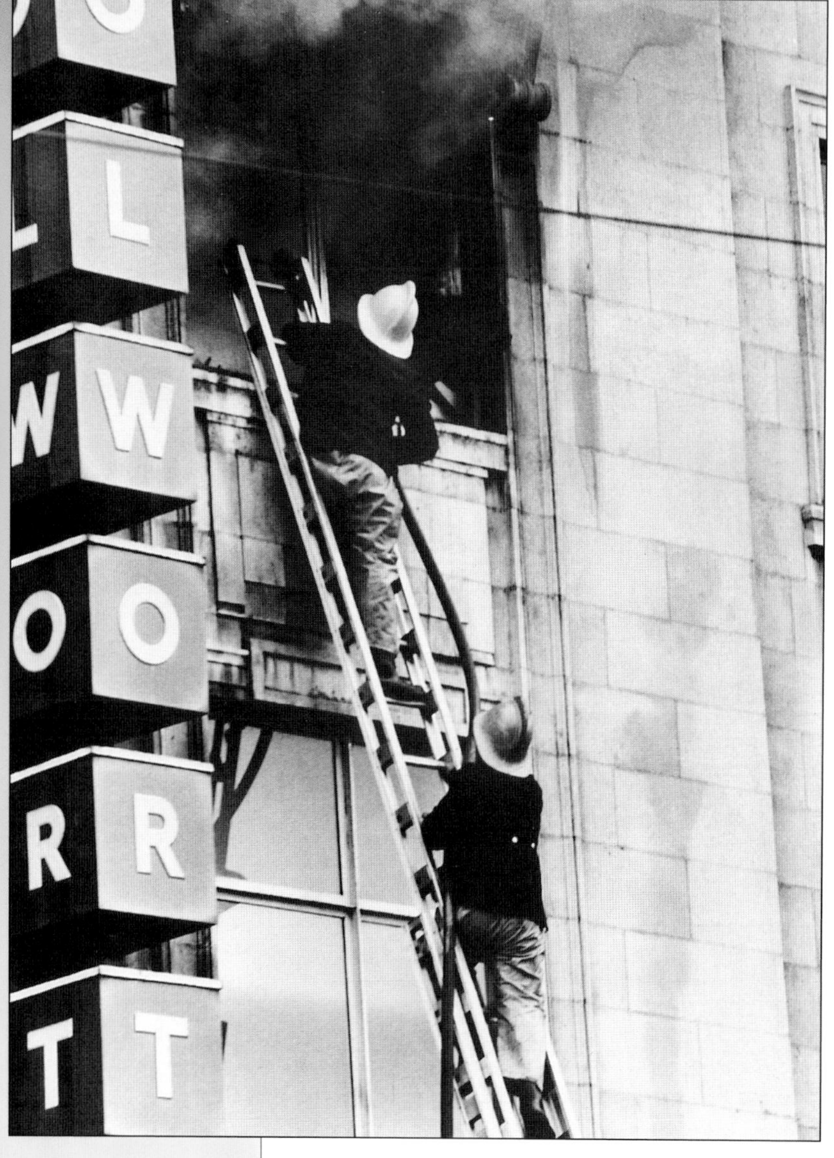

Every available firefighter on the site was now directed to lay out lines to supply three huge foam monitors – increased less than half an hour later to four foam tenders and additional bulk foam compound. By half past midnight 20 pumps were in attendance. Despite the nearby river and the hydrants, water was in short supply for the amount of foam needed and three relays had to be set up to bring water in from half a mile away.

The smoke was still like an atomic mushroom. The scene below was not unlike a war-time disaster, with local families being taken to hospital suffering from cuts and bruises from the flying debris and breathing problems from the toxic smoke. By 0130 hours the factory wall alongside the River Irwell had collapsed, partially blocking the river and also threatening it with chemical pollution. At about the same time, firefighters braved the appallingly dangerous conditions to crawl through and get access to several large trailer containers of chemicals which were being subjected to severe radiated heat, and clear them from the danger zone.

As they left, they opened up another way into the building and revealed yet more metal drums of chemicals, stacked high inside. As if this was not bad enough, there were also stacks of bagged chemicals many of them burning.

The crews continued the attack, siting monitors actually inside the building at one stage, until, thankfully, they sent out the 'stop' message just before 0430. But damping down and watching duties carried on for a further seven hours until they could be sure that there would be no further outbreaks.

In the course of this frightening incident, 45 civilians, three policemen and two firemen were treated in hospital, some 2,000 people were evacuated from nearby homes, and more than 600 houses were damaged by the explosions.

The cause of the fire was, as always, carefully investigated. It was disclosed that not only was sodium chlorate being stored in the building, but a variety of chemicals including magnesium chloride, trichlorobenzene, paradichlorobenzine, orthodichlorobenzene and drums of other flammable liquids as well as some rubber. The brigade had recently been called to the surrounding area for fires caused by arson and the premises had been vandalised several times. It seemed likely that for some unknown reason, gas had built up inside the building which had been ignited by a spark or ember from the pile of burning tyres drifting in, possibly through the damaged roof, and causing the explosion.

In an earlier and long-remembered incident, the big Woolworth's store occupying several storeys in Piccadilly, Manchester, caught fire – again, possibly through arson – in May 1979. The fire had started among upended sofas and beds in the furniture department. Several of them were protected by paper covers and many had polyurethane fillings. Fire crews did their best, but 10 shoppers were killed, trapped and suffocated in the smoke. Another 26 were rescued by the fire service who had, at one stage, to saw through the iron bars across the upper windows of the store to release the shoppers and staff who were trapped inside. A further six people were helped out by firefighters and 47 were taken to hospital, along with 10 firemen.

The fire caused 90 per cent damage to the second floor, where it had started, and its contents. The rest of the building was affected by heat and smoke.

Greater Manchester Fire Service and the Manchester Airport Fire Service joined forces at a major incident on the airfield on 22 August 1985. It was 0715 hours when a 'Full Emergency' call reached the City Service from the Airport Fire Station, indicating that the port engine of a Boeing 737 was on fire.

> ***'Aviation fuel poured through the passengers in a river of flame'***

The City's crews arrived in barely six minutes, but even as they approached the airfield they could see the pall of black smoke indicating that this was more than fire in the port engine. In fact, the fire had caused an explosion which released thousands of litres of aviation fuel. It poured into the fuselage and through the passengers in a river of flame.

While airport firefighters in BA were trying to get in through the starboard wing escape door, four of the City's firefighters were smashing through the front starboard door carrying light water foam branches. In those first horrific moments they could only find one man still breathing, but he was trapped under a pile of bodies. They released him and handed him over to the ambulance personnel who rushed him to hospital.

Outside, the crews had poured oceans of foam over the entire plane and the surrounding area as the aviation fuel continued to leak from the stricken plane. Not until mid-day was the 'stop' message sent and it was two hours later when all the people on board had been accounted for. Of the 131 passengers and six crew, 82 survived and 55 died.

Greater Manchester Fire Service carried out its own investigation into the means of escape from the plane, but the Fire Research Establishment set up a full size model of part of the Boeing's fuselage at its testing ground outside Bedford, to examine particularly the question of whether all airlines should be required to provide smoke hoods for passengers.

Although Manchester has a fair sprinkling of major incidents, most of its calls, like other brigades, are to 'run of the mill' events which provide all their officers with general experience. It is the occasional major disaster which stretches fire officers

A huge fireball bursts over Laporte's chemical works at Warrington, Cheshire, during a large blaze in 1985. A hundred firefighters tackled the outbreak during which a number of other explosions took place. (The Warrington Guardian)

to the full, not least because so few of them have the opportunity to experience them for real.

Among the recommendations after his Inquiry into the King's Cross disaster, Desmond Fennel QC suggested that fire brigades should review their instruction and training in command and control of emergency incidents.

Greater Manchester responded to this by setting up their 'ICCARUS' project – Intelligent Command and Control; Acquisition Review Using Simulation.

This, in fact, is a computerised simulator which can produce all the problems which might arise at an imaginary major incident, changing the picture every time and dropping in all the difficulties and clues which an experienced officer can take in his stride and adapt to, but which might be too much for a less experienced junior officer. Smoke may change colour, with all its implications; there may be a roof collapse; extra crews and equipment may arrive; explosives or similar hazards may crop up in a building; stairs may give way – all these must be responded to quickly and correctly as they come in thick and fast.

The machine can give young officers hands-on experience of a far greater range of incidents than they could normally expect. It is also aimed at increasing their confidence at dealing with the occasional 'big one'. As one officer said 'it gives you everything but the smell'.

CHESHIRE

In April 1992, Cheshire Fire Brigade called in a police marksman to assist its firefighters overcome a rather unusual problem.

The brigade had been called to the

premises of a Winsford company which produced aerosol sprays, polishes and waxes for the motor industry. During a process which involved filling 45 gallon drums with aerosol paint spray, it was noticed that one sealed drum was overheating and beginning to distort. The company chemist believed that a reaction was taking place inside the drum and that there would soon be a high probability of an explosion and fire.

Fire crews worked very fast around the area to lay out hose lines with fixed unattended nozzles. These cooling jets had the effect of reducing the immediate internal pressure on the drum but its reaction within was still active as the drum was now beginning to bulge at the ends.

Further hose lines were positioned throughout the immediate area of the plant to protect it in event of a sudden fire situation breaking out as a result of the drum exploding. While this work was going on, urgent consultations were taking place with the chemist and the Health and Safety Executive. The concern of the fire service was that the drum could obviously not be moved but in the immediate vicinity of the potential 'bomb' were a large quantity of highly flammable liquids.

After further consultations, a decision was taken to call in a police marksman so that the drum could be punctured from a safe distance and so relieve its internal pressure. When the marksman arrived he was briefed on the situation, after which he decided to use a 12-bore shotgun aimed at a mark below the liquid level in the distorted drum.

This meant that the only vantage point from which the marksman could fire with confidence at the 'target' was at an angle towards the drum through a wedged-open door. Once in position, he fired two shots which immediately depressurised the drum and allowed its contents to drain out. From this point on, the serious danger was over, the incident was slowly wound down and crews returned to their stations.

Cheshire's Chief Fire Officer, Dennis Davis, said afterwards: 'This unorthodox approach was used under extremely controlled conditions. The successful outcome of this emergency was a testament to the close co-operation and understanding between all those involved as to exactly what was required and the risks involved'.

In recent years, the fire service has seen itself drawn into fire and rescue situations as a direct result of terrorist activity. This was certainly the case at just after 0400 hours on 26 February 1993 when an IRA bomb exploded at the British Gas production and storage plant at Warrington. Residents throughout the town heard the explosion and no fewer than 709 separate '999' calls were made over the next 30 minutes!

Fire crews from Warrington Fire Station were on the scene within two minutes of the explosion to find three gasholders alight. Even as the crew commander carried out his reconnaissance, one of the gasholders suffered a catastrophic structural roof failure, which caused an enormous fireball to burst forth into the sky as the entire contents of the gasholder burnt off. Although the firefighters were within 100 feet (30 metres) of the gasholder, thankfully they were not injured by the radiated heat of the fireball, even though the sides of the adjacent gasholders were scorched.

Very quickly, a major firefighting effort was mounted but it was only at this stage that it became evident that the explosion was the result of a terrorist device. Further firefighting operations then had to proceed in conjunction with the police and their efforts to ensure that no other explosive devices were present. As it was still dark, CFO Davis ordered a tactical withdrawal of all non-essential firefighters. Police officers organised the evacuation of families living close to the British Gas site, together with the stoppage of all traffic on the British Rail West Coast main line nearby.

'He fired two shots which depressurised the drum'

> *A number of house fires are caused by children*

Soon after 0500, the only fire still burning involved a small gas leak on the side of one gasholder, and this did not produce a significant risk. It was decided to wait until daybreak when a full search of the site could be made for any further bombs.

At dawn, the search began using an army bomb disposal officer and police officers with dogs trained for explosive searches. CFO Davis was also present at this stage. About 40 minutes after the search began, an unexploded device was found together with the evidence of a second smaller explosion. Further searches found more evidence of explosive devices elsewhere in the site complex and it was not until midday that a full clearance was given that the site was now safe.

British Gas engineers had by now been able to decrease the gas pressure on the complex and started the process of lowering the burning gasholder to allow it to self-extinguish in the water seal at its base. Firefighters stood by throughout this operation but residents were allowed back into their homes and trains started to run again. The last flame on the burning gasholder finally flickered out at about 1700 hours.

CFO Davis later commended the Warrington Fire Station Green Watch crew, led by Station Officer Garner, who had been first on the scene, for their total commitment despite the severe shock of the gasholder fireball. It was quite remarkable that there was no loss of life at Warrington; no doubt the bravery and prompt action of the Cheshire firefighters had a part in this.

MERSEYSIDE

The huge port of Liverpool has, for centuries, seen many a fire in its warehouses and on board the thousands of ships which have tied up at its wharves. Today, there is far less shipping traffic, but Merseyside fire crews are still kept busy, particularly in the industrial areas which surround them.

Like many parts of Britain, they have their share of arson incidents, but it was an unusual cause which started a £2.2 million blaze in a cosmetic factory in the early hours of a Monday morning in 1970.

Poor water supplies had meant that fire crews had to relay water from hydrants up to 545 yards (500 metres) away. This, and the lack of dividing walls in the building, added to the highly inflammable materials being contained there, had allowed the fire to 'get away' and cause immense damage.

Investigations afterwards showed that the fork lift trucks used on the site had been 'wired up' on the Friday night to charge their batteries over the weekend. A surge of current had apparently caused several contacts to weld together in the control box and start the expensive blaze.

A surprising number of house fires are caused by children. So much so that in 1988, Merseyside Fire Brigade started a special scheme called 'FACE' – Fire Awareness Child Education – among children aged between four and 12 years old whose parents feared that their obsession with fire might turn them into arsonists.

'We can only deal with children whose parents come and ask us for help,' explained Station Officer Steve Broadhurst of Merseyside, 'and we don't go in to lecture them. We go along to their homes and chat to them with their parents, asking about their interests and family and relaxing them before we start talking about fire. We need their parents' co-operation all the time, and we ask them to turn off the telly now and then and sit round the table and talk to their children.

'We give them little projects to do – pictures to fill in where they have to spot the fire risks – that sort of thing. It may take three months or up to a year, but much depends on the parents. When they feel that the problem has gone, they let us know and we give the child a certificate which enables them to visit the fire station, meet the firefighters and get dressed up in mini uniforms. They see a basic drill and they get involved, holding the hoses and seeing what has to be done. It does seem to work in many cases.'

The fire service works in co-operation with educational and clinical psychologists, care consultants, social service departments, educational welfare guidance departments, the Merseyside police and the burns unit of the major local hospitals. Particularly important is a scheme involving older children who have been taken before the Magistrates Court or the Crown Court charged with arson.

The Juvenile Offenders Fire Safety Course is an option open to judges and magistrates as part of a Supervised Activity Order if they feel a young person might benefit from it and, says Stn/O Broadhurst, 'it isn't a soft option'.

The course comprises a series of meetings with a uniformed fire officer – who has given up spare time and volunteered to help with the project – accompanied by the youngster's youth worker. 'It's a series of chats, backed up by videos, in which we try to get them to understand the effect that setting fire to a school or factory has on so many people in terms of lost jobs, lost opportunities.

'We put it to them in words and situations that they can understand themselves, and then ask them what they would have done to the arsonists if they had caught them. Their answer is almost always "put them inside". We then remind them that they have done just this.'

So far the scheme has proved remarkably successful, with many of the teenagers going back to school and settling down to take their GCSEs. One is now doing 'A' levels in Law, Maths and English, while a 16-year-old has one ambition – to be a firefighter.

LANCASHIRE

They call it 'Death Junction', but Lancashire's fire crews take no pride in having this, Britain's worst motorway blackspot, on their patch. Within two years, between 1985 and 1987, 49 people were killed in road accidents on this stretch of the motorway network between Lancaster and the junction itself at Walton-le-Dale. Twenty-six of them died in two particularly horrific incidents. By a macabre coincidence, the scene of the 'Death Junction' crash on 28 October 1987 was only a few miles south of the spot on the same section of motorway where 13 people had been killed in a similar multiple pile-up almost exactly two years earlier, on 21 October 1985, when a coach ploughed into stationary traffic and 10 cars were demolished.

Spirits dashed by Customs' rule

Hazardous substances are carried up and down our motorways every day of the week and Lancashire's crews are used to coping with everything from spent radiation rods from nuclear power stations to chemicals and wide loads. What brought them particular grief was the day when a large truck crashed on their patch, flooding the carriageway with its gloriously reeking load of golden Scotch whisky.

The allegation that a senior officer's first message read: 'Make pumps four and ginger ale 20' was never substantiated, but there were those who swore that strong firefighters stood by with tears in their eyes as, to prevent any possible avoidance of duty being paid, Customs and Excise staff smashed hundreds of bottles of Scotland's fairest at the side of the road.

One might be forgiven for thinking that fog was the cause of most motorway RTAs. But SDO John Dobbs, whose responsibility for years has been among the fire stations on this stretch of the M6, M61 and M55, says that bright sunshine or heavy rain can prove just as much of a hazard. The only time the weather can really be blamed is after frost, when there is difficulty in manoeuvring vehicles. At other times, accidents usually happen because drivers' attention lapses, they fail to estimate the speed of other cars, the sun is in their eyes, or when traffic slows down because of road works or some other problem ahead.

The call to the particularly horrific 'Death Junction' incident had come in at 1317 hours – lunch time – on 28 October 1987 and SDO Dobbs remembered it well as a bright, sunny day. This time, crews from Chorley and Preston (whole time) and Bamber Bridge (retained) stations set off 'on the bell' with a senior officer. Experience had taught them that in any motorway incident an officer well experienced in this type of rescue was essential.

David Smith was officer in charge of the Chorley fire crews. Before they came near to the section of the road where the crash had been reported, he could see the black smoke rising like a pall over the scene. He knew, immediately, that this was going to be another bad job and was already working out in his mind how to begin coping with it.

As they arrived, he could see that most of the smoke was coming from a fuel tanker which had been involved in a collision with some sort of heavy goods vehicle carrying building material, underneath a motorway link bridge. Instinct, born of experience, flashed warning lights in his mind. The tanker's load was still intact, but the density of the smoke suggested that a lot of oil was burning somewhere close by or beneath it. In a split second, he knew that although in the smoke and chaos he couldn't see any other vehicles, they must be there and on fire.

A few motorists had escaped and were led away by ambulance personnel; four children had been flung from the back of a car and badly burned. It was not easy. There was always a risk of explosion and, added to that, the impact and the intense heat of the flames which roared up from the burning vehicles had badly damaged the bridge so that concrete was falling throughout the operation. Firemen had not only to deal with the damage on the ground but were being hit by lumps of falling masonry.

John Dobbs had arrived almost simultaneously to take command and was relieved to discover that the tanker had not been carrying petrol, which is volatile and highly flammable. Its load of diesel oil was less of an immediate problem and had not been spilt. Like David Smith he was puzzled by the number of vehicles involved. As supporting crews began to pour in, a blanket of foam was laid round the tanker in case its contents started to leak. The raging fires in the cars, which were now obviously causing much of the smoke, were dealt with by foam and cooling jets. Within minutes the main outbreaks were extinguished. Then the next horrifying stage began.

The fire had been so fierce that the cars had been fused together in a mass so tangled that at first the fire officers could

Children were among the 13 people who died when fire broke out after this collision on 21 October 1985, involving a coach on the notorious 'death stretch' of the M6 in Lancashire. Almost two years later, another crash killed 13 people in the same area of motorway. *(Lancashire County Fire Brigade)*

only count the number of wheels in an effort to work out how many vehicles had been involved. There was little chance that anyone could have survived. But because they never give up if there is even the slightest chance of someone being alive in any accident, the crews went in without hesitation and, despite the risk of exploding petrol tanks or the fuel from the tanker igniting, rescued two young girls from a crushed Datsun car. Laying them on the side of the road, they were saddened to discover that one was already dead. The second was rushed to hospital by a waiting ambulance but died soon afterwards.

The rest of the victims were so badly burned as to be virtually unrecognisable. Because of this, one fire officer and one police officer were told to take charge of the work of extricating the motorists. This was done slowly and with great care. Before any body was moved, it was labelled to identify, as far as possible, which car it had come from and who else was in that car. As they worked, the ghastly truth gradually emerged.

A pile of building blocks which had fallen from the lorry had to be removed from a Metro which had also been hit by other vehicles and then totally destroyed by fire. A 74-year-old man was cut from this wreckage.

A transit van had been sandwiched between a van and the wreckage of a Citroen and a Fiesta before being burned. Fire crews had to winch the van clear. Then, working in the still smoking wreckage, they cut the roof away and used 'spreaders' to reach the 44-year-old driver and his 28-year-old passenger. It was only as they climbed into the back of the van that they noticed the load being carried – quantities of lino tiles, still smoking, and two propane cylinders. It was like discovering a time bomb. The overheated containers could have exploded at any time. The crews – in fire service terminology – 'withdrew rapidly', and the cylinders were sprayed with water to cool them before they were safe enough for the firefighters to use a zip gun to cut away the side of the van and retrieve them. They were lifted away with breath-holding care and deposited in a temporary dam which had been erected at a safe distance to contain them under water.

After pulling the van clear, a Citroen car was discovered crushed flat under a Fiesta, a Datsun and the transit. Once more, the spreaders and cutting shears were in action before the charred remains of the driver and his wife could be gently lifted from the front seats – fused together by the flames.

Still there was evidence of another vehicle, so the Citroen was lifted out to disclose a Fiesta with, perhaps, the most poignant scene of the whole incident. Cutting away the metal with shears, and forcing the framework apart with spreaders, the crews came on the badly burned remains of what appeared to be a family outing.

In the follow-up to the crash, it emerged that the father and mother, both aged in their thirties, were taking their two young sons and their two friends out for a day at Blackpool. 'We were all upset by this', recalled SDO Dobbs, 'but it particularly hit the doctor who had attended the scene and was helping to identify the bodies later. Normally he took these things in his stride. They were cadavers and part of his job. This time, the only means of identifying the youngsters was by examining their jeans. He found that in each of their pockets was the same amount of pocket money. They'd obviously been given it before they set off happily for their day's outing. Suddenly, they became real children. He was very affected by it.'

It was just before 1800 hours when the last of this family was released and the 'stop' message was sent from yet another scene of motorway madness.

Lancashire's crews on this notorious stretch of the motorway have specialised training, but have worked out their own systems to deal with each accident as they face it. Trying to reach the scene when all three lanes are usually packed with vehicles is their nightmare. It has to be overcome by using other means of access, particularly the motorway bridges. If there is no other way of reaching the incident, crews park on the bridges and lower their equipment down before running it to the scene.

Apart from the major incidents, they are all too often faced with fires from overheated engines, carelessly dropped cigarette ends or an assortment of other causes. 'There is no particular apprehension among the men. They tend to get "battle weary" from motorway incidents. But the big ones do sometimes take a while for them to get over', said John Dobbs. 'They are obviously upset when people die, and are particularly vulnerable when children are killed, but they get it out of their systems by talking it out among themselves when they're back at the station.

'Even then, it's often just one little thing that gets to them – like the pocket money affected the doctor. With one firefighter, it was the ribbons in the hair of a little girl who had been killed in a crash. She had bright ribbons in her hair and his daughter, who was about the same age, wore ribbons in her hair too. Somehow it was the ribbons which got to him. We all kept an eye on him and tried to help him through and he eventually got over it.'

While Lancashire has plenty to occupy

> ***The villagers had been invited to see the new pumping station***

its firefighters almost daily on the motorway network, there are also general incidents to cope with. Mention Blackpool on the west coast and almost anyone's reaction would be The Tower. Not unlike the Eiffel Tower in Paris, this metal giant is a traditional landmark – but one that needs to be constantly cossetted with inspections and servicing. Of necessity, this happens when the holiday crowds have disappeared, the equally famous illuminations are finished for the season, and winter has set in.

It was on just such a day in December 1991 with a bitter, force eight gale coming off the sea and rain pouring down, that work was in progress when one of the maintenance men collapsed at the very top of The Tower, 800 foot above the promenade.

A Blackpool fire station took the call and the crews arrived only to discover that the service lifts were out of action. There was no alternative. If the man was to be rescued they had to climb a series of unguarded, raking ladders fixed inside the legs of The Tower, carrying resuscitation equipment, a first aid kit and general purpose line with them and with no protection from the elements.

Steadily, the emergency services made their way up. Steadily the others gave up but the firefighters made it to the narrow platform at the top. With the gale howling round their ears and rain beating down, they began resuscitation work, but to no avail. The man had apparently had a heart attack and was already dead. The remaining problem was how to get him down. Between them, and on the brink of hypothermia themselves, the crew slowly manhandled him down the ladder to the ground.

All five firefighters received a well-earned Certificate of Commendation for their 'courage, determination, resourcefulness and professionalism'.

The everyday call to fire in 'domestic premises' can be a false alarm or something so minor that it takes no more than a quick spray of water and an inspection to make sure that it is completely extinguished. On the other hand, it could be a matter of life or death.

It was in Preston that crews were called to a 'house fire with persons' in August 1991. They arrived to find the house burning furiously with thick smoke pouring from all the windows. In spite of the flames and intense heat, two crews wearing breathing apparatus forced their way in. Then, at great risk to themselves, they began to search for the trapped 'persons'. Scattered in four different parts of the house they found the mother and her three children. One by one, they managed to get them out of the inferno and into the cool fresh air where they immediately set about resuscitation before the ambulance arrived to take the family to hospital. Only then did the firefighters discover that the protective outer jackets of their BA had been burned off the cylinders by the intensity of the heat.

Despite their efforts the mother and one child died, but the rest recovered in hospital. An officer and seven firefighters were commended by the Chief Officer for their courage in the incident.

Lancashire crews were called out to the disastrous end of an evening trip out for villagers from the hamlet of St Michael's on Wyre on 23 May 1984. The villagers had been invited to see the new pumping station which had just been built in the lower slopes of the Pennine Hills to help deal with flood waters – always a problem in their neighbourhood.

The cheerful group travelled up from their homes in the countryside behind Blackpool and were welcomed to the Abbeystead Outfall site by local Water Board officials. There was a short introductory address and discussions on the workings of the equipment before the party of some 40 people dispersed between the Wet and Dry rooms – two

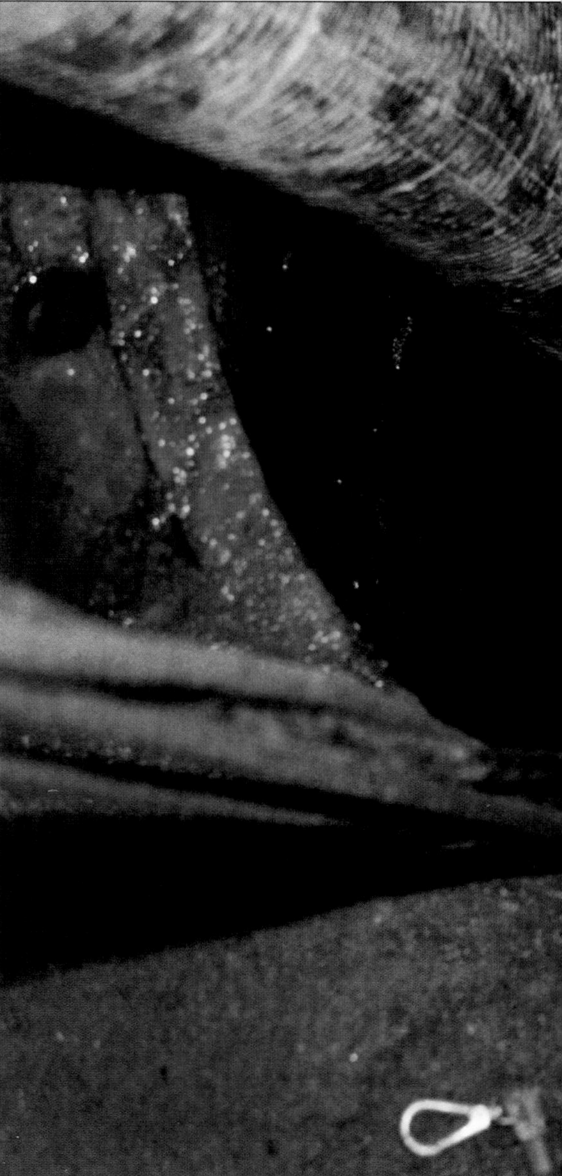

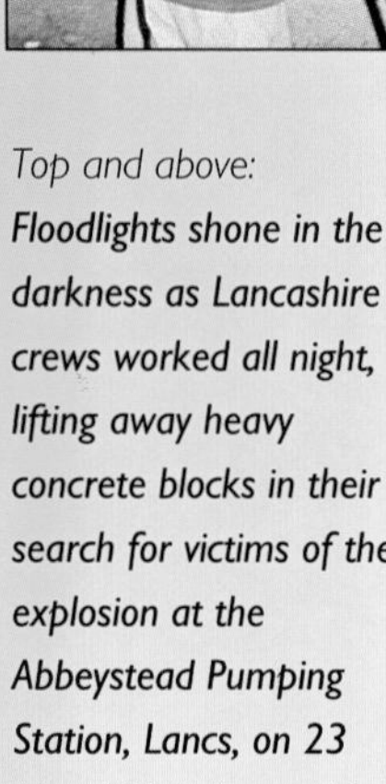

Top and above: ***Floodlights shone in the darkness as Lancashire crews worked all night, lifting away heavy concrete blocks in their search for victims of the explosion at the Abbeystead Pumping Station, Lancs, on 23 May 1984.*** *(Lancashire County Fire Brigade)*

concrete buildings – while their guide went off to telephone the pumping station and ask the operator to start the demonstration.

The operator started the first pump and his indicator showed that water was flowing through, but nothing happened at the other end. After 14 minutes the guide for the waiting visitors sent out another call to the operator telling him that the water still hadn't reached the valve house where they were waiting. To speed up the demonstration he was asked to switch to his second pump. As the visitors stood around, one or two lit cigarettes. Almost immediately there was an enormous explosion which blew the entire concrete complex to pieces. Altogether, 15 people died and 23 were injured, many severely.

So great was the force of the explosion that fire crews who had negotiated the narrow, winding lanes leading to the site, discovered some of the victims lying in nearby fields and blocks of concrete tossed aside like giant dominoes. Nobody could say how many people had been in the chambers at the time of the explosion. The first firefighters had to slide down the broken concrete roof slabs to get into the wreckage where they recovered the first live casualties, partly submerged in water and desperately clinging to the pipework.

It was dangerous work, not only for the casualties but the crews who found

No room for a helmet as this fireman eases himself and his BA down a pipe after the explosion at the Abbeystead Pumping Station. (Lancashire County Fire Brigade)

themselves slipping on the smooth surfaces as water still poured through and the struggle to release the injured continued. Retained firemen with experience of crane and tractor work were particularly valuable in the skilled task of lifting the great beams of concrete away to release the victims below. In all, they removed 30 concrete beams in the course of the rescue. Only when the fire crews and Water Authority workers had shifted tons of earth which had slid into the chambers, were they satisfied that all the bodies had been removed and the incident was closed at 1500 hours the following day.

A lengthy and detailed inquiry into the explosion concluded that the water flowing along the pipe for the first time had forced methane gas, which had penetrated the pipe, along into the chamber where the visitors had been waiting. Smoking had not been prohibited and the lighting of cigarettes had probably caused the methane to explode.

At the Abbeystead disaster, medical crews stayed on duty all night in case any rescue workers were hurt. Luckily they were not needed on this occasion, but quite frequently fire crews do get injured in the course of their work. When the crew of Burnley Fire Station reached a burning house in the town the derelict building was well alight but they could see a man waving from a window. Neighbours had tried to rescue the squatter but their ladders were too short to reach him.

Firefighter J. Sheridan realised that they could not wait for the escape to arrive. He swarmed up the builder's ladder, raked against the house wall, and went in through a window to the room where the man had been seen. In the darkness and smoke, he felt his way through until he found the victim and dragged him to safety. Sadly, the man was dead. Ff Sheridan suffered 27 per cent burns to his legs, hands and neck in the course of the rescue attempt and was detained for some time in the Burns Unit of the Royal Preston Infirmary.

The crew, and particularly Sheridan, were commended for their action at 'a very severe fire situation'.

CUMBRIA

CUMBRIA FIRE SERVICE

Like its neighbour, Northumberland, Cumbria Fire Service has a number of outdoor fires, but for them, it's more heathland – heather and scrub that burns huge areas of the fells into a black and crumbling wasteland.

The night of Monday, 29 June 1992 should have been a midsummer delight of long twilight and warm scented air. Instead, the light faded ominously early and fast as pitch black clouds rolled in. By 2100 hours, the stillness of the air was broken by a crack of thunder – the dramatic prelude for a violent electrical storm. Torrential rain lashed the whole county and as the thunder crashed and reverberated round the massive hills, a double bolt of lightning struck the ground and started fires on two areas, high on the fells. Until then, the weather had been particularly dry. The heather had dried out and, with a strong, warm easterly wind the flames spread fast.

A vigilant farmer at Newbiggin, a Mr Dixon, uneasy at the intensity of the storm, spotted the flames first and called the fire brigade. The nearest crew, Brampton, had already been called out to deal with floods brought on by the downpour so it was five men from Lazonby, the next nearest station, who arrived at the farm.

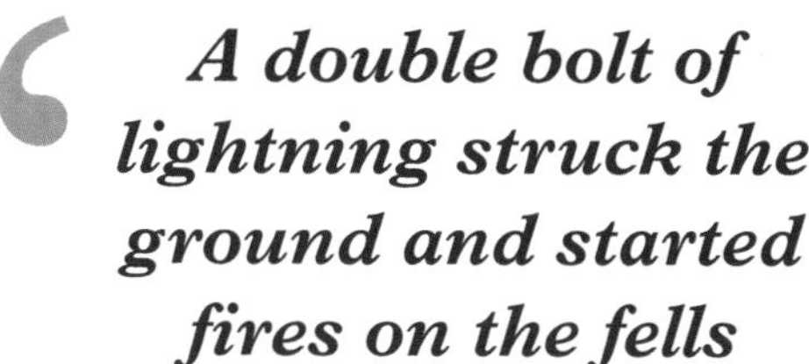
A double bolt of lightning struck the ground and started fires on the fells

Mr Dixon was waiting with transport to drive them up on to the fell and together they went into the attack, choking on the smoke as they beat out the flames. Their rapid action put out the fire in that section, but because speed and non-stop beating had been essential they had no time to report back to base on the situation. They had already spotted another outbreak further on and moved over to attack that.

The Divisional Commander was concerned at not having heard from the crew and at 2300 hours he sent a senior officer to the farm to see what was happening. As he arrived the five firefighters, by now exhausted, were being brought back by the farmer with the news that the second fire was much worse and more help was needed.

It took another six hours before that blaze was under control, but by then they could see that the first outbreak had flared up again. All through that second day, firefighters and farmers joined forces to do battle. By tea-time, as heavy rain began to fall again, everyone hoped that this, along with strategic beating, would be enough to finish the outbreaks in the next 24 hours.

Beating is an exhausting job, particularly with the smoke and the smell of charred heather in the lungs. Late in the evening a helicopter survey suggested that the rain had, indeed, done its job. The fires were out. Mist was rising and all crews were taken off the fell, making their way down the long, steep slope with care as the visibility worsened.

The 'stop' went out for both fires. Ten acres had been destroyed by one outbreak, and 100 acres in the other. The brigade heaved a sigh of relief and settled back to recover – but too soon. Once more the warning bells shrilled and the teleprinters rattled as a new call came through. This time, dense smoke was pouring from the top of Cumrew Fell, an area of outstanding natural beauty and a valuable grouse moor. This was the big one.

Farmers and firefighters scaled the fell once again and realised, immediately, that this time the fire had penetrated down into the dried-out layers of peat. Unless they could soak the ground in water they were in for a long battle, not just soaking the peat but digging it out to make sure that no 'hot spots' were left. Every bit of spare hose from all the surrounding fire stations was rushed up the fell along with new crews.

Water was short but, as so often happens with the part-timers – the retained crews who have other jobs away from firefighting – here the local knowledge, particularly by the retained crews, helped. They knew that on the far side of the fell was a stream which could give them a steady supply, but at a distance. It took 90 minutes of hard work – a remarkably short time considering the difficulty of the terrain where they were working – to set up a relay of hose and start the pumps going to carry water from the stream, across the hillside and into the burning peat through five high-powered jets.

Workshop staff stood by to make sure that the pumps kept going hour after hour all through the next night and into the following day, when fresh crews from all over the county were brought up the fell in the farmers' tractors and trailers to take over.

One of the most useful forms of transport was an all-terrain four wheel motor cycle and trailer, borrowed from a farm. This was invaluable for transporting fuel and equipment. But a JCB digger, brought in to help the crews to dig a trench as a firebreak in the peat, got bogged down so the hand-digging had to go on.

The drama continued for five days, with wearying crews and non-stop pumping until, by the following Sunday morning, the Brampton crew trudged up the fell for the last time. Four more hours of spraying and digging made sure that, at last, the fire was, indeed, dead. After six days, the 'stop' message finally went out and the cost was assessed.

A total of 113 firefighters had been deployed from 11 different stations – Aspatria, Keswick, Millom, Kendal, Staveley, Windermere, Carlisle, Penrith, Appleby, Brampton and Lazonby – fed and watered with 250 meals. Men and women firefighters were up on the fell, full-timers and retained crews – people from all kinds of backgrounds – farm hands, builders, bar staff, a vicar and a journalist among them. Totting up the equipment, they discovered that 32 lengths of hose had been damaged and needed repair out of the 205 lengths which were used. The hose relay had lasted, non-stop, for 30 hours and lifted two and quarter million litres of water into the peat. Added to that, they had used 10 light portable pumps, three controlled dividing breeches, 12 portable UHF radios, one B5 transportable VHF radio, and 22 beaters. The third fire had spread to 70 acres of land earmarked for a future National Park.

The crews were particularly saddened by the effect of the fire on the wildlife. 'We're country people', explained one firefighter. 'Everyone round here knows the birds, and this was an important nesting ground for hen harriers, merlins, peregrine falcons, golden plover, meadow pippits – a whole range of beautiful birds. It was heartbreaking to see it all blackened and dead.'

Country people they may be, but not all Cumbria is wild open space. To the western edge of the county, on the edge of the sea, stands the Sellafield nuclear facility and the Vickers nuclear submarine installation. Both have their own fire services on duty day and night, but trained by Cumbria who are always on stand-by to go in should there be any sort of incident at which their expertise might be needed. Protective clothing is kept at the ready in the plant and the county crews carry out regular training exercises with the industrial teams.

ISLE OF MAN

Mention the Isle of Man in the same breath as the word 'fire' and the reaction will be 'Summerland'.

In many ways Summerland was a pioneer – one of the first big leisure complexes in Britain, built for Trusthouse Forte Leisure Ltd to provide a wide variety of entertainment under one huge roof. The roof itself was a major talking point – transparent and made of acrylic material. Here, holidaymakers could enjoy a marquee show bar, leisure deck, and amusement arcade all connected to a solarium by open 'flying' staircases. The complex opened in July 1971 and was an instant success. Other seaside resorts vowed to imitate it. But on the evening of 2 August 1973, disaster struck.

A group of boys accidentally set fire to a dismantled kiosk on an outside terrace. It was a tiny fire, insignificant in itself, but the flames spread to the main building. What followed was the worst peace-time fire disaster in Britain for 44 years – a disaster which was to change the whole legislation governing fire safety on the island and to leave its influence on mainland Britain too.

At the height of the holiday season, families had finished their evening meal and around 1930 hours many were

Burning molten plastic falling from the ceilings, asphyxiating and explosive vapours, heat and burning debris were among the hazards facing Isle of Man firefighters in August 1973 when the Summerland leisure complex went up in flames and 50 of the 3,000 people who had been in the building were killed. (Adrian Ashurst)

> ***'More than 3,000 people were inside the building'***

strolling along the sea front, heading for an evening's entertainment in the huge, transparent building. A few minutes later, staff noticed a fire spreading along the Mini Golf terrace, raised the alarm among their colleagues in the building, and began tackling the flames with hand extinguishers. It was 20 minutes before the Island's Central Fire Control got a '999' message from a mini-cab driver to say that Summerland was on fire. This was followed quickly with a call from a ship, anchored in Douglas Bay, confirming the news.

The first appliance was already on its way before the automatic alarm from Summerland was activated in Douglas Fire Station at 2005 hours. Sub Officer Quayle, who was riding the first pump, could see that this was going to be bad and called for more back-up even before he reached the blazing building.

Inside were eight different levels. Sub Officer Quayle evacuated the downstairs and upper downstairs levels, but already the heat and burning debris falling from the roof had cut off the main solarium floor at the top. There was total confusion as scattered families tried to find each other, others tripped and fell, all slowing down the process of clearing the building.

Flames were spreading like a lightning strike across the surface of the transparent cladding. This was producing asphyxiating and explosive vapour as the plastic melted and fell in great molten globules onto the stairways and floors below.

Within nine minutes of the first call, every station on the Island had been alerted. Fifteen minutes later they were all mobile – remarkable considering that many of them were retained and volunteer crews.

Water pressure was low as all six nearby fire hydrants were opened up and water board staff rushed in to increase the flow.

Even so, and despite every effort by the fire crews, it was clear that there was no hope of saving the beautiful but flammable building. All they could do was prevent the fire from spreading to other nearby buildings including the Aquadome. In this, at least, they were successful.

By 2110 hours the fire was under control, but it was several days before minor 'hot spots' were completely extinguished. When the first flames had touched the walls, more than 3,000 people were inside the building. Although most managed to escape, 50 died in the inferno. The cost of the fire damage was £1.5 million – an immense sum in those days – added to which was the loss of the amenity for holidaymakers. But above all was the loss of life.

The Commission of Inquiry which was set up after the tragedy sat for five months. In its Report, it blamed three main reasons for the number of deaths: the rapid development of the fire; inadequate means of escape; and the evacuation of the building being 'delayed, unorganised and difficult'.

There had been no fire stops between the outer cladding and the inner lining and the multi-storey part of the building was rapidly engulfed in flames. Although there were 20 'break-glass' fire alarms in Summerland, plus seven staff fire points, all directly connected to Douglas Fire Station, it was 25 minutes after the fire started before any were actuated, and no fire alarm sounded in the building itself. A protected staircase had a permanent opening made in it which allowed smoke through. This, coupled with the failure of the emergency lighting system and the fact that the emergency doors at the bottom of the stairs were bolted, had resulted in the death of 12 people.

But out of a terrible disaster came a whole new view of the danger of fire in public places. The Commission's many recommendations brought new restrictions on the use of plastic in building. They insisted that if any fire alarm system in a public place failed to work it should immediately go into an alarm state and not be able to be switched off by unauthorised persons. Its comments on the training of architects resulted in the Royal Institute of British Architects reviewing its whole professional code of conduct and publishing a booklet of advice for architects on fire awareness.

On the Island itself, the fire service was immediately involved in a new, wide range of safety measures in theatres and public buildings. From Summerland eventually came a whole new legislation bringing powers, nationally, to cover safety and adequate means of escape in public buildings, including hotels and boarding houses.

Holidaymakers watch, horrified, from a safe distance as the Summerland leisure complex in the Isle of Man burns. (Noel Haworth)

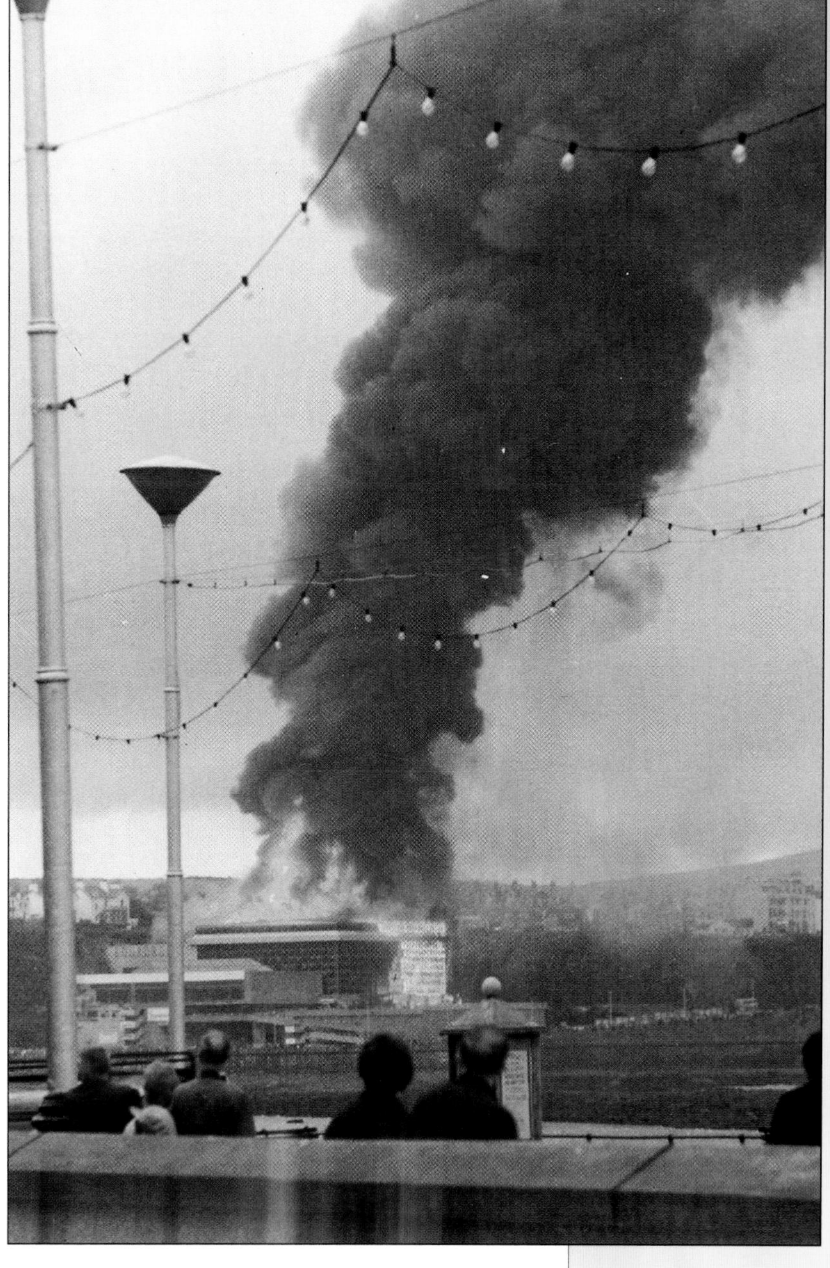

CHAPTER 9

ALL OUT FOR FIRE SAFETY

NORTHERN IRELAND

'The Fire Brigade are the protectors of this society from the hazards of fire and they provide that protection with outstanding courage. Each and every day, whatever the danger, whatever the call of duty, they demonstrate that they are totally committed to serving this community faithfully and well.'

This tribute to the firefighters of Northern Ireland came in 1993 from the Chairman of the Fire Authority for Northern Ireland, Denis Connolly OBE, for their work which covered a whole range of incidents other than those caused by the troubled times which afflict the province.

It had been a year which had seen a highly successful fire safety campaign carried out among children and adults, plus as big a variety of calls as any on mainland Britain.

There was a decrease in the number of calls of more the 2,000 over the previous year – 27,657 altogether. The service was particularly pleased at the drop in false alarms, which had fallen by 466, more than 12 per cent, a figure which they hoped would be cut still further when the 'BTOSS' – British Telecom Operator Services System – came into operation. With this, the operator can see immediately the number of the telephone from which every '999' call is made.

There was no escaping the effect of the terrorist bombing campaigns as the totally neutral fire service went in to put out fires and rescue victims, in many cases at great risk to themselves. Petrol had been sprayed from a slurry tanker at the army observation post in The Square, Crossmaglen, on 12 December 1992 and a bomb had been fastened to the tractor which had dragged it into position. Using water and foam, the fire crews managed to restrict the fire damage to the army position and a nearby shop and house.

In another incident, just before Christmas on 1 December 1992, bombers struck at 0945 hours, soon after the shops had opened, blowing up a travel agent's office in Ann Street, Belfast. The first crews to arrive found one victim, badly burned and covered in blue residue, staggering out of the building. Other workers, equally shocked, were staring helplessly from the first floor windows, trapped as the flames roared beneath them. Their main way of escape – the internal staircase – had been blown away by the explosion.

Regardless of the possible risk of other bombs in the area, firefighters pitched a ladder against the front of the building to rescue some of the trapped and injured, while others made their way in through the back and brought out the rest.

Altogether, the firefighters rescued 49 casualties. Some of them were treated by ambulance crews on the spot, but 27 had to be taken to hospitals with shock, burns, cuts, bruises and smoke inhalation.

The firefighters of the province face plenty of other incidents too. Fire in the unusual modern church of Legahory, at Brownlow, Lurgan, brought a particular hazard for the crews on 3 February 1993. One of the church's main features was its long, steeply sloping roof rising from some 18 feet (5 metres) at the side to nearly 60 feet (18 metres) at the top, which was well alight when the firefighters arrived. Despite this, they managed to contain it, but some 60 per cent was damaged in the outbreak. Although the efforts to put out the fire involved climbing on the steeply raked roof, there were no accidents.

On a lighter note, fire crews from all over Northern Ireland combined in the 'Thumbs up on Monday' campaign, designed to encourage everyone living there to install a smoke alarm and to test it by putting a thumb on the test button every Monday. The idea caught on, more smoke alarms were installed, and for many Ulster men, women, and children, Monday became 'Thumbs up' day.

Above: Thumbs up plus a cheerful smile from Paul McCambridge of Abercorn Primary School, Banbridge, C. Down, as he takes part in the Northern Ireland Fire Brigade's campaign for 'Thumbs up on Monday' to encourage people to press the button on their smoke alarms every Monday to make sure these are still working. (Northern Ireland Fire Brigade)

Oops! But it was no joke when this tanker, full of petrol, failed to take a bend and crashed through the parapet of a bridge at Ederney, Irvinestown, in October 1992, to hang suspended above the river flowing below the road. Firefighters, including one perched on the near perpendicular top of the tanker, risked their lives to prevent it from bursting into flame as they siphoned the bulk of its load into another vehicle before hauling the stranded truck back on to the road. (Northern Ireland Fire Brigade)

> **'Petrol had been sprayed from a slurry tanker at the army observation post, Crossmaglen'**

CHAPTER 10

OVER THE BORDER

SCOTLAND

DUMFRIES AND GALLOWAY

Time was when the country on either side of the England-Scotland border was one of feuds and fighting. Today, Cumbria, in the northernmost part of England, and Dumfries and Galloway, the most southerly area of south west Scotland are – mostly – good friends. Certainly the two fire authorities are always ready to help each other if the need arises. In 1988, the need arose.

Few areas of Britain could be more tranquil than Dumfries and Galloway. Field after field of contented cattle munch their way through the seasons. Sturdy granite and stone houses dot the landscape, many of them fortified like small castles to withstand the stormy raids of the border territory in the past.

Today, trucks from north, south and east trundle along the motorways. The A75 Euroroute from Ireland to Europe comes ashore at Stranraer and Cairnryan, cutting across the south of the region. The A74 links the border between Carlisle, in England, and Glasgow on the Clyde. The Solway, with its long sandy shores, attracts summer tourists to this homeland of 'Rabbie' Burns, Scotland's famous poet. To the west lie the rollers of the Atlantic.

Apart from its motorway incidents, many of this fire authority's 'shouts' are to house and industrial fires, and particularly farm incidents. Typically, in recent years, one of the more memorable fires damaged two shops in the centre of Dumfries when 300 bales of straw fell off a trailer and ignited. Within minutes, choking smoke poured off and much of the town centre was closed while the firefighters worked to dodge the tumbling bales and douse the flames.

In an equally typical local 'shout', a pregnant mare which had been up to her neck in a ditch of water all night, was rescued by firefighters who struggled in the slime until they managed to get a couple of hoses beneath her and haul her to dry land. Three weeks later, the mare gave birth to a pretty foal which, in graceful tribute to its saviours, was named 'Firefighter'.

To the east of the Region lies Lockerbie, population 3,500. This is so small a town that driving along the A74 or sitting in the main line train to London, you can take it all in at a glance, brick-built houses, church, garage, gardens and all round, fields and bleak hillsides, sliced by the A74.

Any incident involving death is sad, but the disaster that hit Lockerbie was particularly shocking. A few seconds either way would, at least, have saved the town. That was not to be.

The date was 21 December 1988. The time just after 1900 hours. All over Britain families were preparing for Christmas, wrapping parcels, decorating the tree, delighting over cards. The Pan Am 747 jumbo jet *Clipper Maid of the Seas*, Flight 103, had taken off late from London's Heathrow Airport with its 259 passengers and crew, heading north for Scotland before veering west and crossing the Atlantic, destination John F. Kennedy Airport, New York.

Most of the travellers had settled down in their seats and were cheerfully anticipating pre-Christmas drinks and a leisurely dinner as the plane crossed the Scottish border 38 minutes into the journey. The lights of Gretna Green twinkled below as it reached 31,000 feet and the pilot prepared to head west. In all this open land, it had to be directly above the small market town of Lockerbie when the bomb, hidden in the hold, exploded.

There were no survivors.

Eye-witnesses speak of aviation fuel and blazing debris raining down from a great fireball in the sky. Within seconds, the fuselage and both wings had thundered into the neat roofs and gardens of Sherwood Crescent, Rosebank Crescent and Park Place, Lockerbie. An above-ground tank holding 15,000 litres (3,300 gallons) of diesel burst into flames at the Townfoot Garage, with fire spreading to a tyre store, an adjoining garage workshop and an assortment of cars.

The cockpit thudded to earth three miles away in a field near Tundergarth Church. The explosion as it hit the ground made a crater 140 feet (43 metres) long by 49 feet (13 metres) wide and up to 29 feet (6 metres) deep. Through all the wide border country, pieces of metal and the bodies of innocent passengers were coming to rest in back gardens, fields and forests from the Atlantic coast almost to the North Sea, so violent was the blast. On the A74 two cars and a van were hit and their occupants ran for their lives. In Sherwood Crescent, Lockerbie, 11 people were killed instantly.

As the rumbling of the crash and the falling debris calmed, there was no need to call out the emergency services. They were already racing to the scene and sending out for help from the rest of the region and beyond.

Dumfries and Galloway Fire Brigade had only one whole-time fire station and 16 retained (part-time) stations, one of them in Lockerbie plus two volunteer units. Scheduled as a 'D' risk it could normally have expected a fire appliance within 20 minutes. Its own equipment comprised a single water tender/ladder appliance manned by one Sub Officer, one retained Leading Fireman and eight retained Firemen. If it needed more, it called in. Tonight the call was loud and intense and not just from the professionals.

The first message to Dumfries HQ came as the debris was still clattering down at 1904 hours when a member of the public grabbed a telephone and reported 'a huge boiler explosion at Westacres, Lockerbie'.

Another followed immediately, telling of 'an explosion and ball of fire at the Express Dairy cheese factory'. More bombarded the exchange with tales of the fireball in the sky and the havoc it had wrought. It was the wife of an off-duty fireman who reported a plane crash.

Action was instant. Even in so rural an area, preparations had been made for this remote possibility. Within minutes, as crews and administrative staff began to pour into the local fire stations, the 'Major Incident Plan' went into operation.

Lockerbie's own appliance had already made its way through the debris and was reporting 'In Attendance'.

Remarkably, an assortment of fire brigade personnel, including officers, happened to have been visiting friends in the area and raced to the site of the crash to make the first assessment and begin evacuating families. It was essential not only to deal with the incident but to check the railway line. Debris on the express track and an unsuspecting driver could have added a second disaster to the first. Then,

'Most of the travellers were cheerfully anticipating pre-Christmas drinks and dinner'

This map of Lockerbie shows where the wreckage of the bomb-shattered Boeing fell on and near the small Scottish town, and where the sources of water supply were positioned. The main A74 road between Glasgow and Carlisle lies to the west (left) and the railway line passes through the centre. (Illustration: Courtesy the Firemaster, Dumfries and Galloway Fire Brigade)

too, there was this strong smell of gas. The mains had been ruptured and here was another potential explosion.

Much expert help was needed and much came. From Dumfries, from Lothian and Borders and Strathclyde the blue lights came flashing while the two-tones of the Cumbrian Fire Service echoed across the Esk as their headlights picked out the 'Welcome to Scotland' sign. Never were the Sassenachs more welcome.

Within half an hour there were 15 and then 20 appliances and crews, all struggling to put out the fires and save who they could from the wreckage. At first it was feared that there might be as heavy a death toll on the ground as had come from the air, but amazingly, only 11 people were killed, and the caravan of ambulances took a total of only five people off to hospital.

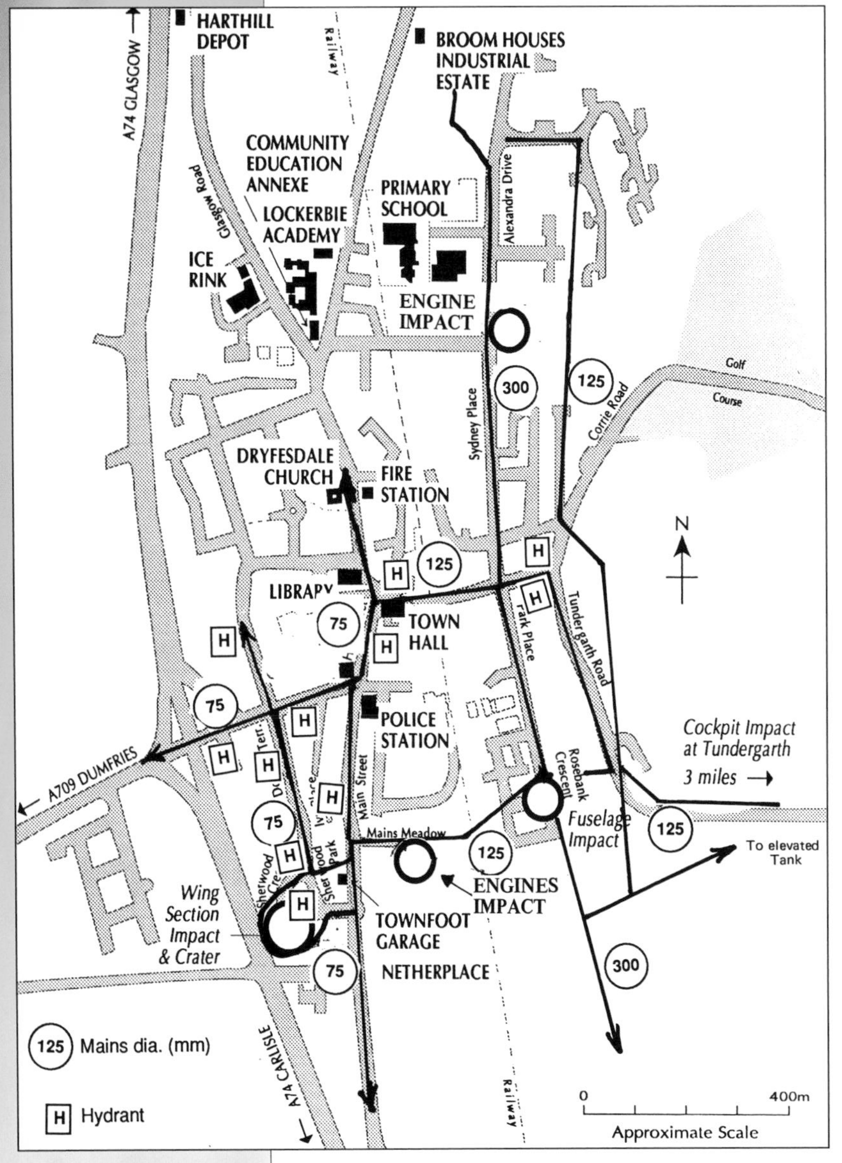

Water was at a premium. The town had no nearby lake or river, the three-inch water main had been destroyed, and fires had been started over an area of 1,000 feet (330 metres) downwind of the crash. Every kind of water container was pressed into service including, at one stage a fleet of milk tankers. Firefighters with police, residents and later, servicemen, fought together to put out as many outbreaks as they could and to rescue as many people as possible. As house after house was searched, confirmed as empty or had its occupants rescued, a piece of timber was placed against each doorway – like some medieval plague cross – a sign to other firefighters that this had been dealt with. Later, reflective tape was fastened across the doors.

Bit by bit the pictured emerged. A huge section of the fuselage with both wings attached had landed on two houses in Sherwood Crescent. The cockpit and forward fuselage had come down three miles east of the town. One of the four engines was embedded in the road by the primary school, three more had landed in open ground close to the railway lines. Two were still on fire and were extinguished by firemen using high pressure hose-reels and portable fire extinguishers, another was cooled off by firemen with a hose-reel, and the fourth posed no fire risk. Bodies, or pieces of bodies of the passengers had fallen throughout the area, making the work of the rescuers even more harrowing.

As the flames died down and with all the survivors accounted for, the gruesome task of gathering up the bodies of the passengers began with extricating the human remains from the cockpit and front fuselage. It was to last for many weeks, and from every part of this wild countryside. In all, 259 passengers and crew and 11 local residents died in the massacre of Lockerbie.

For the firefighters, counselling ser-

Firefighters help in the sad and gruesome work of removing bodies from part of the fuselage of the crashed Boeing as police join them in using salvage sheets to screen the operation from public view. (Courtesy the Firemaster, Dumfries and Galloway Fire Brigade)

vices were set up to help with any trauma effects following their experiences. In his full report on the disaster, the Firemaster noted that two-thirds of the fire service personnel engaged on the incident were retained, but of all the firefighters involved, only a small number made use of the counselling services and help lines.

The Queen, the Prime Minister, Mrs Margaret Thatcher, and the Secretary of State for Scotland, Mr Malcolm Rifkind, all sent their sympathy to the bereaved and praised the work of Lockerbie's heroic rescuers.

LOTHIAN AND BORDERS

Edinburgh boasts the first municipally maintained fire brigade in the whole of Britain. The fire service goes back to a disastrous blaze on 3 February 1700 which damaged or destroyed the greater part of the city. The City Fathers were reported to be 'shocked into thought' and after two years of thinking, they took action. On 21 April 1703 they passed an Act authorising the formation of 'a Company for Quenching of Fire and Rules to be observed by the inhabitants thereanent'.

Among the items it called for were 12 Firemasters, 'each Firemaster having in his hand a batton...and a large hand axe, made with luffs nailed to the shaft, and a sledge hammer, with a hand saw, all marked with the town's mark...' Barrels and 300 buckets of water were to be made available, every citizen was to keep a supply of water in his house for fire extinguishing and occupiers of tenements (some of them were 14 storeys high) had to provide themselves with ropes the height of the building, plus an extra 'four fathoms' to allow for those who could not slide and had to be tied in and lowered. A 'brigade' of auxiliary firefighters was also to be established.

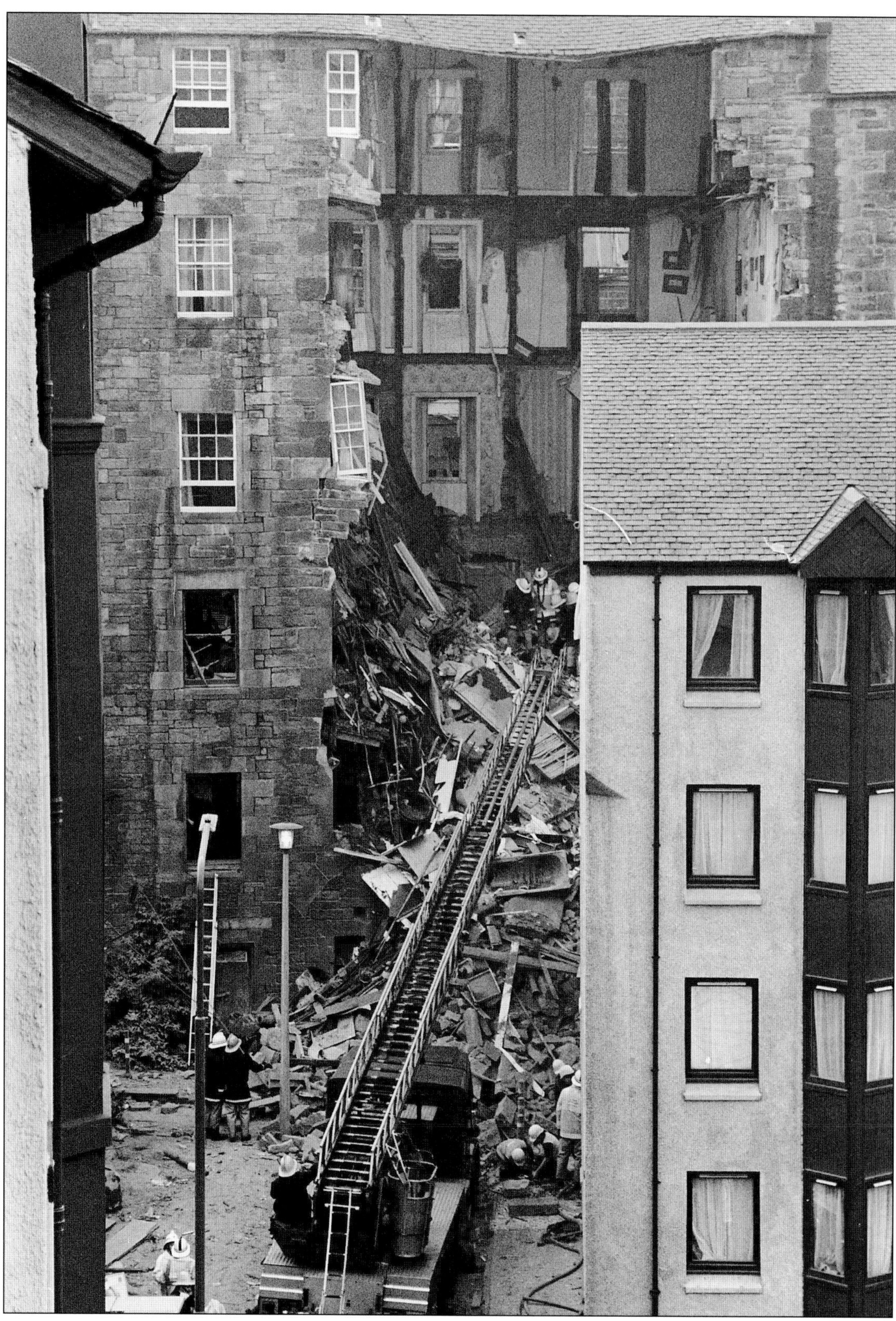

Leaking gas caused the explosion which wrecked this tenement block in Guthrie Street, Edinburgh, in October 1989. Fire crews worked to rescue residents buried in the wreckage, with a fine disregard for their own safety as windows and loose stonework teetered above them. (Lothian and Borders Fire Brigade)

In 1824 another major fire, known as the Great Fire of Edinburgh, destroyed much of the centre of the city. It was following this that the Police Commission was asked to persuade the City Fathers to finance what was to become the first municipally funded fire brigade in the UK. Its leader was a well educated young man called James Braidwood, son of a cabinet-maker but trained as a surveyor.

He was given the title of 'Master of Fire Engines', later to revert to the older title of 'Firemaster of Edinburgh' (which continued until the 1990s when, for political correctness, it was scheduled by the British Government to be changed to 'Chief Fire Officer' in 1996).

A brilliant organiser who became an equally effective fire engineer, he organised and honed his brigade until 1832 when he travelled south to command the combined insurance fire brigades of London and, as the first Chief Fire Officer, build them into the London Fire Engine Establishment. Braidwood was killed by a falling wall as he led the attack on one of the capital's most devastating warehouse fires at Tooley Street on the banks of the Thames. His death precipitated the setting up of London's first municipally funded fire service, the Metropolitan Fire Brigade, to be followed throughout the country by many more cities.

Since then Edinburgh, like other cities, has suffered from the fires brought about by its sheer development. In recent years, the Festival and the growth of Scotland's tourist industry has brought a fair spate of hotel and restaurant fires as well as several incidents in bars and night clubs. An ongoing headache has been its high tenement buildings. In the earliest days, the city was surrounded by a wall within which most of the homes were built. When space ran out, they built upwards. The tall and tightly packed 'closes' and 'wynds' have always caused problems for the city's firefighters.

A startling incident involving these tenements began early on the morning of Wednesday, 4 October 1989 at 27 Guthrie Street, Edinburgh, with the simple and innocent switching on of a light by a resident. The slight spark it produced was enough to ignite the gas which had apparently been leaking from a fractured main and caused an almighty explosion. The first of six calls to Lothian and Borders Fire Brigade rang out soon after 0700 hours. It would be more than 50 hours before the 'stop'.

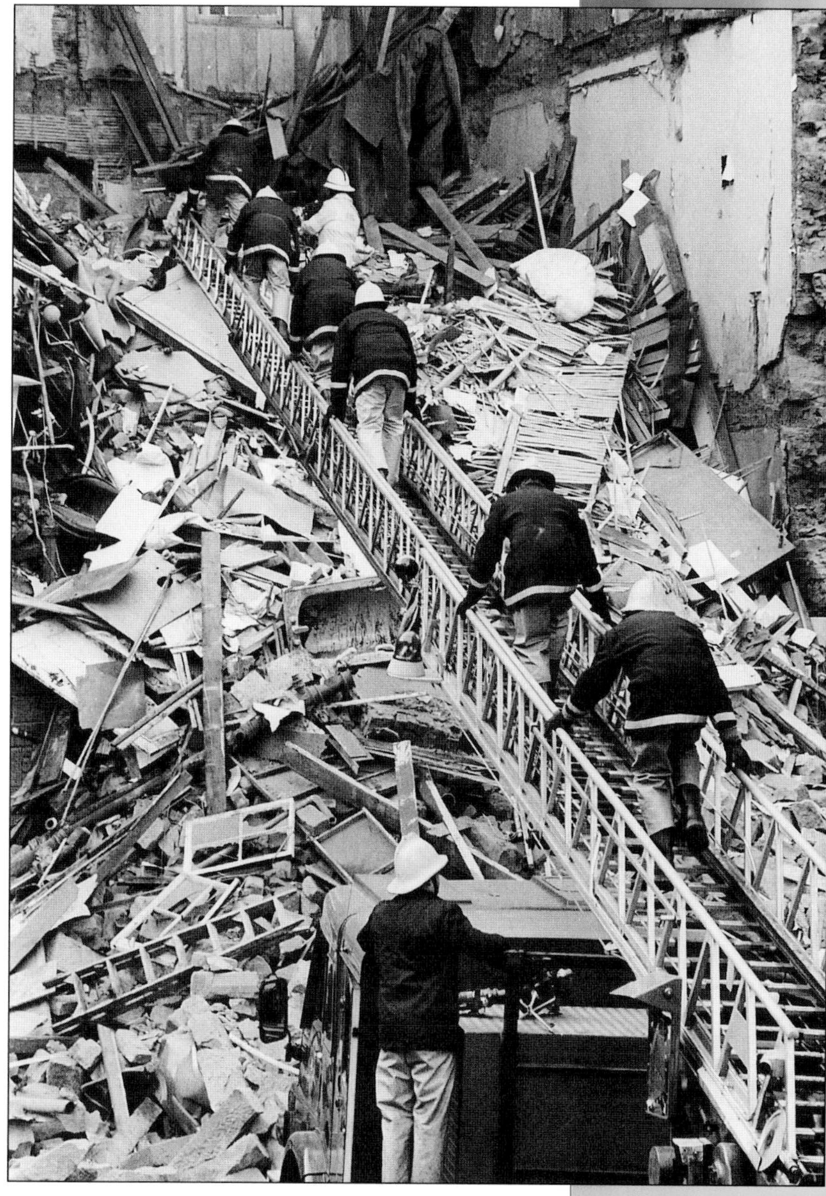

Regardless of the risks of falling masonry, Edinburgh firefighters use a turntable for a bridge as they continue their rescue work after the Guthrie Street explosion in 1989. (Lothian and Borders Fire Brigade)

For a brief moment they thought it might be an exercise – one had by coincidence been planned for 0800 hours that day. Any such illusion disappeared rapidly as Red Watch from Tollcross and MacDonald Road pulled in to Guthrie Street. Following the explosion, the five-storey building had collapsed in a mountain of rubble with the families, who had been having breakfast and starting the day, buried below.

Without knowing whether there might be another explosion the firefighters, joined by back-up crews, piled in and quickly dug out one victim. By now, there was not only the risk of further explosions but lumps of masonry were beginning to

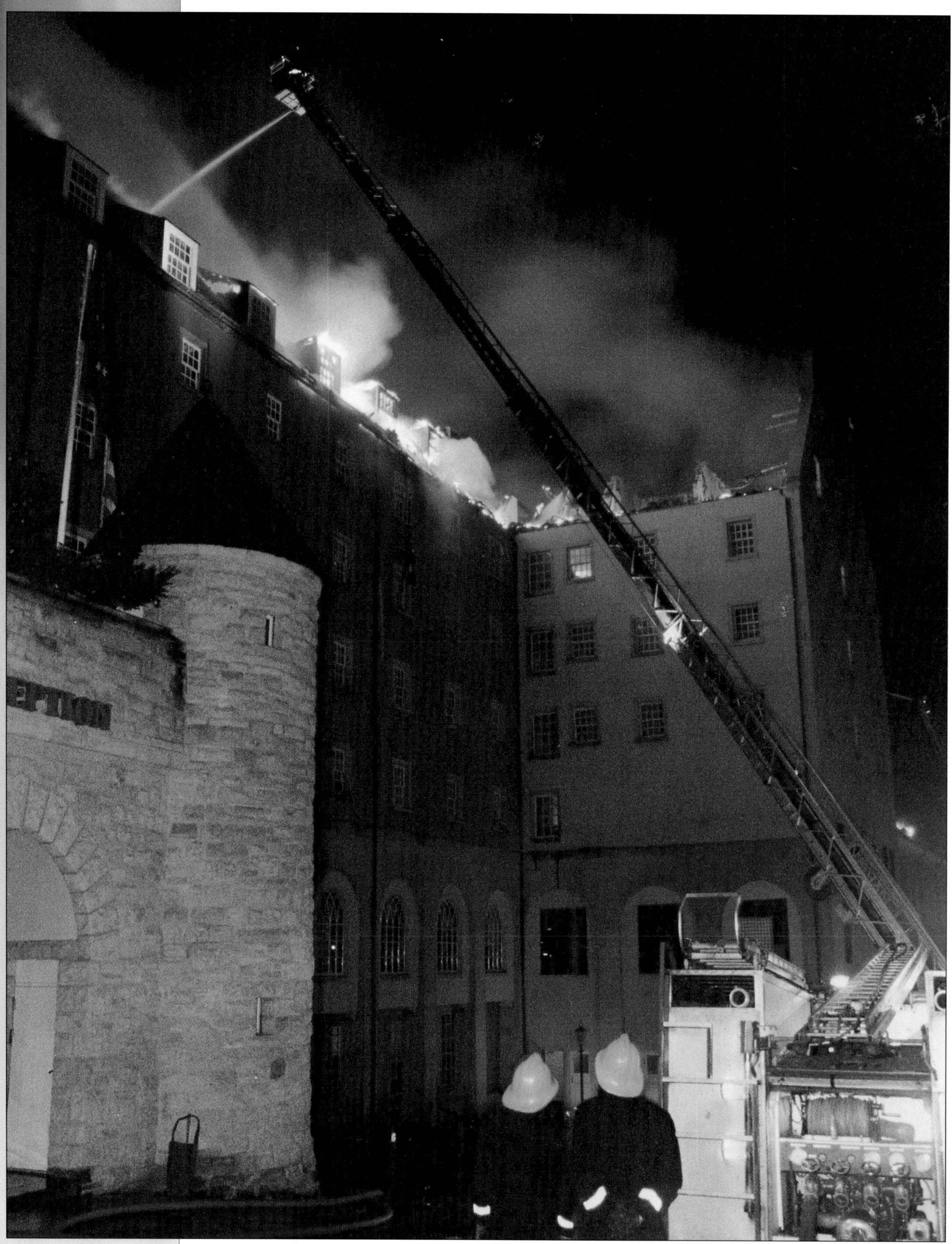

Opposite: ***The Scandic Crown Hotel in Edinburgh at the height of the pre-Christmas fire on 20 December 1992, which damaged its roof and top floors. More than 200 guests were evacuated but nobody was injured in the incident.*** (Lothian and Borders Fire Brigade)

Fireman's raffle prize went up in flames

All through the previous week there had been intense security at the Scandic Crown Hotel, in the heart of Edinburgh, when it was filled with overseas delegates for the European Summit Meeting. Now it was over, the delegates had gone, and the hotel was full of pre-Christmas guests. Fire chiefs began to relax. Then, in the small hours of 20 December 1992, fire broke out in the ducting in the roof space, damaging much of the roof and upper floors of the hotel.

Firefighters and management successfully evacuated the residents, although 12 reported missing meant that every room had to be searched by crews, while the rest fought the fire, before it could be assumed that the absent guests had simply been out all night.

For one firefighter from Tollcross Fire Station, the first to attend, it was a particularly bitter occasion as he helped rake over the ashes. On the previous evening the station had held its Christmas party. He had been delighted to win first prize in the raffle – dinner for two at the Scandic Crown Hotel...

Station Officer David Cooper of Edinburgh and his specially made, life-size puppet Bright Spark put across the message of fire safety to children in day nurseries and primary schools of Lothian and Borders. David has produced a tape of nursery rhyme style fire safety songs which he and a fellow firefighter, Brian Chisholm, have composed for the younger children. There is also a 'rock' number for teenagers. They hope that the music will help create a new generation which respects the danger of fire. (Lothian and Borders Fire Brigade)

tumble from the walls and the roof threateningly bowed.

To speed the rescue work and prevent more harm to anyone still buried below, the crews ran out a turntable ladder across the site, using it as a bridge to crawl over as, in turn, they extricated a further four, alive, from the debris, and two more who had been killed in the fall. It had been a long, dangerous and exhausting episode.

The City has its share of road accidents, its suicides and its household and hotel fires. High on the list for action though, is what they call 'Back to Front Firefighting' – stopping fires from starting. It targets four main points: Loss of Life, Loss of Property, Wilful Fire Raising (arson), and Malicious Calls.

To do this, the fire brigade has got together with the schools and local authorities to teach children, particularly, about the hazards of fire.

They start young, in the nursery schools, and from then the youngsters have lessons in fire prevention at intervals all through their school lives.

Helping with this is Station Officer David Cooper. Dave, a popular figure, has strong feelings about children and fire. So much so that he has written words and music for songs which warn children about fire with music they might hear on top TV shows. For nursery school toddlers, there's *The Get-Out Song*, with its warning: 'Don't try to hide, don't be scared to tell your mum or dad, if there's smoke around, get down on your hands and knees.' Particularly popular with small children is the action song *Firefighters*, written by colleague Brian Chisholm. This starts with 'Five firefighters climbing up a ladder', and the children pretend to climb, continuing down to 'one firefighter drives the engine back to the station', with the whole class making the 'nee-naw' sound of the two-tone.

For the teenagers who, so often, get their kicks from making false alarms,

Scooshers would fit into narrow corners

Glasgow's famous 'Scooshers' were unique in many ways, not least for the fact that when other fire engines were content to flash their blue beacons, Scooshers flashed red, white and blue.

These unusual small fire appliances were built specially for Glasgow Fire Brigade in 1968 by Dennis Bros of Guildford. Until then, the Tinderbox City, as it was known for its constant fires in everything from tenements to heavy industrial sites, had used normal size fire engines. Now it was faced with manoeuvring its appliances around the pedestrian walkways, sharp corners and overhanging balconies of the new, 25-acre Anderson Complex of tower blocks of flats with commercial buildings below.

The answer was the MK I Scoosher – named after the Glasgow slang word for a water pistol. The city's firemen were well accustomed to 'slooshing down' with water. Now they had the machine to do it. Scooshers' unique design provided for a tubular metal hose with a knuckle-type joint which folded into a small space alongside the ladders. The narrow wheel-base machine could wiggle into narrow spaces, slip the ladders off and unfold the boom which was topped with an equally unusual head. This included an infra-red heat detector which could identify exactly where the seat of the fire was located. It would then ring a bell and the operator could, if necessary, use a sword-like implement, fastened alongside the nozzle, to break windows before turning on the water and hitting the fire on target – at the same time saving water and water damage.

Alas, the gallant little Scoosher lasted for only seven years before Glasgow became part of the new, bigger Strathclyde brigade. The Scooshers quietly disappeared and the last one to be seen was in use as a rain machine on a film location.

Falling whisky barrels crushed a turntable ladder as firemen ran for their lives after the explosion at the Arbuckle Smith warehouse. (Glasgow Fire Service)

there's a sequence of heavy rock music with a plaintive 'don't make that call' theme. The whole scheme is now under way and Edinburgh is looking forward to the day when a new generation of fire-aware adults will make it one of the less busy areas for fire calls.

FIFE

Whisky stores, the old linoleum industry in Kircaldy (now mainly manufacturing floor coverings with a plastic base), heavy engineering, flour milling and one of the larger processors of oats for Scotland's famous porridge are all among the potential hazards facing Fife Fire and Rescue Service in an area of 508 square miles, much of which is farm land and forests. Add to that the Navy's nuclear submarine depot at Rosyth, the RAF airfield at Leuchars, and the giant petrochemical complex at Mossmorran, near Cowdenbeath, and there is more than enough to keep its crews busy throughout the year.

But it was a different problem that led to White Watch at Rosyth Fire Station being called out late on the night of 2 April 1991. Maintenance work was in hand on the long road bridge which crosses the Firth of Forth just west of Edinburgh and in the darkness, one of the workmen had fallen from the scaffolding erected around the north tower. He could have tumbled to his death in the waters of the river, far below, but instead, had somehow landed on a girder beneath the carriageway and hung there now, helpless, as two of his colleagues managed to climb down and secure him, but were not able to get him up again.

Two of the Rosyth crew, Firefighters Martin Hargreaves and David McBride, volunteered to be lowered down on Rollgliss line rescue gear and after consulting ambulance personnel, decided to raise

> ***'One of the workmen had fallen from the scaffolding'***

him and his two mates to the road level using the same apparatus. Despite the darkness and a high wind, they carried out the rescue safely and comparatively calmly until boats arrived below the bridge and turned on their searchlights. Only then did the two firefighters look down and realise how far below the water was – and how nervous they suddenly felt!

CENTRAL REGION

In neighbouring Central Region, industrial incidents have, again, caused grief for local fire services. Among its biggest industrial areas, Alloa has the United Glass Company's huge works – certainly the biggest glassworks in Britain and probably in Europe – where, from time to time and despite all precautions, the bottom falls out of a furnace. When this happens, up to 600 tons of molten glass flows out.

This can only be stopped by the fire service, who direct hoses on it to solidify the glass. Although there are no flames or fumes to deal with, there is one major hazard peculiar to these incidents. The glass is so hot that the water boils as it hits the flow. In saving the town from the torrent of glass, a number of firefighters have suffered scalds to their feet as the steaming water reached boiling point and splashed, agonisingly, into their boots.

Further north in the Region, the great oil refinery at Grangemouth has had its problems in the past, generally dealt with quickly by its own fire crews. But there was one occasion in particular when the local fire brigade was asked to help.

A maintenance worker had collapsed half way up the outside of a 200 foot (61 metres) chimney at BP's Grangemouth refinery and was seen from the ground to be swinging loose from the outside ladder, held only by his safety belt. Although a colleague had gone up to help him, more support was needed. With great courage, a Falkirk firefighter, Craig Beauchop, set out on the long climb, in a high wind, and took over from the man's mate. Unfortunately the 35-year-old worker was already dead, but the problem remained of getting him down to ground level. There was only one answer – a helicopter – and while they were waiting for it to come, both the friend and the firefighter stayed with the body until it was safely lifted away.

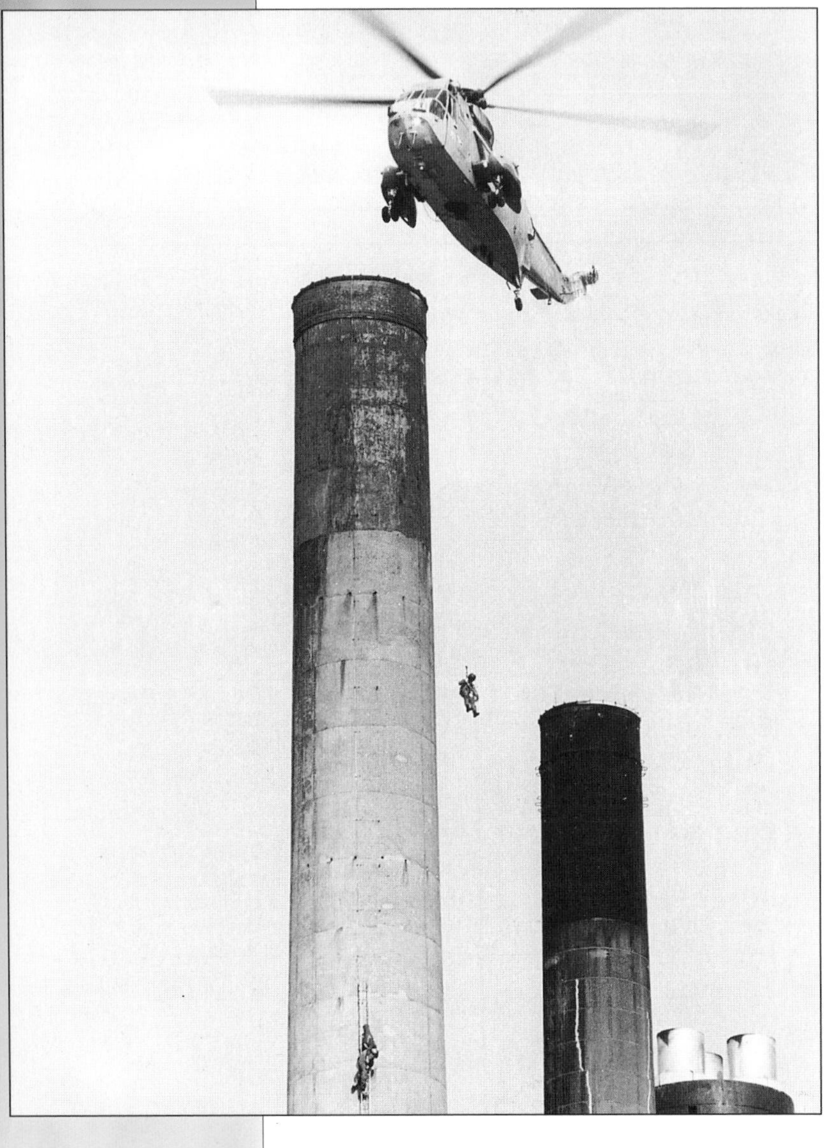

A Royal Navy helicopter team from Prestwick hovers above the 200 foot chimney at BP's Grangemouth refinery as a winchman is lowered to rescue a 35-year-old maintenance worker, Malcolm McKittrick, who collapsed while he was half-way up. One of his colleagues and Firefighter Craig Beauchop of Falkirk Fire Station, supported him until he was winched to safety. (Central Region Fire Brigade)

TAYSIDE

Jute, Jam and Journalism have, for years, been Dundee's main claim to fame. But while jute fires have been a major nightmare for the fire brigades over the years, it was whisky which brought one of the worst disasters ever, when the six-storey bonded store of James Watson, distillers, went up in flames in July 1906. It was surrounded by equally high buildings holding provisions for a co-op, a printing works and a tobacco manufacturer, so it was essential that the fire should be controlled as fast as possible.

With outstanding courage, the firefighters went into action, sweating over their manual and steam pumps to pour water into the blazing storehouse despite the threat of explosion. It was an hour after the fire started that a vat containing 1,000 gallons of whisky blew up, smashing every window in the surrounding area and pouring down the side of the warehouse 'with a roar like Niagara'. All the residents in nearby tenement buildings were evacuated and the firefighters continued gallantly. But, according to the local paper, the *Dundee Advertiser*, they were confronted by an amazing scene which must have reduced strong Scotsmen to tears:

'Slowly creeping to the outmost recesses of the building, the fire...gained access to the large store of liquor housed in the south west corner. As the bottles cracked and the casks burst the liquor poured in large streams from the many windows. The whisky, which was on fire, was a beautiful sight as it fell to the streets in a variety of colours, sometimes purple, occasionally blue of different shades and, again, red. A river of blueish flame, many yards in width, rushed down Trades Lane towards Dock Street and the more the firemen drenched it with water, the more it burned'.

The total fire loss, despite the efforts of the firemen, was £400,000 – a great deal of money in 1906.

Jute fires still present a particular hazard. The bales absorb water, expand rapidly, burst their ties, tumble apart and can buckle walls, eventually bringing down the entire building.

Usually a brigade can expect a fire to be extinguished within 24 hours – sometimes longer – but for the Central Region and Fife firefighters it was a remarkable six days before the 'stop' came at 1318 hours on Sunday, 11 July 1993, for a callout at 1247 hours on the previous Monday, 5 July.

It had started quietly enough with word of some timber scaffolding planks on fire at the coal fired Longannet Power Station, Kincardine, on the northern shores of the River Forth. Crews from Rosyth and Dunfermline in Fife Fire and Rescue Service and Alloa from nearby Central Region, were the first to attend only to find that the works' fire team had coped with the burning planks. However, like all good firefighters, they were curious to discover what had set the planks on fire in the first place, so investigated further. They were not happy to find a hopper containing 20 tonnes of PFA (pulverised fuel ash) designed to extract ash from the flue gases before they went up the chimney and into the atmosphere, was alight. That was not all. The hopper was one of a bank of 48 similar containers and a further 11 were already burning.

It was not only going to be a long process but also a dangerous one. The scene of the operation was at the 60 feet (18 metres) level of the plant. It was not possible to empty the hoppers normally without the risk of spreading the fire. Spraying water on the surface of the hoppers from a higher level would form a crust on top of the coal dust which would prevent it from reaching the lower levels which were burning. This might also produce water gas, a mixture of hydrogen and carbon monoxide, which could cause an explosion.

Jute fires are always a problem for Dundee's firefighters – here the bales are smouldering, swelling and falling as the crews struggle to play their hoses on the fire. (Tayside Region Fire Brigade)

Conveniency – hardly used

Organised firefighting was slow in coming to old Dundee. It seems that it was not until 1775 that the City Fathers invested in firefighting equipment, noting in a manuscript of the period that 'this town is accommodated by two sets of Water Engines for the extinguishing of fires when they break out in the place. This is a conveniency we do not wish to find much use for'.

Chilly workmen lit fire – inside building

Workmen stripping out a disused warehouse, due to be refurbished as flats and offices in the centre of Dundee, found the building too chilly for their liking. So they lit a rubbish fire to keep themselves warm – inside the building.

When they returned from lunch, later, the fire had taken all too well, flames were belching from the upper windows and traffic had stopped while fire crews tackled the inferno from all sides. The fire achieved more than the demolition men – the building collapsed leaving only two floors standing.

Their only safe option was to open a sliding inspection door by using ropes which firefighters could operate from a safe distance and gradually empty the hoppers in a carefully controlled operation. A third firefighter was positioned near the hole with a poker to dislodge any larger material which might slow down the emptying process. Meanwhile, two monitors, water sprays and two hand jets were set up near the slide opening to dampen the burning material as it emerged from the hoppers and to spray the firefighters working there.

The crews had to wear breathing apparatus, work in hot, wet and filthy conditions and could only empty one container at a time before handing on to a relief crew. At intervals, the site chemist, in BA, would go into the hoppers to check by analysing the gas, which hoppers were in most urgent need of being dealt with. The firefighters would confirm this with a thermal imaging camera and their special gas detection equipment.

The work continued, day and night. At several stages there were crises, including one when the smouldering coal dust, pouring from the hopper, escaped with a

Workmen, trying to keep warm, lit a fire inside this building, then went off to lunch. The resulting fire brought more warmth than they had bargained for and a total standstill to Victoria Road, Dundee, in 1993. (The Courier, Dundee)

sudden rush, engulfing four firefighters in a cloud of hot dust which burned their ears and feet. They were all taken to hospital after being treated at the site by the Service Occupational Health Nurse who had been monitoring the conditions under which the firefighters were working.

There was all round relief when finally, the slow, patient but effective procedure paid off and all the fires were reported to be completely extinguished – in time for Sunday dinner.

Fire on Friday 13 April 1962 brought tragedy for the Angus Fire Brigade (later to form part of Tayside Region) in a jute warehouse in Constitution Street, Dundee. More than 2,000 bales of jute were in the building as the fire crews went into action, and 51-year-old DO John Buist who, ironically, specialised in the technique of fighting jute fires, was killed underneath an avalanche of falling bales. 'His specialised knowledge together with his character, which showed great courage and determination, makes his untimely death a great loss,' said the Firemaster, John Jackson.

Two younger firefighters had dived between the bales as jute cascaded round them and lay terrified for six minutes, listening as more bales fell, six inches of water gathered on the floor beneath them and their breathing apparatus gave out. Only the courage of other firefighters in hammering a small hole in a corrugated iron gable, finding the two men and dragging them out from under the smouldering bales as the whole pile collapsed, prevented a death toll of three in the incident.

Thirty years later, in February 1992, Dundee's crews were faced with a similar fire in the packed Manhattan Works jute warehouse after a fork lift truck started a major blaze. Fire chiefs who, at first, feared that they were in for a three-day operation, sighed with relief as the crews worked non-stop throughout one night and extinguished the fire, losing 150 tons but saving 350 tons of the fibre. There was particular praise for a three-man Dundee Plant team who had worked throughout the night driving a JCB that dragged the smouldering bales from the burning warehouse and dumped them on a tip, clear of the building. Supplies to the shopfloor next day were assured and the factory's 300 workers were able to carry on their work normally. Management at the factory described the work of the firefighters as 'superb'.

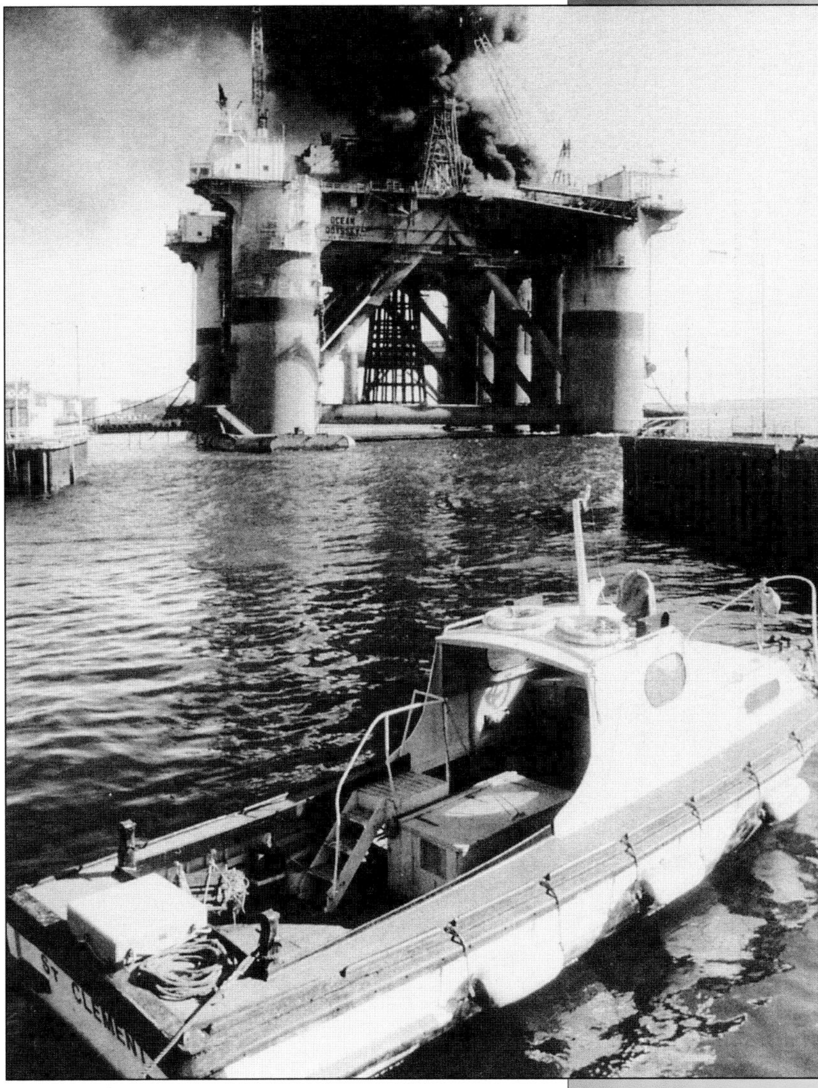

The Ocean Odyssey goes out with a bang. Cutting equipment, being used by demolition workers breaking her up for scrap, set light to part of the stricken rig and Tayside fire crews were called in as black smoke poured across Dundee in March 1989. (Tayside Fire Brigade)

Dundee firefighters again put their lives on the line when fire broke out on the blazing rig *Ocean Odyssey* which had been brought to their harbour in 1989 to be scrapped after the disastrous North Sea blaze which had resulted in the death of the radio officer.

Workmen from the demolition company were using cutting equipment in the rig's engine room when a fire erupted in its diesel-soaked floor. Before long, flames and clouds of dense, acrid black smoke were pouring from the jinxed platform, high above the water. More than 50 firefighters were lifted 100 feet (30.5 metres) by a special hoist to its decks and, in the words of its Firemaster, Alex Winton, 'faced very difficult conditions' to pump thousands of gallons of water from the Tay into the 'very, very severe fire' in the early stages.

The crews had to wear full breathing apparatus to combat the smoke and fumes from the residual oil and found themselves slipping as the decks began to slope on the ebbing tide. As they trained water on the flames, they could hear loud banging noises – the metal of the rig was buckling from the intense heat. In spite of all the difficulties, the fire was surrounded within two and a half hours and the process of 'damping down' the wreckage was begun.

HIGHLANDS AND ISLANDS

With only one full time fire station for the whole area, one might be tempted to think that the Highlands and Islands Region was small. In fact this unique section of Britain's fire service is roughly the same size as the whole of Belgium. It covers 12,000 square miles of the north west of Scotland – one sixth of the total land mass of Great Britain – stretching from the northernmost point of the Shetlands through the Western Isles and down to join Strathclyde at Glencoe and Grampian to the west.

Its one full-time fire station is at the headquarters in Inverness. But the area is dotted with 28 'mother' stations of retained firefighters, and 98 units of more than 1,000 men and women volunteers who train at their own stations, and once a month, visit the retained stations for an update under the care of the retained crews. Their 111 appliances include not only the normal water tenders with ladders but a fleet of light appliances. These carry ladders, hose, detachable and portable pumps and a variety of equipment through the narrow roads and over the mountains of their wild territory.

All the firefighters are called out by personal pager via what is the biggest radio link in Britain – and probably in Europe. It uses 74 different transmitting masts to overcome the problems of the mountains blocking the VHF links.

When the Inverness crew is called out to back up Mallaig it faces a journey of 115 miles, often along single track and mountainous roads. A journey of 50 miles to a fire is not unusual and if helicopters are needed – as often happens when fire breaks out in one of the many huge forests in the Highlands – an assurance has to be given that the landowner will foot the bill.

Cash is always a problem in so scattered a region as this. When its offshore firefighters had to travel out to tackle a fire on a Russian 'klondiker' carrying a cargo of cardboard boxes in its lowest hold, the cost of getting a succession of relief crews out and pumping foam into the ship for several days was £500,000.

Risks in the different areas vary only slightly. Kyle of Lochalsh, for instance, had about 100 calls in a year, 'mostly hill fires with heather burning, road accidents – some of the roads are still single lane with passing places – and a lot of chimney fires. Many people in this part of the country still burn peat to heat their homes so that chimney fires figure large'. Stornoway, one of the busiest retained stations, has around 300 calls a year, mostly to chimney fires from peat.

Employers in the area understand the problems of the volunteers and retained crews, and with such long distances between stations, there is no such thing as

Shellfish attitude

Highlands and Islands firefighters rate among their oddest 'shouts' a road accident involving a lorry which was travelling along the A87 road from Inverness to Kyle when it skidded and overturned. The driver was trapped in his cabin for four and a half hours before fire crews could extricate him from the wreckage. His load – 32 tons of prawns on their way to be frozen – were scattered across the whole area.

> ***A journey of 50 miles to a fire is not unusual***

a relief crew after four hours – or longer. Firefighters stay on duty until they are satisfied that the incident is completely finished. A two-pump fire at the unoccupied Stromferry Hotel was dealt with by crews from Kyle, Broadfoot and Lochcarron who were there from 0845 hours in the morning until 2000 hours.

As inland crews might be called out for motorway disasters, Highlands and Islands coastal crews go out for 'special services' at sea. In March 1994 a German coaster, the *Inger,* on her way from Sweden to Belfast, ran aground at Kylerhea, between the mainland and Skye. She was refloated but found to be holed in three places, so local fire crews went aboard and escorted her to safety, pumping out her bilges all the way to prevent damage to her engines – an 'incident' lasting nine hours.

Among their more unusual 'shouts' came one from a yacht, sailing along the western coast. The crew noticed a remote cottage on fire in the hills above the sea. They called up a sail training ship which in turn called the Oban coastguards who called Fire Control at Inverness and turned out the Mallaig lifeboat. This liaised with the firefighters, carrying their equipment round to the nearest point to the burning cottage where they could land. The fire in the cottage was extinguished, but two people were found dead in the ruins.

GRAMPIAN

Looking at the map, Grampian's fire region covers the top right hand section of Scotland. It takes in a huge area of mountains, forests and rivers, the Queen's home at Balmoral, and 'more castles than you can count', as one firefighter put it. Dominating it all is the great modern phenomenon of the oil rigs – out of sight, offshore in the North Sea, but still influencing the life of the region and particularly of Aberdeen and the surrounding area.

Time was when Aberdeen's firefighters faced a typically local Scottish range of hazards – tenements, big houses, forest fires and fires associated with the warehouses round the harbour. Particularly at risk were the smoke-houses where a fair quota of the catch from the great fishing fleets which sailed home into its port was transformed into such delicacies as smoked haddock, kippers, bloaters, Finnan Haddie and Arbroath smokies. Today's stringent fish quotas in the North Sea have decimated the fish trade, and all too much 'smoking' is carried out artificially these days – but at least there are fewer smokehouse fires.

Today, the range of 'incidents' is as varied as in many other parts of the country. These include road traffic accidents, house fires, and perhaps more chimney fires than some – a total of 1,152 in one recent year and the largest cause of fire in the area. Forest fires in the Grampian mountains behind Aberdeen have brought the need for better equipment. The fire brigade has contracts with private contractors to provide helicopters capable of carrying huge 'buckets' slung beneath them which can pour 5,000 litres of water on the blazing trees in one great 'scoosh'.

Catch a bus in Aberdeen and it could be carrying these vivid fire safety messages. Industrial sponsors locally have, so far, paid for the cost of the bus advertisements which include figures of firefighters in the front and back windows where children can fit their faces into the space under the helmets. There is even a message 'Fit and Maintain a Smoke Alarm' painted on the roof for onlookers in high rise flats and offices. 'It certainly seems to have attracted attention,' observed a fire officer. (Grampian Fire Brigade)

> ***It was quite hair-raising – the sea under the rig was still on fire***

One particularly bizarre accident faced the local firefighters on a suburban road in the outskirts of the city when a liquid gas tanker overturned as it was driving down a hill. The risk of explosion was tremendous. The slightest spark could have set it off. The whole area was cordoned off. Houses were evacuated, and police were standing on duty all round to prevent any car from entering the danger zone when a woman, driving a small car and oblivious to all, broke the cordon and careered off down the hill. For a brief moment, the horrified fire crews thought that she was going to hit the tanker. But then she seemed to realise that something was wrong and stopped in time to be told, firmly, what might have been the consequence of her daydreaming.

Without doubt though, it's oil and gas which have made Aberdeen a boom city in the past 30 years. And, in the tradition of the service in keeping up with developments in whatever the area of the country, the fire brigade has expanded in size and expertise to make sure that it can not only cope but stay several steps ahead.

Aberdeen is a world centre for educating specialists who deal with fires on oil and gas rigs, in oil wells and refineries. Also covered are many other hazards like distilling, storage and transportation of whisky and other spirits and chemicals, and an assortment of other sensitive materials.

Grampian has been there, from the first exploration of the offshore industry in the North Sea to the present day, when many companies pump oil and gas to the Scottish coast – gas to St Fergus, just north of Peterhead and oil to nearby Cruden Bay. St Fergus has four terminals. Shell, Total and Mobil produce the gas, and British Gas gather their supplies from the other three, add the safety smell and pump it into the National Grid at the rate of 75-80 million standard cubic metres per day, which amounts to 40 per cent of the nation's gas.

Each terminal has its own personal fire appliances, manned by trained employees of the company concerned. But Grampian Fire Brigade has fire stations there, too, ready to back up or manage the firefighting side of any incident along with the companies' experts.

The rigs themselves are a two-hour helicopter flight away in the North Sea and their personnel too, are carefully schooled in fire prevention and how to deal with any unexpected incident. Despite this, in July 1988, there was a disastrous explosion under the *Piper Alpha* rig, followed by so fierce an inferno that no firefighter could have dealt with it and in which 167 men died.

Grampian stood by to help out alongside the blazing rig but they were not able to get on board as explosion followed explosion. The heat reached 11,000 degrees Centigrade and metal 'melted like butter'. The *Piper Alpha* fire was dealt with by the American fire expert 'Red' Adair.

Aberdeen fire crews played a greater part when the *Ocean Odyssey* rig reported a 'blow-out' on 22 September 1988. Gas bubbled up from the sea bed below it and crews who flew out reported seeing the sea on fire as the flames leapt up below the metal staging. All the workers on the rig managed to escape but the radio operator courageously went back to transmit a Mayday call and died in the smoke and heat.

Grampian flew 10 firefighters to the rig by helicopter. 'Our job was to rescue the radio operator and do all we could to put out the fire,' said one of the crew, Alistair Swift. 'It was quite hair-raising. The sea under the rig was still on fire. We were dropped on to the fire support ship, the *Stadive*, and then we transferred to the burning rig by a bucket suspended from a 200 ton crane.

'Once on board we discovered the radio operator but he had been overcome and, to our sadness, had died. We hauled our hoses along and explored to see if we could put out any fire in the living quarters. I shall never forget opening the door of one of the cabins.

'On the far side was a shelf with an oilman's full outfit on it. As we walked in the whole thing burst into flames. Opening the door had let in oxygen and everything went up in smoke. Luckily we had our hoses with us and were able to deal with it immediately. The gas burned under the sea for 24 hours until it finally extinguished itself but the decks of the rig were so hot that we had to stand on the hoses to stop our feet from burning.'

The firefighters eventually cut the chain holding the rig in position and made it ready to be towed away to Dundee for demolition.

Not all Grampian's work is in Scotland. For some years now, firefighters from Britain have volunteered to go abroad to help with rescues from disasters including earthquakes and the civilian aftermath of wars. Help had already been given to Mexico and in Armenia, and after the Gulf War the call came for help with the mass evacuation of Kurdish refugees from the terrors of Northern Iraq into Kurdistan.

It was then that the British government set up a national organisation to carry out this emergency work. Sixteen fire brigades throughout Britain offered their co-operation in forming the UK Fire Service Search and Rescue Team. All take it in turns to have a fully trained crew of volunteers equipped and ready to fly to

Grampian's Rescue team outside their 'fire station' in the border region of Kurdistan. (Alistair Swift, Grampian Fire Brigade)

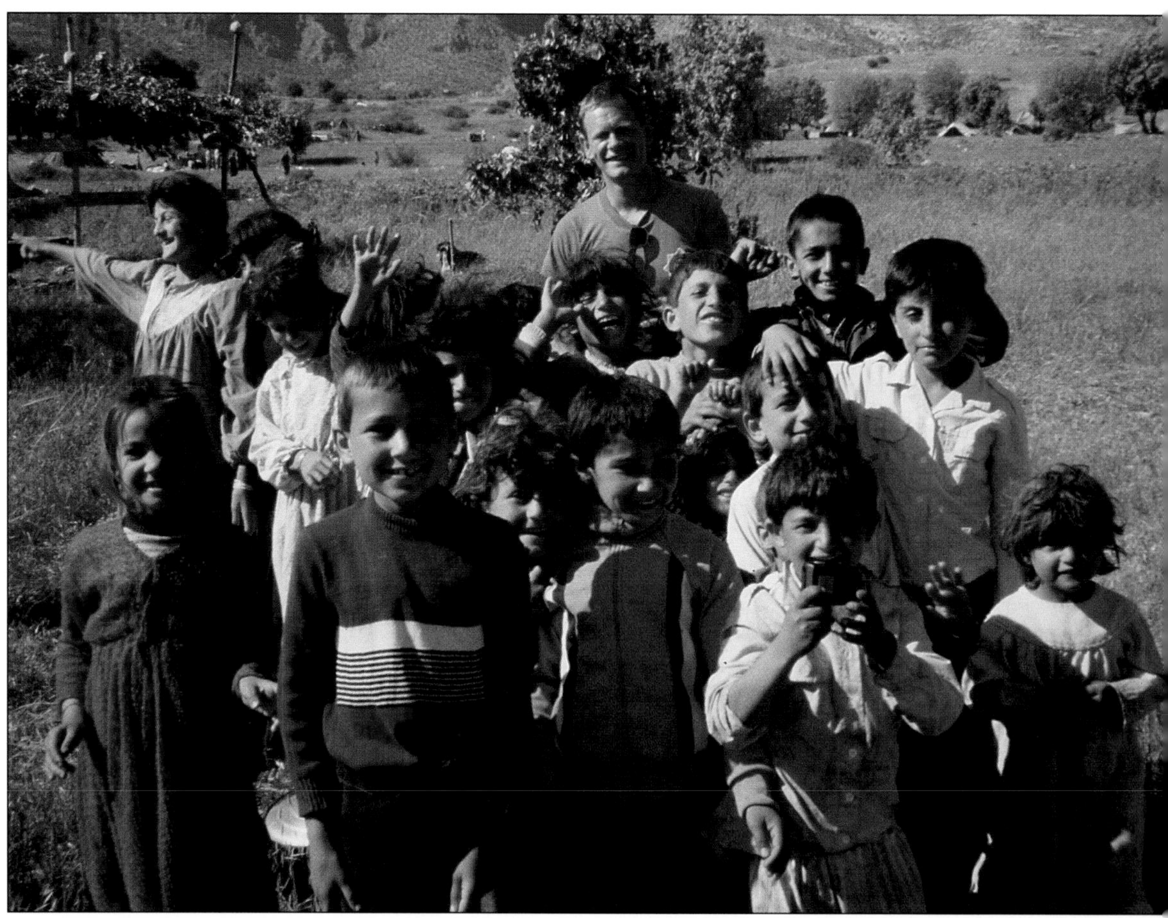

Gary Mills of Grampian with Kurdish children after carrying out a health check. (Alistair Swift, Grampian Fire Brigade)

The Kurdish refugees were delighted to see the men from Aberdeen and shared hospitality with Alistair Swift and Gary Mills in the family tent. (Alistair Swift, Grampian Fire Brigade)

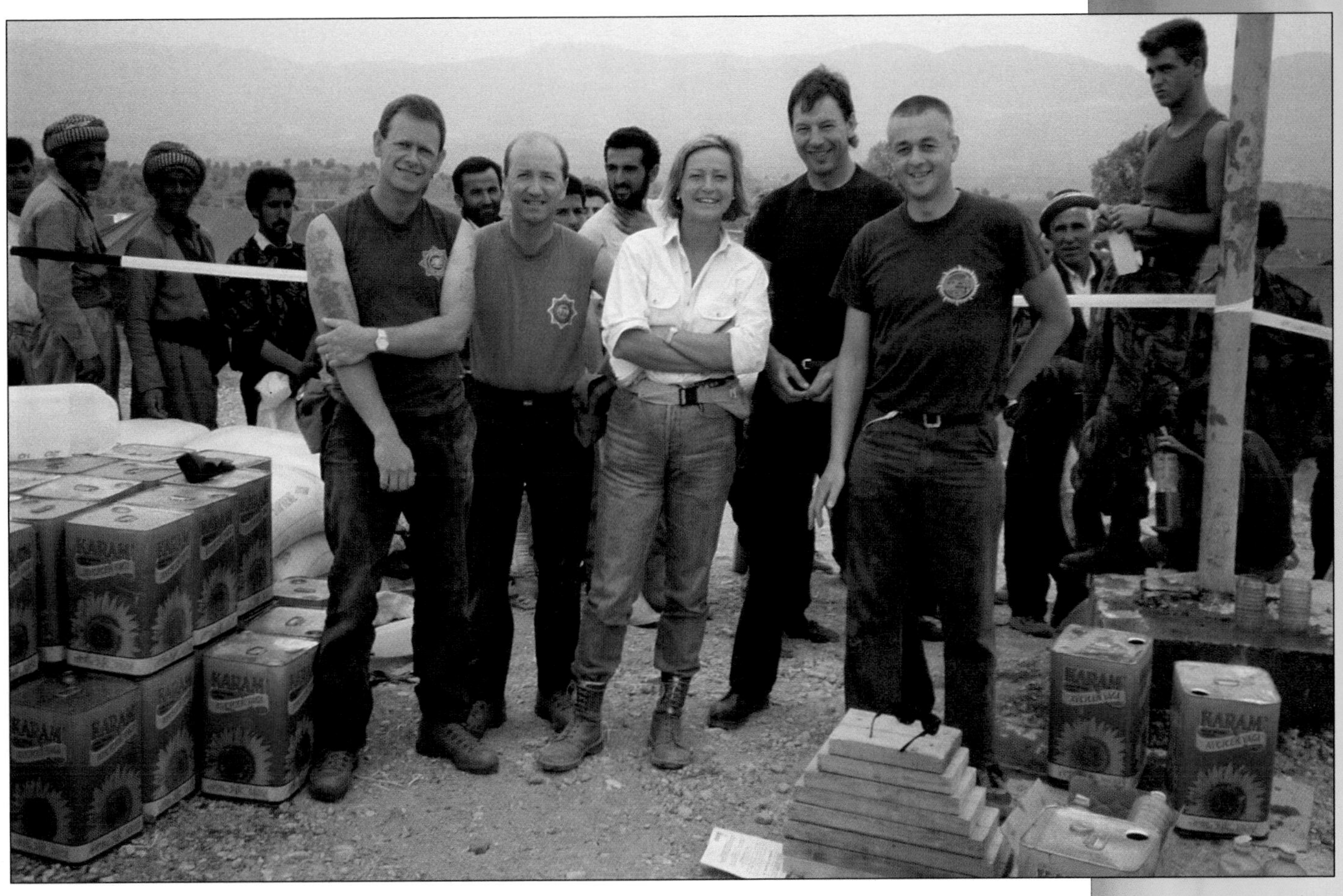

Kate Adie, BBC correspondent, joins Bill Low and Gary Mills of Grampian and two Dyfed firefighters at a food distribution point. (Alistair Swift, Grampian Fire Brigade)

any part of the world at 12 hours' notice. They work on a rota basis, each crew on stand-by for a set period and handing on to another county at the end of that time.

Training includes, now, a special course at the Fire Service College, Moreton-in-Marsh. There, not only are the volunteers given climbing training in the local Cotswold hills, but they are faced with a three-storey building, supposedly collapsed in an earthquake, filled with rubble from which victims are screaming for help in a babel of different languages.

It is typical of the sort of scene which might face them after an earthquake. But the firefighters from Grampian found a different scene when they were sent to Kurdistan.

'Three of us went at a moment's notice,' recalled Station Officer Alistair Swift. 'We were told it would be very cold in the mountains and the Marines were taking Arctic clothing so we wrapped up warm, but found when we got there that it was very hot during the day.' Stripped to their tee shirts with the Aberdeen Fire Brigade motif, they set to work, helping the medical teams, setting up tented villages, feeding the refugees and distributing food supplies.

'Language was not too much of a problem – a surprising number of them had at least a smattering of English,' he said. 'But we were amazed when a small group of refugees, ragged, weary, covered in dust and dirt, staggered over the border to safety one evening. One of them detached himself from the group as he saw us.

'He was in full traditional costume. He and his tribesmen had lost everything they had, but as he saw the Aberdeen logo on our tee shirts he put out a hand and with a big smile said "Fit like!" We couldn't believe our ears. This is a local dialect greeting in Aberdeen. It turned out that not only had he lived in the city for some years and spoke English quite fluently but some of his family still lived in the next road along from my home!'

CHAPTER 11

THE MAKING OF A FIREFIGHTER

RECRUITMENT AND TRAINING

Compared with Victorian times, the basic requisite qualities of a firefighter remain remarkably unchanged. Endurance, courage, strength and the ability to work within a team are all as true for the 1990s as they were in the brass helmet days of the service.

However, modern firefighting and rescue increasingly involves hazards quite unknown to Victorian firemen. Nowadays, burning plastics produce huge quantities of thick, choking, toxic smoke. Chemicals in solid, liquid or gas form can be explosive, flammable, corrosive and toxic. Modern technical processes often use high voltage electricity and radioactive materials.

When such a diverse array of potentially lethal substances and operations become involved in a fire or accident situation, as does happen, firefighters need to be well trained to cope confidently with the most demanding and dangerous scenarios.

With such a wide number of potential 'nasties' likely to be present at a 1990s fire or crash scene, the existing rigorous fire service training standards are constantly being refined to ensure that fire crews have a good knowledge and understanding of physics, chemistry, mechanical engineering and the like.

The UK fire service has had single tier

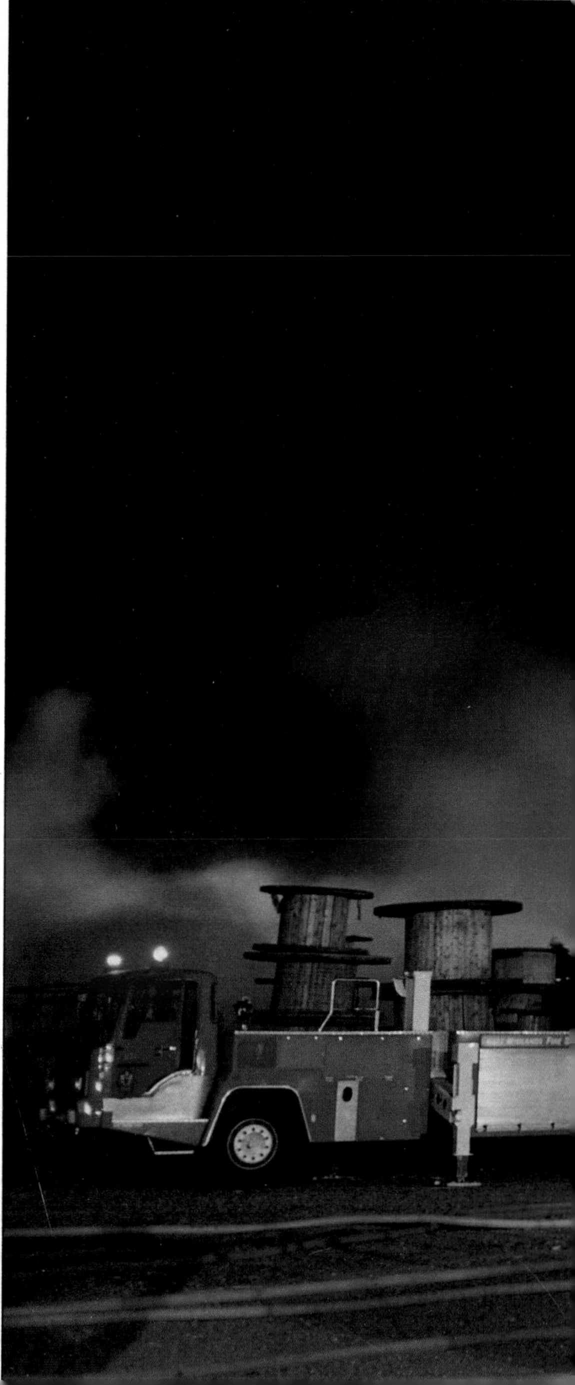

entry since the end of the Second World War. This means that the promotion path through to Chief Fire Officer starts when a recruit firefighter completes his basic course at training school and is posted to his first operational fire station. Thus every one of today's 66 Chief Fire Officers started life as a fireman dealing at the sharp end with fires and crashes, getting smoke in his nostrils, and being very sweaty and grubby at the same time.

Up to the mid 1970s the fire service was a male bastion, but since then a number of female firefighters have progressively joined fire brigades up and down the country.

Recruit training is undertaken at a number of regional training centres. Here, for the first time a recruit will be amid the exciting world of the fire service. There will be fully equipped fire engines of various sorts and large drill ground areas with eight-storey drill towers where ladder skills can be learnt under the watchful eyes of instructors.

A particular section of the outside training area will be used to simulate road crashes: scrap cars have to be cut apart,

One million old tyres were going up in this volcano of flame when West Midlands fire crews put their hydraulic platforms into action at a scrap yard incident. Breathtaking pictorially – and physically – for the firefighters absorbing the smoke and stench of burning rubber. (West Midlands Fire Service)

4,000 recruits applied

The few opportunities to join the fire brigade are snapped up pretty quickly. Essex County Fire and Rescue Service recently advertised in a local newspaper for 24 recruits. Within days, the brigade's Brentwood HQ had over 4,000 applications from budding firefighters.

carefully yet quickly. Special buildings constructed to withstand internal fires simulate the actual awful heat and smoke conditions in which most firefighters work. Other structures allow recruits to practise extinguishing fire with foam, inert gases, and powder methods for those occasions when oil or chemicals are blazing and the use of a water jet would only serve to make the fire explosively worse.

Most courses are residential and last up to 13 weeks. During this time a recruit will be given an intense and comprehensive introduction to the theory of firefighting. Much firefighting still uses water and a recruit has to understand the firefighter's art of getting water from A to B as quickly as possible. There will be equipment such as extinguishers and resuscitators to comprehend, cryptic radio procedures to learn, and the basics of law which govern the way fire brigades operate, besides many other classroom subjects.

Nevertheless, it is the practical side which predominates most of the recruits' course. In the very first week come the initial drills when hose is run out from a hydrant and knuckles are grazed as the hose is unrolled to get a jet of water to work. Early on during the first week recruits will pitch a ladder to the second

Animal rescues are quite a regular occurence for rural firefighters. The West Yorkshire crew pictured here were nicknamed 'Cowlin's Cowmen' after this incident – the Odsal Station Commander (5th from left) was Stn/O Les Cowlin.

Extreme skill – and experience – is required for extinguishing a fire in a ship's hold like this one. Home from the sea in the winter of 1992, with fire in one of her deepest holds, the huge fish factory ship Veronica, *pride of Northern Ireland's merchant navy, lies alongside the quay while firefighters, poised on a hydraulic platform above her decks, tackle the tricky job of putting out the flames. Others are working far down below the decks.* (Northern Ireland Fire Brigade)

floor level of the drill tower and learn the first techniques of safe working from ladders. Any initial fear at this modest height of 35 feet (10.6 metres) will be identified and carefully exorcised by the instructors.

And so the hectic pace accelerates as the course progresses. After several weeks the recruits steadily develop their teamwork skills by using a fire engine as the base of a drill sequence which might include pumping water, pitching a ladder to the third floor and hauling other firefighting gear aloft by line to deal with some imaginary conflagration. By then the teaching of first aid, casualty handling, knots and lines – a firefighter needs to know 24 different knots and hitches and their uses – protective clothing procedures, the intricacies of fire alarms and sprinklers are all bearing fruit.

A firefighter also has to qualify to wear compressed air breathing apparatus, a firefighter's personal life support set. He or she must show that they are safe to work as part of a team amid the smoky, hot and toxic fumes which are the day to day dangerous working environment of the fire service.

Recruit training is a tough time, physically and mentally, as the outside physical effort in all weathers and the classroom work intensify. Regrettably, the sheer pace and disciplinary demands occasionally defeat a recruit who cannot cope with one aspect or another. Generally the young men and women recruits quickly grow in both stature and character. They emerge after 13 weeks as assured, confident, and smartly turned out firefighters, even if their real education is only about to begin.

Once posted to an operational fire station on shift work covering day and night patterns, the recruit has a probationary period of up to two years during which a number of further skills and knowledge, some relating to the local area, are acquired.

Beyond this, for those who wish, there is a career path through the national structure of promotion examinations and those of the professional body – the Institution of Fire Engineers – which also offers a BSc degree in fire engineering.

There are further training courses for qualification as an ordinary driver, an emergency driver (to drive fire engines to '999' calls) and to operate the complex 100 feet (30 metre) hydraulic platforms and turntable ladders used for high-rise rescues.

Tough training is needed to prepare firefighters for a multi-fatal situation like this one. Traffic was stationary on the M42, queueing to enter a side road to the Birmingham Exhibition Centre on 6 November 1990, when it was hit in the rear by a lorry. The point of impact is clear from the skid marks on the road as well as the concentration of resources and equipment needed for the rescue work. (West Midlands Fire Service)

As an individual's career develops he or she will study further at the Fire Service College at Moreton-in-Marsh, Gloucestershire. This is probably the finest fire training establishment in the world. The College courses embrace leadership, command and management, as well as the sciences, fire service legislation, fire safety law, and a range of associated subjects.

Away from the lecture and seminar rooms are a quite staggering variety of 'hot fire' buildings in and around which fire officers are able to develop their skills amid the hostile environment of their dangerous profession. These include factory and industrial buildings, a shopping mall, domestic properties and a 4,000 ton ship.

The College sports its own motorway section where realistic crashes are staged, an airliner, a section of electrified railway line, oil and gas tanks, high voltage electricity grids, and a chemical plant. At any time in the academic year, there will be about 500 students of all ranks present, including a number from overseas brigades, such is the reputation of this British fire training centre.

While all this prepares a professional firefighter for his work, the 'retained' or voluntary arm of the British Fire Service is similarly recruited and trained. Retained firefighters man fire stations in those many small towns and villages in the UK where fire risk is not deemed sufficient to support a permanent professional presence.

These front line 'community' firefighters undertake a basic 60-hour training course before they are posted to a retained station as an operational firefighter. Retained crews usually meet once a week for a drill and general training session.

A retained firefighter lives and works close to his or her local fire station and is issued with a bleeper which in the event of a call summons the crew to the fire sta-

One of the cars, mangled in the wreckage. (West Midlands Fire Service)

tion, much like a lifeboat launch. Retained personnel are paid an annual 'retaining' sum plus call-out fees.

The retained element of the service is, in a sense, the backbone of the British Fire Service, for although a retained crew may only answer perhaps 50 '999' calls a year, they may well come face to face with as many risks and danger in a rural area as does the busy professional city firefighter whose station answers 4,000 calls per annum.

And what will the firefighter recruit, either professional or retained, feel after his or her initial training course and first months as a 'red rider'? The chances are that the motive which drove them to apply to become a firefighter will be stronger than ever. Could it be that it was to escape a humdrum 'nine to five' office job and seek excitement in an often dangerous situation? Or maybe it was that the sheer glamour of being a firefighter and charging about in red fire engines fulfilled a childhood dream. Who can tell?

Whatever the initial motivation, the UK fire service has a remarkably small employment wastage rate and it is not unusual for the majority of recruits to go on to serve their full pensionable 30 years.

It's not all horror. Following a blaze in a barn at a farm at Balsall Common, firefighters pitch in to help feed distressed lambs who have survived the blaze. (West Midlands Fire Service)

CHAPTER 12

LOOKING BACK

A HISTORY OF THE FIRE SERVICE

Few people who hear the howl of the two-tone and see a fire appliance elbowing through the traffic have any idea that this is a service which not only goes back to the ancient Romans, but still attracts the same type of character.

Roman firefighters were well-trained, courageous and devoted to each other and to saving lives. When danger was at its greatest, they knew they could rely on their mates, trusting them, if the need arose, with their own lives. On the other hand, they were a cheerful irreverent lot. The Roman orator Cicero (106-43 BC) recorded one group which set off on a nightly 'watch' tour of the city to check for fires when they discovered smoke billowing above a garden wall. Quick as a flash they burst their way in and had hurled their full supply of water – in buckets – on the source of the fire before discovering that they had ruined a religious sacrifice.

Long before Julius Caesar landed on the shores of Britain, Rome had a fire brigade to cope with the endless succession of fires which bedevilled the city and, at one stage in its history, destroyed large areas of wooden and even stone built houses. Roman firemen were, in those early days, part of the army. The earliest fire force was called the 'familia publica', but after a particularly disastrous blaze in 6 AD, the Emperor Augustus set up a service which lasted for the next 500 years.

Officially they were called 'Vigiles', but because they all carried that earliest item of firefighting equipment – a bucket, in this case made from Esparto grass and tarred to help it hold water – they were known as 'sparteoli', or bucket boys. Their uniform was a toga and sandals. They were highly organised, stationed in a succession of 14 main fire stations, each with a system of sub-stations in the surrounding area, and these ringed the city.

Even Nero, famous for having 'fiddled' while Rome burned, played his part in maintaining the Vigiles. There is a glimpse of this organisation still surviving today in the ruins of their fire station at Ostia, outside Rome. Carved into a stone pillar are the details of their jobs and their equipment. This included hooked poles, blankets, ladders, sponges, brooms, buckets, wickerwork mats, pickaxes and felling-axes – many of them still being used by firefighters today.

Without doubt, the Vigiles came to Britain. They marched across the country with the columns of the Roman Army. Vigiles were entered in the original Army Lists as being stationed in Chester-le-Street and, further north, at Greta Bridge near the Roman Wall in Northumbria, combining their firefighting duties with that of an early type of police force.

> *'In Shakespeare's time the first attempts at fire engines began to appear'*

This medieval illustration shows some of the earliest methods of firefighting – several of which, including the hooked poles and ladders, are still being used.

When the Romans finally returned to their warmer homeland, firefighting deteriorated in Britain to its original 'basics' of buckets, ladders and long poles with hooks on the end, used to pull down burning thatch and dangerous walls. Church bells were used as fire alarms and two are known to have survived. One, in Sherborne Abbey has the inscription *Lord, quench this furious flame, arise, run help put out the same.* Another, in Coventry, reads: *I have been called the common bell To ring when fire breaks out to tell.* Prayers against fire were also said in churches.

William the Conqueror introduced a curfew (from the French 'couvre-feu' – cover fire), and for many years, citizens had to cover or extinguish the fire in their hearths at dusk and try, with friction or tinder or a spot of illegally smuggled embers, to light it again at dawn.

Throughout the country, city after city, with homes usually built of timber in those early days, suffered enormous fires, some of which destroyed almost every building. By the 14th century, edicts were going out from many of the early town councils, demanding that houses should be brick or stone built and that roofs should be covered with tiles or slates rather than thatch. But still the implements were basic, the ladder, the hooked pole and the bucket chain.

In Shakespeare's time, the late 1500s, the first attempts at fire engines began to appear, some home-built but the more sophisticated, at first, being imported. As early as the 1620s, London's aldermen had ordered a dozen or more of the latest 'enjins' from Germany. By 1666, when the Great Fire of London swept the city, more than a score were stationed in the parishes, but were either in too bad a condition to be of any use or with nobody available to man them. For most home owners, it was back to the buckets in a hopeless attempt to save their property.

The great turning point came after that fire. More stringent fire laws resulted in the first major breakthrough in fire related architecture – the Queen Anne house. Brick built, to a depth and strength laid down by law, with reasonable gaps in between, and wider roads instead of cramped lanes, this was the beginning of today's universally applied building regulations.

The Great Fire brought another new idea: fire insurance. Almost as soon as the flames had died down, an enterprising businessman, Nicholas Barbon (a Puritan, he had been christened 'If Christ Had Not Died Thou Wouldst Have Been Damned' but was usually known for his sharp business methods as 'Damned Barbon') set up 'The Fire Office' in London – a scheme for insuring houses and businesses against fire. Within a very short time, others followed and before long, half a dozen fire insurance offices were competing for clients. Indignantly, Barbon struck back with a new advertising gimmick – a band of 'lusty watermen' trained in fighting fires. Watermen were preferred because they were accustomed to manhandling furniture on and off their boats, which were the transport of the city at that time. Whatever their job or their city, the trained, professional firefighter had arrived.

Until now, water had been pumped by hand through rigid metal nozzles on top of the 'enjins', but the Dutch, who were great firefighting inventors, were beginning to experiment with flexible hosepipes made by sewing or riveting lengths of leather into tubes. William of Orange brought the first samples to Britain and they were quickly nicknamed 'the great sucking worms'.

These were in considerable demand as fire after fire was reported from cities throughout the country. But it was a particularly memorable conflagration in London's dock area that destroyed the homes of hundreds of families, killing many people and making thousands homeless which forced Queen Anne and her government to decide that urgent action was needed. They ordered that every parish should have a fire pump and that parishioners should be ready to use it to fight fires in their neighbourhood.

> ***'London firemen were always chosen from the ranks of retired sailors'***

For more than a century, these were to be the main source of firefighting in Britain – along with the insurance firemen, in brightly coloured uniforms, wearing the badge of their company. Among them were the Hand-in-Hand, the Phoenix, the Royal Exchange and, still surviving to this day, The Sun. Each householder who insured with a company was given a mark to fix to the front wall as visible proof when the fire engine galloped up – or was hauled along by hand – that here lived a policy holder who was entitled to have his fire put out. Even today, all over the country, fire marks can still be seen on the walls of some older houses – usually set high out of reach as they are valuable collectors' items.

As times changed and industry spread, so the fire services developed to keep pace with them. The history of each brigade is a clear key to the changing pattern of life in its area. The growth of industry, the opening up of the British Empire, the development of steam power for transport, steam-powered trains and ships, all produced more buildings, more goods, more warehouses and storage depots and more hazards for the firemen of Britain.

When Queen Victoria came to the throne in 1837, many of the insurance brigades had already combined to form larger fire brigades. Edinburgh was one of the earliest of these, and the first to form a fire service paid for by the community. Its Firemaster, James Braidwood, had developed Edinburgh's force into a remarkably trained and efficient unit, cutting his professional teeth on the Great Fire of Edinburgh in 1824 before leaving to take over the insurance brigade in London, the London Fire Engine Estab- lishment. His men fought disastrous fires in the Houses of Parliament, the Tower of London, the Royal Exchange and a never ending succession of huge warehouses along the Thames. Braidwood himself was killed by a falling wall at one of the biggest-ever fires in the capital, Tooley Street, where a long line of warehouses, downstream of London Bridge, burned for nearly a month.

Braidwood's death and the enormous price which had to be paid out for the damage caused by the Tooley Street fire, spelled the end of the insurance companies' responsibility for firefighting in London. In 1866 the capital had its first municipally funded fire service – the Metropolitan Fire Brigade.

Its leader, the dashing Captain Eyre Massey Shaw, ordered – and was reluctantly allowed – more and better fire stations and equipment, including steam-powered fire floats for the dockside fires on the Thames, and magnificent steam-pumped engines drawn by galloping horses. London firemen were, at his insistence, always chosen from the ranks of retired sailors who had served their time in the Navy: they were accustomed to climbing rigging in atrocious conditions, to strict discipline, and to appallingly long working hours.

Shaw was always short of men. Among the volunteers who helped out at fires in London were the Prince of Wales, later to be King Edward VII, the Earl of Caithness and the Duke of Sutherland. All wore the uniform of the MFB and its heroic and memorable distinguishing brass helmet – which was later to be copied by almost all other fire brigades in the country. (Not until the 1930s, with the rapid development of electric power and the deaths of some firemen, killed when the trailing cables brushed against their metal headgear, was this famous symbol of the firefighter replaced by helmets of non-conducting material.)

By the early 1900s, most of the larger brigades in the country were experimenting with petrol-powered fire appliances. In the early 1920s most of the traditional horses had been pensioned off and their old 'steamers' replaced by motorised vehicles. By now, too, the 'hi-hi' men, the trumpets and the rattles which had cleared the way for fire engines in the past, had been replaced by hand rung bells.

The First World War saw many firemen called up for service in the armed forces. Their places were taken by untrained conscripts from such unlikely sources as postmen in London and dustmen in Aberdeen. When the first bombs fell in London, any professional firemen who had survived the horrors of trench warfare were hastily brought back to cope with the ensuing air raids.

The mid-30s, with its threat of a possible Second World War, brought the first enclosed fire pump – and one which carried its own supply of water. In the past, firemen had returned from fires with their uniforms so wet that in winter they could stand them up, frozen solid, in the station yards. Now, at last they could travel to and from a fire without being exposed to the elements.

Not until 1938, after nearly a century of petitions and warnings from leading fire officers, did the government finally take

Research matched new materials

By early this century research into fires was developing almost as fast as such new perils as matches, explosives, paraffin, and petrol refinery and storage. Other hazards included the exceptionally inflammable celluloid (which was being used to make films for the new-fangled cinemas) and a variety of dangerous materials, like the seemingly innocuous flannel. This was widely acclaimed as soft and warm for babies' clothes and ladies' petticoats – despite its horrifying death toll.

Fire pours from one of the burning towers as the great Crystal Palace at Sydenham, London, went up in flames in November 1936. The fire could be seen miles away in North London and the heat was so intense that fire crews wore their brass helmets back to front to protect their faces, but they were powerless to prevent most of the building from being destroyed.

firefighting seriously. At last, they realised that there was a real risk of fire-bomb attacks from a possible enemy and that the country's fire service was in no state to cope with it.

There were, by now, more than 1,600 diverse fire brigades in Britain. Their equipment ranged from the sophisticated pumps and long, turntable ladders of the big cities to the still horse-drawn and even hand-operated manual pumps of some of the smaller villages. The Fire Brigades Act of 1938 went some way towards up-dating fire protection. An auxiliary fire service was also inaugurated which, for the first time, included women – but only in non-operational duties. That these would include the despatch riders who eventually wove their motor bikes through the exploding bombs of the blitz attacks on so many British towns with supreme courage, had not been anticipated.

Only in 1941, when the awesome incendiary and high explosive raids had struck throughout the country, was a National Fire Service formed and every fire brigade came under the control of the Home Office.

By 1948, with the war over, the Service was re-organised. Many of the smaller brigades were lost for ever, absorbed first into the new 'regions' and later into counties.

Their officers put the experience of war to good use and looked to the future. New materials, new production methods, a huge increase in road transport, and more chemicals were all threatening a whole range of hazards. Worst of all was the hangover from Hiroshima – nuclear power. In 1958, the '999' system was instituted to help the public call out the emergency services and with it came the increasing need not just for firefighting.

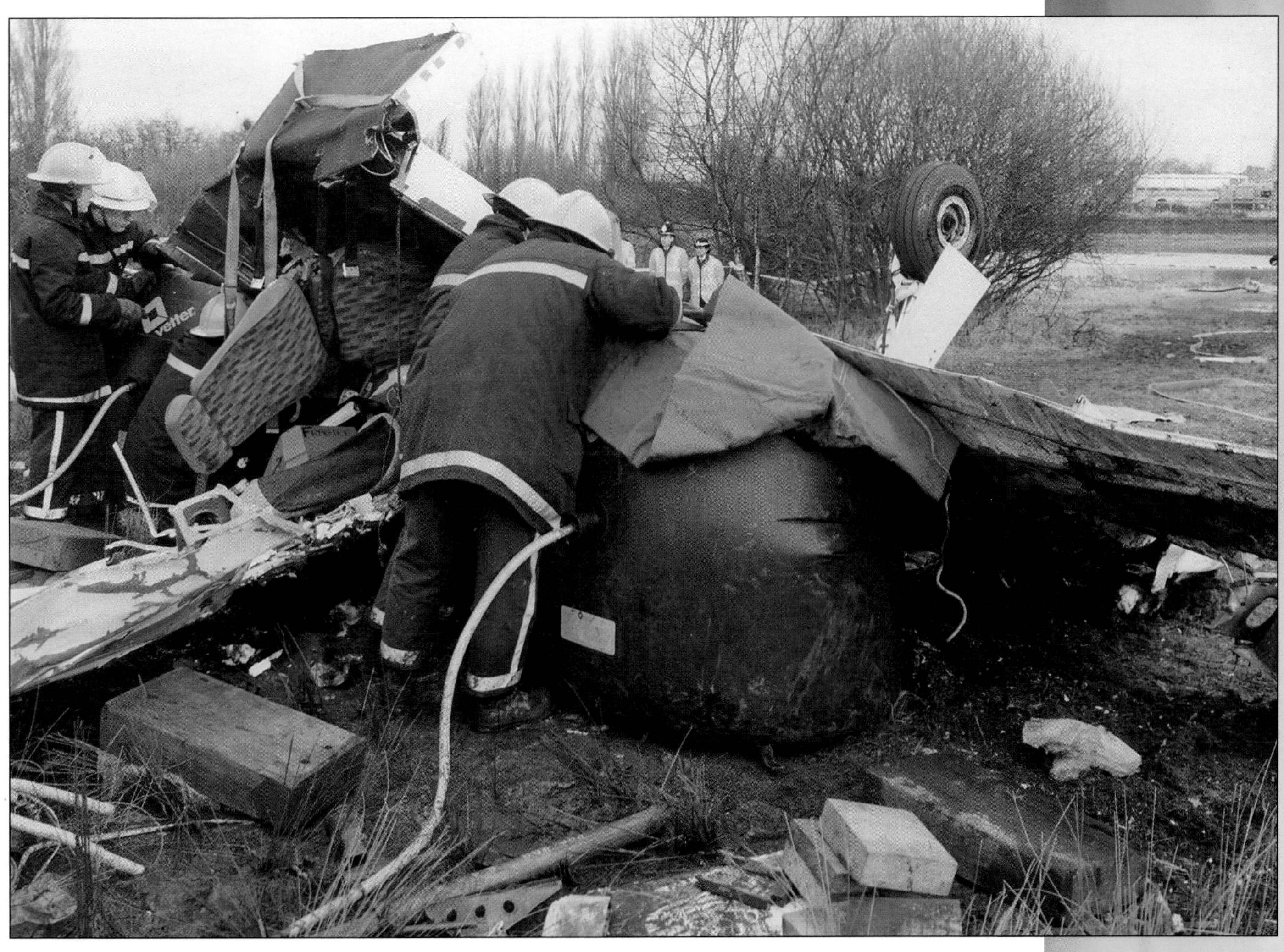

Large airbags were inflated beneath this upturned light aircraft which landed on waste ground at Sneayd Lane, Bloxwich, to the north of Birmingham, in January 1994. Supporting the weight of the plane, they helped firefighters' efforts to rescue the pilot and passengers. (West Midlands Fire Service)

For the first time virtually every brigade, especially those covering urban areas, began to respond to a growing number of non-fire '999' calls; the fire service termed these emergencies 'special service' calls.

To illustrate this growth, during 1937 the entire London Fire Brigade, the largest body of professional firefighters in the country, answered a mere 123 such calls. By 1974 this London total had accelerated to almost 15,000 and 10 years later the number of special service calls dealt with by London crews had doubled to over 30,000 individual cries for urgent, non-fire assistance from the public.

The quite phenomenal rise continued each year across the area protected by the London Fire Brigade. Today over 63,000 emergency turnouts are made by London firefighters to special service '999' calls.

This enormous growth is also reflected in every other fire brigade up and down the country where about 30 per cent of a brigade's total annual '999' calls are now to special services. This had led to a situation where Britain's firefighters nowadays rescue more men, women and children from special service incidents than from purely fire situations. But what precisely are special service calls?

With the development of today's road networks, much of the work involves gruesome road traffic accidents (RTAs). Here the first priority for fire crews will be to free driver and passengers from the crumpled and bloodstained wreckage of their car, which is often one of a number of vehicles involved in a multiple crash.

Other '999' calls summon firefighters to leaking toxic chemicals. This might be a corrosive acid dripping from a damaged valve on a road or rail tanker, or an explosive gas cloud which has escaped from a

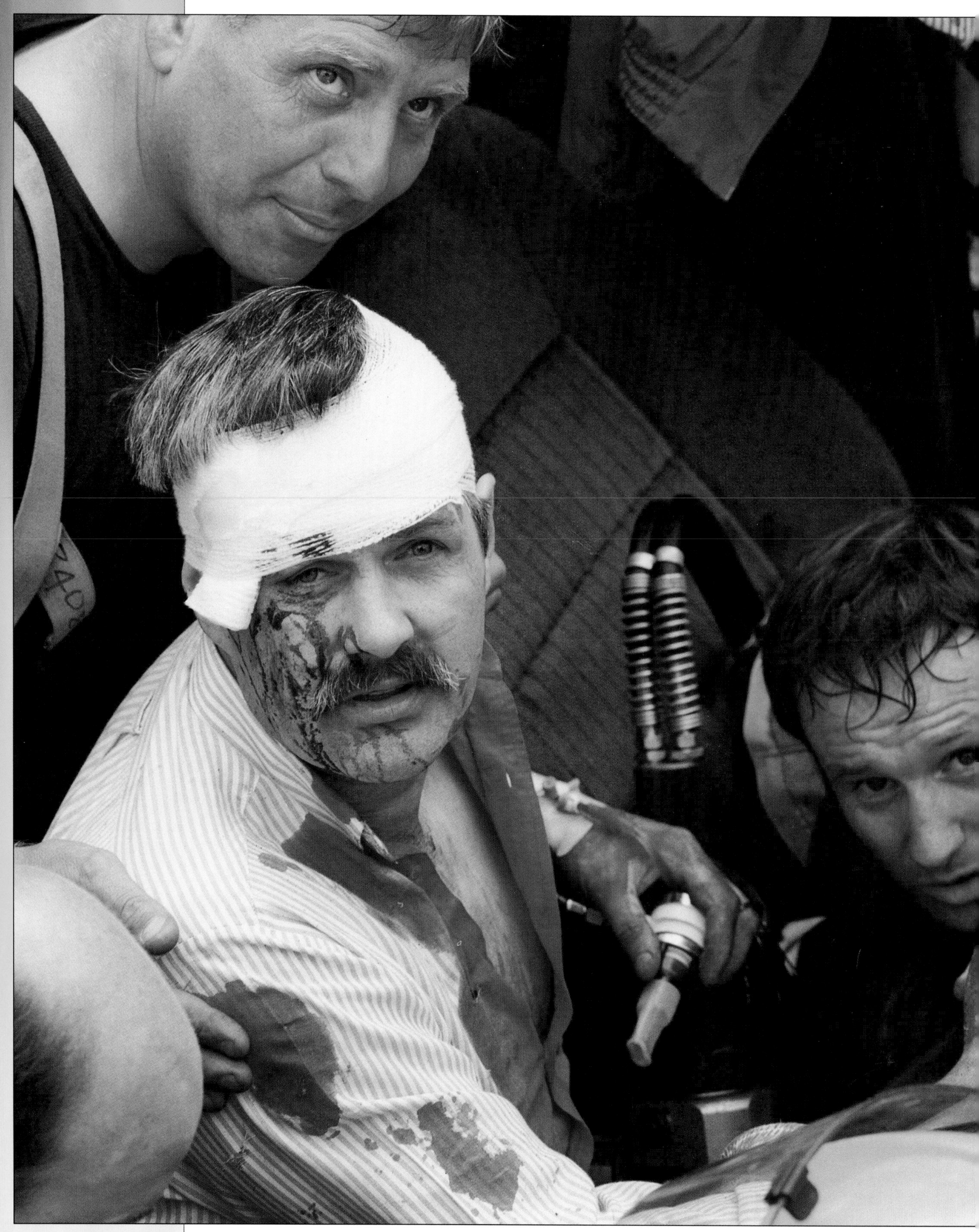

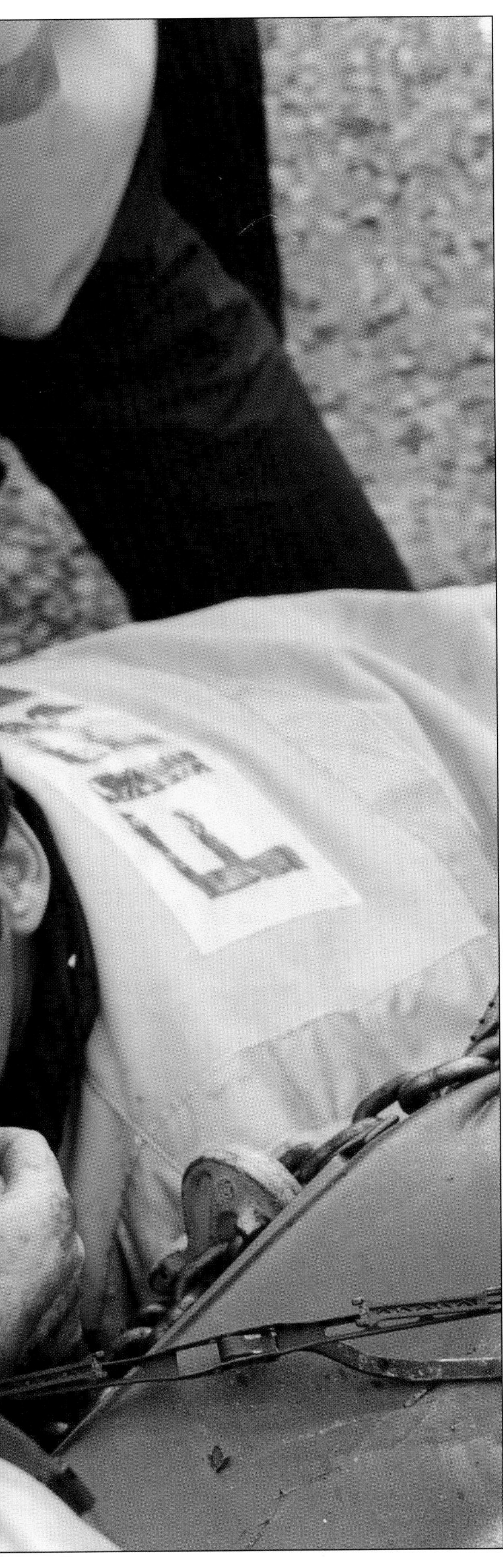

chemical works and is blowing towards a housing estate nearby. Evacuation of the public will be necessary, while firefighters don special protective suits and breathing sets to deal with the dangerous situation.

At these incidents, fire crews will need to understand the particular chemistry of the hazardous material involved. For example some liquids will explode violently if water is applied.

The emergency may be to a factory worker trapped in machinery, or perhaps under a fork lift truck after a moment's carelessness, or to a building site worker, buried when the sides of a trench have fallen in without warning.

Leakages of gas can cause explosions powerful enough to demolish entire buildings. If such a drama happens at night in a block of flats it is likely that many residents will be buried under tons of rubble; a high wind may have brought down a section of scaffolding and pedestrians could be underneath the tangled mass of twisted steel tubing; a car which has skidded on ice and plunged into a river will see firefighters arrive speedily on the scene.

These are a few not unusual examples of special service emergencies which modern day fire crews have to deal with. Life is at immediate risk and dependent on the immediate actions of fire crews. As with a spreading fire where thickening smoke traps people on upper floors above the blaze, firefighters may have only seconds in which to act if they are to save life and limb.

Somewhat different are the potential suicides perched on high bridges or on window ledges. These sad people will be talked to and patiently listened to by fire crews; a quite different, softer approach will be needed here and it is likely that several hours may pass before – if the talk-

> **‘Leakages of gas can cause explosions powerful enough to demolish buildings’**

*Opposite: **This one's for real! Ambulance workers tended his injuries, inserted a drip and gave him a tube to draw on pain-killing medication. Concern and compassion show on the faces of West Midlands crews who had just cut away the roof of the man's car and were comforting him as they struggled to release his feet from the wreckage. He had been the innocent victim of a multiple collision on the M5 in July 1992 after a lorry's heavy load had shifted.** (West Midlands Fire Service)*

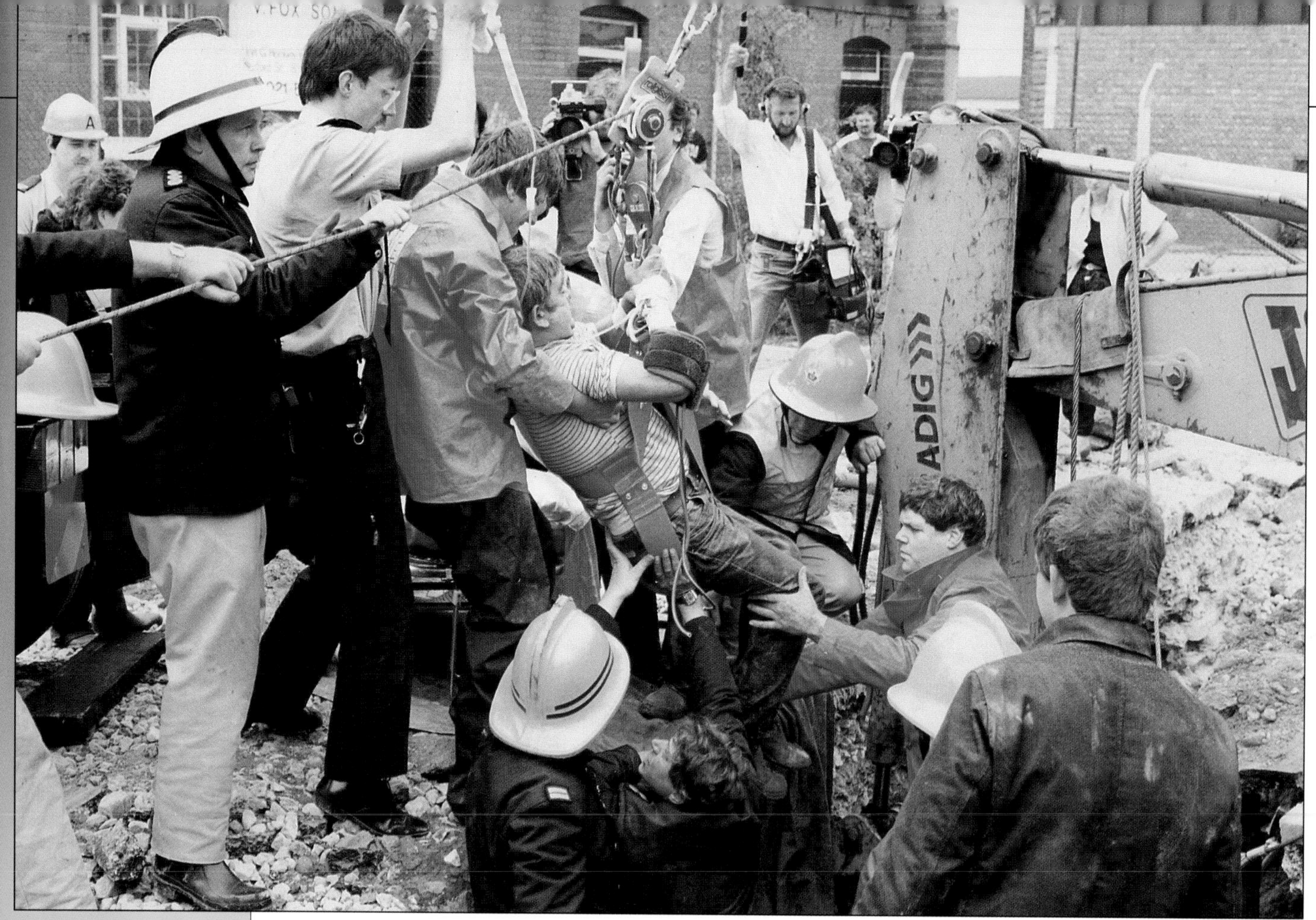

Master of all trades

In rural areas, firefighters are sometimes called to rescue horses stuck in deep muddy ditches, or cows which have fallen into foul-smelling farm slurry pits. And everywhere, in city, town and village, children frequently get stuck on ledges, down wells, in pipes, or have fingers trapped in bicycles or swings.

Freak weather may bring lightning strikes, flooding and landslips, each bringing a new challenge for the fire service.

The sheer variety and complexities of special service '999' calls is almost endless, as is the level of human carelessness, folly and misfortune which causes accidents and emergencies to occur in the first place. All this growing and widening range of emergency work over the past decades has led to the need for today's firefighter to be a real master-of-all-trades. Ingenuity and improvisation handed down from the past will be to the fore at every new incident.

The 1990s firefighter needs to be engineer, electrician, chemist, builder, doctor and psychologist all rolled into one. What a far cry from the days of brass helmets and steam powered fire pumps when the sole task of firemen in city and parish alike was simply to be ready for the old enemy – fire.

ing is successful – the person is carefully helped down to safety.

Occasionally there comes a major disaster to further test the skills of all the emergency services. The dramatic images of the 1975 Moorgate London Underground crash with 42 fatalities and 76 injured; the bombing of the Grand Hotel, Brighton, in 1984; or the 1989 Boeing 737 crash onto the M1 motorway at Kegworth – they all serve to show just what sudden mayhem can be caused amid our sophisticated modern world.

Most special service rescues tend to be protracted affairs. Cutting apart a crushed car with a family inside after it has run underneath a 38 ton truck calls for particular skills and personal discipline, as well as some very specialist equipment.

Some non-fire '999' calls do not pose an immediate threat to life and limb but still are likely to provide plenty of problems for fire crews. An electricity power cut or malfunction will see lift-cars suddenly halt between floors in urban high rise buildings, trapping the passengers inside.

Opposite: ***A last pull. The workman had been trapped in a collapsed trench for more than an hour – long enough for television news cameras to reach the scene. West Midlands fire crews, working above and below ground, had used all their expertise, including a complicated winch system, to release him. Limp and exhausted, he was finally safe.*** *(West Midlands Fire Service)*

A dramatic view of a hydraulic platform in action as it hangs in a cloud of smoke, damping down after a major fire in the West Midlands in 1991. *(West Midlands Fire Service)*

CHAPTER 13

SPECIAL RISKS

CHANNEL TUNNEL, INDUSTRIAL SITES, GAS AND OIL RIGS, AIRPORTS, HOUSES OF PARLIAMENT

CHANNEL TUNNEL

Over and above the normal call of duty are some areas of firefighting which demand a particular brand of courage or expertise – and probably both. They include the crews who are responsible for safety in the Channel Tunnel, for our airports, for the special hazards of oil and gas rigs, nuclear and chemical industrial sites. Many of these establishments have their own firefighters, specially trained in the specific expertise which would be demanded if an accident were to take place. But almost always they rely on the back-up of their local fire brigades who often work in close co-operation with them, knowing their problems and how to help deal with these.

Kent Fire Brigade, for instance, has worked closely with the government and with Eurotunnel to make sure that everything possible has been done to protect workers and travellers in the Channel Tunnel. In doing this, they link with their counterparts in France and all their officers are now required to learn French.

Responsibility for fire safety and fire precautions within the tunnel rests with the owners, Eurotunnel. Eurotunnel have been intensely aware, throughout the planning and building, of the need for fire prevention, fire protection and, if the worst should come to the worst, for firefighting.

Apart from the construction material of the tunnels, all of which is fireproof, a third tunnel has been constructed not only for maintenance but for evacuating passengers in the remote event of all the precautions in the running tunnels failing.

All the material used in the rolling stock is fire-resistant and will not produce toxic fumes. As soon as loading is finished at the terminals, fire barriers are lowered across each end of the wagons with emergency doors at the side to allow passengers to move from one wagon to another in case of trouble.

Reckoning that the main hazard will come from passengers' vehicles, smoking is totally banned and so is lifting the bonnet to work on car engines. Attendants will be moving from wagon to wagon throughout the journey to make sure that these vital bans are observed.

Any kind of dangerous smoke or vapour is picked up instantly by detectors and passengers are then warned to pass through to the next wagon.

Cars travelling on wagons stand in shallow troughs which will catch any fuel which might be leaking. Should this catch fire, special aqueous foam is injected to douse the flames immediately and extinguishers are available for staff or passengers to use. If, in spite of all this, a fire becomes life-threatening, a special gas, Halon 1301, is automatically discharged at low concentration and, although this could alarm passengers, it would not harm the atmosphere and it would give them ample time to reach the next wagon in safety. The fire barriers, like the wagons, retain smoke and flames for half an hour and by then, the train would have left the tunnel. The burning wagon would then be shuttled into a siding where it would be dealt with by the emergency services.

In the unlikely event that none of this was effective, three stages of evacuation have been planned.

1. Passengers move from wagon to wagon while the train continues out of the tunnel.

2. This would be triggered if the burning wagon could not be moved. Wagons are coupled in sets of three which can be uncoupled from inside. Passengers would be moved into the safe wagons which would be hauled back to where they had come from by the rear engine or forward to the other side by the leading engine, with the signalling system arranged to take account of such an emergency and react accordingly.

3. If, by some remote chance, the entire train could not be moved, passengers would move along the shuttle to the coach which was opposite a 'cross passage'. From here, they would go out on to a walkway at the side of the tunnel and follow signs leading to doors which would take them into the service tunnel, where smoke and fumes are kept back by higher air pressure. From there, they would pass into a special train in the far tunnel which would evacuate them.

Special fire engines have been built for use in the tunnel and these can be driven from either end of the vehicle, as there is no room to turn round. The basic vehicle is the same for maintenance work, firefighting, ambulance or communications. The firefighting body which fits on to it carries a crew of six plus 500 litres of foam concentrate; 12 x 45 mm (1¾ in) hose and 12 x 70 mm (2¾ in) hose; one breathing apparatus set per firefighter plus spare cylinders; cutting and lifting tools; chemical splash suits and general hand tools.

Eight 'STTS' (Service Tunnel Trans-

The fire engine they hope will never be used in the Channel Tunnel. This unusual chassis, loaded with a 'pod' containing specialist fire and rescue equipment, stands ready for action. Its 'push me-pull you' shape is designed to allow it to move backwards and forwards without turning in the pressurised service tunnel which runs between the two train lines.

port System) vehicles will be available, four at Folkestone and four at Calais.

Kent Fire Brigade has been on standby for the Tunnel throughout its construction, with long-term BA teams and oxygen at the ready. Altogether, 52 firefighters divided into four watches of 13 firefighters each, crew the station 24 hours of every day of the year. Already a close 'entente' has been set up with their counterparts at the Calais end and there have been social events to bring them together against such time when they may have to meet in action.

No matter how carefully the plans and training are made to prevent accidents taking place, the unthinkable can – and does – happen from time to time, and not least in the huge modern developments of oil and gas rigs.

ABERDEEN

Aberdeen is recognised now, worldwide, as the oil and gas capital of Europe. Many rigs are sited off its coast in the North Sea, but the town also has a specialist centre set up to provide training in the theory and the practical work of dealing with the sort of fire which might break out not only on the rigs but in many other places of work. These include ships, whisky distilleries or transportation, hospitals – in fact, anywhere that might pose a particular hazard.

The centre has a strategic alliance with many of the leading international organisations dealing with firefighting, safety and survival training and firefighting training. Among these are the Houston Fire Department in Texas; Calgary Fire Department in Alberta; Westpoint Safety Services; Alberta Survival Systems; Nova Scotia and the Marine Institute, Newfoundland.

Many industries including power stations, hospitals, forestry operators and factories send their workers on the courses relating to their own particular hazards. The cost of the course is a fraction of the cost of the fire which the knowledge gained might prevent.

The consequences of fire can gravely damage the full range of industry. This is why wise employers are turning to the experts for advice on prevention.

AIRPORTS

One of the specific areas in which fire could be disastrous is in air transport. Particular care is taken through the Civil Aviation Authority to prevent fires in airports. Working along with all the other countries in the United Nations, Britain's airports follow strict guidelines on safety, particularly as it concerns fire.

Off to an early start to their holidays, taking off from Manchester Airport soon after 0700 hours on 22 August 1985, 131 passengers and six crew were aboard this Boeing 737 when fire broke out in the port engine, followed by an explosion. The BAA Fire Service rushed to the scene, followed by Greater Manchester Fire Service, but despite their desperate efforts, 55 people died in the smoke and flames which swept through the fuselage. Twenty-five died from inhalation of fumes, 21 from fumes and fire, and nine from the fire alone. Fuel had spilled from the aircraft's tanks after the explosion and a carpet of foam was laid to prevent it from spreading further. Here, crews damp down and remove passengers' luggage from the wreckage. Following the incident, lengthy research into passenger safety and the possible use of smoke hoods, was carried out by the government research department, and a number of improvements to passenger safety became law. (Greater Manchester Fire Service)

Under these regulations, all airfields which are used by paying passengers must comply with set rules. The size of the airports obviously varies, so there are nine different categories. For each one, rules are based on the size of plane, in length and width, which is expected to land there.

Gatwick, one of the biggest airfields in Britain, comes under category 9. The airport fire station stands on the edge of the airfield and its crews must be able to reach a plane in distress within two minutes, and certainly not more than three minutes, of its landing. A minimum of 24,300 litres of water must be available, along with 1,430 litres of foam concentrate, and the fire appliances must be able to pump this at the rate of 9,000 litres a minute.

Gatwick Fire Station has its own control tower. Any pilot in trouble can talk not only to the main airport control staff but to the senior fire officer on duty, seeking his advice if necessary. If there is the possibility of an emergency landing, the decision will be taken jointly with the pilot and the fire officer.

When such a call is made, a particular telephone is used. This warns the firefighters of trouble, and simultaneously opens the huge folding doors of the fire station to reveal a line of giant fire appliances. Each one is able to carry sufficient water to keep its foam flowing long enough to put out any aircraft fire. The floor of the appliance bay is heated and the engines are linked to a permanent electricity supply so that there is no question of a non-starter. As the call comes through on the station loudspeakers, the crews rush to the driving cabins where their breathing apparatus is fixed behind the seats, ready to slip on and be ready by the time they reach the stricken aircraft.

67 toilet fires

The work of all airport firefighters is vitally important. Because of them, fire and accidents at airports and in British aircraft are kept to a minimum. But they do still happen. In five years, the CAA reported 95 galley fires; 67 fires in toilets; 26 incidents in the main passenger cabin; 34 in passenger hand baggage; and 325 in aircraft engines. Mostly these involved minor fire and smoke, and were dealt with by the flight crews.

Fire crews are on duty day and night. They not only deal with problems in aircraft but in the airport buildings themselves where they tackle any fire which might break out, and help with passengers who might be in difficulties. 'Thousands of people pass through the world's airports every day,' explained a senior fire officer. 'Some are experienced business people for whom it is an everyday event, but for many, particularly holidaymakers, it may

Ready for action in any emergency – Gatwick's formidable array of fire engines lines up outside the appliance bay alongside the main runways.

British Airport Authority's Fire Service has 424 officers and crew covering its seven airports. Gatwick, second only to Heathrow (which is the largest airport in the world), has 81 officers and crew to provide 24-hour cover for aircraft landing and taking off, and for the airport buildings. It also provides a full training programme of four weeks basic course for the other BAA airports fire crews. Training includes simulated underwing, undercarriage and two different types of fires, as well as fuel spillage emergencies.

The airport's eight firefighting appliances include three Meteors, four Javelins and one Nubian Major. These are kept ready for the 'off' at all hours. Meteors, the lightest, can pump out 20,727 litres of foam per minute. The Javelin carries 10,000 litres of water. It has a monitor on its cab roof which can shoot out 45,400 litres of foam per minute. Although each vehicle weighs 30.48 tonnes they can accelerate from 0-80 kph in 30.48 seconds. (BAA)

be the first time or a once a year adventure. For some, the excitement and stress is too much, so we go in and deal with heart attacks and other illnesses. All our crews are highly trained in first aid and in the use of defibrillators.

'Remarkably, a few sick people choose to commit suicide in an airport, and we have to cope with them too. Usually it is a cry for help and we pass them on to the medical services, but occasionally they succeed and, again, we deal with this.'

The airport fire crews have close links with their nearby county brigades, who attend as soon as they are called. But the airport crews must be first on the scene.

Airport fire services deal with the planes on the ground. The airlines themselves are responsible for passengers within the aircraft, for their surroundings and for making sure that they escape if there is an emergency landing.

Take British Airways as an example. According to internationally accepted regulations, British Airways regularly inspects the airports at which its planes land to make sure that these comply with all the safety rules. There are also strict regulations on packaging any items of freight which are carried by British Airways aircraft – in order to prevent leakage or possible fire.

British Airways has good cause. As the biggest international cargo airline, as well as carrying 26 million passengers a year over a distance equivalent to a journey to the moon and back, it has planes landing at 153 destinations in 69 countries. British

British Airways Fire Service appliances line up alongside Concorde at Heathrow Airport. (British Airways Fire Service)

Airways has its own fire station operating out of Heathrow, London, in addition to co-operating with the British Airports Authority fire service at the airport and the local authority fire services from adjoining London and Surrey.

Their crews provide 24 hours a day cover throughout the year. They are concerned not just with aircraft – which include Concorde – but inspecting, testing, maintaining records of sprinkler and detection systems and fire alarms as well as keeping an eye on operations like aircraft painting which could be hazardous.

Why do fires happen? Ask the passengers. The CAA has produced a note on causes of fire in all the airlines which showed:

- At least 13 cases of passengers falling asleep and dropping lighted cigarettes down the side of their seats.

- Two toilet fires caused by passengers burning passports (to avoid immigration difficulties).

- One involving petrol leaking from a Microlight aircraft being carried in the hold.

- One 13-year-old boy (old enough to know better) who was striking matches in the toilet and dropping them.

- One passenger heating drugs in the toilet.

- One young woman singeing her hair in what was, apparently, a new fashion technique.

All were dealt with successfully.

OTHER SPECIAL RISKS

Other examples of special risks involve petrochemical manufacture and storage, nuclear installations, medical research establishments, and construction sites involving tunnelling such as for new sewer schemes.

There are a number of large petro-

Opposite: ***Explosions and toxic smoke faced Manchester's crews tackling this huge fire in a haulier's store at Flax Street, Salford, in 1982. Local families were evacuated after their homes were damaged in the explosions and clouds of toxic smoke spread over the area. Here, firefighters huddle against a pallet as they direct a jet on to lorries full of chemicals parked in the yard.*** *(Greater Manchester Fire Service)*

chemical risks in the UK. These pose a particular hazard to firefighters due to their fire and explosive potential. A number of chemicals in solid, liquid or gaseous form are dangerous even in a spill or leakage situation. Some substances can be lethal simply on human skin contact or ingestion.

Nuclear power stations are, of course, operated under very strict safety standards. This also applies to the transportation of nuclear fuel to and from power stations, and to the storage on site of quantities of radioactive materials associated with the nuclear generation of electricity.

Medical research establishments pose special biological hazards for fire crews. In laboratories, there are likely to be organisms in culture, which in a fire or spillage situation would demand great caution from firefighters during any firefighting or clearing up operation.

Palace of Westminster has own uniformed fire brigade

Parliament has no divine protection from fire. In 1834 much of the building at Westminster was destroyed by a tremendous conflagration after a clerk decided to get rid of a load of old wooden 'tally' sticks by burning them in a furnace which became overheated. Since then, apart from wartime bomb damage, there has been no big fire although in March 1992, the Chamber of the House of Commons had to be evacuated after fire broke out on the floor above it.

Few people know, however, that Parliament has its own uniformed fire brigade. The Parliamentary Fire Section, an arm of the Security Force, has 30 fire officers working in three watches under their Principal Fire Officer, John Peen. It responds some 400 times a year to small fires, smells of burning, smoke, suspect packages and other emergencies within the Palace of Westminster.

Its Fire Safety Manager, Ronald Bentley, himself a former London fireman, says that, night and day, the Palace of Westminster and its outbuildings are covered by uniformed patrols of firemen. All of them have had careers in the fire service – mostly in Central London. Every inch of their area is inspected every year and 'there is an incredible amount of experience and knowledge between these men and their officers which permits them to recognise fire risks – in other words to deal with a fire before it has started.' Added to that, they maintain more than a thousand fire extinguishers, test over 200 hose reels and 500 fire alarm callpoints as well as training hundreds of staff in the use of firefighting equipment every year.

All the fire alarms in what is known as 'the Parliamentary Estate' now terminate at two VDU screens in the Metroplitan Police Security Room. A rota of firemen makes sure that these are constantly manned. It is also one of very few premises in the whole of London to be linked by direct line to the London Fire Brigade's Command and Mobilising Centre, without having to dial '999' and go through the exchange first.

Even so, the LFB crews have no automatic right to enter the buildings. If they are called out, they are met at the gates by the Parliamentary Firemen who give them a situation report and guide them to the scene. London's automatic response to a call to Parliament is four pumps, one aerial ladder and a fireboat which moors off the Chancellor's Steps in case they need to attack the incident from the Thames.

Fire at Cox's Chemicals factory in Shropshire made national news when it went up in spectacular flames in February 1993. Crews were hard put to get within range of the buildings as they struggled down the adjoining lanes. (Shropshire Fire and Rescue Service)

Although fires and emergencies on construction sites are somewhat less complicated, when a fire breaks out in a tunnel there can be problems not readily found elsewhere. By their nature, entry into tunnels is usually difficult and restricted, with access down deep vertical shafts. Many tunnelling sites are kept under positive pressure, ie: the atmosphere inside the tunnel is at a higher pressure than outside. This is normal where tunnel digging is likely to encounter wet subsoil and helps to minimise localised flooding as the tunnel progresses. Unfortunately, this adversely affects the use of firefighters' breathing sets, and tunnel fires can be notoriously difficult to extinguish. Thick smoke can be spread by ventilation and natural draughts long distances remote from any fire. This was amply demonstrated during the King's Cross underground tragedy in London in 1987.

To help firefighters deal with incidents at such a range of special risk sites, much research and development of suitable equipment has taken place. As a result, fire crews have over the years been progressively issued with various types of protective suits, more sophisticated breathing apparatus, and more effective monitoring devices to detect the location of gas leaks or radioactive sources.

There is also much work put in by fire brigades on regular training sessions. Often this takes place at the special risk site, working alongside specialist personnel with their invaluable technical knowledge. Nowadays, most UK fire brigades have their own uniformed specialist hazards officer, often backed up by a chemist. During these exercises and other visits, firefighters make themselves familiar with the general layout of the plant, its access points and water supplies. The ongoing training of fire crews includes sessions on the precise nature of special risks on a particular fire station's area.

CHAPTER 14

FIRE FACTS

HUMAN AND MATERIAL COSTS, ARSON

The physical cost of fire has to be measured in both human and material terms.

Firstly, there are fire deaths which in 1992, the most recent year for which statistics are currently available, totalled 789 men, women and children. By any standards, this is an appalling loss of life, but the 1992 total was, in fact, the lowest number of annual UK fire deaths since 1967. However, this was more than offset by the 14,700 serious non-fatal fire casualties which for 1992 were some of the highest on record. During 1992, two firefighters were killed in action. This compared with four in 1991, and six in 1990. 1992 also saw 861 firefighters seriously injured.

Secondly, an enormous amount of money literally goes up in smoke each year. The direct annual UK fire loss broke all records in 1991 when it reached £1 billion. Fortunately, the 1992 figures were significantly down at £850 million. It was the first time for some years that the sum had shown a downward trend. Perhaps the hard work put in by firefighters in getting the fire safety message across to the community is beginning to pay off.

Unfortunately, the direct fire loss total does not include intangibles such as the cost of lost jobs when a factory closes after a fire, or lost future orders. Taking such

Prevention is the name of the game here. Fire safety starts early in the West Midlands where they have their own Young Firefighters' organisation. Boys and girls attend training sessions, learning about fire safety and protection throughout the year. Here they enjoy their annual 'Muster Day'. (West Midlands Fire Service)

factors in as well would produce a much higher annual fire loss figure.

In 1992, UK firefighters attended 425,600 fires, two per cent fewer than in 1991. This was primarily due to the wet weather which reduced the number of grass and heathland fires. There were 107,300 fires in occupied buildings: 65,000 of these were in dwellings. A happier estimation is that by 1992, almost half of all homes had a smoke detector fitted. The number of people alerted to house fires by their smoke alarms tripled between 1988 and 1992.

But accidental fires in dwellings were most likely to be caused by the misuse of electrical equipment, such as cookers being left on, or heaters being knocked over. Faults in appliances were the second most frequent cause of fire in the home, with careless use of cigarettes third.

In 1992, for the second year there was an increase in the number of fires started by washing machines, refrigerators, electric blankets and tumble dryers. A worrying fact was that during the year the num-

'Arson costs £100 million a year'

Half arson fires are in schools

By 1990, fire statistics in the UK showed that arson was spiralling up to record levels, causing losses of £100 million a year – and that 49 per cent of deliberately started fires occurred in schools. Children of all ages were among the culprits, but many were 'curiosity firesetters' – aged between five and 10 years, who came from 'stable families'. Some 40 per cent of the children had significant emotional difficulties, and problems at home, at school and with their peers. Most needed professional mental health counselling.

Several areas, including Merseyside and Tyne and Wear, are pioneering programmes to try to prevent child arson.

Children playing with matches has been one of the biggest causes of fire in the UK for more than a century. Many have died in the outbreaks they have started themselves.

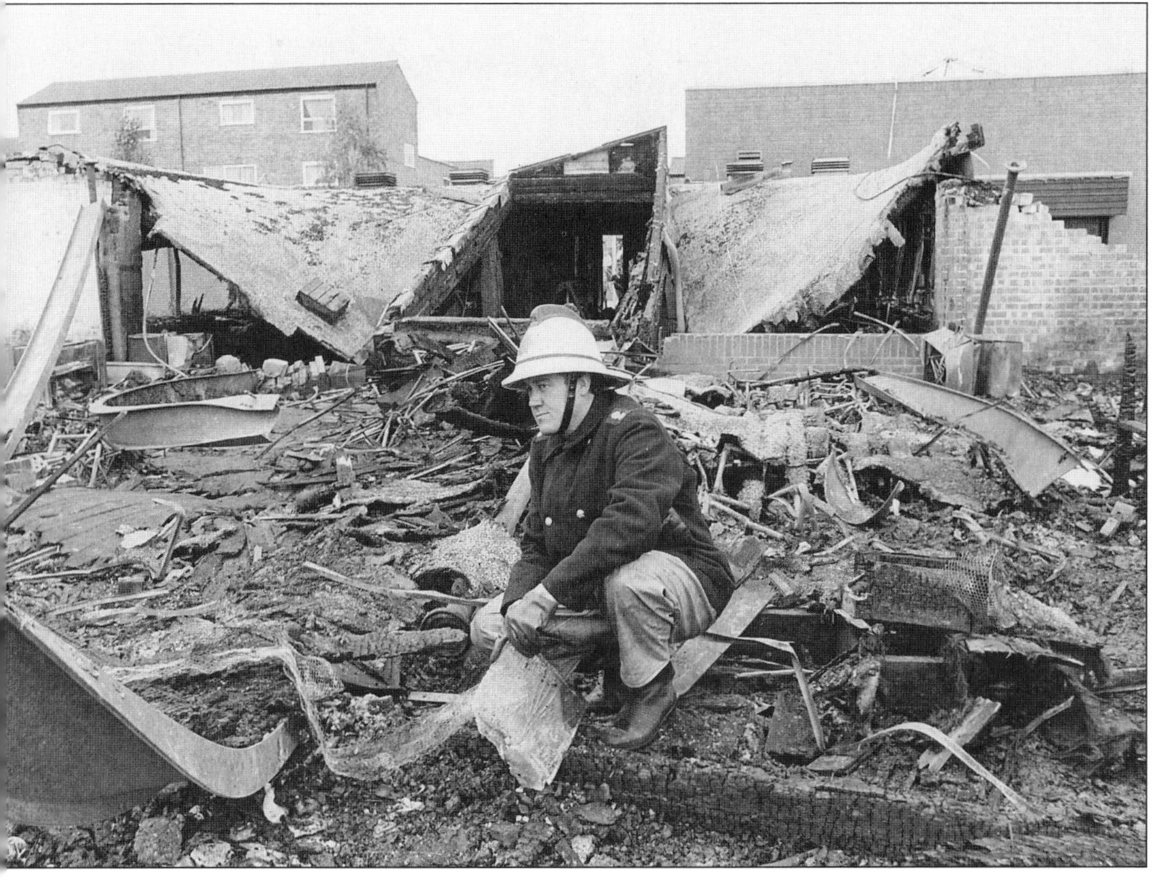

What a waste! This Station Officer sits wearily in the ruins of a primary school, tired and saddened by the stupidity of arson. In 1993, the cost of fires in schools totalled £28 million and in 37 of them there was more than a quarter of a million pounds worth of damage, apart from the loss of work and stress on staff and pupils. Merseyside Fire Service has now started a scheme to try to explain to young arsonists the effects of their mischief and who has to pay for it. (Peterborough Evening Telegraph)

Fireman Sam, Welephant and friends enjoy themselves at the 1993 West Midlands Young Firefighters' Muster Day. It looks fun but serves an important role. (West Midlands Fire Service)

Gray's allergy – to fire and practical jokers!

So great was the fear of fire in Thomas Gray, who wrote the famous poem *An Elegy in a Country Churchyard*, that when he was living in Peterhouse College, Cambridge, in 1756 he had iron bars set across the top of his window from which hung a rope as a primitive fire escape. Hearing the cry of 'Fire! Fire!' in the middle of the night, he leapt from his bed and, still in his nightshirt, slid down the rope to land in a huge vat of cold water, put there by his friends as a practical joke.

Legend has it that he was so annoyed that he moved from Peterhouse to Pembroke College where, in 1760, he wrote to another friend: 'I beg you to bespeak me a Rope-Ladder (for my Neighbours everyday make great progress in drunkenness...) it must be full 36 Foot long, or a little more, but as light and manageable as may be, easy to unroll and not likely to entangle. I never saw one but I suppose it must have strong hooks, or something equivalent, a-top, to throw over an iron bar to be fix'd withinside of my window'.

He had good cause. In 1768 the rooms opposite his were destroyed by fire. He escaped, with a word of tribute for two neighbours who had been studying late into the night and 'raised the alarm to the college and the town' and to 'the very speedy and excellent assistance of engines and men'.

ber of house fires caused by children playing with smoking materials rose by 400 to 3,300 incidents.

Against the sorry statistics, it is easy to get sound advice in order to reduce the risk of fire. There is a wealth of free leaflets and practical guidance available at every fire station across the UK.

By the 1990s, arson was responsible for nearly a quarter of all the fires in Britain. Unemployment and firms going bust were among the reasons suggested for this record level of fire-raising attacks.

In 1993, insurance companies paid out £300 million in compensation for fire damage. In the 10 years between 1983 and 1993 the number of arson attacks doubled.

There seemed to be little doubt that arson figured in the general increase in crime, with more fires started as mindless vandalism by bored children and teenagers and by criminals trying to cover their tracks as well as sacked employees taking out their vengeance on the bosses who dismissed them.

Another suggested cause was the num-

Blazer of glory?

Statistics show that only 14.5 per cent of fire-raisers are women. Male arsonists' peak ages are between 16 and 25, while for women there is no particular age. Feminine efforts tend to be more dramatic and seem to be done to attract attention, create excitement or, above all, as revenge against husbands or lovers. They are less interested in the arrival of the fire engines than men, and often set fire to their own homes and dress up for the occasion. Some are associated with suicide.

ber of mentally disturbed patients being discharged from hospitals into the community without sufficient supervision.

In 1991 there were 24,862 attacks of arson compared with 26,300 in 1992. A decade earlier, in 1981 there were 12,772 arson cases and in 1971, 5,288. By 1994, arson was the cause of 24 per cent of all fires in occupied buildings.

What the Fire Service costs

The cost of providing a public fire service in Britain comes from local and central Government funding. It is remarkably modest compared with the expenditure necessary to run other community services.

Lincolnshire, for example, is a large yet rural county with an average size fire brigade.

1993/94 revenue cost of
Lincolnshire Fire Brigade = £11,036,000

Other services expenditure in Lincolnshire:
(after specific grant allowances)

Education: £213,580,000

Social Services: £43,165,000

Highways : £32,810,000

Police: £28,321,000

The 1993/94 budget of the London Fire Brigade, the largest in Britain, was £250,500,000.

Must be adaptable and outgoing

From a fireman's wife:

It's definitely a case of 'love me, love my job' when you fall in love with a fireman. Right from the beginning, with the passing out parade, you become more and more embroiled in the Service, helping on fire station open days and Christmas parties and standing out in all weathers to cheer him on at sporting events.

As time goes by and your beloved goes in search of promotion, you go in search of new houses, new schools for the children – and new friends for yourself. It never ends. Wives of retained men suffer broken nights sleep when the phone by the bed rings in the early hours. And they have to be prepared to be abandoned without warning in the middle of an evening out.

Senior officers' wives fare no better. The higher ranking your husband is, the more moves you will probably have made. Sometimes they seem to be continually on duty and the family is unable to move without Fire Control knowing. You certainly have to be adaptable and learn to be outgoing, but on the plus side there is great friendship within the Service and pride in your man.

I was the one who suffered the shakes

From a fireman's girlfriend:

A wife or a girlfriend has to come to terms with the fact that a fireman does a dangerous job, but that they do it as safely as possible. However, there are times when reality confronts you. By far the worst time for me was when I realised just how much danger he had been in.

My future husband was on night duty and did not phone to wake me as usual. On my way to work I saw fire engines and hoses strewn across the road as the bus I was on passed the end of the street where the blaze had been fought. I wondered how long they had been there.

Later in the morning my telephone call came and he reassured me that he was safe, but that some of his colleagues had been trapped and one killed. He sounded so tired. It was not until late in the afternoon that he was able to see me briefly before going on duty for his second night and by then I had seen the evening newspapers and the television news and I realised the enormity of it all.

I was the one who suffered the shakes and delayed reaction, having it brought home to me that not only could I have really lost him, but that I loved him dearly.

They were his family – the Watch

From a fireman's ex-wife:

I don't think I realised what I was letting myself in for but I soon found out. You don't just marry a man – you have to share him with the fire brigade. They were his family – the Watch. They worked together, they ate together, they exercised together, some of them were studying and all helping each other. They even slept in the same dormitory.

When someone died in a fire they talked it all through together. And it wasn't just when he was on duty. Every week, there was a birthday, a stag party, a celebration of some sort or something to get out of their system and always with a 'get together' at the pub and home late for supper.

Of course, they aren't all the same, but I certainly couldn't take it any longer. I can't help feeling that you have to be a very special person to stay married to a fireman. I wasn't!

POSTSCRIPT

The real life accounts of fires and rescues which appear throughout this book set out some of the stories behind the work of the British Fire Service, but let it not be thought that the fires and rescues described here are special. Some incidents were major in terms of firefighting teams needed to bring a particular blaze under control. Some were minor and dealt with by the first crew at the scene. Occasionally, some '999' calls led to the ultimate sacrifice: fire crews usually head straight into the danger from which everyone else is fleeing. They pay a high price.

A Government Inquiry into the fire service reported that: '...on occasions a firefighter must voluntarily face extremities of danger which confront few people in time of peace...'

This should be a comfort to the public. For the number of fires, subsequent deaths and casualties, together with the appalling financial cost of fire damage, has soared to record heights in recent years.

Sadly, it is a fact that somewhere, at this very moment, an electrical plug is overheating in an overloaded circuit, or a glowing cigarette end has fallen down the back of a foam filled sofa. Before long, the smouldering fire will kindle and gather strength before suddenly bursting into a fiery mass with huge volumes of thick black toxic smoke capable of suffocating in seconds. For it is usually smoke which is the killer, not the flames.

If the threat to life is not from fire it may be a car crash on the motorways or rural lanes of Britain in which driver and passengers are trapped and injured inside the crushed wreckage. Hopefully, a prompt '999' call will be made and the fire service – working with the other emergency services – will be rapidly on their way to yet another situation where human drama may be played out.

The nation's fire crews never become completely inured to the suffering and distress which surrounds much of their work. It is a different set of men, women and children involved every time.

Thankfully, there are happier sides to being a firefighter. It might well be the utter satisfaction of saving life, either in a fire or accident situation, or the successful extrication of a cow from a slurry pit, or a kitten snatched from up a tree.

The British Fire Service and those who wear its uniform can perhaps best be described as a modern-day mix between the Sixth Cavalry, and St. George. The fire dragon and its threat to human life and property has to be beaten – constantly.

By any standard the achievements and service provided by the British firefighter is quite remarkable. Without any doubt whatsoever, it really is 'One Hell of a Job'.

APPENDIX

BRIGADE DETAILS, COUNTY BY COUNTY, FOR 1994

COUNTY OF AVON FIRE BRIGADE. HQ Temple Back, Bristol

Area 512 sqm. Risks: A-C. Calls 15,356, spec 2,382; false 6,542. Estab: 660 w/t; 212 p/t. Appl: 42 Wrt; 15 WrL, 4 TL, 2 HP, 3 RT, 10 Psu, 1 CU, 1 HL, 2 HRT, 1 CIU, 1 MRT, BA 232 air. Radio: Home Office AM. Stations: W/t Temple, Southmead, Avonmouth, Patchway, Bath, Brislington, Speedwell, Kingswood, Weston-super-Mare, Bedminster. D/m Yate. P/t Thornbury, Radstock, Paulton, Keynsham, Clevedon, Portishead, Pill, Chew Magna, Blagdon, Winscombe, Yatton, Nailsea.

BEDFORDSHIRE COUNTY FIRE AND RESCUE SERVICE HQ Kempston, Bedford

Area 123,461 hectares. Risks B-D. Calls 6,770, spec 927, false 2,681. Estab: 315 w/t; 161 p/t. Appl: 3 HP, 26 WrL (rescue), 2 Wrl, 2 WrC, 7 L4P, 2 4x4, 35 PP, 2 rescue units, demountables – 1 Cav, 2 CIU, 2 SU, 2 FoU, 1 CU, 22 ancillary, BA 125 air. Radio: 86 Home Office VHF, 72 Pye VHF, 91 Motorola HT600E. Stations: W/t Bedford, Dunstable, Kempston, Luton, Stopsley. D/m Leighton Buzzard, Toddington. P/t Ampthill, Biggleswade, Harrold, Potton, Sandy, Shefford, Woburn.

ROYAL BERKSHIRE FIRE AND RESCUE SERVICE. HQ Reading

Area 125,886 hectares. Risks: A-D. Calls 15,460, spec 1,515, false 5,573. Estab: 436 w/t; 156 p/t. Appl: 20 PL, 2 P, 2 WrT, 1 L4P, 1 FoT, 2 RSV, 1 BAT, 1 SAL, 1 CU, 2 HP, 15 PCV, 1 CAV, 1 CIU, 62 W cars, BA 148 air. Radio: Home Office AM. Stations: W/t Newbury, Caversham Road, Dee Road, Bracknell, Whitley Wood, Wokingham Road, Windsor, Slough, Langley, Maidenhead. P/t Hungerford, Lambourn, Pangbourne, Mortimer, Crowthorne, Sonning, Wargrave, Wokingham, Ascot, Cookham.

BUCKINGHAMSHIRE FIRE AND RESCUE SERVICE. HQ Aylesbury

Area 725 sqm. Risks B-D. Calls 8,277, spec 2,178, false 3,324. Estab: 316 w/t, 254 p/t. Appl: 11 RP, 18 WrL, 5 P, 4 L4T, 20 SU, 1 HP, 1 CU, 1 CAV, 1 HL, 2 WrC, 1 rescue boat, 5 PCV, 3 4x4 pick-up, 1 caravan unit, BA 156 air. Radio: Home Office VHF/AM. Stations: W/t, Bletchley, Broughton, Aylesbury, Great Holm, High Wycombe. D/m Amersham, Beaconsfield, Buckingham, Gerrards Cross, Newport Pagnell. P/t Olney, Woburn Sands, Winslow, Wolverton, Waddesdon, Whitchurch, Brill, Haddenham, Princes Risborough, Great Missenden, Chesham, Burnham, Marlow, Stokenchurch.

CAMBRIDGESHIRE FIRE AND RESCUE SERVICE. HQ Huntingdon

Area 1,316 sqm. Risks: B-D. Calls 9,552, spec 1,539, false 4,686. Estab: 290 w/t, 380 r/t, 20 Vol. Appl: 2 TL, 2 RV, 1 SRU, 1 CCU, 3 WrC, 1 HSRU, 1 RB, 1 Prime Mover, 30 WrLR, 3 WrL, 16 WrTR, 9 WrT. BA 184 air. Radio: Home Office AM. Stations: W/t Cambridge, Peterborough (Dogsthorpe), Peterborough (Stanground), Huntingdon. D/m Ely, St Neots, Wisbech. R/t Cottenham, Sutton, Littleport, Soham, Burwell, Swaffham, Bulbeck, Linton, Sawston, Gamlingay, Papworth Everard, Yaxley, Whittlesey, Thorney, March, Manea, Chatteris, Ramsey, Sawtry, Kimbolton, St Ives.
Volunteer: Peterborough Volunteer Fire Brigade.

CHESHIRE FIRE BRIGADE. HQ Chester

Area 233,000 hectares. Calls 14,285, spec 1,584, false, 5,595. Estab: 642 w/t, 204 p/t. Appl: 46 WrL, 9 L4T, 4 RT, 1 TL, 3 HP, 2 CU, 2 FoT, 1 PetC, 2 Special Incident Units. BA 270 comp. air. Radio Home Office. Stations : W/t Birchwood, Chester, Ellesmere Port, Macclesfield, Runcorn, Warrington, Widnes, Wilmslow. D/m Congleton, Frodsham, Knutsford, Northwich, Stockton Heath, Winsford. P/t Audlem, Bollington, Holmes Chapel, Malpas, Middlewich, Nantwich, Poynton, Sandbach, Tarporley.

CLEVELAND COUNTY FIRE BRIGADE. HQ Hartlepool

Area: 59,090 hectares. Risks: special, A-D. Calls: 15,560. Estab: 643 w/t, 72 p/t. Appl: 11 WrL, 12 WrT, 3 ET, 2 FoT, 1 HP (98), 1 HP (90), 1 HP (77), 2 L6V, 2 FBT. BA 140 CA poss. Pressure, 95. poss pressure escape sets. Stations: W/t Middlesbrough, Grangetown, Redcar, Coulby Newham, Marine, Stockton, Thornaby, Billingham, Stranton. R/t Guisborough, Saltburn, Skelton, Loftus, Yarm, Headland.

COUNTY OF CLWYD FIRE BRIGADE. HQ Rhyl

Area: 936.11 sqm. Risks: C-D. Calls: 6,766, spec 754, false, 2,942. Estab: 434, 187 w/t, 225 p/t. Appl: 30 WrL, 2 HP, 1 FoT, 5 L4P, 2 ET, 1 CU, 1 CIU, 1 ALP. BA 144 air. Radio: Home Office AM. Stations: W/t Wrexham, Deeside, Rhyl. P/t Flint, Buckley, Mold, Johnstown, Chirk, Llangollen, Corwen, Prestatyn, St Asaph, Abergele, Denbigh, Ruthin, Cerrig-y-Drudion, Holywell.

CORNWALL COUNTY FIRE BRIGADE. HQ Truro

Area: 1,370 sqm. Risks: B-D. Calls: 5,759, spec 894, false 1,868. Estab: 691. 177 w/t, 432 p/t. Appl: 38 WrL, 11 WrT, 1 HP, 1 P, 3 ET, 2 FoTr, 3 WrC, 33 L4P. BA 200 air. Radio AM Microwave. FM. Stations: W/t Truro, Falmouth, Penzance, Camborne, Newquay, Bodmin, St Austell. P/t St Ives, Helston, Redruth, Penryn, St Mawes, Perranporth, St Keverne, Mullion, St Just, St Columb, Liskeard, Bude, Looe, Launceston, Padstow, Wadebridge, Mevagissey, Delabole, Torpoint, Saltash, Callington, Fowey, St Dennis, Polruan, Lostwithiel.

CUMBRIA COUNTY FIRE SERVICE. HQ Cockermouth

Area: 2,680 sqm. Risks: B-D. Calls: 7,853, spec 818, false 3,392. Estab: 756. 286 w/t, 439 p/t. Appl: 10 WrL, 46 WrT, 3 TL, 3 FoT, 6 rescue units, 2 CIU, 4LP4P, 60 LPP, BA 252 air. Radio: Home Office AM. Stations: W/t Workington, Whitehaven, Barrow-in-Furness, Barrow, Kendal, Carlisle. P/t Ambleside, Arnside, Broughton, Coniston, Dalton, Grange, Kirkby Lonsdale, Milnthorpe, Sedbergh, Staveley, Ulverston, Walney, Windermere, Alston, Appleby, Brampton, Kirkby Stephen, Lazonby, Longtown, Patterdale, Penrith, Shap.

DERBYSHIRE FIRE AND RESCUE SERVICE. HQ Littleover

Area: 1,016 sqm. Risks: A-D. Calls: 18,716, spec 1518, false 6,339, others 10,859. Estab: 515 w/t, 408 p/t. Appl: 54 WrL, 3 TL, 2 HP, 3 WrC, 2 BAT, 2 FST, 1 L4P, 1 CAV, 1 CU, 2 DecU, 1 RecVeh. BA 242 air. Radio: Home Office AM. Stations: W/t Buxton, New Mills, Glossop, Matlock, Long Eaton, Ripley, Chesterfield, Ascot Drive, Derby, Nottingham Road, Derby, Kingsway, Derby, Swadlincote. P/t Whaley Bridge, Chapel, Bradwell, Hathersage, Bakewell, Ashbourne, Wirksworth, Alfreton, Crich, Belper, Duffield, Heanor, Dronfield, Staveley, Clowne, Bolsover, Shirebrook, Clay Cross, Melbourne.

DEVON FIRE AND RESCUE SERVICE. HQ Exeter

Area: 2,591 sqm. Risks: A-D. Calls: 14,534, spec 1,926, false 5,889. Estab: 1,353, 547 W/t, 780 P/t. 10 Vol. Appl: 103 WrL, 3 HP (28.2m), 3 TL, 4 HL, 131 LPP, 4 ET, 1 L4P, 150 other vehicles. BA 418 air. Radio: Home Office AM. Stations: W/t Exeter, Torquay, Plympton, Camels Head, Crownhill, Greenbank, Plymstock. D/m Barnstaple, Ilfracombe, Exmouth, Paignton. P/t Appledore, Bideford, Braunton, Chulmleigh, Combe Martin, Hartland, Hatherleigh, Holsworthy, Lynton, North Tawton, Okehampton, South Molton, Torrington, Woolacombe, Ashburton, Bovey Tracey, Brixham, Buckfastleigh, Chagford, Dartmouth, Dawlish, Kingsbridge, Moretonhampstead, Newton Abbot, Teignmouth, Totnes, Salcombe, Axminster, Bampton, Budleigh Salterton, Colyton, Crediton, Cullompton, Honiton, Ottery St Mary, Seaton, Sidmouth, Tiverton, Topsham, Witheridge, Bere Alston, Ivybridge, Modbury, Princetown, Tavistock, Yelverton. Volunteer: Kingston.

DORSET FIRE BRIGADE. HQ Dorchester

Area: 265,376 hectares. Risks: B-D. Calls: 7,943 (fires 1,632, chimney 557, small fires 1,234, false alarms 3,363, spec RTA 280, others 877). Estab: 307 w/t, 364 p/t. Appl: 1 TL, 2 HP, 14 WrT, 27 WrL, 3 L6P, 19 L4T, 2 RT, 1 FoT, 1 CU, 2 PCV, 2 SV, 1 WrC (9,000 litres), 1 BAT. BA 200 air. Radio: AM. Stations: W/t Weymouth, Springbourne, Christchurch, Redhill Park, Westbourne, Poole, Hamworthy. P/t Beaminster, Blandford, Bridport, Charmouth, Dorchester, Gillingham, Lyme Regis, Maiden Newton, Portland, Shaftesbury, Sherborne, Sturminster Newton, Bere Regis, Cranborne, Ferndown (nucleus manned), Swanage, Verwood, Wareham, Wimborne.

DURHAM COUNTY FIRE AND RESCUE BRIGADE. HQ Durham

Area: 243,365 hectares. Risks: B-D. Calls: 11,490, spec 728, false 4,637. Estab: 442 w/t, 228 p/t. Appl: 43 WrL, 6 specials, 105 mobile radio units. BA 206 air. Radio: Home Office AM. Stations: W/t Consett, Stanley, Fence Houses, Seaham, Peterlee, Durham, Bishop Auckland, Darlington, Newton Aycliffe. R/t Wheatley Hill, Langley Park, Crook, Spennymoor, Sedgefield, Stanhope, Middleton-in-Teesdale, Barnard Castle.

DYFED COUNTY FIRE BRIGADE. HQ Carmarthen

Area: 2,226 sqm. Risks: B-D. Calls: 8,514, spec 1,207, false 2,246. Estab: 228 w/t, 342 p/t. Appl: 34 WV, 5 UV, 3 SV, 38 WrL, 5 PL, 33 ET, 1 FPBus, 1 FPVan, 1 FPUnit, 1BL, 1 CU, 2 Prime Movers, 1 FoT, 1 FEV, 1 MRU, 1 HP, 1 L4P, 1 L4R, 2 TL, 48 PP, 7 L4V, Pods – BA Training, 1 CaV, 1 WrC, 1 FoT, Decontamination. BA 2 air. Radio: Home Office AM. Stations: W/t Llanelli, Carmarthen, Ammanford, Haverfordwest, Milford Haven, Pembroke Dock, Aberystwyth. P/t Kidwelly, Pontyates, Tumble, Llandeilo, Llandovery, Llandyssul, Newcastle Emlyn, Narberth, Tenby, Whitland, Cardigan, Fishguard, St Davids, Crymych, Caldy Island Volunteer Unit, Tregaron, New Quay, Aberaeron, Lampeter, Borth Local Volunteer Fire Unit.

ESSEX COUNTY FIRE AND RESCUE SERVICE. HQ Hutton, Brentwood

Area: 367,192 hectares. Risks: B-D. Calls: 20,275, spec 3,335, false 8,859. Estab: 924 w/t 406 p/t. Appl: 41 Wrt, 57 RP, 2 HP, 3 ALP, 3 LWrT, 3 LU, 1 RV, 1 FBt, 96 PP, 5 RT, 4 FoTr, 2 FoT, 2 FTank, 1 HL, 1 CU. BA 390 air. Stations: W/t Clacton, Colchester, Chelmsford, Great Baddow, Leigh, Southend, Basildon, Brentwood, Canvey Island, Grays, Hadleigh, Tilbury, Harlow Central, Loughton, Ongar. D/m Dovercourt, South Woodham

Ferrers, Waltham Abbey. P/t Braintree, Brightlingsea, Coggeshall, Frinton, Halstead, Manningtree, Sible Hedingham, Tiptree, West Mersea, Wethersfield, Witham, Wivenhoe, Burnham, Hawkwell, Maldon, Rayleigh, Rochford, Shoeburyness, Tillingham, Tollesbury, Billericay, Corringham, Ingatestone, Wickford, Dunmow, Epping, Harlow, Leaden Roding, Newport, Saffron Walden, Stansted, Thaxted.

MID GLAMORGAN FIRE SERVICE. HQ Pontyclun

Area: 393 sqm. Risks: B-D. Calls: 12,588, spec 1,180, false 4,150. Estab: 342 w/t, 264 p/t. Appl: 40 WrL, 15 L4V, 3 HP, 3 RT, 2 FoT, 1 RU, 16 UV, 46 WV, 4 PCV, 1 WrC, 6 demountable appliances with control unit, salvage, BA unit, Chemical unit, canteen and lighting pods. BA 160 air. Radio: Home Office and IAL 'Firewatch' System. Stations: W/t Merthyr Tydfil, Pontypridd, Aberdare, Caerphilly, Bargoed, Bridgend, Tonypandy, Maesteg. P/t Pontyclun, Hirwaun, Abercynon, Treharris, Rhymney, Porthcawl, Kenfig Hill, Pencoed, Ogmore Vale, Pontycymmer, Treorchy, Ferndale, Porth, Gilfach Goch.

SOUTH GLAMORGAN FIRE AND RESCUE SERVICE. HQ Cardiff

Area: 41,622 hectares. Risks: A-D. Calls: 8,194, spec 851, false 3,726. Estab: 325 w/t, 20 p/t. Appl: 15 WrL, 1 TL (30m), 1 HP, 2 ETs, 1 SRU, 2FoT, 1 DCU, 1 HL, 7 LP, 2 L4V, 2 RO/RO (with CU, BA, CIU and 2 GP pods), 41 others. BA 81 air. Radio: Home Office AM. Stations: W/t Central, Roath, Whitchurch, Ely, Barry, Penarth. D/m Cowbridge. P/t Llantwit Major.

WEST GLAMORGAN COUNTY FIRE SERVICE. HQ Morriston, Swansea

Area: 315 sqm. Risks: A-D. Calls: 7,866, spec 1,045, false 2,882. Estab: 247 w/t, 111p/t. Appl: 18 WrTL, 1 TL, 1 HP, 6 L4P, 3 L4V, 20 WCar, 9UV, 4 Rolonof (Prime Movers), 1 RAV, 8 pods (2 FoT, WC, Bat, CIU, HL, CU, CaV). BA 98 air. Radio: Home Office AM. Stations: W/t Neath, Port Talbot, Parc Tawe, Sketty Green, Morriston, Pontardawe. R/t Glynneath, Cymmer, Reynoldstown, Seven Sisters, Gorseinon, Pontardulais.

GLOUCESTERSHIRE FIRE AND RESCUE SERVICE. HQ Cheltenham

Area: 264,901 hectares. Risks B-D. Calls: 7,006 (fire 2,902, spec 1,172, false 2,932). Estab: 229 w/t, 271 r/t. Appl: 31 WrL, 9 RIV, 1 Tl, 1 HP, 1 ET, 3 RA, 1 ISU, 1 DCU, 1 FoT, 1 CU. BA 170 Sabre Centurion sets, 2 Sabre Centurion air lines. Radio: Home Office AM. Stations: W/t Gloucester, Stroud, Cheltenham. D/m Cirencester. R/t Lydney, Coleford, Cinderford, Newent, Painswick, Nailsworth, Wotton-under-Edge, Dursley, Tewkesbury, Winchcombe, Chipping Campden, Moreton-in-Marsh, Stow-on-the-Wold, Northleach, Fairford, Tetbury.

GUERNSEY FIRE BRIGADE. HQ St. Peter Port

Area: 30 sqm. Risks C + special. Calls: 1,461, spec 393, false 615. Estab: 55 w/t, 13 p/t. Appl: 1 ComU, 3WrL, 2 WrC, 2 L4P, 1TL, 1 ET, 1 L4V, 4 WCar, 1 UV, 1 TrPM, 1 TrPL, 2 FoTr, 1 STr, 1 HLTr, 1 HMTr, 1 LUTr, 16 LPP. BA 36 air. Station: W/t Town Arsenal.

GWENT FIRE BRIGADE. HQ Pontypool

Area: 137,700 hectares. Risks: B-D. Calls: 8,314, spec 489, false 3,626. Estab: 289 w/t, 156 r/t. Appl: 31 WrL, 2 HP, 2 RT, 15 L4P, 1 FoT (van), 1 CU, 1 CIU, 1 CaV, 1 FPTr. BA 155 air. Radio: Storno FM. Stations: W/t Cwmbran, Maindee, Malpas, New Inn. D/m Abercarn, Abertillery, Caldicot, Cefn Forest, Duffryn, Ebbw Vale. R/t Abergavenny, Abersychan, Blaenavon, Blaina, Brynmawr, Chepstow, Monmouth, Risca, Tredegar, Usk.

GWYNEDD FIRE SERVICE. HQ Caernarfon

Area: 1,492 sqm. Risks: B-D. Calls: 3,961, spec 493, false 1,612. Estab: 100 w/t, 418 p/t. Appl: 28 WrL, 3 WrT, 8 L4P, 2 TL,1 CIU, 4 PCV, 1 Comm Unit. CABA 180. Radio: Home Office AM/FM. Stations: W/t Holyhead, Bangor, Caernarfon, Llandudno, Dolgellau. P/t Amlwch, Llangefni, Rhosneigr, Llanfairfechan, Menai Bridge, Beaumaris, Benllech, Llanberis, Nefyn, Abersoch, Pwllheli, Porthmadog, Conwy, Llanrwst, Betws-y-Coed, Aberdovey, Bala, Tywyn, Barmouth, Harlech, Blaenau Ffestiniog.

HAMPSHIRE FIRE AND RESCUE SERVICE. HQ Eastleigh

Area: 377,900 hectares. Risks: B-D. Calls: 18,850, spec 1,980, false 6,294, malicious 779. Estab: 784 w/t, 698 p/t. Appl: 106 P, 6 RT, 6 WrC, 3 ET, 1 CU, 2 TL (30), 5 HP (21), 7 L4P, 10 L4T, 1 CV, 1 Inshore Fireboat, 1 Recovery Unit, 1 Fire Safety Exhib Unit. BA 350 air. Radio: Home Office AM. Stations: W/t Basingstoke, Rushmoor, Gosport, Copnor, Cosham, Southsea, Fareham, Eastleigh, St Mary's, Redbridge, Woolston. D/m Havant, Winchester, Andover, Lyndhurst, Fawley. P/t Fleet, Alton, Whitchurch, Grayshott, Hartley Wintney, Kingsclere, Odiham, Overton, Tadley, Liphook, Yateley, Bordon, Waterlooville, Hayling Island, Wickham, Horndean, Emsworth, Titchfield, Portchester, Petersfield, Hamble, Romsey, Stockbridge, Sutton Scotney, Alresford, Twyford, Botley, West End, Bishops Waltham, Droxford, Lymington, Hythe, Ringwood, Totton, Fordingbridge, Beaulieu, Brockenhurst, New Milton, Burley.

HEREFORD AND WORCESTER FIRE BRIGADE. HQ Worcester

Area: 392,678 hectares. Risks: B-D. Calls: 8,468. Estab: 349 w/t, 369 r/t, Appl: 52 WrL, 2 TL, 2 HP, 1 CU, 3 ET, 3 WC, 1 L4P, 2 L6P, 80 cars, vans, etc. BA 240 air. Radio: Home Office AM. Stations: W/t Kidderminster, Redditch, Worcester, Hereford. D/m Bromsgrove, Droitwich, Evesham, Malvern. P/t Stourport, Bewdley, Pebworth, Broadway, Pershore, Upton-upon-Severn, Ledbury, Bromyard, Fownhope, Ross-on-Wye, Whitchurch, Ewyas Harold, Eardisley, Kington, Kingsland, Leominster, Tenbury Wells.

HERTFORDSHIRE FIRE AND RESCUE SERVICE. HQ Hertford

Area: 631 sqm. Risks: B-D. Calls: 13,492 (spec 2,756, false 5,761, fires 4,219, out of county 756). Estab: 591 w/t, 225 p/t. Appl: 3 WrE, 17 WrL, 23 WrT, 3 HP, 37 wireless cars, 1 DecontamU, 2 ST, 1 ErT, 1 Exhibition Unit. Stations: W/t Hemel Hempstead, Rickmansworth, Watford, Garston, St Albans, Borehamwood, Potters Bar, Cheshunt, Welwyn Garden City, Stevenage, Hertford, Baldock. D/m Hatfield, Bishops Stortford, Hitchin, Royston. R/t Markyate, Tring, Berkhamsted, Bovingdon, Kings Langley, Bushey, Redbourn, Radlett, Hoddesdon, Welwyn, Wheathampstead, Harpenden, Ware, Much Hadham, Sawbridgeworth, Buntingford.

HUMBERSIDE FIRE BRIGADE. HQ Hull

Area: 1,365 sqm. Risks: A-D. Calls: 16,029 (spec 1,636, false 6,502). Estab: 744 w/t, 328 p/t. Appl: 65 WrT, 19 special, 64 others. BA 276 air. Radio: Home Office AM. Stations: Hull Central, Hull West, Hull North, Beverley, Brough, Market Weighton, Pocklington, East Hull, Bransholme, Bridlington, Driffield, Sledmere, Hornsea, Withernsea, Patrington, Preston, Grimsby Peaks Lane, Grimsby Cromwell Road, Cleethorpes, Immingham, Waltham, Barton, Scunthorpe, Goole, Snaith, Crowle, Epworth, Kirton in Lindsey, Winterton, Howden, Brigg.

ISLE OF MAN FIRE AND RESCUE SERVICE. HQ Douglas

Area: 227 sqm. Risks: B-D. Calls: 1,158 (spec 195, false/malicious 49). Estab: 55 w/t, 96 r/t. Appl: 4 WrTL, 4 WrT, 1 TLP (100 ft), 1 HP (75 ft), 1 PE, 2 RTA, 1 FoT/HL, 3 Pa (4x4), 1 LPA (4x4), 3 LPA (6x6), 1 HRU. BA 64 air. Stations: W/t Douglas. R/t Castletown, Kirk Michael, Laxey, Peel, Port Erin, Ramsay.

ISLE OF WIGHT FIRE AND RESCUE SERVICE. HQ Newport

Area: 38,013 hectares. Risks: B-D. Calls: 1,911 (spec 342, false 553). Estab: 50 w/t, 168 p/t. Appl: 12 WrL, 7 WrT, 1 RT, 1 BA/CIU, 2 WrC, 2 HP, 1 FST, 27 PP, 1 L4V, 1 PCV, 2 UV. BA 96 air. Radio: Home Office AM. Stations: W/t Newport. P/t Newport, Cowes, East Cowes, Ryde, Bembridge, Sandown, Shanklin, Ventnor, Freshwater, Yarmouth.

ISLES OF SCILLY FIRE BRIGADE. HQ Truro

Area: 6 sqm. Risks: C-D. Calls: 48 (spec 29, false 4, fire 1). Estab: 1 w/t, 32 p/t. Appl: 2 WrT, 1 L4T, 1 L4P, 8 PP. BA 16. Stations: p/t St Mary's, Tresco, St Martin's, St Agnes, Bryher.

JERSEY FIRE SERVICE. HQ St Helier

Area: 45 sqm. Risks: B-D. Calls: 2,511 (spec 1,062, false 910); Estab: 74 w/t, 42 p/t. Appl: 6 WrL, 2 WrC, 1 ET, 1 FoT, 1 HP (93), 2 TV, 8 cars, 2 vans, 2 TrPM, 2 TrPL, 12 LPP, 2 marine rescue craft. Stations: W/t St Helier. D/m St Brelade.

KENT FIRE BRIGADE. HQ Maidstone

Area: 373,192 hectares. Risks: B-D. Calls: 35,390 (spec 3,043, false 8,632, fires 9,019); Estab: 950 w/t, 704 p/t. Appl: 28 RWrL, 14 WrL, 61 WrT, 2 WU, 7 HV, 10 PM, 2 FU, 3 Land Rover, 2 HU, 1 BAU, 1 ETU, 3 ISU, 2 ICCU, 1 MRU, 3 GPU, 5 light boats, 2 BA Mobile Workshop Vans, 3 FEMS Mobile Workshop Vans, 6 MWks, 450 CABA, 40 LDBA, 92 ancillary vehicles. CABA 450. Stations: W/t Dartford, Thames-side, Strood, Medway, Maidstone, Tunbridge Wells, Margate, Thanet, Ramsgate, Canterbury, Dover, Folkestone. D/m Sheppey, Sittingbourne, Faversham, Sevenoaks, Tonbridge, Larkfield, Ashford, Whitstable, Herne Bay, Deal. P/t Teynham, Eastchurch, Queenborough, Rainham, Chatham, Gillingham, Halling, Hoo, Cliffe, Grain, Swanscombe, Chilham, Tenterden, Wye, Charing, Lenham, Headcorn, Cranbrook, Hawkhurst, Marden, Matfield, Paddock Wood, Southborough, Rusthall, Edenbridge, Westerham, Seal, Borough Green, Aldington, Horton Kirby, Swanley, New Romney, Westgate, Sandwich, Sturry, Wingham, Eastry, Aylesham, Whitfield, St Margarets, Hythe, Dymchurch, Lydd.

LANCASHIRE COUNTY FIRE BRIGADE. HQ Preston

Area: 306,951 hectares; Risks: B-D. Calls: 47,476 (spec 3,036, good intent 7,058, mechanical 1,989, malicious 4,745). Estab: 996 W/t, 479 P/t. Appl: 87 PA, 6 TL, 6 ET, 3 FoT, 1 CU/CAV, 1 L4P, 1 L4V, 1 CIU, 1 BA unit, 91 ancillary. BA 338. Radio: Private FM. Stations: W/t Lancaster, Morecambe, Blackpool (Bispham), Blackpool (South Shore), Fleetwood, St. Annes, Accrington, Blackburn, Rawtenstall, Darwen, Burnley, Nelson, Preston, Chorley, Skelmersdale, Penwortham. D/m Bacup, Ormskirk, Fulwood, Leyland. P/t Bolton le Sands, Carnforth, Silverdale, Hornby, Garstang, Preesall, Wesham, Lytham, Great Harwood, Haslingden, Oswaldtwistle, Padiham, Clitheroe, Barnoldswick, Earby, Colne, Bamber Bridge, Tarleton, Longridge.

LEICESTERSHIRE FIRE AND RESCUE SERVICE. HQ Leicester

Area: 985 sqm. Calls 13,151 (spec 1,766, false 5,138); Estab: 467 w/t, 216 p/t . Appl: 39 WrL, 2 ET/CU, 1 CU, 2 RV, 2 FST, 1 TL, 1 HP, 1 CIU, 1 CAV, BA 170 air. Radio: Home Office AM. Stations: W/t Loughborough, Coalville, Hastings Road, Leicester, Aikman Avenue, Leicester, Lancaster Road, Leicester, Wigston, Oakham, Hinckley. P/t Melton Mowbray, Syston, Ashby De La Zouch, Moira, Shepshed, Billesdon, Uppingham, Kibworth Beauchamp, Market Harborough, Lutterworth, Market Bosworth.

LINCOLNSHIRE FIRE BRIGADE. HQ Lincoln

Area: 591,470 hectares; Risks: B-D; calls 6,591; Estab: 193 w/t, 516 p/t. Appl: 71 plus 30 ancillary, BA 232 air. Radio: Home Office AM. Stations: W/t Lincoln, w/t-d/m Gainsborough, Skegness, Boston, Spalding, Grantham, p/t Bardney, Caistor, Market Rasen, N. Hykeham, Saxilby, Waddington, Wragby, Alford, Binbrook, Horncastle, Louth, Mablethorpe, North Somercotes, Spilsby, Wainfleet, Crowland, Donington, Holbeach, Kirton, Leverton, Long Sutton, Woodhall Spa, Billingborough, Billinghay, Bourne, Brant Broughton, Corby Glen, Market Deeping, Metheringham, Sleaford, Stamford.

LONDON FIRE BRIGADE. HQ Albert Embankment

Area: 157,944 hectares. Risks: Calls 243,840 (fires 44,295, spec 58,900); Estab: operational 6,388, non-operational 340. Appl: 269 P, 11 TL, 13 HP, 6 ACP, 6 AFC, 6 HRU, 6 CSU, 3 MRS, 49 MDC, 31 VB, 16 PCB, 1 COM1, 6 FCB, 5 FIB, 24 HDC, 12 HLB, 6 DCB, 5 ACB, 1 EUB, 4 BFB, 6 BATB, 2 Fbt, 158 ancillaries. Radio: Home Office AM. Stations: W/t Stanmore, Harrow, Ruislip, Northolt, Wembley, Hillingdon, Park Royal, Willesden, Hayes, Southall, Ealing, Acton, North Kensington, Kensington, Hammersmith, Chelsea, Fulham, Chiswick, Heston, Feltham, Enfield, Barnet, Southgate, Edmonton, Mill Hill, Finchley, Hornsey, Tottenham, Hendon, West Hampstead, Belsize, Kentish Town, Holloway, Islington, Paddington, Manchester Square, Euston, Barbican, Clerkenwell, Dowgate, Soho, Knightsbridge, Westminster, Stoke Newington, Kingsland, Shoreditch, Whitechapel, Chingford, Walthamstow, Leyton, Leytonstone, Bow, Homerton, Bethnal Green, Shadwell, Woodford, Stratford, Poplar, Millwall, Plaistow, Silvertown, Hainault, Ilford, Barking, Dagenham, Romford, Hornchurch, East Ham, Wennington, Southwark, Dockhead, Old Kent Road, Deptford, Peckham, New Cross, Forest Hill, Greenwich, East Greenwich, Woolwich, Lee Green, Lewisham, Downham, Beckenham, Bromley, Biggin Hill, Eltham, Shooters Hill, Erith, Plumstead, Bexley, Sidcup, Orpington, Lambeth, Battersea, Clapham, Brixton, Richmond, Wandsworth, Tooting, West Norwood, Twickenham, Kingston, New Malden, Wimbledon, Mitcham, Norbury, Sutton, Wallington, Croydon, Woodside, Purley, Surbiton, Addington.

GREATER MANCHESTER COUNTY FIRE SERVICE. HQ Swinton, Manchester

Area: 500 sqm. Risks: A-D. Calls: 64,254 (spec 6,693, false mechanical, 4,404, false malicious 11,972, good intent 11,866, fires 29,319). Estab: w/t 2,217. Appl: 68 WrL, 5 TL, 5 EST, 1 CU, 1 CaV, 1 HLL, 3 FoT, 4 L4P, 1 Tractor, 2 BAT, 2 Tr, 97 LPP, 3 ALPlat, 1 rescue boat, 1 HX FoT. BA 463 C/A (positive pressure). Stations: W/t Salford, Broughton, Agecroft, Eccles, Stretford, Sale, Altrincham, Moor Lane, Bolton, Crompton Way, Bolton, Farnworth, Wigan, Atherton, Leigh, Rochdale, Heywood, Oldham, Hollins, Bury, Chadderton, Whitefield, Whitehill Street, West Stockport, King Street, Stockport, Lisburn Lane, Moss Side, Withington, Wythenshawe, Cheadle, Thompson Street, Manchester, Blackley, Philips Park, Gorton, Ashton-under-Lyne, Stalybridge, Hyde, Mossley, D/m Irlam, Hindley, Ramsbottom, P/t Littleborough, N/m Horwich, Marple.

MERSEYSIDE FIRE BRIGADE. HQ Liverpool

Area: 64,650 hectares. Risks: A-D. Calls: 45,818 (spec 6,140, false 14,576). Estab: w/t 1,607. Appl : 63 WrT, 4 TL, 3 FoT/T, 3 CU/ET, 1 ET, 2 HL, 1 DecontamU, 1 HiExU, 1 MPU, 1 MU, 1 CV, 2 L4P. BA 350 air. Radio: 4 channel VHF. Stations: Bankhall, Buckley Hill, Longmoor Lane, Storrington Avenue, Crosby, Southport, Formby, Kirkby, Canning Place, West Derby Road, Exmouth Street, Upton, Bebington, Heswall, West Kirby, Wallasey, High Park Street, Mather Avenue, Conleach Road, Banks Road, Derby Lane, Childwall Valley Road, Parr Stocks Road, St Helens, Borron Road, Newton le Willows, Huyton Lane, Millfields, St Helens.

WEST MIDLANDS FIRE SERVICE. HQ Birmingham

Area: 346 sqm. Risks: A-D. Calls: 53,094 (fires 20,479, spec 6,342, false 24,948, RTA 1,325); Estab: W/t 2,107 p/t 12. Appl: 1 PL, 95 PRL, 8 HP, 5 TL, 1 RV, 2 BA main control units, 8 demountable, 3 command: foam distribution, 3 incident support, 2 hazardous substances, 2 major rescue, 3 plant bed, 2 GP body, 1 rope rescue, 3 fire safety display unit, 2 skid steel loader. Radio: Home Office AM. Stations: W/t Central, Aston, Sutton Coldfield, Erdington, Perry Barr, Ward End, Handsworth, Solihull, Sheldon, Coventry, Canley, Foleshill, Binley, Bickenhill, Highgate, Harborne, Smethwick, Bournbrook, Kings Norton, Northfield, Ladywood, Billesley, Hay Mills, Oldbury, Brierley Hill, Halesowen, Stourbridge, Cradley Heath, Tipton, West Bromwich, Dudley, Walsall, Bloxwich, Willenhall, Aldridge, Wolverhampton, Fallings Park, Bilston, Tettenhall, Wednesbury, P/t Sedgeley.

NORFOLK FIRE SERVICE. HQ Norwich

Area: 536,953 hectares. Risks: B-D. Calls 9,215 (spec 1,505, false 3,503). Estab: w/t 292, p/t 463. Appl: 65 WrT, 3 HP, 2 FST, 1 CIU, 5 ET, 1 CU, 1 WrC. BA 272 positive pressure. Radio: Home Office AM. Stations: W/t Kings Lynn, Norwich City, Sprowston, Great Yarmouth, D/m Thetford, Gorleston, R/t Downham Market, Outwell, Sandringham, Terrington, West Walton, Attleborough, East Harling, Methwold, Swaffham, Watton, Dereham, Fakenham, Holt, Massingham, Reepham, Wells, Diss, Harleston, Hethersett, Hingham, Long Stratton, Wymondham, Acle, Martham, Aylsham, Cromer, Mundesley, N. Walsham, Sheringham, Stalham, Wroxham.

NORTHAMPTONSHIRE FIRE AND RESCUE SERVICE. HQ Northampton

Area: 236,913 hectares. Calls 7,742 (spec 1,234, false 3,040); Estab: w/t 295, p/t 235. Appl: 33 P, 1 TL (100), 1 HP (100), 1 ET. BA 159 air. Radio: Private FM. Stations: W/t Northampton (Mounts), Northampton (Mereway), Moulton, Kettering, Corby, Wellingborough, D/m Daventry, Rushden, P/t Towcester, Woodford Halse, Long Buckby, Guilsborough, Brixworth, Brackley, Rothwell, Oundle, Thrapston, Raunds, Burton Latimer, Desborough, Earls Barton, Irthlingborough.

NORTHUMBERLAND FIRE AND RESCUE SERVICE. HQ Morpeth

Area 1,943 sqm. Risks: C-D; Estab: w/t 205, p/t 155. Appl: 28 WrL, 7 Support/Trng units, 19 Vehicles/Trailers. BA 114 air. Radio: Home Office FM. Stations: W/t Ashington, Morpeth, Blyth, Cramlington, D/m Berwick, Hexham, P/t Amble, Rothbury, Alnwick, Prudhoe, Ponteland, Bellingham, Haltwhistle, Allendale, Hayden Bridge, Wooler, Belford, Seahouses.

NOTTINGHAMSHIRE FIRE AND RESCUE SERVICE. HQ Nottingham

Area 216,362 hectares. Risks: A-D; Calls 15,049 (fires 7,002, spec 1,686, false 5,967, OB 394). Estab: w/t 614, p/t 332. Appl: 37 WrL, 1 TL, 2 HP, 5 RT, 8 WrT, 3 PM. BA

180 air. Radio: Private AM. Stations: W/t Mansfield, Ashfield, Worksop, Retford, Newark, Central Nottingham, West Bridgford, Stockhill Nottingham, Dunkirk Nottingham, Beeston, Arnold, Carlton, R/t Blidworth, Edwinstowe, Warsop, Harworth, Misterton, Tuxford, Southwell, Collingham, Stapleford, Eastwood, Hucknall, East Leake, Bingham.

OXFORDSHIRE FIRE SERVICE. HQ Kidlington, Oxford

Area 260,782 hectares. Calls 9,293. Estab: w/t 233, p/t 336. Appl: 42 WrL, 1 TL (30 metre), 1 HP (28 metre), 1 R/T, 46 PP, 3 tractor units, 1 ST, 1 CU, 1 WrC, 1 FT, 1 CIU, 1 CaV, 1 flat bed, 1 Display Unit. BA 172. Radio: Home Office. Stations: W/t Banbury, Kidlington, Rewley Road, Oxford, The Slade, Oxford, Abingdon, Didcot, P/t Hook Norton, Chipping Norton, Charlbury, Woodstock, Bicester, Deddington, Witney, Bampton, Burford, Eynsham, Faringdon, Wantage, Goring, Henley, Thame, Wheatley, Watlington, Wallingford.

POWYS FIRE SERVICE. HQ Builth Wells

Area 1,960 sqm. Risks: C-D. Calls 1,636 (spec 374, false 490). Estab: w/t 31, p/t 257. Appl: 26 WrL, 2 WrT, 1 HP, 2 TrU, 2 FoT, 2 WrC, 2 LRT, 6 L4P, 2 L4T, 2 L4V. BA 107 air. Radio: Home Office AM. Stations: Newtown, Machynlleth, Montgomery, Welshpool, Llanfair Caereinion, Llanfyllin, Llandiloes, Llandrindod Wells, Knighton, Rhayader, Presteigne, Builth Wells, Llanwrtyd Wells, Brecon, Abercrave, Crickhowell, Talgarth, Hay-on-Wye.

SHROPSHIRE FIRE AND RESCUE SERVICE. HQ Shrewsbury

Area 862,429 acres. Risks: B-D. Calls 5,806 (spec 636, false 2,372). Estab: w/t 208, p/t 312. Appl: 9 WrT, 30 WrL, 2 ET, 1 TLP, 1 ALP, 3 Pm, 4 Pods (TSU, ISU, EFU, CU), 5 L4P. BA 150 air. Radio: Home Office AM. Stations: W/t Shrewsbury, Telford Central, Wellington, P/t Oswestry, Ellesmere, Wem, Whitchurch, Ludlow, Bishop's Castle, Church Stretton, Craven Arms, Baschurch, Clun, Minsterley, Prees, Market Drayton, Hodnet, Newport, Albrighton, Much Wenlock, Bridgnorth, Cleobury Mortimer, Tweedale.

SOMERSET FIRE BRIGADE. HQ Taunton

Area 1,335 sqm. Risks: B-D. Calls 5,840 (spec 744, false 2,469). Estab: w/t 173, p/t 404. Appl: 25 WrT, 23 WrL, 26 L4V, 3 HP, 2 WrC, 1 HFST, 2 RT, 1 L4P, 1 CU, 2 FSU, 1 BL, 19 ancillary. BA 210. Radio: Home Office AM. Stations: W/t Yeovil, Taunton, Bridgwater, P/t Crewkerne, Martock, Somerton, Street, Glastonbury, Wells, Shepton Mallet, Castle Cary, Wincanton, Frome, Ilminster, Chard, Dulverton, Burnham-on-Sea, Wellington, Wiveliscombe, Williton, Nether Stowey, Minehead, Porlock, Cheddar.

STAFFORDSHIRE FIRE AND RESCUE SERVICE. HQ Stone

Area 1,069 sqm. Risks: various. Calls 14,277 (spec 2,017, false 5,797, O/B 472, fires 5,941). Estab: w/t 495, p/t 424. Appl: 28 WrL, 31 WrT, 3 HP, 2 TL, 2 FST, 6 RT, 2 SIU, 2 WrC, 1 CaV, 1 CU, 3 ATV, 1 lorry, 1 MDU (special incident unit). 4 MW, 1RV. BA 240. Radio: Home Office AM. Stations: W/t Burslem, Hanley, Longton, Newcastle-under-Lyme, Burton-on-Trent, Stafford, D/m Kidsgrove, Leek, Cannock, Lichfield, Tamworth, P/t Ashley, Biddulph, Cheadle, Ipstones, Longnor, Abbots Bromley, Barton-under-Needwood, Brewood, Chase Terrace, Codsall, Eccleshall, Gnosall, Kinver, Penkridge, Rugeley, Stone, Tutbury, Uttoxeter, Wombourne.

SUFFOLK COUNTY FIRE SERVICE. HQ Ipswich

Area 1,470 sqm. Risks: A-D. Calls 8,410 (spec 1,149, false 2,759, malicious 632, GI 1,480, def alarms 647). Estab: w/t 262, p/t 421. Appl: 2 TL, 52 WrL (4 reserve), 1 WrT, 1 RT, 5 FCPodU, 45 cars, 3 PCV, 2 SV, 21 GP vans, 62 LP, 1 BAT, 1 WrC, 4 load lorries with 'Rolonof' demount eqpt (demount pods in use), 1 HL, 3 Smoke Trngpods, 1 CIU, 1 CanPod, 1 WrT (1,000 gallons), 3 LoadCPods, 1 CU, 2 small inshore FBt. BA 216 air. Radio: Home Office AM. Stations: W/t Colchester Road, Ipswich, Princes Street, Ipswich, Normanhurst, Lowestoft, Parkway, Bury St Edmunds, D/m Felixstowe, Newmarket, Sudbury, Haverhill, P/t Holbrook, Beccles, Bungay, Leiston, Southwold, Halesworth, Woodbridge, Framlingham, Orford, Clifton Road, Wrentham, Aldeburgh, Saxmundham, Mildenhall, Brandon, Ixworth, Elmswell, Long Melford, Clare, Wickhambrook, Eye, Nayland, Hadleigh, Needham Market, Stowmarket, Debenham, Stradbroke.

SURREY FIRE AND RESCUE SERVICE. HQ Reigate

Area 167,924 hectares. Risks: B-D. Calls 15,208. Estab: w/t 734, p/t 144. Appl: 54 WrL, 3 HP, 20 specials. BA 180 compressed air. Radio: Storno FM. Stations: W/t Reigate, Dorking, Epsom, Leatherhead, Godstone, Guildford, Painshill (Cobham), Farnham, Woking, Haslemere, Chertsey, Egham, Sunbury, Walton, Esher, Camberley, Staines, P/t Lingfield, Oxted, Cranleigh, Godalming, Dunsfold, Gomshall, Chobham.

EAST SUSSEX COUNTY FIRE BRIGADE. HQ Lewes

Area 179,529. Risks: B-D. Calls 10,018 (spec 2,303, false 3,332). Appl: 46 WrL, 4 TL, 2 HP, 30 SV, 1 FoT, 1 WrC, 1 CU, 1 Animal RV, 1 H4P, 1 L4PT, 34 cars, 5 PCV, 34 UV, 2 GPL, 3 SV, 1 stores van. BA 198 air. Radio: Home Office AM. Stations: W/t Eastbourne, Hastings, Hove, Preston Circus, Roedean, The Ridge, D/m Bexhill, Crowborough, Lewes, Newhaven, Uckfield, N/m Battle, P/t Barcombe, Broad Oak, Burwash, Forest Row, Hailsham, Heathfield, Herstmonceux, Mayfield, Pevensey, Rye, Seaford, Wadhurst.

WEST SUSSEX FIRE BRIGADE. HQ Chichester

Area 769 sqm. Risks: B-D. Calls 11,033. Estab: w/t 396, p/t 310. Appl: 46 WrL, 10 L4T, 3 HP, 3 RT, 2 CU, 1 L4V, 2 WrT, 3 BACV, 1 CaV, 1 FoT, 1 CT, 1 HL, 1 WrC. BA 216 air. Radio: Home Office AM. Stations: W/t Chichester, Bognor Regis, Worthing, Shoreham-by-Sea, Crawley, Horsham, Horley, D/m East Grinstead, Haywards Heath, P/t East Preston, Lancing, Findon, Arundel, Littlehampton, Selsey, East Wittering, Bosham, Midhurst, Petworth, Partridge Green, Steyning, Billingshurst, Storrington, Turners Hill, Burgess Hill, Henfield, Keymer, Hurstpierpoint.

TYNE AND WEAR METROPOLITAN FIRE BRIGADE. HQ Newcastle-upon-Tyne

Area 208 sqm. Risks: A-D. Calls 35,567. Estab: w/t 1,107, p/t 24. Appl: 46 WT, 2 FoT, 4 TL (100 ft), 2 ET, 1 CU, 3 RT, 1 ST, 2 Fbt, 58 LV. BA 309 air. Radio: Private. Stations: W/t Newcastle West, Newcastle Central, Gosforth, Newcastle East, Wallsend, Tynemouth, West Denton, Swalwell, Gateshead, Washington, Sunderland, Hebburn, Sunderland West, Sunderland Central, Sunderland North, Sunderland South, South Shields, P/t Chopwell, Birtley.

WARWICKSHIRE FIRE AND RESCUE SERVICE. HQ Leamington Spa

Area 197,747 hectares. Risks: B-D. Calls 6,467 (spec 737, false 2,991). Estab: w/t 325, p/t 170. Appl: 14 WrL, 21 WrT, 2 HP, 1 CU, 1 BAT, 2 GPL, 13 cars, 4 PCV, 14 UV, 41

PP, 8 Gen, Demountable system comprising 4 prime movers, 2 ET, 1 FoT, 2 WrC. BA 180 air. Radio: Home Office AM. Stations: W/t Leamington Spa, Stratford-upon-Avon, Nuneaton, Rugby, D/m Bedworth, Coleshill, Atherstone, P/t Warwick, Kenilworth, Southam, Fenny Compton, Kineton, Tysoe, Shipston-on-Stour, Bidford-on-Avon, Alcester, Studley, Henley-in-Arden, Polesworth, Brinklow.

WILTSHIRE FIRE BRIGADE. HQ Devizes

Area 1,295 sqm. Risks: B-D. Calls 8,466 (spec 1,240, false 3,951). Estab: w/t 206, p/t 319. Appl: 24 WrL/Rescue, 4 WrL, 8 compacts, 4 RT, 1 P/HP, 1 HP, 2 DCU, 4 WrC, 1 FU, 1 CP, 1 CUCaV, 1 PM. BA 170. Radio: Home Office AM. Stations: W/t Swindon, Stratton, Salisbury, D/m Chippenham, Westlea, Amesbury, Trowbridge, P/t Cricklade, Marlborough, Wootton Bassett, Corsham, Malmesbury, Calne, Ramsbury, Wilton Tisbury, Mere, Ludgershall, Pewsey, Bradford-on-Avon, Melksham, Westbury, Warminster, Devizes.

NORTH YORKSHIRE FIRE AND RESCUE SERVICE. HQ Northallerton

Area 831,235 hectares. Risks: B-E. Calls 8,470. Estab: w/t 398, p/t 425. Appl: 69 WrL, 4 L4R, 4 TL, 6 ET, 4 MW, 3 PCV, 1 CU, 1 FST, 1 CaV, 1 WrC, 2 flat bed, 4 transporter, 1 exhibition unit, 1 Argocat, 88 ancillary. BA 254 air. Radio: Home Office AM. Stations: W/t Harrogate, Scarborough, York, Acomb, D/m Ripon, Richmond, Malton, Whitby, Northallerton, Selby, Tadcaster, P/t Knaresborough, Masham, Summerbridge, Skipton, Bentham, Settle, Bedale, Hawes, Leyburn, Reeth, Pickering, Sherburn, Snainton, Filey, Danby, Lythe, Robin Hood's Bay, Stokesley, Helmsley, Kirkbymoorside, Boroughbridge, Easingwold, Thirsk.

SOUTH YORKSHIRE FIRE AND RESCUE SERVICE. HQ Sheffield

Area 156,046 hectares. Risks: A-D. Calls 21,824 (fires 10,019, spec 2,067, false 9,738). Estab: w/t 1,042, p/t 124. Appl: 37 WrL, 3 TLP, 3 HP, 4 ET, 5 RAV, 1 CU, 1 BAT, 2 GPL, 3 PCV, 43 UV, 4 L4V, 2 Rolonof vehicles + 5 pods, BA 306 plus 2 sets airline equipment. Stations: W/t Barnsley, Royston, Doncaster, Adwick-le-Street, Mexborough, Thorne, Rotherham, Oaks Lane, Brampton Bierlow, Edlington, Sheffield Central, Rivelin Valley, Lowedges Road, Ringinglow Road, Maltby, Darnall Road, Elm Lane, Mansfield Road, High Green, Mosborough, P/t Askern, Rossington, Stocksbridge, Kiveton Park, N/m Penistone.

WEST YORKSHIRE FIRE SERVICE. HQ Birkenshaw

Area 787 sqm. Risks: A-D. Calls 42,963. Estab: w/t 1,815, p/t 156. Stations: W/t Leeds Bramley, Hunslet, Morley, Moortown, Stanks, Garforth, Wetherby, Gipton Cookridge, Bradford, Pudsey, Rawdon, Fairweather Green, Idle, Bingley, Shipley, Keighley, Odsal, Halifax, Todmorden, Elland, Slaithwaite, Illingworth, Cleckheaton, Brighouse, Holmfirth, Skelmanthorpe, Huddersfield, Wakefield, Ossett, Rothwell, Castleford, South Elmsall, Pontefract, Knottingley, Batley, Dewsbury, R/t Silsden, Ilkley, Otley, Haworth, Hebden Bridge, Mytholmroyd, Marsden, Meltham, Normanton, Hemsworth, Featherstone, Mirfield.

SCOTLAND

CENTRAL REGION FIRE BRIGADE. HQ Falkirk

Area 1,051 sqm. Risks: A-D. Calls 4,266. Estab: w/t 240, p/t 160. Appl: 16 WrL, 11 WrT, 1 HP (85ft), 1 FST, 1 MIV, 2 SSU, 1 CaV, 1 L4T, 1 WrC, 2 LFAppl. BA 131. Radio: Private, 60 mobile sets. Stations: W/t Falkirk, Stirling, Alloa, Bo'ness, P/t Balfron, Bridge of Allan, Denny, Larbert, Slamannan, Tillicoultry, Aberfoyle, Callander, Doune, Dunblane, Killin, Vol/stat Tyndrum, Crianlarich, Lochearnhead.

DUMFRIES AND GALLOWAY FIRE BRIGADE. HQ Dumfries

Area 2,480 sqm. Risks: B-D. Estab: w/t 96, p/t 209. Appl: 1 ALP, 1 TL, 20 WrL, 6 WrT, 2 ET, 1 CIU, 1 ICU. BA 160 air. Radio: Private. Stations: W/t Dumfries, R/t Thornhill, Sanquhar, Moffat, Lockerbie, Langholm, Gretna, Annan, Newton Stewart, Stanraer, Whithorn, Gatehouse, Kirkcudbright, Castle Douglas, New Galloway, Dalbeattie, vol/stat Eskdalemuir, Drummore.

FIFE FIRE AND RESCUE SERVICE. HQ Kirkaldy

Area 508 sqm. Risks: A-D. Calls 6,496 (spec 440, false 2,685). Estab: w/t 376, r/t 95. Appl: 20 WrL, 10 WrT, 2 HP (27.8 metres), 1 FoT, 1 CU, 1 ET, 1 HC, 1 MW, 1 ESU, 3 WCars. BA 197 air. Radio: Private. Stations: W/t Dunfermline, Glenrothes, Kirkaldy, Lochgelly, Methil, Rosyth, R/t Anstruther, Auchtermuchty, Burntisland, Cupar, Newburgh, St. Andrews, St. Monans, Tayport.

GRAMPIAN FIRE BRIGADE. HQ Aberdeen

Area 3,360 sqm. Risks: A-D. Calls 7,424 (spec 742, false 2,848). Estab: w/t 354, p/t 476, vol 34. Appl: 48 WrL, 19 WrT, 1 HP, 2 TL, 1 DCU, 3 RU, 1 Stonefield, 3 prime movers with demountable – flat bed, chemical unit, canteen unit, BA unit, foam unit, control unit, BA training unit, fire safety unit, helicopter support unit, 3 Landrovers, 1 stonefield line rescue unit, 1 ATV, 1 Kawasaki Mule, 22 W/cars, 18 vans, 1 53-seater bus, 70 LPP, 75 E/Gen, 7 BA compressors. BA 270 PP. Stations: W/t North Anderson Drive, Aberdeen, King Street, Aberdeen, Altens, Aberdeen, D/m Elgin, R/t Insch, Turriff, Macduff, Fraserburgh, Peterhead, Maud, Ellon, Oldmeldrum, Inverurie, Kintore, Dyce, Alford, Strathdon, Braemar, Ballater, Aboyne, Banchory, Laurencekirk, Inverbervie, Lossiemouth, Forres, Tomintoul, Dufftown, Aberlour, Keith, Rothes, Fochabers, Buckie, Cullen, Portsoy, Banff, Aberchirder, Huntly, vol/stat Balmoral, Gordonstoun.

HIGHLANDS AND ISLANDS FIRE BRIGADE. HQ Inverness

Area 12,000 sqm approx. Risks: B-D. Calls 4,913. Estab: w/t 99, p/t 381, vol 931. Appl: 50 WrL, 1 ET, 1 HP ,(85 ft), 30 P, 1 FoT, 1 CU, 234 LPP, 7 HX, 3 car, 1 GPL, 1 L4V, 1 PCV, 1 WrC, 2 Argo, 1 Muskog, 1 x 28m combined HP/TL. BA 227 air. Radio: Private. Stations: W/t Inverness, R/t Aviemore, Broadford, Fort William, Grantown-on-Spey, Inverness, Kingussie, Kinlochleven, Kyle of Lochalsh, Mallaig, Nairn, Portree, Benbecula, Dingwall, Fortrose, Invergordon, Stornoway, Tain, Ullapool, Gairloch, Brae, Dornoch, Golspie, Kirkwall, Lairg, Lerwick, Stromness, Thurso, Wick, Vol/stat, Acharacle, Ardgour, Beauly, Boat of Garten, Cannich, Carrbridge, Drumnadrochit, Dunvegan, Eigg, Fort Augustus, Foyers, Glenborrodale, Glendale, Glenelg, Kilchoan, Kinlochmoidart, Kyleakin, Lochaline, Muck, Nethybridge, Newtonmore, Raasay, Ratagan, Salen, Sleat, Spean Bridge, Staffin, Strontian, Struan, Uig, Waternish, Knoydart, Achiltibuie, Applecross, Aultbea, Balintore, Bayhead, Berneray, Castlebay, Cromarty, Eriskay, Great Bernera, Kinlochewe, Leverburgh, Lochboisdale, Lochcarron, Lochmaddy, Portmahomack, Port of Ness, Scalpay, Shawbost, Shieldaig,

South Lochs, Strathconon, Strathpeffer, Tarbert, Torridon, Valtos, Achfary, Baltasound, Bettyhill, Bixter, Bonar Bridge, Bressay, Dunbeath, Durness, Eday, Fair Isle, Fetlar, Flotta, Hamnovoe, Helmsdale, Hillswick, Kinlochbervie, Lochinver, Longhope, Lybster, Mid Yell, Mossbank, North Ronaldsay, Rousay, St. Margaret's Hope, Sanday, Sandwick, Scalloway, Scourie, Shapinsay, Stronsay, Sumburgh, Tongue, Walls, Westray, Whalsay, John O'Groats, Foula, Skerries, Papa Stour.

LOTHIAN AND BORDERS FIRE BRIGADE. HQ Edinburgh

Area 2,500 sqm. Risks: A-D. Calls 16,856. Estab: w/t 721, p/t 295. Appl: 3 TL, 3 HP, 3 ET, 1 FST, 11 WrT, 23 WrL, 22 WrL/ET, 2 PCV, 2 GPL, 53 car, 56 LPP, 24 V, 1 CU. BA 300 air. Radio: Private. Stations: W/t Bathgate, Crewe, Toll, Dalkeith, Galashiels, Hawick, Liberton, Livingston, McDonald Road, Marionville, Musselburgh, Sighthill, Tollcross, P/t Broxburn, Coldstream, Dunbar, Duns, East Linton, Eyemouth, Haddington, Innerleithen, Jedburgh, Kelso, Linlithgow, Melrose, Newcastleton, North Berwick, Peebles, Penicuik, Selkirk, South Queensferry, Tranent, West Calder, West Linton, Whitburn.

STRATHCLYDE FIRE BRIGADE. HQ Hamilton

Area 5,348 sqm. Risks: A-D. Calls 62,396 (spec 3,850, false 32,364). Estab: w/t 2,233, p/t 619, vol 265. Appl: 157 P, 5 TL, 5 HP, 8 RRU, 1 HRV, 1 CU, 1 TSU, 106 UV, 6 PVC, 1 ST, 2 FST, 5 MW, 6 GPL, 2 HGVTrng, 37 car, 9 VSU, 3 CaTr, 6 BaTr, 3 FoTr. BA 719 air. Radio: 564 mobiles, 474 hand portables, 48 base units. Stations: W/t Cowcaddens, Easterhouse, Springburn, North West, Knightswood, West, Govan, Pollok, Castlemilk, Polmadie, Cambuslang, Parkhead, Calton, Johnstone, Barrhead, Clarkston, Paisley, Renfrew, Port Glasgow, Greenock, Ayr, Kilmarnock, Irvine, Ardrossan, Dreghorn, Hamilton, Motherwell, Bellshill, Coatbridge, East Kilbride, Lanark, Clydebank, Bishopbriggs, Kirkintilloch, Cumbernauld, Milngavie, Helensburgh, Dumbarton, P/t Gourock, Maybole, Girvan, Colmonell, Dalmellington, New Cumnock, Cumnock, Muirkirk, Mauchline, Newmilns, Stewarton, Dalry, Beith, Kilbirnie, Largs, Skelmorlie, Millport, Brodick, Lamlash,Troon, Shotts, Larkhall, Strathaven, Lesmahagow, Douglas, Abington, Biggar, Carluke, Stepps, Kilsyth, Balloch, Arrochar, Oban, Tobermory, Bowmore, Lochgilphead, Tarbert, Campbeltown, Tighnabruaich, Inverary, Rothesay, Dunoon, Cove, Gairlochhead.

TAYSIDE FIRE BRIGADE. HQ Dundee

Area 7,000 sqkm. Risks: A-D. Calls 8,313 (spec 573, false/good intent 1,815, malicious 1,024). Estab: w/t 396, p/t 255, vols 44. Appl: 44 WrL, 1 TL, 3 HP, 2 FST, 2 ET, 1 Command control unit, 5 RAV, 30 others. BA 188. Radio: 100 Private FM. Stations: W/t Blackness Road, Dundee, Macalpine Road, Dundee, Kingsway East, Dundee, Monifieth, Arbroath, Perth, P/t Montrose, Brechin, Forfar, Kirriemuir, Carnoustie, Auchterarder, Crieff, Comrie, Dunkeld, Aberfeldy, Pitlochry, Coupar Angus, Blairgowrie, Alyth, Kinross, Vol/stat Airlie Estates, Kirkmichael, Glenshee, Kinloch Rannoch.

NORTHERN IRELAND

NORTHERN IRELAND FIRE BRIGADE. HQ Lisburn

Area 5,450 sqm. Risks: A-D. Calls 27,288. Estab: w/t 847, r/t 1,023. Appl: 101 WrL, 45 PL, 4 TL, 3 HP, 4 FoT, 3 ET, 11 ESU, 2 RU, 3 LV, 8 L4V, 2 L4P, 3 CAV, BA 630 CA. Radio: Private. Stations: W/t 10, R/t 53, vol 1.

INDEX